FROM THE ASHES

Sarah Jaffe

FROM THE ASHES

Grief and Revolution in a World on Fire

BOLD TYPE BOOKS
NEW YORK

Bold Type Books
Hachette Book Group
1290 Avenue of the Americas, New York, NY 10104
www.boldtypebooks.org
@BoldTypeBooks

Printed in the United States of America

First Edition: September 2024

Published by Bold Type Books, an imprint of Hachette Book Group, Inc. Bold Type Books is a co-publishing venture of the Type Media Center and Perseus Books.

Print book interior design by Sheryl Kober.

Library of Congress Cataloging-in-Publication Data

Names: Jaffe, Sarah, 1980– author.
Title: From the ashes : grief and revolution in a world on fire / Sarah Jaffe.
Description: First edition. | New York : Bold Type Books, 2024. | Includes bibliographical references and index.
Identifiers: LCCN 2024002964 | ISBN 9781541703490 (hardcover) | ISBN 9781541703513 (ebook)
Subjects: LCSH: Grief—Social aspects. | Memorialization.
Classification: LCC BF575.G7 J34 2024 | DDC 155.9/37—dc23/eng/20240506
LC record available at https://lccn.loc.gov/2024002964

ISBNs: 9781541703490 (hardcover), 9781541703513 (ebook)

LSC-C

Printing 1, 2024

For the grievers: Angelica, Antonia, Ethan, Joshua, Laura, Natasha, Samhita, and especially Dania

Contents

Where life is precious, life is precious.

—Ruth Wilson Gilmore

Introduction

Haunted

A police car on fire is the perfect embodiment of grief.

The smoke is darker than we are used to. It curls up into a 2 p.m. sky in Philadelphia and I think, *This time is different.* The burning car is an icon of a pain that feels like it can and will destroy the world, a symbol of the uselessness of power in the face of loss. The world as it is did not protect your love, your son, your sister, so what good is it, anyway? Why not consign it all to the fire?

The burning car is not just an expression of grief for a person or group of people but a release of the idea of America, of a particular consensus that had never really existed but was taught to us nevertheless as though the repetition could make it real. As though there had been a shiny and clean American Dream that was available to all of us if we tried hard enough. The burning spread around the world, because it is not just America in the flames.

The burning will be written off as rage, but the truth is there is so much rage inside of grief. Anger that boils up in your chest and demands to be let out. The target, if there is one, is probably out of reach so it will just come out when you least want it to if you don't find a way to aim. What no one tells you about rage is that it is overwhelming, but it is not directionless; you can explain exactly why you feel it even as it makes your body shake and twist. Rage, they say, as if rage is for the less-than-human, a base emotion, as if it doesn't take human comprehension to feel such a powerful thing. Rage is perfectly correct when you have felt a loss this big and when you know in your bones that more are coming. When you know the next one could be your brother sister cousin lover friend, could be you.

The police car afire was the most potent visual symbol of 2020, of a moment when so many people had so little left to lose. But 2020 wasn't an anomaly or a freak year in an otherwise forward march of progress. The pandemic might have been new, but the unequal exposure to its ravages was formed centuries earlier, and the protests might have been bigger in 2020 than they had been in 2014, in 2016, but the world has never stopped reminding us that things can get worse as easily as they can get better. The crises outlasted 2020, and the pandemic was absorbed into the new normal much as the climate crisis has been, even as the death toll mounts, the heat waves rage, the violence continues. There is so much still to grieve, and we have taken so little time—we are allowed so little time—in which to do it. We are told to return to normal, and yet normal was already killing so many of us.

When my father died, in 2018, I was upended by grief. Nothing I had read or experienced before prepared me for how absolutely undone I would be, how shattered. How *physical* it was, how it affected my breathing, my heart rate, my ability to sleep and to walk and to be touched by the people who loved me, to make eye contact and hold a gaze. How it took the taste of food from my mouth, how I felt like a child again begging someone to make it all right and at the same time how I felt ancient wisdom at the back of my skull, the knowledge of something that no one could have explained to me, that I had to go through. Years later a friend would say, *I am still in the land of the dead*, and I would know how she felt. Ghosts walked with me.

It was an absolute break with what had come before, with who I had been before.

It was wrenching. But it also, in moments, opened up a vast space of possibility. Having lost someone I could not fathom a life without, could I picture instead something totally different? Could I imagine my life absolutely otherwise? Could we all, if we acknowledged our grief rather than shambling on like zombies, imagine collectively something new?

As I picked up the pieces of my life, I began to see traces of grief everywhere. And yet the world as we know it makes so little space for mourning. This fundamental contradiction seemed to me suddenly to be at the heart of every rebellion, every political battle, every bit of the spectacular violence speeding up all over the world. I found it at the heart of every story I was covering as a reporter, even before the pandemic began. I went on a journey through the land of the dead, learning about grief, my own and other people's, and this book you hold in your hands is the result.

It is a more personal story than I have told before, and I remain uneasy with this. Uneasy with taking up space, and uncomfortable with my own vulnerability. I could and indeed have gathered theorists and experts around me, clothed myself in their brilliance and hidden myself from you to a degree, but it was in reporting this book that I found I had to share my story first. It was cruel to sit with a stranger as they told me the most intimate details of the worst moments of their lives and to pretend at objectivity. It was impossible to hold to some kind of journalistic distance, to not reach for a hand when tears came to someone's eyes, and it was impossible to ask the questions I wanted to ask without offering my own story first, my own pain, so that they knew I was not simply rubbernecking but was a fellow traveler, and that maybe together we could understand our own hearts better. And that I had to offer my story on the page as well, that I had to be brave enough to offer myself up first for examination. To counter, as Saidiya Hartman and Christina Sharpe have written, "the violence of abstraction."[1]

My own griefs were, in a word, ordinary. And yet they turned my life upside down. Losing a parent who had been ill a while, the end of a relationship that had long withered, these are the kinds of unavoidable losses in any human life. They attuned me, in a fresher, sharper way, to all the unnecessary grief around me, to the crueler losses by far that other people were living with, to all the premature deaths and violence and dispossession that *did not have to happen*, not then, not that way. Janet Malcolm famously wrote, "Every journalist who is not too stupid or too full of himself to notice what is going on knows that what he does is morally indefensible." She may have been right; including my own story in this book is my attempt to be less of a monster.[2]

I needed to tell this story, to intertwine my own with those of others because, as Cristina Rivera Garza wrote, "We always grieve for someone and with someone. Grieving connects us in ways that are subtly and candidly material." Because grieving isolates yet it convolutes, too, and writing is oddly similar. Gathering the details for this book was deeply social; it was an excuse to meet so many people, to sit and talk in cafés and offices and living rooms and parks in places I had never been before, to feel over and over the awkward desire to reach through the screen of a video call to comfort, to soothe. And then to sit down and write meant to peel off my own scabs and bleed afresh, to reread those conversations and discover in them not just the stories of others but the story of myself, too, told over and over in subtly different ways as I learned, as I became the person who could do this writing at all. Who could offer this thing to you.[3]

The bulk of it, though, is about those people who sat with me. About the transformations they have gone through, the ways they made sense of what had happened to them or learned to live with the senselessness. The things they taught me, the worlds they built on the other side of catastrophe. Their stories are grouped roughly into five chapters, five threads of reckoning with the crises of the twenty-first century. There are many, many more stories to tell than the ones I have woven into this book, and I made the choices I did in part simply to hold the scope to something manageable. I was also limited, naturally, by the willingness of strangers and friends to open up to me, to sit and excavate their heartbreak for my recorder. I am and will remain endlessly grateful to everyone who has chosen to tell me their story, for this book and over the years.

I also have five themes, five theses, or perhaps a grammar of grief, to lay out here before we dive into the stories.

1. Grief Is a Rupture

It is a sudden, abrupt, even violent break from the status quo—even if you were expecting it, even if you had felt it before. Before I experienced real grief, I thought that I would be sad for a while. I was not expecting the howling storm, the black hole it opened up around me and inside me. Grief *is* rage and anger and frustration and sadness and sometimes a kind of horrible joy; it is less an emotion than a state of being. It is a being-undone. It is a realization of one's own vulnerability.

It was Judith Butler's writing on grief that first helped me understand what was happening, that first felt like something other than the terrible cliches that abound. Butler, a philosopher of gender and the body, was able to capture something about the bodily nature of mourning, about the process that was happening unconsciously in my cells and organs. That it was an ecstatic process, like rage or desire, that brought me outside of myself, that seemed to loosen me from the physical world at the same time as my body's mechanics insisted on my attention.[4]

I expected too that my grief would lessen by the day, that it would be a sort of process with steps and stages, maybe even identifiable ones, and yet it was profoundly nonlinear. Indeed, it disrupted my very sense of time, my perception of days or hours passing. I experienced some moments at a remove and lived others so fiercely I thought they would be the end of me. I still find it sideswiping me, five years later; it is distant enough now that it takes me a while, when it happens, to recognize it as my grief biting into me again.[5]

Researchers have documented all of this, I learned, eventually. The brain fog and the unevenness, and the fact that the "stages" don't work that way in the least; that everyone will experience grief differently, even when they are experiencing the same loss. That other people can help but sometimes their attempts to help will hurt. I learned terms like "disenfranchised grief," for a loss that "is not or cannot be openly acknowledged, socially sanctioned or publicly mourned," and "ambiguous loss," when a relationship is "disrupted or broken due to physical absence or psychological absence," when the person being mourned is not present but still alive or still present but not themselves, from therapists and grief experts like Jess Kuttner and MaryGrace DiMaria, people who reached out to me after reading my first published attempts at grappling with the subject. Pauline Boss, the woman who coined the term "ambiguous loss," explained that "closure" is all but impossible, a cruel expectation to place on ourselves. That rather than seeking an end to the process, we could heal by giving it new meaning, by seeking justice.[6]

The whole thing was outside of my control, and control was the thing I had learned to value the most. It was a lesson my father had taught me, and now he was gone.

It was not the experts who soothed me with their answers (even when their answers were "there are no answers"). It was the writers in whose pages I found my state echoed back to me. Walter Benjamin, a man who knew something about grief. I could not read his works without thinking about the way he'd died, a German Jew fleeing Paris ahead of the Gestapo, sending his books ahead of him, acquiring the visas he needed from the United States but denied an exit visa, trapped, opting to end his own life. Trying to read him without talking to his ghost was impossible. "Didn't the dead person's name, the last time you uttered it, sound differently in your mouth?" he wrote, of the moment we learn of a death. "Don't you see in the flames a sign from yesterday evening, in a language you only now understand?" His books seemed gifts from the community of the dead; as he noted, "*Ad plures ire* was the Latin expression for dying." To go among the many.[7]

"Rupture" is a political term as well as a personal one; as China Miéville pointed out, it is a key term used in the *Communist Manifesto*. It is the idea that a political transformation must be total, a complete break, a leap into a future we cannot see or even imagine from where we stand. The break that is grief, that is a death, a loss of a home or another pillar of one's existence, is a similar kind of severance. It is a loss and an opening up simultaneously, an opening up that is terrifying and also necessary.[8]

In accepting loss we make possible the future.[9]

This book is animated by the living, but I want to say a few words about ghosts. Ghosts as the people and things that are both here and not here, the dead that refuse to stay dead. That return to tell us something is wrong. Ghosts hover along borders and hide in dark crannies and appear in the corner of your eye. A ghost is a trace of the past that won't let go. Ghosts trouble the rupture.[10]

And our world is so very full of ghosts. It has to be, after all, because it is built on foundations of violence. Avery Gordon, in her book *Ghostly Matters*, makes this clear: "Haunting is one way in which abusive systems of power make themselves known and their impacts felt in everyday life, especially when they are supposedly over and done with (slavery, for instance) or when their oppressive nature is denied (as in free labor or national security)." Haunting is the way those experiences linger and refuse to be erased.[11]

So grief is a rupture, but the dead do not let go of us cleanly. The haunting demands something of us still, even after a change that we might believe could not possibly be bigger. We carry our ghosts with us everywhere. As Walter Benjamin wrote in his perhaps most famous piece, "On the Concept of History," the dead have a claim on us. It is not just for ourselves and our children but also for the dead that we fight. So in telling the stories of the people I met in this book, I must also tell the stories of the ghosts that haunt them, the ghosts of loved ones and ancestors and decisions made by people who never loved them but nevertheless shaped their lives and all of our lives too. I have tried to do justice to these people I never met, to refuse in Peter Mitchell's words to "reduce them to the trauma of their dying," not to turn them into symbols or fetishes but always to remember that they were people just like me with loves and flaws and ghosts of their own.[12]

In this book I am writing about individuals' grief, including my own, but I am also writing about something collective formed out of all those losses. About the way loss and death and destruction shape our society and have done since the beginning of the thing we call capitalism. The particular way it does so now, at this moment of many crises and looming planetary catastrophe. The way so many of us keenly sense our own disposability. I am, then, writing about grief as what Welsh critic Raymond

Williams called a "structure of feeling" that because grief is multiple can be seen in varying ways all across our world. It is threaded through our politics and our personal lives, the ways we behave and the things we repress. It is wound throughout our common sense. It is within all the moments of rupture that have taken the establishment pundits by surprise over the past few decades. To see this structure of feeling, one has to let go of a comfortable set of rules about the way the world is and open oneself to the possibility of it being undone. The comfortable struggle to do this; it is the grievers who see it first.[13]

2. Grief Is About the Future

When my father died I was prepared to be very sad, perhaps for a long time. I was prepared to cry racking sobs and to be unable to move. But the most striking part of grieving was that it wiped out my ability to see the future. The world as I had known it was gone. I could barely imagine the next sunrise, let alone a month, a year down the line. Grief, I had thought, would be about the past, about memories that would wash over me and bring tears and anguish. I was stunned by how much grieving was about what came next and learning how to believe in a future that would not be like my past had been.

When someone dies far too young, it is easier to understand that loss in the future tense. The death of a child leaves the mourners with almost nothing to hold on to but their imaginings of the future that would have been. When journalist Dawn Foster died aged just thirty-four in 2021, everyone who loved her or valued her work mourned the books and articles she would never write. I, who did not know her well, still wonder what she would think or say about this or that. The loss of Dawn filled me with anger and a determination once again to break open the particular pieties of our field. Journalism flatters itself that it is about "speaking truth to power" and a hundred other saccharine lies but did not give her the recognition for doing so—and more importantly the money, the stability, the *care* she deserved. We are poorer for the lack of her voice. This is true of Dawn in particular, and it is true of everyone who dies too young.[14]

In "Mourning and Melancholia" Sigmund Freud described the process of grieving: "Reality-testing has revealed that the beloved object no longer exists, and demands that the libido as a whole sever its bonds with that object." The process of mourning is of severing an attachment to the past; though Freud mentions "expectation" connected to the lost object, he misses almost entirely the way that grief is future oriented. In this, he also misses the transformation it effects, the way mourning is filled with ambivalence and flux and nothing about it resolves so much as it becomes a piece of you, a metal street sign around which a tree has grown. I did not recognize anything about my own experience in this much-cited piece.[15]

Recent psychological research on what some call "complicated grief" (similar, I think, to what Freud called melancholia) confirmed what I had experienced, what people had told me of their own experiences: research subjects struggled to imagine a future, particularly to imagine a future without their lost loved ones. Such difficulty, the researchers added, "may contribute to a sense of lost identity." The need, I think, to delineate a kind of bad grief, a pathology, from Freud to the present, is a distraction, a distinction without meaning when you are stranded in the fog, trying to learn to move forward all over again.[16]

I spoke with psychoanalyst and author Josh Cohen about Freud and grief, and he pointed out the way that grief *is* excess, that the process of mourning is not linear, not short, not resolvable; it will be with us in some way for the rest of our lives, it will *be* us for the rest of our lives. It will be our future. And it is not a bad thing, to not want to detach. It is not a bad thing, sometimes, to be haunted.[17]

We make our futures but not in circumstances of our own choosing. We carry the dead with us, but we have not had the time to mourn them properly, our attention sapped by the proliferating demands of work, families, debt, more work, social media, and yet more work. Politicians seem unable to offer us more than slight improvements or threats. We live in a stretched-out present.[18]

Today the challenge we face is a sort of centrist melancholia: an insistence that nothing after all needs to change that much. The declaration of the "end of history" was bad enough, but to cling to this non-change or perhaps anti-change now when it is abundantly clear that the future will not look like the past, if for no other reason than the climate is now rapidly changing, feels disconnected from reality. It is the refusal to believe in transformation that worries me now, the refusal to admit that the future we were promised was better than this. The "slow cancellation of the future" is the dominant structure of feeling now for all but the wealthiest, a feeling of possibilities ebbing away.[19]

Mourning may wipe out desire for a time, as it wipes out anything future oriented. But within disappointment, defeat, and loss, a space is opened up for the radically new if we can hold on long enough to begin to see it.[20]

3. Grief Is Not Work

We often talk about grieving as though there is something one must *do* to grieve. As though we must apply our conscious effort to the process like it is a job. I expected that, when my father died after a year of illness, I would be somehow prepared to be good at grief. That it was something I could learn the way I had learned to be a good listener, to meet deadlines, to write other people's stories in ways that felt correct to them. That I could apply myself and get through it faster.

I could not. Because grief is not *work*.

The writer Namwali Serpell pointed me to an essay on drift and the middle voice, which has, I think, colored everything I have written since then. It was called "Drift as a Planetary Phenomenon" by Bronislaw Szerszynski, and it concerned movement and the way the earth was built and suggested a different way of understanding time. Szerszynski pointed to the "middle voice" largely missing from modern European languages, from English, something between the active and the passive: "Passive and active voices both divide the world clearly into agent and patient, and just differ in which they make the subject of the verb: thus we might use the active-voice formulation 'the wind drives the snow,' or the passive-voice version 'the snow is driven by the wind.'" Active voice is the voice of volition, of capitalism, of the explorer, the powerful; we are warned as writers not to use the passive voice, not to skip over the agent of the action, though this is routinely violated in what scholars have called the "exonerative tense," for example, when a police officer shoots someone. There is assumed (see what I did there?) to always be an active person involved, one we can point to. But what of the middle?[21]

Many languages, Szerszynski explained, have a middle voice, which is less concerned with agency. In the middle, "the subject does not 'do' or have something 'done to' them; neither can they simply opt out from or reverse the action of which they are a part. They undergo change while engaged in interactive processes from which they cannot simply withdraw; they are not and cannot be exterior to the process." This, Serpell suggested, is what grief is like. You are grieving but grieving is also *doing you*. A transformation is happening from which you cannot withdraw, in which you are a participant but you are out of control.[22]

I hate being out of control as much as anyone raised by my father would have. I was raised to believe in hard work, that it would bring me success and that there was nothing I could not do if I put my mind to it. Yet I had to let go of this and learn to drift. And in doing so to be more sensitive to drifting things.[23]

Szerszynski noted that drifting can be a state that comes from marginality—the vagrant or "drifter"—but it can also be a pleasure. I learned too to let my aimlessness be a kind of luxury. I had enough money put aside to take some time away from work to let grief wash over me. I learned to let the people who loved me just love me, to accept, eventually, that love too was a middle voice, that I did not have to earn it in order to be cared for.[24]

What I needed most of all was to be able *not* to work when the waves came for me, to let myself float.

Josh Cohen, himself the author of a book on work or rather nonwork, suggested that the pause, the break from work, of grief or otherwise, can be a political act. With him, I believe that, rather than productive (or even counterproductive), releasing and mourning is in fact defiantly *anti*-productive, the opposite of work and growth. That it is profoundly social as much as it is physical and embodied, and that it demands time out of the everyday flow of life, a respite from labor rather than a form of it, a period where we are allowed to simply be human and experience the darkest parts of what that means.[25]

Forcing ourselves back to productivity and false happiness is a thousand times more destructive than what we might feel and learn and do if we were allowed to stop. If we were given the time to grieve properly, what might we decide to change?

Working people barely get any time off for bereavement, though. The labor movement has fought at times for the right to grieve, but it has mostly been unsuccessful because, Erik Baker suggested, "grief is a threat to the peculiar way capitalism expects workers to relate to their time." Grief resists being contained, and this makes mourners troublesome workers. If we get bereavement time at all, it will be strictly delimited: this family member but not that one, a partner but only if you're married. Not time to grieve, only to attend a funeral.[26]

Because of course grief does come with rituals, which are something to do that requires time away from work. There is the Jewish practice of sitting shiva, a weeklong period where mourners abstain from work and accept calls from the community; callers bring food and accompany the bereaved as they feel the loss. Mourning rituals are numerous, practiced by all cultures, though in so many different ways. There is silence and there is keening; there are prayers and dances; there are burials and burnings; there are many processes of preparing the dead.[27]

The rituals exist precisely because productivity is impossible but following rules is just about doable. In our secular world the rituals too are often individualized, centering the story of a particular life, perhaps with directions left behind by the dead. (My grandmother laid out specific instructions that she would be buried in her favorite hot-pink pantsuit.)[28]

Since Walter Benjamin's time Western society has been losing its familiarity with the dead. Benjamin noted, "In the course of the nineteenth century bourgeois society has, by means of hygienic and social, private and public institutions . . . [made] it possible for people to avoid the sight of the dying." Dying has been pushed even further from us in the years since; deaths happen in hospitals and nursing homes, specialized locations that sterilize grief. Colonial occupiers liked to "civilize" the people they dominated by stifling grief rituals that seemed too unruly. Public lamentations, particularly by women, were banned in India under British rule; before India they had been suppressed in Ireland as well. Funerals became sites of resistance, places where political communities could form. Elegies were often written as political propaganda.[29]

Grief rituals have long been the province of women, the home the place where grief is held. The home the opposite of the workplace and women's domain, and women's work long considered not-work. Women's assumed proficiency at caring extended to caring for the dead. In the nineteenth-century United States, Spiritualism became a religious and political movement based on direct communication with the dead; there were a variety of ways that ghosts could talk, but mostly they talked to—and through—women. Queen Victoria even embraced it; the Victorian era was perhaps the last period of splashy public mourning in the West, when the dead could be romanticized rather than hustled offstage. When mourning was a respected occupation, rather than an indication one was skiving off work. Books offered detailed rituals; mourning fashion was available for purchase; locks of hair taken from the dead were made into mourning jewelry.[30]

But even today, while mourning publicly is mostly abjured, women are still the ones who accompany the ill and the dying, who administer medicine and food and sponge baths and love. This work that is not considered work is undervalued even when done for a wage, shaped by hundreds of years of expectation that the work of care, for children or for the dying, will be done out of love. Emotional life is drawn into the workplace and the logics of the workplace in turn into our emotional lives. Care work is devalued under capitalism, left to the lowest-paid and most easily exploited workers (often immigrant women of color), and those with status tend to avoid it. Even care for children—to whom at least lip service is paid as "the future"—is undervalued; care for the dying rates hardly at all. And so often we who set aside productive labor to sit at the bedsides of the dying want, rather than to be paid for that time, to have time that does not require such scrupulous accounting at all.[31]

In my writing about labors of love and my grieving, I came to desperately want to reclaim love *from* work. There is something real in the tension between love and money, paid and unpaid labor, the demands for genuine love from paid laborers and unpaid work from those who love. This is, I think, why I embraced the concept of the middle voice, a tense that capitalism cannot assimilate, for grief and for love. Because these contradictions do not have easy solutions in the world we inhabit, and that makes them potentially rebellious.

4. Grief Is Anathema to Capitalism

A friend who knew I was writing a book about grief sent me a screenshot via Twitter of a stack of brochures for something called "Dove Actually." It appeared to offer a service where you could "release a dove in memory of a loved one" as "a way to say goodbye." The terrible pun struck me as a useful example of how impossible it is to sell products to ease the pain of loss.[32]

Funerals, obviously, are a business and can be quite expensive; death doulas and counselors and support groups can provide much-needed care; but when it comes to commodities, there just isn't much that you can buy that will make it less awful that your person is gone. And yet so many keep trying. Though Freud himself argued that mourning was normal, its cure simply time, these days, you can get a diagnosis and a prescription to help you through. In 2022, the latest set of updates to the *Diagnostic and Statistical Manual of Mental Disorders* included "prolonged grief disorder," which the *New York Times* pronounced "an answer" to the question,

"How long should it take to grieve?" The answer, apparently, was, "a year." While *DSM* inclusion often has more to do with clinicians' ability to bill insurance companies for treatment, the decision still angered many practitioners, who "fear grief will be seen as a growth market by drug companies that will try to persuade the public that they need medical treatment to emerge from mourning."[33]

There's nothing wrong with getting help, in therapeutic or even pharmaceutical form, when it feels impossible to go on. But the pressure to treat grief as an illness has more to do with the needs of capitalism than the needs of the human heart. People are not interchangeable, let alone replaceable by things, and it is not pathological—as Freud correctly noted—to mourn a death for what seems a long time, in some ways for the rest of your life. Grief reminds us that we are intertwined.[34]

The gap, the strangeness exposed by the "Dove Actually" is a kind of haunting. It exposes a basic truth of capitalist social relations: in this world, though we are deeply reliant on other people's labor and love to survive, so much of that work comes to us disguised in *things*. In commodities.[35]

A coat (or magazine, or video game, or meal delivered to your door) hides inside it all the people who worked on it, people we are prevented from caring about directly by supply chains and processes we mostly know little about, people whose lives and deaths occur *somewhere else* but whose presence enlivens the things we buy and sell. This is what Marxists call the fetishism of the commodity.[36]

It is a short step from experiencing human relations mediated by commodities to treating humans as commodities ourselves, replaceable, interchangeable. Such commodification shows up all over if we are looking for it. Employee injury law, where prices are assigned to body parts and to entire lives, is one place to see it. Legal scholar Nate Holdren, who studied the process of assigning prices to human bodies, wrote that commodifying people "requires overlooking the individuality, singularity, and, so to speak, infinitude of human persons. Commodified persons are in a sense always nameless and faceless, which is to say, unrecognized." And if unrecognized, ungrievable. Injured or just aging workers are simply discarded as surplus, replaced by younger or faster or just cheaper people, maybe people somewhere else.[37]

The moments when we see through the veil that shelters these processes from view can be disorienting, troubling. But they also create the potential for change. How did we come to treat human bodies and lives this way? This is the question at the heart of this book.[38]

To make the claim for the value of an individual human life is on some level to go beyond the rational, to appeal to emotion, at the very least, and often to something spiritual. It is also to challenge us to see ourselves, once again, in one another. Max Weber famously spoke of "the disenchantment of the world," the process of extracting the mystery from our lives, treating the world as a subject to be dissected on a table. This was not simply the progress of rationalism against religion; it was, rather, a deeper sense: if life has no meaning, it has no value; if it has no value, it has no meaning. We might use the old term "alienation."[39]

The process of disenchantment, of alienation from the world, the land, and each other, has been going on for centuries. The Black Death, the fourteenth-century plague, turned life upside down; familiarity with death, Silvia Federici wrote, "undermined social discipline," as people preferred to enjoy their lives rather than dedicate them to work. The beginnings of capitalism in the subsequent centuries required workers to be re-disciplined, removed from the land and means of self-sufficiency, directed into the workplace and into productivity. The discipline of the body was key to this process. But rationalization did not eradicate the anxieties around death.[40]

Religion was there to offer a solution: work hard in this world, and you'll get your rewards in the next one. But religion itself was made and remade into more austere forms, more individualized, more suited to Enlightenment science and to capitalist production. Nineteenth-century mourners fought this change by intensifying their own mourning in what would be a losing battle, but they also turned to politics and social reform efforts that concentrated on uplifting the living.[41]

There is a reason that Karl Marx used so many gothic metaphors, wrote of werewolves and vampires and specters, when he was describing capitalism. It is not just because he, like me, loved spooky stories; it was an attempt to denaturalize the processes of the system, to awaken his readers to its monstrosities. Most famously, of course, he wrote, "Capital is dead labour, that, vampire-like, only lives by sucking living labour, and lives the more, the more labour it sucks." Vampires may not be real, but dead labor certainly is, as are the bodies of those drained of blood by the system.[42]

But Marx and his coauthor, comrade, and best friend Friedrich Engels also used a spooky metaphor for the change that they aimed to bring: the infamous specter of communism, haunting Europe in the opening of the *Communist Manifesto*. As China Miéville noted, Marx and Engels "revel in that foreboding spectrality invoked, that flattering vesting in communism of dread powers." The specter of the *Manifesto* is not a ghost of the past but a glimpse of the future that hovers just out of sight, teasing us, daring us to make its prophecy come true.[43]

Marx, the supreme rational analyst, encouraging "ruthless criticism of all that exists" nevertheless understood the ways that the irrational is always present in our choices and our actions. Walter Benjamin sought to make those irrationalities visible, to show us the ways that capitalism is haunted and to remind us that its haunts are worth understanding. That the cracks in the structure are where the ghosts hide, and they can help us figure out how to bring the thing down.[44]

Because capitalism is happy to exist without most of us. It is a system that requires workers in order to create value, and a system that requires us to work in order to get the money we need to buy things to survive, but it is also a system that is looking at every turn not just to pay us less than we need to survive but to replace people with robots, algorithms, and other forms of dead labor.[45]

At the beginning of wage labor, the choice was simple: work or starve. And yet many people chose to become vagrants rather than to get a job. It took punishment, violence, witch hunts, hangings to convince people that work was the preferable option. In the eighteenth century, the proletariat was caught between, in historian Peter Linebaugh's words, "the organized death of living labour (capital punishment) and the oppression of the living by dead labour (the punishment of capital)." Some of the deaths intended to send a message; others merely incidental, the cost of doing business. Both sent a message that was received loud and clear. Yet all that punishment broke people, and humans don't work if we're broken. Labor reforms were won through workers' struggles for freedom but aided by the fact that capital needed workers to function—even as the workplace disposed of people faster than they could be replaced. The contradiction at the heart of the system, which remains true today: it needs us but it kills us.[46]

So capital conceded, allowed for shorter working hours or banning child labor or a raised wage or health care, publicly or privately funded, as needed to maintain the workforce, but it never ceased trying to win the overall war. Winning entailed either replacing human labor with machines or forcing humans to become so machinelike that the difference doesn't matter.

The system was designed for endless accumulation, and it turns out that can happen whether many of us live or die. The COVID pandemic proved this to us, but it was already broadly true. Capital can even find a way to make money off our deaths: financiers have turned life insurance into securities, sources of profit. Money does not have to "produce" anything to find a return; income can be generated without any social value. Or it can appear to be doing socially necessary work—as in the care economy—while in fact squeezing both workers and recipients of care for every last penny. It is a system for making the unbearable profitable.[47]

The unbearable takes many forms. It adapts. We will follow many threads of it through this book; follow the slave ship and the colonizers, the police force and the prison, the plague and the industrial workplace and the pollution heating the world.

The modern state is built on what Achille Mbembe called "necropolitics": it finds its "ultimate expression of sovereignty" in "the power and the capacity to dictate who may live and who must die." Linebaugh, thinking along similar lines, referred to it as "thanatocracy," rule by the spectacular dealing of death. The state is justified not just by its use of violence (war, policing, execution) but also by the division of humanity into groups more or less susceptible to death. More or less disposable.[48]

But there is also the ordinary unbearable, the way we are ground down too by being incorporated into the process. The workplace can kill spectacularly—about five thousand people a year die of workplace injuries in the United States, or about one every two hours—but more often it just shortens your life in a thousand imperceptible ways. The classic workplace struggle over the length of the working day, Marx wrote, is a struggle for life: capital "extends the labourer's time of production during a given period by shortening his actual life-time."[49]

It was Engels who named the process, or rather discovered the name, as he credited the term to the workers themselves, the workers who spoke to him for his book *The Condition of the Working Class in England.* The son of a factory owner himself, Engels studied the homes and workplaces, the streets and shops where the English workers spent their days and often died young, and deemed it "social murder":[50]

> But when society places hundreds of proletarians in such a position that they inevitably meet a too early and an unnatural death, one that is quite as much a death by violence as that by the sword or bullet; when it deprives thousands of the necessaries of life, places them under conditions in which they cannot live—forces them, through the strong arm of the law, to remain in such conditions until that death ensues which is the inevitable consequence—knows that these thousands of victims must perish, and yet permits these conditions to remain, its deed is murder just as surely as the deed of the single individual; disguised, malicious murder, murder against which none can defend himself, which does not seem what it is, because no man sees the murderer, because the death of the victim seems a natural one, since the offense is more one of omission than of commission. But murder it remains.[51]

The world has changed since Engels's day, and yet capitalism has never managed to banish the slum and the sweatshop entirely. It has rearranged the structures of social murder, in response to crises and protests and regulation, but it never stopped the killing. Holdren, who spent the pandemic years examining the concept and process of social murder, told me, "There's a throughline of continuous death, but there's not a requirement of death by machinery or a requirement of death by overwork. So, what capitalism will do is it will move the death and destruction around."[52]

The killing is often moved offscreen, as it were, out of sight. Our contact with it returns to the indirect, through the food or clothing or cars we buy rather than our own experience. The deaths happen elsewhere: more than 1,100 people died in the 2013 Rana Plaza factory collapse in Bangladesh. They happen here but to migrant workers: 59,000 meatpacking workers in the United States got COVID in the first pandemic year, and 269 died. The air and water kill slowly: nine million deaths per year from air pollution worldwide, the hundreds worried about their water after a train carrying chemicals derailed in East Palestine, Ohio. Other deaths are fast: seventy-two died when the Grenfell Tower in London burned, its destruction accelerated by flammable cladding put up on the cheap.[53]

The most recent reshuffle, though many would argue we're undergoing another one right now, was called "neoliberalism." (Some prefer "late capitalism," though I have come to think that term far too optimistic, foreshadowing as it does the thing's possibly imminent end.) Political theologian Adam Kotsko explains neoliberalism as "a combination of policy agenda and moral ethos," a push not just toward maximal privatization of resources but also toward justifying the system's inequalities by generating blame. "Neoliberalism," he wrote, "makes demons of us all, confronting us with forced choices that serve to redirect the blame for social problems onto the ostensible poor decision making of individuals." Freedom, the ultimate good that neoliberals gesture to, means being free to suffer the consequences of our actions, free from protection and a safety net. Free the way a tightrope walker is free.[54]

Freedom, in this way of thinking, comes with costs, costs that we must always be assumed to understand in advance. The cost of taking a certain job, of having sex, of moving or socializing or anything we might enjoy, measured against its potential fallout, our ability to make more money. Neoliberalism expects us to be happy and tells us that it is entirely our own fault if we are not. Yet it has grown increasingly punitive in recent years as it fails to provide the happiness and freedom it promised. Dealt a death blow by the 2008 financial crisis, the system staggers on, a zombie that offers only to eat you faster or more slowly.[55]

This demonization renders so many of us ungrievable, at fault in our own deaths: Gay men were assumed to have chosen the risk of HIV and therefore deserved to get AIDS, and Black men who do not submit to police officers in a way the officers deem sufficient are deserving of a bullet. The freedom they are presumed to have is only the freedom to die.[56]

Social worker and organizer MaryGrace DiMaria linked such blame to disenfranchised grief: "If someone dies from an overdose, that is disenfranchised completely. The blame is on the family: 'why didn't you do more? You could have done this and that and that.'" The obsession with who is worthy of support, of a job and social payments and a home, she said, leads to a lot of shame and hidden grief, to a hierarchy of lives and of deaths.[57]

Those who cannot be mourned remain with us as ghosts. We, the living, are constructed by the ghosts we choose to see, to honor. We are haunted by hundreds of years of history, by the ghosts within the objects we buy and the relations we are subject to. Capitalism cannot mourn; it can only continue the circuit, the production of profit, and whether we live or die is meaningless to it unless our lives or deaths are making money.[58]

5. Grief Is a (Collective) Becoming

We are denied the particularities of our lives and deaths in a world that makes us interchangeable, but by making us interchangeable, capitalism has also made us dangerous. If we are so alike, why should we not band together? With so little to lose, why not turn the whole thing upside down? As drifting things, we are blown together by forces that seem outside of our control, but if we can find the role we play in the process, we can turn collective mourning into revolt.[59]

Grief is so singular, particular, bodily. Each person lost is a whole universe, yes, but each person who mourns them will do so differently. Grieving alone will be necessary, and yet doing so together also necessary. We have to, Holdren suggested, create a space to value our own lives—our day-to-day existences, victories and losses, pleasures and small luxuries—a space that is also public and politicized and part of something bigger than ourselves. "What any individual can do about this feels like it would obliterate the individual," he said, "which is why it can't be an individual response."[60]

This is why my friends who had lost a parent all reached out to me when my father died and I in turn have reached out to others who have been through it since. Because the strange bodily-ness of grief, the way that it takes you, wherever you are—in the middle of crowds, once moderating a panel, so many times while sitting in front of your computer desperately trying to write—is frightening unless someone else tells you, *me too*. Unless they tell you, as Jess Kuttner told me, trying to suppress it will not work; it will come out somewhere else in the body, sometimes as pain or even illness.

To claim time for grief is to claim time for a whole spectrum of human feeling otherwise banished from public life. What people might call the darker emotions, or what Andrea Long Chu memorably called "negative passions," are still significant and worth feeling even as they are discomfiting. That is precisely their value. They teach us to experience the world differently.[61]

Cat Salonek told me a story about a friend of hers from high school who was stabbed after their senior year. Salonek had "squeaked by" in school and gotten accepted to college; she was white and her friend was Black. "I just didn't understand why I made it out and other people didn't," she said. But she began to learn about the structures of power that exposed some more than others to violence and premature death. She became an organizer: "My mission is to make it a world where all the angsty teenagers can actually live into their potential despite whatever angstiness they're going to get themselves into."

Grief does not necessarily make us better. It can and will make us angry and bitter, despairing and isolated. These are phases, maybe, but we can get stuck there. As Olúfẹ́mi O. Táíwò wrote, "Pain, whether born of oppression or not, is a poor teacher. Suffering is partial, shortsighted, and self-absorbed. We shouldn't have a politics that expects different." Loss and trauma, he suggested, are building blocks. We can build different things of the same materials. They can connect us to others, if we let them, or we can turn inward and let them fester. We can let the knowledge of our own vulnerability that grief brings open us up to one another, recognize that vulnerability in the people around us, reach outward for connection. Or we can cling to the uniqueness of our pain and use it as a weapon to wield against others, see in their humanity a threat to our own.[62]

This is precisely why collective mourning is necessary. Because it is an assertion of a different logic, one that says that these lives matter—that asserts their value over the value of profits. To take the space and the time to sit with what has happened, to talk about it in public, is to challenge the logic of productivity that hustles people back into the workplace after a loss. It is to share what we have learned. It is, as nurse Elizabeth Lalasz told me in the midst of a COVID-19 wave, to look at reality and also to wonder how we might change it.

To call for public, collective grieving is not simply to call for emotional catharsis. Rather, it is to say that this lack of attention to our losses in all their layers both springs from and leads to concrete failures of public health, safety, and care. If we do not grieve what we have lost, we will simply remain stuck in this doom loop, repeating cycles of death, and this will only get worse with the accelerating climate crisis.[63]

We lose so much in this life before it ends: loved ones, homes, jobs, entire communities. Some of those things we will grieve deeply, others we will leave behind gladly, many we will relate to as some kind of in-between. We are haunted by the ghosts of the choices we didn't make, yes, but also haunted by the choices made for us, the choices made sometimes before we were born and sometimes by distant, powerful others. By the kinds of impersonal decisions that quietly kill. In this book I try to tell many of those stories, and while I am sharing my own story too in these pages, I do so not to overshadow the others but to make myself vulnerable alongside them. If this book is different from the ones that I have written before, it is because I am no longer the person who wrote those books. I share some of her obsessions and her passions; some of the people who loved her still love me. But I have been changed by grief, and I cannot write exactly as I have before. Writing, Hélène Cixous suggested, begins with the dead; I do not know whether this is true, but I do know that I started this book alongside ghosts.[64]

I know that grief ended my ability to be in the world in a certain way. It eroded my capacity for bullshit, my tolerance for lies, my patience for people who want only to extract. The awareness that life is too fucking short became very real to me. It also taught me to love better and harder and to accept the love I was offered; it taught me to take risks and to beware the pleasures of doom. To cling fiercely to hope. *Hope is a discipline*, my friend and organizing hero Mariame Kaba says, and I try to remember that when everything feels dark.[65]

Because the universe is perverse and sometimes magical, I fell in love with someone who was deeply grieving while I was writing this book. Before he ever kissed me, I read something he wrote about grief, and unlike so much of what I read it felt true in my chest, and when he kissed me he asked if I was there because of his book and the answer wasn't yes but it wasn't no either and anyway he broke my heart before I finished the writing and taught me even more about grief that way. One of those things is that Freud's description of mourning is closer actually to heartbreak, to ambiguous loss. That in heartbreak you will struggle to let go, to detach your future from the one you planned together or even just the one you fantasized alone. And still it is not work, because love is not work any more than grief.

Nor is solidarity. It exists in the middle voice, something that you do, kind of, that is done to you, sort of, that is both at the same time and thus somehow bigger. It is impossible to do it one way; it exists as a relation, a reminder that we are never truly alone. We are remade by desire as well as by grief. We are remade together even though our losses are specifically our own. Mourning is, as Cristina Rivera Garza put it, a way of unknowing our individual selves. A becoming.[66]

A becoming, together.

Walter Benjamin wrote that "the spark of hope" can be fanned only by those "firmly convinced that *even the dead* will not be safe from the enemy if he wins. And this enemy has not ceased to be victorious." That solidarity with the dead who came before is part of his project and mine; his understanding that "the 'state of emergency' in which we live is not the exception but the rule" is necessary in order to turn the current crises to our advantage. We have to at once understand the specificities of today's grievances and their roots in structures past, in order to approach something like justice, for the dead and the living alike.[67]

In his addendum to the "Philosophy of History," Benjamin suggested, "Perhaps revolutions are an attempt by the passengers on this train—namely, the human race—to activate the emergency brake." When I first began to think politically about grief, sometime deep in its fog, I thought of this line. In its halting of everything, in its particular rupture, grief, I think still, could be revolutionary.[68]

I have covered social movements for the better part of two decades, and one thing that the ones that stuck had in common was that they provided solidarity in a material way. They offered care that was physical: food, a place to sleep, masks and hand sanitizer during COVID-19. They offered life, even when protesting a death. We lack a word in English for this kind of life making, like the missing middle voice. I have struggled in writing this book with the need for such a word, one that encapsulates the kind of world I want to live in and the way I want to live in it. It does not exist, I think, because we are not there yet.[69]

But in the streets and the camps that I visited while working on this book, in the spaces we made when I sat with someone and told them of my grief and they told me of theirs, I glimpsed it. In the struggles that did not shy away from public mourning as well as political militancy, I began to feel it.[70]

Break I

When I learned my father was sick, I was at a retreat not far from where I lived with some people I loved and one I would learn to love and a whole lot of strangers, and I had to perform.

When I found out he would die, I was on my way to Passover dinner with some of those same people, and I kept going, kept driving, I went.

It was what he would have done. It was what he told me to do. He was wrong.

It was the summer of 2017, and as usual my mother didn't call me immediately with the news that she'd taken him to the hospital. Not that there's ever a good way to get that call, but when she did call me and I walked out onto the lawn alone during a break to call her back, he had already been sick for days, and this time it was something new, not the heart and lung problems that we had known about for decades (he was a lifelong smoker, tried to quit several times, but mostly resorted to hiding the smoking from us rather than actually giving it up; I was the one to catch him each time). This time it was kidney disease, strangely advanced, unexpected.

I did what I always did in a crisis, what he taught me to do: I kept going, kept working. My mother had told me not to come home, there was nothing

I could do, so I did not go. Then. I performed, instead. I made new friends or at least new comrades, organized an informal lunch caucus; I hovered around an acquaintance that I was feeling more and more drawn to.

I was used to my father being sick. His first heart surgery came when I was in my second year of university, twelve hours from home in New Orleans, and then too my mother said, *There's nothing you can do, stay at school, keep working.* I remember curling in bed with an even-then-ex-boyfriend and waiting for the call to tell me he was out of the procedure and trying not to picture him with his chest cracked open. Gave up my own occasional cigarette when I saw the scar it left.

That wasn't the last heart surgery either.

In my twenties, I had been floating around a post-9/11 recession country trying to figure out why my sort of fancy degree didn't get me any sort of a job, waiting tables, drinking too much, and wondering what the hell to do now that I was ostensibly an adult, I landed home for a holiday and was put to work in the family business. My parents ran a bicycle shop then; before we moved to South Carolina it had been restaurants, a step up from my father's parents' Jewish deli outside of Boston (later I would search the web for mentions of the deli and find that they had been named the Best Bagels in Boston in 1980, the year I was born). The bike shop catered to tourists and I hated catering to tourists but I hated it marginally less than restaurant work, it turned out, and my mother's shoulder and neck problems were just surfacing so I filled a necessary gap in the running of the thing. I moved home, planning to stay the summer, save money, drift somewhere new in the fall.

I stayed three years as my father fell apart. I caught him smoking again but mostly I watched his supernatural work ethic crumble and slowly took on all his responsibilities. Fred—the manager—and I would conspire to shove my dad out the door for a half day once a week (the shop was open seven days a week, and he stayed for all of it). It was grief, I think, at first, that broke him.

His own parents had died within brief months of each other and there had been no funeral. He was their only child (a brother had died young), and so it was on him to go down to Florida, pack their apartment, carry out their wishes, come home with the few things that he wanted to keep. Some jewelry, some art, my grandfather's needlepoints. No funeral. Just his unspoken grief, kept inside.

I did not recognize it then. I was sad when they died, but I was not undone by it the way my father seemed to be, and it seemed to strike him later than I expected—he kept going for a while.

But it was not only grief; it was the old illness in his body. Or rather, the two are not separable. Grief is all throughout the body. His damaged heart breaking down.

Two years into my time looking after the business and my parents I decided that the thing to do would be to go back to school so I studied obsessively and took the GRE and applied to programs all over, in English literature, in creative writing, in journalism. School I understood, I was good at, though by then I was also good at various things to do with a bicycle and a small business and even, rather shockingly, managing a small staff of mostly men my age or so. I had proved what I needed to to my father, I thought, shown him that it wasn't a lack of hard work that had made my postcollege years a scramble. I had earned the right to make my life what I wanted, and writing in those days was what brought me joy and pleasure, and so I was off to school. The journalism program that accepted me offered me a teaching spot and it was in a city my then-boyfriend deemed acceptable so we were off at the end of August. But by then my father was really sick. Not just face in hands in the back room at the bike shop when he was pretending to work sick but can't-breathe sick.

He was still in the hospital when I left, well enough to tell me that I had done enough and I needed to go. Go to school, back to work, improve yourself. There's nothing more you can do.

He recovered, mostly, from what turned out to be a vicious pneumonia. I got a graduate degree in journalism and moved to New York City, got a series of jobs, wrote a book, broke up with one person and met the one I thought I'd be with forever. That man and I packed our things and moved north of the city to a house in the Hudson Valley, just us and a dog. It was a good life for a while.

It wasn't that the election of Donald Trump changed everything, though I fought more aggressively with my father over that election than I ever had before. He had always been a Republican but the kind of Massachusetts Republican who wants to keep his own taxes low and believed down deep in his third-generation-small-businessman bones that everything he had, he'd worked for. I couldn't accept he'd actually voted for . . . for that, even though I knew all about what he'd voted for before. *How could a Jew vote for this politics how could you say things to me about new refugees and migrants that they used to say about us?* He'd joke about his communist daughter even as I was running his small business better than he had. I earned his respect on the shop floor, but when my job became politics, that was different, that was work he did not recognize, and we grew apart. I did what he had, over and over, told me to do, and I worked hard. I freelanced away my weekends while holding down a full-time job, paid down my student debt, made a life. But I could not change his mind.

So when he went into the hospital that summer, I took my mother's call at a retreat organized by an international network to bring together people from North America and Europe over the threat of the far right; my father and I were strained because he'd voted for the same people I was working to defeat.

I did go home not long after that, saw him in the care home the hospital released him to, cried and struggled to know what to do with myself, with the racing heartbeat and the insomnia, the sadness and the fear, the impossibility of him getting better, the equal impossibility of him being gone. I hid it well, I think, though it seemed to me it was written all over my face, the line that began to etch itself off-center between my brows. I waited for the phone to ring.

For a little while it seemed he was getting better. The care home released him to my mother with a now-permanent portable oxygen tank and not much to say for a while. Then suddenly he was better, he was happier, even if he had to do dialysis and even though he hated feeling useless.

He was capable of going through the mountain of paperwork generated from selling the bike shop to his friendly competition so that he could ostensibly retire and enjoy himself. He would never be fully himself again, but he was a man in his seventies, and for a while we thought we would have him longer.

Then he had a fall, and he was back in the hospital, and the care home, and back again to the hospital.

It was his decision to die. To stop the dialysis and the other attempts to bring him home. The United States won't let you actively kill yourself, but it does give you the right to stop treatment. It was Passover when my mother called to tell me what he had decided, and my boyfriend and I went to dinner that night with the friend who taught me to knit the blanket I had made to throw over my father's lap in the chair at home while he watched golf, and I held my tears, mostly. We broke the matzo and drank the wine and ate the bitter herbs and said the prayers that I had learned from my father's family and I prayed, maybe, to the G-d he never believed in. I bought a plane ticket for the next day and went home to say goodbye.

We said goodnight one night—he could no longer speak but at least made eye contact—and at five the next morning the phone rang, and I crawled onto the couch where my sister had been sleeping and we held each other until our mother came and told us what we already knew.

She started cleaning immediately.

That he had been ready should have made things easier. Maybe it did; I have nothing to compare it to, or rather, it is not possible to compare it to the grief for friends I lost shockingly young to violent accidents.

All I know is that it broke me.

There are so many smarmy things written about grief, so many cliches and platitudes, so many things passed around as deep insight that sounded to me when I was deep in it—that still sound to me now, with my chest thrumming as I write this—like so many Hallmark cards. What I know about grief is that the cliches won't help. Grief will undo you, break you down, and if you are lucky enough, maybe it will remake you at the end. That you will remake yourself.

I did not know that then, but I know it now.

A friend who had not been close messaged me to say that there were two things he had learned from losing his mother that he wanted to share: *Whatever you are feeling is OK*, and *You will manage other people's feelings as much as your own*. Two weeks on I would write back to him and add a third: *You will be shocked by who will show up for you, and equally shocked by who will fail you*.

The man who was supposed to love me did not understand why I was so undone. People I barely knew flooded me with messages from silly to heartfelt. The only people who knew what to say were those who had been there.

I was OK. I was not OK. I was in shock. I was normal. I had a hole in my chest where the scar on his chest had been. I could not breathe. I had to remind myself to exhale fully, but when I did I could not hold myself together. I slept with a hand pressed to that place between my breasts. I kept working. Of course I did.

I left the man I wrote into my father's obituary as *partner* because although we would never be married, he deserved, I thought, to have status that sounded equal to that of my sister's husband. The relationship I had thought was forever could not, it turned out, survive my loss. I did not know how to ask for what I needed, but I knew that I needed more than his unwillingness to interrupt his routine to at least witness my devastation. If I was going to have to take care of myself through it, I could at least stop taking care of him. I moved back to the city alone. I fell stupidly in love with the person who knew what to say, knew that I needed hippo videos and poetry in equal measure. I could not be with him. I had a series of heartbreaks on top of heartbreaks; grief was already spilling over everywhere so why not pour more on top?

I wanted to stop hurting but I couldn't stop hurting myself. I filled notebooks with pain and trusted the wrong people and I began to realize that I was no longer an entertaining trainwreck, that my excess was exhausting.

There were a few exceptions to that rule, a few people who held me together. I remember a night in a cab with two dear friends—a couple—

who pressed me between them to give me as much human contact and warmth as they possibly could, and when I thanked them later the one simply said, *This is what friends are for.* I remember the first time the hippo-videos-and-poetry man kissed me and the hole in my chest closed for a night. I landed in Italy for another talk, another performance, a trip I had almost refused because I could barely speak only to find that food tasted good again and to recognize after a friend pointed it out that a new man was flirting with me. I remember the earthshaking sex in his hotel room and walking away with a smile. I remember the people who skipped events to walk with me and the friend who sent me a grief worksheet that included all the things happening to my body in its long list of symptoms. *Grief is in the body.* Of course.

I would have ten homes with twelve housemates in five years in four states and two countries and several months where I just hopped from house-sit to house-sit to hotel to couch-surf. I would rebuild myself and break that version too. I would write a whole book and watch it emerge in a pandemic. I would hold myself together, and I would fall in love with the men who held me when I cried, and I would be too much for nearly everyone. I would see the newspaper tell me that there was a new diagnosis of *prolonged grief disorder*, but then someone else told me, *Grief is excessive or else it isn't grief.* Of course I was disordered, but wasn't that the whole goddamn point?

I tried to hide it and realized that I succeeded too well, that everyone thought I was fine.

I was fine. It did not kill me. I survived all that. I could survive anything. I still wanted to watch everything burn.

CHAPTER 1

Burn

State violence, solidarity, and rebellion

1.1 Aflame

Let us return to that police car on fire.

It was 2020 and I was wearing a cloth mask that I could pull down to gulp water at a safe distance from other people, and we had gathered on the steps of the Philadelphia art museum and it was still the first lockdown, technically, and so I had not gotten yet to the point where I flinched at the nearness of strangers. At first it was like the other mass marches of the movement for Black lives in that it was angry and mournful and calm and dignified. But the streets were so otherwise empty, the broken windows, the graffiti everywhere. "Vengeance for George Floyd" scrawled in white paint on a window that might have been a bank. We followed the thick black smoke to the police car on fire and watched a group of young people—so impossibly young—walk slowly, deliberately distanced, arms raised, down the street, and the police car that was not on fire backed up from them until they took the intersection and began to dance.

The thick black smoke coated my nostrils and throat even through the mask. A girl on crutches blocked the path of a motorcyclist in the street so the march could pass.

Days later we marched again, more of us, clogging the steps of the art museum that Rocky once ran up. Faces covered, masked against the virus, people held cardboard signs that said "reparations now" and "rise up" and "no justice no peace" and "racism is a public health emergency." Little red letters on that one also said "I have sunscreen and ibuprofen if you need." There were doctors and nurses wearing their scrubs and street medics with red-duct-tape crosses on their T-shirt sleeves and people pulling wagons or pushing grocery carts with bottled water and hand sanitizer and masks to give away. I would see a big white CARE NOT COPS banner over and over again.[1]

When we reached City Hall on June 6, under a massive yellow ABOLISH THE POLICE banner, people were handing out hot food, which seemed like a miracle: that underneath a row of police in riot gear lining the level where Frank Rizzo's statue had been, there were folding tables and portable heat sources and aluminum catering trays of free food. It was a little piece of the world the protesters wanted to build even if it was under the looming threat of crackdown, even if the smiles of the people who handed out plates were hidden under N95 masks. It was the concrete practice of making Black lives matter, in Philadelphia, in Minneapolis, everywhere. It was a promise that we could care for each other.[2]

In between the marches in the streets in 2020, young activists were reading and holding teach-ins and trading books. Abolitionist geographer Ruth Wilson Gilmore became within the movement for Black lives a household name; her work finding its intended audience because she has always been an organizer as well as a theorist. Gilmore is known for many things, but one of them is her oft-repeated definition of racism as "the state-sanctioned and/or extralegal production and exploitation of group-differentiated vulnerabilities to premature death."[3]

It is those group-differentiated vulnerabilities that the millions in the streets were protesting when they insisted that Black lives matter. It was a movement that had grown tired of grieving, tired of the loss and the death and the repression that comes when you dare to say that those premature deaths were brutal and cruel and unwarranted. That this is what racism is as well: the concentration of people in the neighborhoods and the jobs and the streets that kill, places that were defunded long ago.

Gilmore also has a term for this: she calls it, as will I, following her, "organized abandonment."[4]

Organized abandonment is the necessary precondition for an unequal world, for the continued exploitation of so many in order to make life not just comfortable for others but to speed the accumulation of capital by a tiny few. Racism is the process by which that abandonment is made acceptable. It is produced differently in different places, produced by historic events and the way relations of power shift and change.[5]

That's how systems work, or rather how they conscript us into doing their work for them. The police officer who put his knee on George Floyd's neck, the police officers who fired into Breonna Taylor's apartment in a raid the *New York Times* described as "compromised by poor planning and reckless execution" didn't invent racism or policing or the guns they held in their hands; they were doing their jobs, jobs that taught one of them to act with "an extreme indifference to the value of human life" and another to "[abandon] his sworn oath to uphold the sanctity of life."[6]

The violence is justified because police, we hear, are there to protect us from "criminals," but "criminal" is a matter of perspective. Participants in uprisings are branded *looters*, the same way Black people in New Orleans after Hurricane Katrina were. As if Black people's acts of freedom have not been considered stealing since they were enslaved and "stole" themselves away from bondage.[7]

The production of criminals is, Gilmore wrote, the process of creating public enemies and of individualizing disorder. It is, like racism, geographically distinct and shifting in time: think of the uneven spread of marijuana legalization, how something is a crime one day and not the next, illegal in one state and fine just across an invisible border. If protesters are criminals, then mass disobedient protests and the burning of a police station are not justified. If they are criminals, why bother grieving their deaths?[8]

If people are branded "criminals," they can be locked away for years of slow death, their friends lovers cousins wives left to grieve even as they attempt to hold on. Yet prison removes people from one place that is in crisis and places them in another; it does not solve problems, but like most solutions of capitalism, it resolves one series of contradictions by creating a new set.[9]

The money that states spend on prisons is what might, with a different set of priorities, be spent on services that people need. *Care not cops.* This is what the movements mean when they say, "defund the police" or "divest/invest": that the decision to spend our collective wealth on cops and prisons to manage the people who are surplus to production could have been made otherwise.[10]

Racism is vulnerability to premature death. It is a process of justifying deaths when they happen, of justifying the use of violence by state or nonstate actors (Officer Derek Chauvin or Officer Brett Hankison or self-appointed neighborhood watchman George Zimmerman or former Marine Daniel Penny), of declaring that the people they killed were not grievable. Some of you might say that George Floyd or Breonna Taylor or Trayvon Martin or Jordan Neely did not do the thing they were supposed to have done when they were killed, and yet what if they did? The punishment for making and using a counterfeit twenty-dollar bill, as George Floyd was accused of doing, or for selling drugs, which was the thing Breonna Taylor's ex-boyfriend was suspected of doing, or bothering people on a subway as Jordan Neely supposedly did is not slow public torturous death or being gunned down in one's bed. Innocence is not enough. Innocence is produced in social spaces as much as race is, as much as criminals are. The rules of who and what can be innocent change constantly; Michael Brown was described as "no angel" in the *New York Times*, as if he ought to have been one. The young organizers who took to the streets and the subway tracks to demand justice for George Floyd and Breonna Taylor and Trayvon Martin and Jordan Neely insisted that their lives mattered whether or not they were innocent. They were worth grieving because they had lived and been loved, and the system that justified their deaths, *the whole damn system was guilty as hell.*[11]

That system we call capitalism, which some of us call *racial capitalism*, following Cedric Robinson, who meant not only the way the slave ship and the plantation were embedded into the thing from the beginning but also the way existing differences between people, real or imagined, get exaggerated into "race," and race in turn is used to rationalize the inequalities we live and die with. "Capitalism requires inequality and racism enshrines it," Gilmore reminds us. It is a system that requires human sacrifice. It does not necessarily require police murders or prisons; those are the fixes for our current iteration of the thing, worse in the United States than most anywhere else in the world. In other times and places, it has meant apartheid, pogroms, segregation, slavery, mass executions, settlers destroying Native homes and food sources. But it does require death making.[12]

And so in 2020 in particular more people realized this than had ever before, realized it as they were trapped behind screens in pandemic lockdown with nothing to do but to consider the world they lived in and whether normal had ever been anything but a different kind of hell, realized it as they kept going to work and their bosses denied them sick time. Realized in their misery that others were miserable too, different but parallel, that as Gargi Bhattacharyya wrote, "heartbrokenness is the class consciousness of racial capitalism," that in our heartbreak we could come together. The people who came out to protest in 2020 defied simple color lines. The demonstrations were proof that Black lives matter not only to Black people but to many of us, that we too grieve, we take our place in the second line, we remember, we demand justice.[13]

1.2 Family

Nyliayh and Darrius Stewart grew up like brother and sister, though they were cousins. Their mothers were sisters who stayed close as they raised their children. "Everybody said we looked like twins," Nyliayh told me. They lived and played together in Memphis, and then Nyliayh returned to Mississippi, where she was born, for high school, and one night she woke up to hear her sister screaming. Her cousin was dead. "I just broke down. It was terrifying."

The story as she knows it is that Darrius was in a car with his friends. They were pulled over for a broken taillight, and the police asked everyone to produce ID; Darrius didn't have his, so his friends went down the road to his mother's house to get it, leaving Darrius in the custody of the police. When they returned, he was dead. Eyewitnesses later testified to an official investigation that Stewart was turning to flee when he was shot. One of those witnesses said they heard Stewart yell, "I can't breathe" before the second bullet hit him.[14]

Darrius was nineteen. Nyliayh was sixteen. "It was terrifying. I was going into my senior year the next school year because it happened in the summer, and I didn't even want to go to school. I had never lost anybody that close to me."

There were protests in Memphis when Darrius was killed and an investigation that recommended charging the officer, Connor Schilling, with "voluntary manslaughter and employment of a firearm during the commission of a dangerous felony," but the grand jury did not indict. "I feel like it wasn't manslaughter. It was first-degree murder. It was murder," Nyliayh said. "He was unarmed, and I've never known the police to pull over a car and ask for everybody's identity. They were stereotyped. It was a car full of young Black boys."

Nyliayh, small and pretty and poised, was telling me a story she has told many times. Her family was and remains close, and they carry the loss with them still; she doesn't even like to speak of Darrius to her auntie, his mother, because it is too hard for her. She spent her senior year in a deep depression, at first refusing to talk about what had happened. "I really had nobody to talk to because I'm the strong friend. I'm who everybody comes to talk to. They don't expect me to be down; it's like they don't know what to do. So it was a process I had to go through by myself. I think that was the hardest year of my life."

The summer of 2020, the year of the pandemic and the George Floyd rebellion, was the five-year anniversary of Darrius Stewart's death, and the family, as they did each year, held a vigil at the site of his killing. It was at that vigil that Nyliayh met one of the founders of Decarcerate Memphis. The organization was fighting for changes to policing in Memphis, changes beyond the body cameras that had been instituted after Darrius was killed. Nyliayh joined the organization, and, when Memphis police killed Tyre Nichols in 2023, her testimony before the city council helped to pass a ban on the kinds of pretextual traffic stops that had led to Darrius's death.[15]

Nyliayh is proud of the effort to change the law, but it also hurts. "My cousin would still be here today if that law would've been passed eight years ago. I don't want to sound harsh when I say it. It's something that I personally can't celebrate for myself because it seems like a slap in the face to my family. I am happy that it would save others. But it's not a celebration to me.

"Why does someone have to die for them to see these are problems?"

Darrius Stewart's death was a spark that blazed into more and bigger protests. The momentum carried through 2015, from rallies at the Shelby County Criminal Justice Center to businesses and tourist centers, including Graceland, the home-turned-museum of Elvis Presley, and when Alton Sterling was killed by police in Baton Rouge and Philando Castile was killed in Minnesota in July 2016, a march that was headed for the Civil Rights Museum changed direction and took over the I-40 bridge. Al Lewis, old enough to have childhood memories of when Martin Luther King Jr. came to town for the sanitation strike, said of the bridge moment, "For me that was the most powerful thing that ever happened in Memphis, including Dr. King coming and getting killed."[16]

But when the crowds fade, Nyliayh and her family still live with the grief. Nyliayh had known young people, schoolmates, who died violently before, and that had been bad, but it was nothing like the kind of deep gutting bodily grief that came from losing someone she was raised with. She finds herself at a loss for words when friends lose someone. "I can't talk about it. I can't talk about death. I don't know what to say. I don't know what to tell you because I can't . . . I'm not going to tell you everything's going to be okay because I don't know your grief. I don't know how you're going to grieve."

Nyliayh Stewart lives with an impossible burden and a kind of moral authority she would trade away in a heartbeat to bring her cousin back. It is a burden shared by Samaria Rice, whose son Tamir was twelve when he was shot by a Cleveland police officer, who spoke of that struggle to Imani Perry. "There is a certain way you have to go in front of the media to let them know that you want justice for your baby," she said. Black mothers, Christina Sharpe wrote in her exquisite book *In the Wake*, carry a particular burden because they live with the knowledge that such things can happen to them at any moment. The responsibility of being "mothers of the movement" is a kind of caring work that these mothers never asked for, a triply cruel burden on top of the other demands made of them in a world that extracts their work and their love, and that it all be performed under constant surveillance. It is a demand for perfection that no one could possibly meet.[17]

It is not only that Black family members have to defend their loved ones against the assumptions of criminality; it is that they have to also prove their right to grieve. Claudia Rankine wrote, "Michael Brown's mother, Lesley McSpadden, was kept away from her son's body because it was evidence. She was denied the rights of a mother, a sad fact reminiscent of pre–Civil War times, when as a slave she would have had no legal claim to her offspring. McSpadden learned of her new identity as a mother of a dead son from bystanders." Michael Brown's body was left for hours in the street; when he was finally taken inside, it took two weeks before McSpadden was allowed to see him. There was a movement in his name shaking the world by that time, but there were also vendors selling

T-shirts with his name on them. "Not only were the procedures around her son's corpse out of her hands; his name had been commoditized and assimilated into our modes of capitalism."[18]

Racism is vulnerability to premature death. Rankine's words linger: "The condition of black life is one of mourning."[19]

While it is not always the mother leading the battle, the campaigns for justice are so often led by a woman. Mothers daughters aunts sisters. Marcia Rigg, one of the chairs of the United Families and Friends Campaign—a network of those bereaved by deaths in police, prison, and psychiatric custody in Britain—described the organization as a place of support as well as political struggle, somewhere that grieving people "can meet other families, share their stories, share their pain, and have somebody else to talk to that understands what they've been going through." It is an extraordinary kind of love that this world demands of people like Rigg, whose brother Sean was killed in Brixton Police Station in South London in 2008, or Nyliayh Stewart, Samaria Rice, or Judy Scott, who was on the phone with her fifty-year-old son Walter as he was killed by police in North Charleston, South Carolina, in 2015. Scott looked the police officer who killed Walter in the eye in court and told him she forgave him, but what a cruel demand it is that anyone forgive such a loss, what a superhuman kind of love we expect of Black women like her.[20]

And yet those mothers sisters cousins friends have risen to that impossible bar over and over again.[21]

In claiming their right to love their sons brothers nephews partners, the family and friends of the people killed sometimes find themselves in tension with other parts of the movement for Black lives. Samaria Rice called out those who were, in her words, "hustling Black death," disconnected from the real lives of those grieving, the real knowledge of just who has been lost. Her statement, alongside Lisa Simpson, the mother of Richard Risher, killed by the LAPD in 2016, read in part:[22]

> We condemn capitalism's monetization of Black people's death and dying through the following modes of violence: "celebrity activism,"

> along with fundraising without transparency. We need structured distribution of funds to Black working class families and grassroots organizations. Families of those who are killed by the police—and whose loved ones' deaths spark mass movements—continue to navigate political misrepresentation, battle zones of police repression, homelessness, and poverty, while Black "leadership" that has not been selected by the masses flourishes through celebrity status. These families must be provided the resources to sustain themselves, their families, and their work dedicated to building community infrastructure. . . . Stop celebrity activism; stop corporate investments that support lobbyists for this norm; put an end to the political-economy's parasitism on Black death and poverty.

Her words are a sharp description of how the system into which she was thrust operates. As Selma James wrote years ago: "Every time we build a movement a few people get jobs, and those who get the jobs claim that this was the objective of the movement, this was the change."[23]

This is a process, as Olúfẹ́mi O. Táíwò wrote, of "elite capture," of the way the well positioned or relatively privileged ("relatively" is important here; privilege is always a relation rather than a measure of absolutes) tend to gain control of financial benefits or political projects. The era of the influencer, given leadership status based on social media clout, has magnified this problem a hundredfold; busy people latch onto a few voices to tell them what to think, deferring to others deciding that those voices speak for a broader and much more heterogenous movement, group, ethnicity, collective. Whether the group from which the speaker is extracted itself has any basis in reality rarely matters.[24]

Indeed, this also describes the way that certain mothers or family members are elevated, listened to, treated as respectable. Mothers themselves, as Rice noted in her conversation with Perry, are not a monolith. And yet it is true that, in Perry's words, "there are market exchanges happening; people are making money because news agencies, publishers, and civic and professional organizations need interpreters of this moment." Of that money and attention-that-is-money in this economy, "the vast majority goes to a professional class of spokespeople: organizers, writers, and academics. And the killings continue. So whether we deliberately hustle Black death or not, it is without question a nefarious hustle."[25]

Public grieving-as-protest (or as-riot) challenges the boundaries of what and whom we are permitted to grieve. It is an attempt, though imperfect, to share some of the burden that Nyliayh Stewart and Samaria Rice and Lesley McSpadden and Marcia Rigg carry. The solidarity we can offer comes from putting our own vulnerability on the line in honor of what someone else has suffered, is suffering, will suffer. Most of us have not, will not, cannot know what they feel, and so invariably we will make mistakes; but we must, I think, do a better job of holding those whose impossible losses sparked the movement in the first place.[26]

I remain haunted by a photo of graffiti from the George Floyd uprising that I saw online; trying to find that original picture, I found multiple versions of it, all striking: "All mothers were summoned when he called out for his mama."[27]

What is the family but the group of people for whom it is permissible to grieve?

The outpouring into the streets in collective public mourning is a statement of kinship beyond the nuclear family, beyond the extended family, beyond the bounds of the weird family called "race." It is a statement of the most basic solidarity: an injury to one is an injury to all. That we are in fact responsible to and undone by one another. That the rage and pain and gutted-ness of the immediately affected, those mothers sisters cousins lovers, will not be a burden to be carried alone. Such generosity was everywhere in the streets in 2014, 2015, 2020, as everywhere people cared for each other, shared tips on battling tear gas, picked each other up from the ground, brought food and water and in the pandemic times, masks and hand sanitizer. Grief both could and could not be shared.[28]

Abolitionist organizer Mariame Kaba has worked with many families who have lost people and who are survivors of violence, navigating the varying understandings of what "justice" might look like. One success—though it took decades—was the campaign for reparations for survivors of police torture in Chicago. For the men who were tortured into false confessions and imprisoned, there was so much rage and a tiny sliver of hope that their fight to be exonerated would succeed.[29]

The survivors understandably wanted the men who tortured them to be convicted and imprisoned in turn: that was their vision of justice. But Kaba felt distant from the early campaign because as an abolitionist she could not support the demand for more incarceration; she sought instead other ways to help. "The question then becomes, how do you respectfully find something so that you can still be in relation with them?" she said. "Just because somebody's grieving intensely and wants revenge, you don't have to say, 'I will also fight for revenge.' You can say, 'I hear you, valid. You are right to feel your feelings. Now here's what I can offer. Do you want that?'"

The reparations campaign became a form of justice that she and the survivors could come together around. Standish Willis, an attorney who'd fought battle after battle for the torture survivors, was the one to say that the legal realm was perhaps exhausted and what they needed was a political fight, a reparations framework and an international lens through which to shame Chicago officials into action. This was just after the Abu Ghraib scandal had rocked the United States and the world, and it inspired the survivors to take their demands for justice to the UN Committee Against Torture.[30]

The international shame campaign worked, to a degree. Jon Burge, the police commander and head of the torture ring, faced charges and was convicted—for lying about torture, rather than the torture itself. The survivors and their families felt their sustaining rage turn to a deep emptiness. Justice required something more. Joey Mogul, another attorney, suggested an artistic project, which Kaba joined. Mogul created the first reparations ordinance as part of that art project, which became the first draft of the eventual law.

This was happening as the streets were filling with protesters over the deaths of Trayvon Martin and Jordan Davis, and in Chicago young people whom Kaba had organized with were mourning one of their own, Dominique Franklin Jr., Damo to his friends, who died after police used a Taser on him. "I had all these young people in front of me, and they were just nihilistic. I was terrified. I use that word very specifically. I was terrified at the reaction, because it wasn't anger. It was complete, fuck the world in a way that I had not seen before in them," Kaba said.[31]

She recalled returning home to her partner after a meeting with Damo's friends. "He could see something was really wrong. I started crying immediately and I said, 'I'm scared. I'm terrified. I don't know what they're going to do with themselves.' I was afraid that people might do harm to themselves . . . and end up further ensnared by the system," she said. When her partner looked at her and calmly said, "What do you know how to do?" she said, "I lost it." Her partner let her vent all her rage and grief and then left her alone. Calming down, her eyes fell on the bookshelf across the room and lit on William Patterson's *We Charge Genocide*, the petition carried to the United Nations in 1951 by Patterson and Paul Robeson, documenting American racism in detail and demanding repair. "I pulled it and I said, 'Let's go to Switzerland.'"[32]

All of the disparate threads began to make sense to her. The torture survivors' need for justice, Damo's friends' need for an outlet for their grief, a community's need to be heard. At the first meeting, around fifty people showed up; young people and lawyers and seasoned organizers together to hear her pitch for what would become We Charge Genocide the organization, which would present its case to the United Nations in November of that year. Energized by the uprisings after the deaths of Michael Brown and Eric Garner that summer, the young organization would pour all of its members' rage and grief into building a demand for reparations that would win.[33]

In 2015, the ordinance passed. It included money—nearly $100,000 for each of the fifty-seven documented torture survivors—and free tuition at Chicago junior colleges for survivors and their families, as well as a counseling center. It included a public memorial—yet to be built in 2023—and a curriculum for the public schools to teach the history of police torture.[34]

People who are grieving, Kaba said, need a "soft place to land." The reparations struggle and its success became a place where people who had been hurt could heal together, and the torture justice center is now a place for the survivors and their families to help one another, to learn about the breadth and depth of the emotions they are feeling, now that they have time to feel.

A radical movement that truly meets people's needs, geographer and organizer Adam Elliott-Cooper suggested to me, must be a thing that people can turn to in pain as well as joy, that can hold their mourning, because it says all aspects of their lives matter. The movement can create its own spaces, its own inquiries and memorials and ordinances that begin as art projects and wind up as demands.[35]

And yet the movement must also sometimes face up to its inability to provide everything for everyone. Ciara Taylor was one of a group of young people who, in the aftermath of Trayvon Martin's killing, organized a march from Daytona to Sanford, Florida, where Martin had died. It felt to her like a reawakening, that moment in time, and a deep sense of community amid a convergence of struggles—inspired by the Arab Spring and the Occupy and immigrant rights movements and shaped by the 2008 economic collapse. But she also wishes, with hindsight, "that we just fully were able to understand the situation that we were in in that moment, and what we were up against." Their understanding of the pieces of a system that would confound their demands over and over again, the structures of the state, the nature of racial capitalism, was incomplete. They were also not from Sanford and did not understand that community either: "We found out while we were in Sanford that the people of Sanford had been wanting to speak with their local law enforcement and their representatives for a long time before

Trayvon was there, before Trayvon was killed and certainly before a rag-tag bunch of students just sort of descended upon their town and kind of super-heroed on our way in."

Rather than giving up, though, Taylor and the others founded an organization called the Dream Defenders and rooted themselves in communities around Florida, dedicated to building power in those communities and developing leaders who could build a lasting movement across the state. In those heady early moments, she said, it felt like the edifices they were fighting were about to fall, "like everything was on the verge of happening tomorrow." The reality was very different. They had to learn to build for the long haul.

The political establishment will elevate certain leaders, reporters will pick spokespeople whether or not the movement does (I am certainly no better than anyone for this), and those leaders will feel pitted against one another too. As historian Donna Murch wrote, there have been many tensions within the larger movement for Black lives, between founders and employees, paid and unpaid organizers, abolitionists and reformers, "between building a larger movement and claiming intellectual property," and always where the money lands. Murch pointed to the Dream Defenders' decision to take a social media break and focus on deep community building as a way to turn from the cult of online celebrity, of organizers-as-influencers, into something more lasting.[36]

The movement is not a monolith; that's easy to say. The movement is an ecosystem, a network made up of networks, a series of streams flowing into a river that eventually reaches the sea. There will be different tactics and strategies and structures of feeling in the thing as it moves, and sometimes the best we can do is to let go of some of these binaries or at least the idea that one or the other is exclusively right.[37]

Grief is a rupture. It makes unthinkable the future that you thought you would have. Rebellion is a rupture too, one where a collection of people come together to say, to demand, to insist that the past future is no longer one they will accept.

* * *

In Memphis there is a house that used to be a stop on the Underground Railroad. They call it Slave Haven now; it is a museum you can visit. Alice Pettit and Beth Hoffberg took me there, and my eye landed on a reproduction of a poster for a raffle that had as its prizes "Dark bay horse, 'Star' and Mulatto girl, 'Sarah.'" My name. A prize like a horse to be won. We walked down stairs into a low-ceilinged basement where once enslaved people had breathed quietly, hiding, resting between stops on their journey north. We peered out between loosened bricks to see a tiny bit of light.[38]

I was there to talk to Hoffberg about today's horrors, not the horrors of the past, though they would echo in our conversation. She hadn't wanted to watch the video of the police beating Tyre Nichols, but her partner at the time was a journalist and he was Black and his job demanded that he watch them and she wanted to hold him through it, so she made a space in her apartment where they would not normally sit—"this can sit here, and you don't ever have to be in this exact space again like this," she said—and they watched the videos while outside the protesters took the I-55 bridge.[39]

The videos by 2023 had a horrible sort of routine to them, released like a movie premiere with promotions and a showtime. The videos haunting, the death happening over and over again. "The City of Memphis has made an exhibition of the footage," Doreen St. Felix wrote in the *New Yorker*. The releases "carefully choreographed," allowing public officials to claim the side of justice even as they prepare to crack down on protests.[40]

Hoffberg spent the night looking at Nichols's photography website, his Facebook page; she read his posts and his stories and realized how many of his photos had been taken at the park where she walked her dog every day, realized afresh how awful what she had just seen was. "If someone in my family had experienced this, I wouldn't want strangers to just . . . watch this video," she said. "People should have access to see it in terms of holding the police accountable. But we shouldn't be able to witness other people being murdered." The horror of the moment drove her to join the protests and to try to honor the man she tried to know from the art and skateboarding and writing he had done while he was alive, the things that gave him joy and made him specifically irreplaceable.

If we linger on the expression of suffering, the results of violence, the images of the bereaved mothers sisters daughters cousins partners, it may be that we will only be able to imagine more suffering, that the images will simply produce fear, despair, complacency. Yet the photographs too have the power to reach beyond their immediate context, to touch and shock. Mamie Till Mobley, whose son Emmett was murdered far from home for paying attention of some sort to a white woman, insisted on an open casket at the funeral, showing what white people had done to her child, showing, as Joy James said, that "there's nothing holy except for your love and rage." Mobley's love and rage went around the world.[41]

Beth Hoffberg wanted the world to know Tyre Nichols through the photos he had taken, not the video of his death. She walked me down to Fourth Bluff Park to show me where they set up the enlarged prints of his best work ninety days after his death to remind the city that a person had been killed, a person who deserved to be remembered and mourned. The park is gorgeous, overlooking the Mississippi River, which I followed from New Orleans to Minneapolis and back. It used to be called Confederate Park, and I can't forget that any more than I can forget why I was in Memphis.

The three-month anniversary of Tyre Nichols's death was also Easter Sunday, and so Hoffberg and L. J. Abraham and Amber Sherman planned a weekend to celebrate his life and to build up to a pivotal City Council meeting where they were demanding changes to the law that might have prevented his death. They wanted to show him as a complex person, not to prove that he was respectable enough to be honored, but because when he died a whole universe died. Because he had, on his website, invited people to see *the world through his eyes*: "My vision is to bring my viewers deep into what i am seeing through my eye and out through my lens. People have a story to tell why not capture it instead of doing the 'norm' and writing it down or speaking it. I hope to one day let people see what i see and to hopefully admire my work based on the quality and ideals of my work. So on that note enjoy my page and let me know what you think."[42]

Hoffberg reached out to Nichols's family through their attorneys to ensure they would approve of her printing his photos and setting up the event, and then she and Abraham and Sherman invited people to speak at sunset and to release lanterns above the Mississippi and honor different parts of who Nichols was. His parents and grandmother and aunt passed through the space quietly at different times. There was a prayer, and a letter from Nichols's friend in California, and an affirmation Nichols had written, and Hoffberg played sound bowls, and they released twenty-nine lanterns, one for each year of his life. On his website Nichols had asked people to let him know what they thought of his photos, so at the event the organizers handed out cards, and people wrote down and shared their thoughts. And then they asked people to attend the City Council meeting for a different form of action and grief.[43]

Decarcerate Memphis had decided to focus on pretextual traffic stops before Tyre Nichols was killed, inspired by what had happened to Darrius Stewart and too many others around the country. They delved deep into what little information was available in Memphis about traffic stops and who was stopped and where and how often they were arrested or hurt or killed. They also held brake light clinics, fixing lights on people's cars for free to take away one more reason for police to stop Black drivers. The goal of abolitionist organizations like Decarcerate is not police "reform" but rather to chip away at police power and reduce the amount of interactions the police have with people while creating alternative institutions—like the brake light clinic—that solve problems.[44]

In November Decarcerate put out its report *Driving While BIPOC*, analyzing all the data on traffic stops and making policy suggestions. They presented the report to the council in December; the council, Decarcerate member Adam Nelson said, made sympathetic noises, but the organizers all assumed they would spend a year just asking for data transparency. The uprising after Tyre Nichols was killed changed everything. Nelson and the others joined the street protests, supported the family's demands—to charge the officers who killed him, to name all the public personnel who were on the scene when he was beaten and release their files, and to end the SCORPION unit (Street Crimes Operation to Restore Peace in Our Neighborhoods, a mouthful of a name that seems to imply many things at once). They also added their own demands, prewritten ordinances for data transparency and to ban pretextual stops as well as the use of unmarked cars and plainclothes officers in traffic enforcement.[45]

The bills passed their first vote on February 7, but the Memphis process demands three votes to pass something into law, and so across Memphis the organizers had to keep up the energy; they had to fight to keep the bills on the agenda, to keep them from being watered down, and ultimately even to stop a bill that had Tyre Nichols's name on it but nothing that his family or the community had demanded. Eventually, the pretextual stops ban was passed, bringing the total of reform ordinances to six.[46]

After the win comes the letdown or the reconciliation or both. It is the feeling, as Nyliayh Stewart said, that you are proud of the win but still angry at what it took, the months and years of painful work and the deaths and putting your grief on display to the world. There's frustration that the laws passed are imperfect. There's the real tension and splits within a community held together by momentum that come up when the momentum fades. Communities are formed in the struggle, Nelson noted, but those communities change and sometimes fall apart.

I think of the common chant "If there ain't no justice then there ain't no peace." It is a political demand of course, that the streets will not be quiet and the fire will not go out until there is justice, but it is also a statement of what grief feels like when the loss is a violence. How do you rest and feel at ease without justice—except what even would justice be? A little piece of justice can still bring you no peace.[47]

"The word fighting is active, it's aggressive, it has this sense of anger with it, and we should be angry," Beth Hoffberg said. But, she noted, anger can subsume other emotions that are just as important to feel. It can be exhausting, she noted: "I think that's probably part of what leads to a lot of activism burnout, frankly."[48]

Al Lewis lived that struggle his whole life. As a teenager, he listened in on his parents' conversations as they did the work of the movement that brought Dr. King to the city. He became a labor movement troublemaker as an adult postal worker, and now many of the young people in the movement call him "OG." "I went into healing work because I wanted to heal myself," he told me, and so he cofounded an organization called Inward Journey, which works on generational trauma among Black people, teaching history to support people in collective grief that dates back to the slave ship and the people huddled in that basement waiting to be helped up and over the Ohio River and on northward. Grief the United States has no interest in addressing.

Lewis was retired and recovering from back surgery when he got a call from younger activist Keedran Franklin in the wake of Darrius Stewart's killing, and he advised Franklin to broaden the protests from the police buildings to local businesses who, he said, "control the politicians who control the police." They targeted Graceland and called the protest that led to the taking of the I-40 bridge. "This reignited a spirit not just in Black people, but in everybody, and particularly young people," Lewis said. Politicians and police leaders tried to pacify them after the bridge but offered nothing material, and so they turned back to "organizing around economic apartheid."[49]

When the George Floyd rebellion hit and young people who had not been active before burst into the streets, Lewis and the others offered to train whoever was interested in direct action tactics. "We were preparing for thirty or forty. Five hundred or more people showed up. Mostly white, mostly young. And I'm sure that scared the power base here because that's their grandchildren. We were telling them about the systems that their grandparents had created and evolved, and we were showing them how to challenge those systems."

While Lewis, like Nyliayh Stewart, is proud of the justice work he's done, he looked around Memphis and still saw so much pain, so much violence, and not all of it from police. "It's still the poorest metro area in the country. We are eaten up with systemic, epidemic ignorance from a school system that is betraying our students. . . . Part of the reason we are seeing this wave of violence, this is nihilism." Gunshot wounds, even if they don't kill, are devastating, and yet Lewis noted the state has only made it easier for young people to get guns. His eyes filled with tears as he told me, "I think we deserve to see each other in a different way. I think we deserve to love each other in a different way. People that haven't been taught how to love ourselves. I'm a native Memphian but I don't love what's happening here, and I want to love it again before I go."[50]

Lewis carried so much grief for so much of his life. "People didn't ask me what happened; they just asked me what was wrong. I thought they meant I must be wrong," he said. In his work, he has struggled alongside his elders and young people, alongside religious leaders and street gang leaders, young people who live in a system "that was designed for them not to get a shot. And they know it was designed that they not get a shot, and they're pushing back."

So what is justice for Memphis, for Tyre Nichols and Darrius Stewart and for the people they were taken from? St. Louis organizer and lawyer Derecka Purnell wrote, "Justice is a process where people decide and create the conditions that help us thrive and it involves the people who are most impacted by those conditions." To Al Lewis, real justice isn't nonprofits, and it isn't a few ordinances: "It's going to take a Marshall Plan–level thought-out process. If we don't continually monitor what's going on with us as we're trying to recreate something, we'll find out that we have recreated the same thing, just a different version."[51]

1.3 Justice

Aviah Sarah Day grew up in an England shaped by There Is No Alternative, a country carved into austerity by Margaret Thatcher and patrolled by police determined not to see repeats of the rebellions in Black communities that roiled the 1980s. She was told like all children of the '80s to work hard and go to university and rise out of her family's circumstances and carry them with her if she could. "No one was talking about class or race," she said.[52]

It was not until the student protests and anti-austerity movement arose in the wake of the 2008 crash that she found her place: she was recruited by the direct action group UK Uncut. At the same time, she was working in the domestic violence sector and watching austerity devastate the programs that people relied on for safety. She, like others who worked in women's refuges and services, had also relied on them in the past, and so the loss felt particularly grim. Sisters Uncut was born in November 2014 out of the demand to keep those services open, the understanding that funding was a political, an ideological choice. The group was also inspired by campaigns like the one led by the family of Stephen Lawrence, a young Black man murdered by racist vigilantes in 1993, and the community defense work done in the wake of the police killing of Mark Duggan, a young Black man from Tottenham killed by police in 2011, and the uprising that followed. That analysis would lead them, eventually, to abolition.[53]

The group dyed the fountains of Trafalgar Square red to chants of "they cut we bleed"; they staged a die-in at the premiere of the film *Suffragette*, saying "dead women can't vote." They joined forces with migrant solidarity groups and with the United Families and Friends Campaign and Black Lives Matter UK. In 2016, Sarah Reed, a young Black woman, was found dead in Holloway Prison, and Sisters Uncut protested outside of the prison. When the prison was closed shortly after, Sisters Uncut became part of a campaign to turn the building not into luxury condos but into a community space where people like Reed could get care. The North London chapter of Sisters Uncut occupied the visitor's center at Holloway, lifting up the demands of the community campaign for affordable housing and a community center and, in an "abolitionist rehearsal," turning their occupation itself into a space for care.[54]

It had taken years, but Sisters Uncut had become an abolitionist collective, one that applied its understanding of policing to the often punitive nature of the very domestic violence sector it had been organized to save. As a teenager, Day recalled being evicted from a women's refuge; as she and Sisters

Uncut went deeper into their antiracist organizing, they began to see the way that gender too was violently policed, particularly for Black and migrant women, the way that people who experienced domestic violence would often be arrested as well, separated from support, brutalized as Sarah Reed had been. Meanwhile, the perpetrators were let off the hook all too often.

In 2020, the George Floyd uprisings reached Britain too, and as was usual by that point the Conservative government responded with yet another bill limiting the rights of protesters. The bill was moving through Parliament when Sarah Everard went missing.[55]

Everard was white; she was young, successful, blonde—the kind of woman the newspapers notice and who would be described in court as a "wholly blameless victim," in marked contrast to the coverage of Mark Duggan or Sarah Reed. It was March 3, 2021, when she didn't come home. COVID restrictions were still in effect, and so the first group to announce a vigil for Everard, Reclaim These Streets, was browbeaten by police into canceling; while Reclaim went to court and lost, Sisters Uncut decided to go anyway. "We thought politically it was incredibly important to turn out and to push back against the police narrative that all protest and gathering was illegal," Day said. "So many women were online saying, 'I'm going to turn up anyway,' we thought, 'There needs to be some kind of organized presence there.'"[56]

The news that a police officer, Wayne Couzens, had been arrested for Everard's murder was rocket fuel to the fire. "It was one of those weird organic moments where all of these things just kind of happen at the same time," Day said. The attempt to shut down the vigil using COVID powers as justification overlapped with the fact that Couzens had used expanded powers granted the police under COVID to kidnap, rape, and murder Everard. When the vigil happened on Clapham Common, the police turned up with more violence, official this time.[57]

Day recalled the beautiful chaos of the evening before the police charged in. The feeling in the air completely changed. Officers began grabbing and pointing at people. "Initially the atmosphere was really somber and reflective and quiet and just sad. And then it turned into this utter rage. I didn't see any protestors touching a police officer at all. But the atmosphere was just rage. Women were shouting, 'Let us speak. Let us speak.' I could see in people's faces just utter rage that they had interrupted this moment of peaceful reflection and mourning. I saw a woman confronting a police officer and just screaming at him like, 'You did fuck all when I was raped. I came to you, you did fuck all.' They just started ramping people up in the Bandstand and arresting them and dragging them off."

Social media was exploding, calling for police commissioner Cressida Dick to resign, sharing a picture of red-haired, COVID-masked Patsy Stevenson being held down by police. Day got a text from a friend in Black Lives Matter UK, saying, "You've got to do a protest tomorrow." She realized they were right.[58]

"Thank goodness for Sisters Uncut," said Adam Elliott-Cooper, who had been organizing with BLM UK at the time. The organization refused to allow a "bad apple" narrative around Couzens and highlighted the fact that his colleagues on the force knew of his tendencies, nicknaming him "the Rapist." They pointed to the violence at the vigil and connected it to the destruction of care services, the failure of police when it came to sexual violence. They underscored the patriarchal nature of policing and created a "mainstream awareness that the police are chauvinistic and the perpetrators of gender-based violence." Because Sarah Everard was white, she was middle class, she was much harder for the police to demonize.[59]

Everard's respectability was historically produced though, just as much as Mark Duggan's purported criminality had been. To have the criminal you must have the victim; to have the colony you must have the metropole. The white women who came to the vigil for Sarah Everard may not have expected violence, but when they stepped outside of the bounds set by the police and the government, they slipped to the other side of the line, becoming, for a moment, as much of a target as Black teenagers in Tottenham, although unlike those young people, they were able to regain their respectability in the press the next day.

At the vigil, it became clear that people had woken up to something that Sisters Uncut, a group led by Black women like Day, had long known, and the movement would grow if they could welcome those people in.

That white women could find themselves on the other side of the line was not a win. The movement wanted to eradicate that violence, at the hands of the state or anyone else. "We do not want parity in mourning for another dead sister," Day and Shanice Octavia McBean wrote later. Instead, they turned their attention—and that of a newfound audience across the world—to the Police, Crime, Sentencing and Courts bill. "We knew that the vigil was a testing ground," Day told me.[60]

While the bill ultimately passed into law, it did so in the face of a large and growing movement that had brought new people to abolitionist consciousness. It brought white women into solidarity with Black organizers, sex-worker and disability-justice activists, and brought Gypsy, Roma, and Traveller communities—targeted especially in the bill—into conversation with them all. Women's confidence in the police plummeted: one poll found that 47 percent of women had lost trust in cops after Everard's murder. The movement rejected the promise of more police in response to the death of a woman at the hands of police.[61]

Alongside protests meant to stop or slow the policing bill's progress—including an action where they set off a thousand rape alarms outside Charing Cross Police Station after an investigation found that "multiple officers from this station joked about domestic violence, child abuse and rape"—Sisters Uncut launched a Copwatch network, organizing ordinary people to voluntarily record and witness police activity, in order to prevent violence but also to withdraw consent, which is one of the central conceits of the British state: that public consent is necessary for policing. Cressida Dick was indeed pushed out of her post, though the broader issues did not start with her or end with her departure.[62]

"Something feels like it has been bubbling over the surface for the last couple of years," Day said. Normally submerged class relations felt more visible, more raw. The thing about impunity is, it doesn't stay where you want it to. Wayne Couzens used his badge and impunity to commit what everyone recognized as murder, and it made people reconsider other moments of violence, made them realize, as Ruth Wilson Gilmore and Craig Gilmore wrote, that killing is, for police, "all, we might say, in a day's work."[63]

1.4 Abolition

It is not easy to get to the Philando Castile memorial, along the busy four-lane road where he was killed. Everything near it is private: apartment homes, condos. I parked in the lot for a condo building and walked over as the wind picked up and stood by the sculptures and signs and the message from his mother, and I thought about the story I read about Valerie Castile's decision to pour her grief into feeding the kids in the state of Minnesota. Philando had been a cafeteria manager at a St. Paul elementary school when he was shot by a police officer, and it was during the outpouring of love from his school community that his mother learned that he would pay for students' lunches out of his own pocket if they did not have money. She started a foundation and raised $200,000 to forgive school lunch debt (a horrific phrase) at local schools, and she backed a bill passed by the state legislature to provide free breakfast and lunch to all kids in the state. No more lunch debt. Philando's legacy and Valerie's.[64]

While I was in Minnesota, the state legislature finally passed a raft of bills that had been priorities for Twin Cities organizers for more than a decade. The lunch debt bill was one of them; others focused on labor law reform, conditions at Amazon warehouses, legalizing marijuana, protecting the right to an abortion, restoring the vote to people on probation for felony offenses, and more. Normally when legislators say what they have done is "transformational" it is so much smoke and mirrors, but the state of Minnesota looked very different after the slate of legislation passed. And yet there is still so very much more to be done.[65]

When we met, after my trip to Castile's memorial, Rod Adams was back in Minneapolis after years away and back to organizing. One of his earliest memories as a child was watching TV in his grandmother's house and his uncle bolting in the door saying "Rod, they're after me." He recalled, "Three seconds later, three Chicago police officers ran into my grandmother's house and beat the shit out of my uncle and tossed him out of a second floor window. So my entire life, I grew up in fear of the police."

He'd grown up around organizers but as a teenager left political work behind. It didn't help that he'd had to move around after his grandmother's home was foreclosed on: South Bend, Indiana, and then St. Paul, Minnesota. He spent some time in juvie as a kid, struggled to get a decent job, and took six years to get an associate's degree while working to take care of himself and his daughter. It wasn't until he sliced the top of his thumb off at a food service job and was told to slap another rubber glove on and keep working that, he said, "I left work that day and I Googled 'worker's rights.'" That search led him to Minnesota Neighborhoods Organizing for Change, or NOC. Every issue that they discussed, he said, was something his family had faced: housing, lousy jobs, racism, schools, policing. They offered him a job as an organizer, and he never looked back. While he was working there, on what became the fifteen-dollar minimum wage campaign, Minneapolis police shot Jamar Clark. A group of organizers, some of whom founded the Black Visions collective afterward, led an occupation of the Fourth Precinct that lasted eighteen days. "We had hundreds of community members who would camp outside," Adams recalled. "It was a bunch of organizers and a bunch of activists, a lot of folks who were there were housing insecure and houseless. They came because there was food every night. There were fires. There was warmth." It was a cold Minnesota November, in 2015, and the police used rubber bullets and tear gas, and in the midst of telling me the story Adams paused and apologized for getting choked up. The occupation was hard and made harder by a group of masked white men who turned up to shoot at protesters. One of those shot was Cameron Clark, Jamar Clark's cousin.[66]

That was the beginning of Defund the Police in Minnesota: from that moment Adams and others were thinking about abolition and more concretely working to move money away from police budgets. They succeeded in getting $1.5 million shifted from the police budget into community projects. "That's when we really knew that a different world was possible," Adams said. Yet it was also hard and demoralizing, and then Philando Castile was killed, shortly after Clark. When NOC, which had given him an organizing home, collapsed after a staffer was accused of improper conduct, Adams felt unmoored, overcome, and so when a friend called and offered him a job in Detroit, he went.[67]

He realized slowly that he was carrying a lot of pain from those years. "This work is highly emotional. It's highly relationship oriented," he said. "The movement loses people every single day because there isn't enough space to discuss grief and discuss the ways in which we should show up for each other." He was able to heal a bit in Detroit, but on May 25, when he saw that George Floyd had been killed, he booked a ticket back to Minneapolis.

There is always something magic about an uprising that catches fire even when organizers have been working for years to throw off sparks. "Those protests were everything," Jen Arnold, the cofounder of Inquilinxs Unidxs Por Justicia (Tenants United for Justice, or IX), recalled; they were chaotic and beautiful and terrifying at once. The police repression was horrific, and she recalled getting tear gassed with strangers and walking one woman home at the end of the night after breathing the same gas. IX and worker center Centro de Trabajadores Unidos en la Lucha (CTUL) share an office on the block where George Floyd was killed, which had been closed for COVID but was informally opened to the community and became a hub for everything from food and water distribution to fleeing tear gas.[68]

No one organization could have hoped to hold it all, and no one tried; they simply showed up and did what they could. Communities set up patrols to keep the neighborhoods safe; Cat Salonek, who with Tending the Soil maintains a coalition with IX and CTUL and many other organizations, was part of a group they called the Minneapolis Fire Squad that dispatched volunteers to handle the fires that were being set by white supremacists who had of course returned in force. They found actual bombs—not just Molotov cocktails but rusty oil drums with liquid in the bottom. "We had helped dispose of a couple and brought them to the fire department and the fire department was like, 'Do not pick these up anymore. They could explode you and the area around you.'"

The uprising built on existing movement infrastructure and added the volatile mix of angry, cooped-up people already facing down mass death unequally distributed. And when the crowds in the streets finally shrank, the organizers were still there, working amid the ashes. Rod Adams was back and working alongside Black Visions collective and others who had created an abolitionist organizing table, doing the dual work of policy proposals at the city and state level while also doing mutual aid work on the streets. "I was going to these rooms, and there were no working-class Black folks," he said. "There were no low-income, no income Black folks, 'cause they weren't included in the conversation. I felt remiss to go to north Minneapolis and knock on folks' doors and talk about abolition. They don't know exactly what it is." He launched the New Justice Project (NJP) to do that work, beginning in September 2021. "It started off with the idea of having a worker center that would work with both at-risk youth, formerly incarcerated folks, to push back on recidivism, and provide resources to people—put them in a position to not have to look to the streets and alternative economies as their way of life."

NJP, he hoped, would connect people to good jobs but also listen to them about their other needs, from restoring the vote to rent stabilization to disrupting violence. It would help to counter the nihilism he too saw. A lot of "we told you so's" happened in 2021 after the referendum to replace the Minneapolis Police Department with a Department of Public Safety failed. The lesson Adams took from that loss was that the community needed to see changes that made them feel safe and secure before they could think of abolishing the police. For him, that meant working in Black communities in Minneapolis to build a pathway to abolition based on real needs.[69]

Jen Arnold and I walked down the street from what is, according to the massive handmade signs topped with sculptural fists, the Free State of George Floyd or just George Floyd Square, past the ongoing memorial where Floyd was killed and where fresh flowers are all over the sidewalk, over the street painted with names of people killed by police, and down to a makeshift cemetery in a park, with plastic tombstones for dozens of people killed by police and vigilantes. Darrius Stewart's name was there; Nyliayh had seen a photo. Jamar Clark and Philando Castile and Breonna Taylor and Sandra Bland and Tony McDade and Walter Scott and Ma'Khia Bryant and Emmett Till. I paused at the stone of Henry Glover, shot by a police officer in New Orleans after Hurricane Katrina submerged the city. "SAY THEIR NAMES," the sign implored, and I thought not for the first time that if we started to say the names, we would never be able to stop.[70]

"When we say rupture, that's what it is," Arnold said. "Everything comes loose. We will have moments like this probably in our lifetime for different reasons, and it would be nice to be able to meet them. And it's so hard to meet them because they throw everybody's nervous systems at once into panic. You're sick to your stomach all the time. Because you'd wake up in the morning and you'd smell smoke and you'd go down the block and the dollar store at the end of the block was burned down."

What to do with the burned buildings—particularly the burned police precinct—has been the subject of intense debate. Will the city once again rebuild luxury condos and paper over the wounds? A community forum, Arnold said, to decide a new police precinct location dredged up all the trauma and rage, and city staff seemed shocked to receive pushback. Amid the "back to normal" story being told by politicians, there is no room for grief and trauma and certainly no need for healing.[71]

It is not a coincidence that W. E. B. Du Bois wrote about "abolition democracy" while writing of the period known as Reconstruction, a too-short glimmer of what could have been before the government pivoted to focus on westward expansion, sending Union generals—including William Tecumseh Sherman of "40 acres and a mule" fame—to fight Native people. Black communities were left unsupported, fumbling for justice. Activists and writers have called the period marked by the movement for Black lives a "Third Reconstruction," the second having been the time most Americans are taught to call the Civil Rights Movement. Now as then, it is mostly happening from the ground up, as young people and elders alike lose faith in the political system to do right by them. A neighbor of Adams's, a sixty-seven-year-old Black woman, told him, "I went and marched every single day. I gave out food. When all of the stores were closed in Minneapolis because of the uprising, I drove people to the grocery stores to make sure my community ate. So if these folks don't do anything for my community, you lost my trust." Organized or unorganized, the abandonment stings.[72]

In Minnesota, NJP and IX and CTUL are part of a broader movement that is practicing what Aviah Sarah Day and Shanice McBean called "abolitionist rehearsals," bringing people together not simply to reimagine what safety and security might be without police but to practice different ways of living together. Police are many things, but one of the things they are is a structure that cannot admit any vulnerability; this is why they deal death at the smallest, even the nonexistent, threat. And yet the first step in being in true community is admitting that we are and will always be vulnerable to being undone by one another.[73]

It is personal for Adams. "I am a felon. I'm getting it expunged now. And we had an expunging affair where I brought my entire family. 'Cause all my siblings are felons. My mother, two years after I was born, spent three years in prison. My dad was in prison for seven years of the first ten years of my life," he said. "These are the dynamics I grew up with. So when I show in a room, the difference between me and some academic is the fact that, like, there are very real consequences of my everyday life. When I talk about this work being sacred, that's why it's sacred for me." Adams is thirty-four; his daughter is sixteen. "I would love to see the world in which, in our time, we will see a world in which we don't have police. To do that, we have to answer all these questions around the economy. Around housing. Around health care. What is our plan around democracy?"

Abolitionism is no less than this: brick by brick, building infrastructures of care that replace the need for armed forces of order. "We live in a country where it's easier to get an AR-15 than a place to sleep at night," Adams said, and there are people all over who want to keep it that way. Organizing, then, has to build a kind of trust that has never existed before. "When something goes wrong in their community, the first place they're going, the first call that they make, is going to be to your organization, 'cause they trust you."[74]

1.5 The State

On October 28, 2023, Sisters Uncut and hundreds of allies arrived at Waterloo Station in London, flooding in from all sides and sitting down on the floor. Aviah Sarah Day was there behind a banner that read, "BLACK JEWISH ALLIANCE," demanding a ceasefire, an end to the State of Israel's bombardment of the Gaza Strip.[75]

Thousands had marched earlier in the day behind Palestinian flags and called for peace, for an end to the siege, for an end to the stranglehold that existed long before Hamas militants broke down the fence that held Gaza apart from the world, killed hundreds of people, took more hostage, and engaged the Israeli military in fighting that killed hundreds more.[76]

"Reality is shaped by when you start the clock," the organization Jewish Voice for Peace reminded us after the October 7 attacks. For much of the world, the clock seemed to start on October 7, as world leaders denounced Hamas, Israel declared war, and the US and British governments promised support and resources. A global anti-war movement thought dead leapt into action, too, as Jewish groups like the one Aviah Sarah Day cofounded in London stepped up to demand that Jewish grief not be weaponized to level Gaza, a tiny territory housing more than two million people on a twenty-five-mile stretch of land; 1.9 million of those people "internally displaced" as I wrote this, a euphemism that feels especially cruel given how small the strip of land really is, how tight its borders, 250,000 homes destroyed, people living crammed in tents desperate for food and care.[77]

Start the clock on October 27: Jewish activists led a sit-in at Grand Central Station in New York. They dropped a banner reading, "Never Again for Anyone," over the board announcing the New Haven Line's train departures. Descendants of Holocaust survivors were some of the three hundred or so arrested for refusing to move. October 29: a video from Italy, thousands marching past Roman ruins demanding ceasefire. November 2: a group of Jewish activists gathered to pray for peace in St Pancras station in London, wearing tallit and kippah. Police attempted to shut them down, one of many strange incidents of police shutting down Jewish prayer for a cause deemed antisemitic by the leaders of Britain, the United States, and Israel.[78]

November 3: The air smelled like smoke in New Orleans, turning my throat scratchy and leaving my eyes watering, and as I returned home from the march, warplanes swooped overhead, a regular occurrence, just a training exercise, but nonetheless one that felt particularly ominous, as did lettering on a police horse's breastplate that read, "TROUBLE." The horse and motorcycle officers kept their distance from the crowd, allowing the protesters to take Canal Street and march up and down the breadth of the French Quarter, the calls of "free free Palestine!" and "trade for needs, not for war!" echoing off the tallest buildings. The protest targeted the port from which the chemicals and oil from Louisiana's petrochemical industry are shipped, the port where one speaker said the white phosphorous being used in Gaza was shipped out, the white phosphorous made in Pine Bluff, Arkansas. White phosphorous that has been used indiscriminately in civilian areas in Gaza, according to Amnesty International.[79]

We lived, those of us who felt a personal stake in the conflict but were far away, in a constant present marked by the strange temporality of social media. We got to know Gazan journalists through the posts they made, always in English, always aware of who their audience was as they lived in the moments between bombs. As they tried to save one another; as they stared at empty grocery-store shelves and captured rainwater. Marching, yelling till our throats were raw for ceasefire, for an end to the siege, the occupation, the displacement, the endless horrors felt better than staring at the computer, watching videos of people desperately digging friends and neighbors from rubble in between the targeted ads offering Black Friday sales. One of the Gazan reporters I followed on Instagram started every post, "Hello, my name is Bisan from Gaza and I am still alive." I took to praying for Bisan, for Plestia, for Motaz, these young people forced to be so unbelievably brave. I lit Shabbat candles for the first time alone in my house.[80]

November 6: Friends, neighbors, my favorite drag queen, hundreds and hundreds of Jewish strangers sat in at the Statue of Liberty. They carried a massive banner reading, "MOURN THE DEAD AND FIGHT LIKE HELL FOR THE LIVING." Their shirts read "Not in Our Name" on the front and "Jews Say Cease Fire Now" on the back. People politicized by Michael Brown's death, who remembered Palestinian live streamer Bassem Masri, always on the ground in those 2014 actions in Ferguson, blocked the entrances to Boeing's factory outside St. Louis, demanding it halt the construction of weapons for war.[81]

Eva Borgwardt, the political director of Jewish direct action group IfNotNow, asked me whether I was eating, how I was sleeping, before our interview began. IfNotNow was born in 2014 out of another Israeli bombing campaign in Gaza; young Jewish activists organized Mourner's Kaddish protests, demanding an end to the bombing, the occupation, and freedom and dignity for Jews and Palestinians alike. Their name, Borgwardt explained, and their values came from Rabbi Hillel's three questions: *If I'm not for myself, who will be for me? If I'm only for myself, what am I? And if not now, when?*[82]

"This is a Jewish liberation movement. We show up for others to achieve Jewish liberation. And Jewish liberation and Palestinian liberation are intertwined," she told me. In the years that followed 2014—also the year when Michael Brown was killed, when Black Lives Matter came to public consciousness as a movement—IfNotNow organized alongside other racial justice movements. The rise of the far right in the United States and around the world, the antisemitism at its core, brought home to many young Ashkenazi Jews that their safety truly was bound up with that of Black and migrant and queer and marginalized people. The networks built through the Trump years prepared IfNotNow and others to step up as the bombs once again rained on Gaza.

November 11: Armistice Day, and hundreds of thousands, perhaps a million, marched in London for peace. I watched the march on Instagram alongside the video from Motaz of Palestinians marching south, waving white flags, fleeing the destruction of their homes under Israeli orders. The awful symmetry wrenching. There were so many in the streets, but the destruction did not end.[83]

November 13: Rabbis prayed at Congress, forearms wrapped in tefillin, carrying the Torah and a banner unfurled from Torah-like scrolls, reading, "Torah is a source of life, not death." So many Jewish prayers for Palestinians, a thing we had been told was impossible. Rabbis for Ceasefire hosted an online *shloshim* gathering, writing, "Shloshim serves as a kind of portal between the depths of our most acute mourning and our first steps towards action. According to Jewish tradition, at the end of our thirty-day mourning period, our task shifts, and we return with heavy hearts to our daily lives, to ensure through our actions that our loved one's memories 'be for a blessing.' Through our cascading grief, we will transition together towards the pursuit of peace."[84]

November 25: Walking in Vermont together on Thanksgiving weekend, Hisham Awartani, Tahseen Ali Ahmad, and Kinnan Abdalhamid, three Palestinian college students studying in the United States, were shot. Awartani, who was paralyzed after the shooting, wrote later, "It is of no importance that the person who shot me was not Israeli, because the hate that made this possible was made in Israel. It dehumanized Palestinians on an industrial scale, and was sent to the U.S. in neat little airwave packages. This hate is what makes the ongoing genocide in Gaza acceptable; a Palestinian is not human." But, he continued, "It was never about me." Joining his fellow Brown University students in protest earlier that November, he wrote, he was handed a list of the dead from Gaza's Health Ministry, and on that list of 6,500 names at the time there were thirteen Hishams who had been killed by Israeli bombs. There were seventeen with Hisham as a middle name. "Had I been one of those Hishams in Gaza my picture would not have been on the BBC or CNN. Instead of being interviewed, my mother would be fleeing south or already killed, trapped under the rubble with me," he wrote. "I am the Hisham you know. I lived."[85]

It is easy to lapse into cliches when writing about Palestine. It is harder to say, this is a thoroughly modern conflict. It arises not from some mythical ancient hatred but from struggles over land and self-determination, power and race making, grief over death and displacement not thousands of years old but in living memory in Gaza, in Jerusalem, in the Jewish and Palestinian diasporas. The clock started not in antiquity but in the 1880s or so, in Enlightenment Europe where Jewish people still faced violence and exclusion, where solidifying nationalisms shaped the desire of some Jewish thinkers for a state of their own. The bombs falling now are a result of an injustice done at the very founding of the state, in my parents' lifetime.[86]

We must be able to say that Zionism is a political movement that relies on a modern conception of the nation-state shoehorned into biblical prophecy, a conception that has waxed and waned in popularity but is rising again in our time of border walls and militarized policing, of ethno-nationalisms from India to the United States, Hungary to Israel. Like other political movements (indeed, like the opponents it refers to always as terrorists), it can be scrutinized, questioned, critiqued, and it often has, by Jews first and foremost. The silencing of that critique, often under the claim that it is antisemitic, is one of the reasons the violence has not stopped.[87]

Hamas is always the answer, but what was the question? Hamas is described by Israeli leaders as the epitome of unthinkable evil; it is compared to ISIS, to the Nazis. But Hamas is a symptom and a recent one, not an atavistic throwback but an organization with goals and strategies that ritual denunciations will not erase. If Hamas is the answer, then anything done by the Israeli state is fine. As scholar Jacqueline Rose noted, "When you accuse someone of evil, history disappears."[88]

But the State of Israel is haunted, and the more its leaders insist that they are righteous, the more we can hear the ghosts rattling.[89]

I returned to Rose over and over in those early days, for her deep reading of the founders and leaders of Zionism in their own words, the way she delicately picked apart the problems with the ideology and the mass psychology of the state without ever letting go of the understanding that Jewish people—like her, like me—have had real reasons to fear for our safety. She explained that the pathology of the State of Israel shows us the pathology at the heart of the modern nation—its fantasies of independence at the barrel of a gun, its denial of interdependence and its own misdeeds; its imagined internal unity and projected rage: these are not Jewish pathologies or even just Israeli ones. They are at the heart of the kind of nationalism we see arising in so many places now, nationalisms that see even internal dissent and disorder as threats to the very existence of the state.[90]

So we got the spectacle, from October and November 2023 bleeding into 2024 and perhaps still ongoing as you read this, of pure kettle logic: a nation that denies the mass expulsion of Palestinians in 1948 that Palestinians call the Nakba and yet pledges at the same time to do it again. A nation eternally the victim and yet eternally triumphant.[91]

Even people who accept that the United States is a settler-colonial nation that founded its much-touted freedom on its ability to clear out the Indigenous population sometimes balk at seeing Israel this way. How can Jewish people fleeing pogroms and concentration camps be at the same time colonizers? It can help a bit to understand that other people colonized Palestine first, that the British were in control and deigned to hand it to Jews, but Zionism's founders were always clear that a Jewish state populated by migrants from Europe would be a little outpost of Europeanness in the Middle East, "a rampart of Europe against Asia," in the words of the man often called the "father of political Zionism," Theodor Herzl. The Jews were played off against other, less desirable minorities, and Zionism was a wager that European Jews would be allowed whiteness, Europeanness, once they were positioned a safe distance away.[92]

By contrast to Palestinians, whose feelings are erased or deemed incomprehensible, Jewish feelings are often discussed as if we are not just a monolith but one creature with many limbs, as if we all share feelings and thoughts, as if our reaction is predetermined somewhere in our bones. We are all supposed to grieve the same. And we are all supposed to be grieving the Holocaust. Gillian Rose (philosopher and sister to Jacqueline) called it "Holocaust piety," this tendency to invoke mass industrialized murder to short-circuit discussion and rout it into melancholia, which halts scrutiny and critique. It turns the Holocaust from a material event in which millions of Jews and also Roma, Black, queer, and disabled people and Communists and other political rebels were killed by other real humans into something almost supernatural.[93]

It is obvious that the Holocaust haunts the State of Israel, that it is never far from the discussion. And yet haunting is a consequence of an unfinished process: an unfinished mourning, an unoffered justice. The head of the Yad Vashem Holocaust memorial, after Israel's ambassador to the United Nations gave a speech wearing the yellow star forced on Jews by the Nazis, tweeted that such a display "disgraces both Holocaust victims and Israel. The yellow star symbolizes the Jewish people's helplessness and the Jews being at the mercy of others. Today we have an independent state and a strong army. We are the masters of our fate." The Holocaust has turned into a source of shame, as if it was Jewish weakness that created Hitler.[94]

Jacqueline Rose had pointed out this strange association years ago. In *The Last Resistance*, she wrote, "It is a recurrent theme throughout Zionist writing, and I believe the key to much of Zionism's own ruthlessness towards the Palestinians, that persecution of the Jews was experienced as moral disgrace. What is short-circuited in this logic is grief." Militancy as a substitute for mourning. "Never again" as a promise of vengeance, though that vengeance has been misplaced. The Holocaust becomes a form of redemption that makes all violence committed by Jews in its aftermath forgivable. Already forgiven. "Disaster," Rose added, "must not be turned into an identity."[95]

Israel wants to claim all Jews for itself and to say that all Jews viscerally felt it when 1,200 Jews were killed. Epigenetic trauma and other such terms figure heavily. Adam Shatz wrote that Hamas's attack on October 7 "touched the rawest part of [Jewish people's] psyche: their fear of annihilation." I find myself flinching from this identification. If I have such intergenerational trauma in my bones and blood, it is activated when I see video of children shuddering in the wake of bomb blasts and pictures of hundreds, thousands marching away from their homes with only the things they can carry. It is multiplied by the feeling that the government that drives these actions uses me and mine as cover. Because I cannot say that I have a mystical connection with all Jews that is activated whenever Jews are killed, but I can say that I was raised to believe in life, that I learned as a child and was reminded when speaking with Jess Kuttner for this book that Jewish texts teach us that every life is a whole world. As Rabbi Elliot Kukla wrote, "each of us contains distinctive cities of relationships, irreplaceable geographies of passions, and deep oceans of memories." Because like him I feel a sense of moral injury that the lessons I learned of justice from Jewish teachings are being weaponized to wage war in the name of some safety for me that I would not want, even if it were possible, at this cost.[96]

Because I do not believe that Jewish suffering is unique.[97]

Israel, Gabriel Winant wrote, "is a machine for the conversion of grief into power." Expressions of mourning for Israeli lives lost get conscripted—often against the grievers' will—into the justification for more violence, more "security." We saw this on horrible display in 2023 as the families of those killed or taken hostage by Hamas themselves pleaded for peace. Noy Katsman said of his brother Hayim, "I don't want anything to happen to people in Gaza like it happened to my brother, and I'm sure he wouldn't have either."[98]

The Israeli state processes each loss into its war machine. In this grinder individual people get lost: the families of many of the hostages taken on October 7 screaming for a political deal, learning that their loved ones too are underneath the buildings leveled by Israeli bombs in Gaza. That many of the hostages had been on Israel's political left, harsh critics of the Netanyahu administration and vocal supporters of Palestinian rights, was both a cruel irony and, some speculated, a reason that the government did not prioritize their safe return. But their families' demand for "everyone for everyone," the release of Palestinians held by Israel in exchange for those held by Hamas, scholar Dan Berger suggested, contained an abolitionist vision, a flicker of a different world.[99]

It is not Jews whom Israel protects. It is not even really Israelis. Rather it is the idea of Israel, which is itself a shifting and changing thing, not a memorial to the dead of the Holocaust but rather a proof that some Jews can fight back. It is a place now where grief is stifled, displaced, exported. Where a side effect of that unacknowledged grief is the production, always, of fear. Fear of Hamas, within the boundaries of the state, fear of antisemitism, for the Jewish community still living more or less comfortably in diaspora. To keep that fear coming we are told over and over again that any expression of support for Palestinians—the tiny Palestinian flag handed to me by a smiling woman in hijab on a march in New Orleans, the shawl off her own back another offered me, the kaffiyeh given to me by a Palestinian friend—is antisemitism in action.[100]

We in the diaspora must be kept afraid to keep the flow of settlers coming. And I have been afraid perhaps for the first time, as a white Jewish person who does not mark myself as such with clothing or jewelry. But it is not Palestinian marches that make me feel this way. It is the far right, which often points to Israel as an example of the kind of ethnostate it would like to see and aims to wipe us out where we live now. It is the man who stopped me as I walked down the street with that kaffiyeh, to shout at me for wearing it.[101]

It is not Jewish grief that matters, not if the police will shut us down in our mourning when we dare to grieve for the wrong people. It is, instead, Jewish dead that are useful. What a profoundly horrific realization.

A friend told me not long ago that she thinks it isn't grief unless you have a stake in it; in this case my stake in all of this is that I am Jewish and American and my country sends the white phosphorous from my city and my representatives vote for it and their staffers sound sad when they answer the phone and take down my name and my insistence that they note that I am Jewish. That I was raised to think the State of Israel was there to protect me, but I do not want a protection that could come with the leveling of hospitals and city blocks and the expulsion of the people who were born in what was then a colonial property before it was given to the Jews as the world's shittiest form of reparations. I do not believe that protection is possible that way; October 7, as Eva Borgwardt told me, shattered that cruel illusion.

I think now it was just a way to defray guilt. German police arrest German Jews for protesting the slaughter in Gaza and pat themselves on the back for having purged their antisemitism so well. I get a message from a stranger on Instagram who reminds me that Palestinians, Arabs are Semitic too. That our liberation is bound up together. That "Free Palestine!" is a threat only to those who think freedom means the freedom to oppress others.[102]

My grief is nothing compared to that of the Gazans dodging bombs that fall on hospitals and schools and UN compounds. "Is there a word for grieving in advance?" Nicki Kattoura and Nada Abuasi wrote of Palestinian life in 2023. The word "grief," they noted, comes from the same root word as "gravity," a force that makes everything heavy. Devin Atallah added, "We know deep in our bodies that to grieve we must have access to the fluidity of time stolen from us along with our land." What is grief time when the bombs keep falling? When you have to keep digging, keep running, keep putting out the fires?[103]

November 29, I watched a video from Bisan. She began, as always, "This is Bisan from Gaza and I am still alive." Israeli bombs, she said, had destroyed the Central Archive in Gaza City. "The future is unknown, the present is destroyed and the past is no longer our past. We don't know anything about our city," she said, her eyes filling with tears. It was the last day of the brief truce. The destruction was due to begin again.[104]

One magazine transcribed voice notes from Gazans and ran them all together, a diary of horrors: "Israel is bombing even small things," one said. "Whenever we heard the rockets coming, we started to run, but we didn't know where to go. We took a rest for one minute and then another rocket dropped, then one minute more, then another one, and then another one. We woke up, but I think our hearts died from what happened yesterday," another said. "The neighborhood where I live was bombed with white phosphorus, which violates international humanitarian law. But nothing is too illegal to be used on us Gazans. We are not Europeans after all," a third reported. She was just sixteen and had lived through seven bombardments of her home.[105]

"If my voice reaches you, know that this area and these people have faced genocide. This genocide is not an exaggeration—it's a reality," another said. A US citizen with family in Gaza, trapped there when the bombing began, begged to get a message to President Biden. A doctor, the same age as me, asked, "Why is it so easy for the international community to deal with us as inhuman creatures?"[106]

Palestinians, poet and psychologist Hala Alyan wrote, are forced always to audition for empathy. To beg to be seen as humans. But as always, she noted, it matters where you start the tape. Where you start the clock. Andreas Malm described Palestinian politics as "post-apocalyptic: it is about surviving after the end of the world and, in the best case, salvaging something out of all that has been lost."[107]

If capitalism has always been racial, those racial lines have always been false, mobile, shifting. An Ashkenazi Jew like my father found himself on different sides of the color line at different stages of his life despite his "white" skin; I find myself wondering at times which side, still, I am on. In the eyes of the beholder, in any case. In terms of politics, there is no doubt for me anymore that choosing whiteness is choosing death. And yet I cannot really choose. Which side of the line the world places me on is not up to me.

Aviah Sarah Day like me grew up Jewish, though the world often sees her first as Black and like many Jews of color she is asked to prove her Jewishness too. Her ancestors like mine were called "rats," "vermin," for being Jewish, and now that language is being used for Palestinian people, the destruction of Palestinian families. This is what brought her to the streets in 2023. This is why she helped create the Black-Jewish Alliance: to fight antisemitism as part of a broader struggle to end racial hierarchies wherever they exist, from Palestine to East London.[108]

Those racial hierarchies ensnare us all and legitimate violence over and over again, in shifting ways but repeating patterns. Antisemitism is real and brutal, and while it has its particular shapes—the conspiratorial, the fantasies of hidden networks of Jewish power controlling money and media and somehow pulling the strings of immigration—it is part of a repertoire of racisms that interact and influence one another. Most obviously, antisemitism and Islamophobia are each other's mirror image these days, and we will not put an end to one without grappling with the other.[109]

In the United States, the racial justice movement that has caught fire in the past decade has been taking lessons from Palestinians. When the tear gas came to the streets of Ferguson, Palestinians tweeted to the Black protesters in the streets their support and tips for how best to deal with the chemicals. One of the founding members, alongside Ciara Taylor, of the Dream Defenders was Ahmad Abuznaid, now director of the US Campaign for Palestinian Rights. The Dream Defenders have taken several delegations to Palestine, building material relationships of solidarity rooted in care and an understanding that the militarized police they both struggle against are sharing tactics too. Organizers in Durham, North Carolina, campaigned successfully to end police training exchanges with the Israeli security forces; Durham's then–police chief, Cerelyn Davis, had participated in one of these programs in 2013. In 2021, she left Durham for Memphis.[110]

The goal of the campaign to end the police exchange, one organizer said, was to "build an internationalist movement to build a better world for everyone that's safe, where we have structures that support us, where we have healthcare and housing, and where we're not being threatened by state violence."[111]

The connections between Israel and the United States are material—in October 2023 the Biden administration rushed to send billions of dollars more in funding and weapons to Israel to conduct its campaign on Gaza and as this book went to press in February 2024 Congress was debating another $14 billion—and ideological. They are both settler countries that tell stories of being the promised land, expanding their borders at the expense of the people who were already there. "Settler colonialism is always an ongoing project, but it's also one that it can't be 100 percent successful," scholar and organizer Laura Goldblatt told me. Native people in the United States are still here, still present, still demanding justice, and even if Israel entirely levels Gaza, there will still be Palestinian people in the world calling for the return of their homes.[112]

They are countries, too, where politics has plunged to the right in recent years but where even the liberal parties uphold the structures of violence that maintain racial hierarchy. Where a matrix of racisms are embedded into the political system and flare up from time to time.

Antisemitism is part of the machine of white nationalism, not a creation of Palestinians or, it should be said, a product of the Israeli government's actions. And yet those actions do make Jews less safe; while Israel does not speak for all Jews and indeed its government has fierce opponents even within the country, its claims to speak and act for us implicate us in its actions. This is why Jewish activists have been so forceful in demanding ceasefire, in saying "not in our names," in pointing out the ways, as Borgwardt did, that Zionism is used as a cover by the same white Christian nationalist movement that points to its "fervent support for Israel as a way to deflect and cover up its deep antisemitism."[113]

There are more professed Christian Zionists in the world than there are Jews. Many evangelical Christians saw the formation of Israel as the fulfillment of part of an End Times prophecy. It doesn't end well for the Jews in that story, but no matter: Israeli leaders have cozied up to the Christian Zionists, even the ones whose antisemitism is fairly obvious. Pastor John Hagee, given pride of place in November's "March for Israel" (not a single rabbi spoke) has written that Hitler was a "half-breed Jew" sent by God as a "hunter" to drive Jewish people toward "the only home God ever intended for the Jews to have—Israel." But as long as he supports current Israeli policy, that's fine with Benjamin Netanyahu, who has a long relationship with the pastor. As journalist Elle Hardy wrote, "Historically, Jews have all too often been portrayed as less than human; today's Christian Zionists superhumanise them, which may be an improvement on the past, but is no less antisemitic. . . . In this conception, the Jewish people are instruments, a literal means to the End."[114]

There are two views on offer of what will keep Jews safe. One of them, seen at the "March for Israel," requires "proximity and access to power structures and through militarization, police walls, et cetera, and domination and criminalization, caging of people who may be a threat to us," Borgwardt said. "This is also how white Christian supremacy operates and how the United States of America approaches the question of safety."

But the route that IfNotNow, Jewish Voice for Peace, the Black-Jewish Alliance, Sisters Uncut, the Dream Defenders, and others take is diametrically opposite: a coalition of groups calling for justice, showing up for themselves and for one another and for Palestinians under siege, for everyone who is targeted by white supremacy. "Really what that boils down to is, can we get Jewish safety directly at the expense of other people, or is Jewish safety intertwined with the safety of all other people?" Borgwardt continued.[115]

I think the flip side to the weaponized grief that is no grief at all peddled by the Israeli state is the Palestinian concept of the martyr. In English the word has Christian resonance, but in Palestine, as Bassem Saad wrote, it is a political term. "Martyrdom refuses to make passivity and innocence prerequisite criteria for recognizing victimhood. It insists that a death took place in struggle." *Shahid* in Arabic, the word more literally means "witness." Saad continued, "Both the Arabic and Greek etymologies of the term, *shahada* and *martur*, entail an act of witnessing. Open to interpretation is whether the deceased is a witness to earthly injustice alone or whether they are also witnessed by God in their passing. But the martyr is surely to be witnessed by those belonging to the political community that they leave behind." To recognize the dead in their thousands as martyrs in the struggle is to recognize that something more than normal mourning is called for. The injustice must be righted, the struggle must continue.[116]

October 7 was not the beginning of the story, but it was a rupture that has not ended as I write this; it has grown and grown with every death, more than 30,000 killed in Israeli attacks on Gaza at the moment I write this, 70,000 wounded or more, some untold number still lost in the rubble. Each one a whole world. The whole world asked to make it stop, to pick a side. To watch as South Africa took Israel to the International Court of Justice in the Hague to answer charges of genocide. As people who inarguably understood apartheid and racist violence and colonization took to the imperfect world stage with meticulously detailed records of death dealing and destruction of homes, libraries, hospitals, historical records, so much more. As the ICJ issued its first finding, that it was "plausible" that Israel was committing genocide, and demanded the state "take all measures within its power" to prevent genocidal acts in Gaza, to "prevent and punish the direct and public incitement to commit genocide," and to guarantee the "provision of urgently needed basic services and humanitarian assistance" to Palestinians. The court could take years to issue a final ruling, and in the meantime the killing still did not stop, but even international institutions built by the West are limited in their power. Even as they still bear weight. "We charge genocide," as legal scholar Darryl Li wrote, had moved "from a protest chant to a formal hearing" in the high court. It was not a solution, but it was another indication of the rupture happening, the change coming. A reminder that, as the other time-honored protest chant goes, *the whole world is watching*.[117]

Around the world the protests for Palestine dwarfed the "March for Israel" because, Aviah Sarah Day said, "we are increasingly able to see our disposability to capitalism," and in Gaza we are getting a real-time demonstration. "Every time we see the utter disposability of Palestinian lives," she continued, "we're also reckoning with our own disposability."[118]

Break II

My family doesn't do grief.

My mother skipped her own mother's funeral, in the brick church in New Hampshire built with bricks from her grandfather's brickyard. There was no funeral for my father's parents, he just packed their things and crawled into himself. I do not remember how my mother grieved her mother, though I know she did. I just did not see it. We don't show emotion in my family.

So I should not have been surprised when my mother's desire to wait a bit to hold a funeral for my father stayed on hold while my life fell apart. If it were to happen, I would have been the one to do it, to make the calls and the plans, and I simply could not. I was too busy finding a place to live, remembering how to be alone, releasing the future I thought I had. I could not carry the weight of my family this time. I had done it for years.

Instead I held rituals myself, or with friends. On Rosh Hashanah my friend and I broke bread and tossed it in the Hudson River outside my latest sublet and I cried into my dog's fur. On my father's yahrzeit (the Yiddish term for the Jewish commemoration of the day of someone's death) friends held me and we ate and they listened while I told stories. I do not know how my mother grieved but I learned that sometimes the last people who can hold you when you need it are the other people mourning the same loss.

Grief was a fog I lived in. I could not see in front of me so I stayed still until someone offered me a hand to the next step. I had editors who liked me so enough work came my way to pay the suddenly inflated single-in-New-York bills. I had friends who liked me so I left the house and I ate and I did not have to hold my chest together all the time. I forgot for a while, I laughed, I got drunk, I kissed the wrong people. I moved and moved again, lived out of a storage unit and my ex's house, spent an entire month on the road between New York and Madison, Wisconsin, on a whim, recorded work from rented rooms, and walked the dog on lake shores. Nothing felt like home so I was at home everywhere. I made "rootless cosmopolitan" jokes myself.

When I was sixteen my parents moved our family to South Carolina after my entire life in one of two Boston suburbs (*best bagels in Boston*). I clung desperately to the life I had only begun to understand was mine until the last possible moment. I did not understand what I went through as a kind of grief, only that I was too much for my teenage friends, that everyone wondered what the hell was wrong with me.

I was sixteen. I was a theater kid, a school newspaper kid, a weird kid who wore too much black and put together a thing we didn't even know yet to call a zine with the other weird kids and wrote terrible poetry in an overpriced hardback journal and kept my crushes to myself. I divided my time between trying to be seen and trying to be hidden. I both believed and did not believe my parents when for years they discussed moving away, and when the process finally began, when they finally sold their house at a huge loss and began to pack it and sell or give things away and my mother and sister left, when we left the house and my father and I stayed behind with some friends of his so he could wind down what was left of the business and I could finish the school year, I refused to believe that it was really going to happen. I thought, somehow, we would stay.

The family friends my father and I stayed with hated me after a while. I drooped and made too many tearful phone calls that were technically long distance, abused their hospitality, though they never said so to my face. I overheard it one night.

My friends at school hated me after a while, or at least found me a convenient target. It was so easy to make me cry.

We did not stay.

I had never had my little heart broken by teenage boyfriends, not yet anyway—that would come later—had not yet lost anyone close to me, so I had nothing to compare the feeling of loss to. I felt disordered; my parents wanted to send me to therapy, but that sounded like hell: *you want me to actually talk about my feelings, how could I possibly do that, I've never done that.*

When we were finally gone, reunited with my mother and my sister, who already had new friends, I tried to reinvent myself briefly, but that didn't work and I reverted to type, to theater and writing and wearing lots of black. It wasn't so bad, or maybe it was so bad but I learned how to manage, to make friends, to use the skill I already had at hiding my feelings to make sure I got along with people.

I did not see my parents grieve their old lives, but they must have. They must have done that alone or with one another, at night or behind closed doors or while I was out doing teenager things. I remember my mother's hurt at the friends who did not write or call afterward. I do not remember my father showing emotion at all, but I caught him smoking again while waiting to drive me to school. He shrugged, admitted he'd never really quit. I did not see him show emotion about the business that had collapsed or the house that he'd been underwater on, only saw him throw himself into his new work.

South Carolina became home, I suppose. By the time I applied to universities, I did not think of going back to Boston. New York was the closest I tried, and I chose New Orleans instead, farther south, something new, a risk I could take though I was scared again. No one ever told me it was grief that I went through, the kind of ambiguous loss where the thing I lost was still there but I would not have a place in it anymore. When I went "home" to visit, my friends had moved on. My crush was seeing a girl who looked like me.

I learned to take moving lightly, to pack my things and exchange a few goodbye kisses and shove my cat in a carrier and hit the road. I did not grieve another home until I left the one I had made with my partner, two hours or so north of New York City, overlooking the river. Cheaper on our freelance incomes, with office space for both of us and a backyard for the dog. The night I realized that I had to leave, weeks after my father died, my partner was not there. He'd left again on another work trip right after the first one he'd gone on right after I came home from saying goodbye to my father. I tossed and turned and stared at the ceiling and held my chest together and thought wildly about what it would mean to leave. Where would I go? Where was home, now? Did I have one?

It was my mother finally who pointed out to me that I was essentially getting divorced, that the legal entanglement I had avoided was not actually the hardest part of ending something that was supposed to last forever. Even as she also thought I was acting out, pushing away the people who loved me in my grief. He did love me, I know that, but he did not love me in my grief because he could not see it. Because he packed and went on those trips. Because he cheerily, finally, told me at a party in front of friends that he would have to miss my birthday for a meeting, and I sat down at a table and one of those friends told me that she was going away for the summer and I could stay in her Brooklyn apartment if I wanted to.

The next day I told him I was leaving and I told her yes.

It wasn't home, that place where I landed, but it was beautiful if small and it was near a park for the dog and it was around the corner from someone I didn't know what to call yet but wanted to be close to all the same. I cried in that bed and wrote long journal entries on the table that doubled as a desk and one night that new man came over and drank wine at the desk that doubled as a table and he said something about moving to Europe and it occurred to me briefly that I too could leave this place entirely.

I'd done it enough by then, hadn't I?

I could not leave my grief behind but I could leave anyway. Eventually I would leave New York too, I would understand why my new almost-lover had to go and write him from a hotel room years later to tell him so. I would understand why my parents needed to leave the home they'd built. I would reach for a new home in a strange place and build myself a new support system among strangers and love people who were a different kind of family.

I would throw more bread in the water, put my father's photo on a desk or mantel or altar everywhere I went, with candles and trinkets that I picked up: a stone from an Irish beach, a flower from a London tree blooming in an extra-warm February. Rather than outrun my grief, I gave it new spaces to dwell in, found it in different parts of my body at unexpected times: a knot in my jaw that a lover massaged away, a day that my chest clenched so tight my housemate brought me a hot water bottle to sit with.

I could not leave what hurt behind me, so eventually I learned to live with it, to recognize it when it arrived. I learned to talk to it, to rarely but sometimes be grateful for it.

CHAPTER 2

Flow

Migration, home, and freedom

2.1 Border

Five rich men disappeared in a tourist submersible, and the rich world was obsessed with them. In the same week 750 poor people were crammed onto a fishing boat called the *Adriana* that the rich world let sink.

On the sub were two billionaires, two millionaires, and a millionaire's son. One of the millionaires and his son were from Pakistan, the same country from which many of the migrants on the *Adriana* had come, looking for refuge in Europe. On the sub they sought adventure, a quick trip down to the wreckage of the *Titanic*, where, famously, the rich people got the lifeboats and the poor were left to drown. On the *Adriana* they sought a different life, a risky voyage that they hoped would finally pay off with safety at the end. They had already left everything behind. One hundred and four of them were saved. The rest lost at sea.[1]

The rescue operation for the sub was international, pricey, expansive. By contrast, Mohammed, a survivor of the *Adriana*, said that helicopters and ships passed them by as their overfilled boat stalled, their distress calls ignored, and that when the Greek coast guard finally arrived, "they were right next to us when it capsized. In the moment it sank, they moved away from us. They deliberately made us sink." (The Greek government denied this.) The *Washington Post*, in a detailed investigation, suggested that "the deadliest Mediterranean shipwreck in years was a preventable tragedy." An anonymous former Mediterranean coast guard official told the *Post*, "It's an open secret that no country wants to take them."[2]

The sinking of the *Adriana* was possibly "the worst tragedy ever" in that sea, according to one EU official, yet it was also not rare. Protesters in Thessaloniki, in response to the sinking, marched to the port with a massive banner reading, "Tourists enjoy your cruise in Europe's biggest migrant's cemetery," words echoing those of Pope Francis before his 2021 visit to migrant camps in Greece.[3]

Carola Rackete, a German ship captain, called them "ghost boats," the various rickety vessels or rafts that carry desperate migrants across the sea, that too often do not survive the journey. Rackete's time leading rescues on the *Sea-Watch 3* coincided with the growing shift toward criminalizing this desperate passage. It was June 2019 when her ship rescued fifty-three people from a raft floating between Libya and Lampedusa, an island in the Mediterranean, part of Italy, where the relatively new government included the hard-right anti-migrant party, the Lega. Its loudest voice, Matteo Salvini, was the interior minister. Some of the people who boarded the *Sea-Watch 3* from the raft were sick, some injured, some pregnant, some young children. Rackete was forbidden from landing her vessel at Lampedusa, but after days in limbo, she did so anyway.[4]

Other countries refused or ignored distress calls from Rackete's ship. She would face charges for "promoting illegal immigration," but rescuing people in distress at sea, she noted, is an obligation under Article 98 of the UN Convention on the Law of the Sea. She pointed out that simply banning the boats would not stop them: "No one signs up for something like this for the sake of adventure, or on some insubstantial whim. You can't scare people into staying at home when their lives were already at risk there." *No one leaves home unless / home is the mouth of a shark,* British Somali poet Warsan Shire wrote. Yet when and if they make it to a European port, migrants are required to tell their stories over and over so that comfortable officials can parse meaning and weigh desperation, gauging whether the reasons a person has left her home are good enough, by which we mean sufficiently horrifying, to give them leave to stay.[5]

Rackete was released, eventually; a judge ruled that her actions in docking at Lampedusa were justified. By 2021, the last charges against her had been dropped, and Salvini faced charges of his own over his refusal to allow migrants to land in Italian ports.[6]

But the borders have not softened. Rather, they keep expanding. When I spoke to Rackete in 2023 over a jittery Zoom connection, she told me that Frontex—the European border patrol—is extending its reach deeper into Africa, surveilling the movements of migrants and signing contracts with countries like Ghana and Senegal. Like US border patrol agencies, Frontex has grown more and more powerful as politicians get louder about migrants, painting them as a security threat rather than as humans moving from place to place for a variety of reasons, as Europeans themselves have done with impunity for centuries. "De facto, the asylum system already doesn't work or the Geneva Convention isn't applied anymore," she said. "Not in the US nor in Europe, nor in Australia. It's already kind of dead, and we are still keeping it alive a little bit with our efforts."[7]

It is easier, Rackete noted, to create a court case against someone like her for something they did or to claim that migrants are breaking the law by moving. It is harder to prosecute someone for what they failed to do, for neglect, for leaving boats drifting in the waves for hours days weeks while pretending not to have heard distress calls. In 2019, Salvini in Italy felt like an outlier, but in 2023, she said, "It just seems like the fascist tendency right now is far, far greater and far more notable across Europe." Center-left parties, in hopes of capturing back some of the vote from the right, capitulate on immigration, making scapegoats of those who take to the seas.

Rackete and Pia Klemp, another ship's captain, were offered the Grand Vermeil Medal by the mayor of Paris in 2019, but like Rackete, Klemp insisted she was no hero. "Paris, I'm not a humanitarian. I am not there to 'aid.' I stand with you in solidarity," she wrote. "We do not need medals. We do not need authorities deciding about who is a 'hero' and who is 'illegal.'" Their sea rescues, Rackete said, are a form of triage, one person at a time, not a structural solution but important, nevertheless, to prove that it is possible to make a difference, that regular people (not heroes) can push back against the impersonal forces of border and state and capital. In her book, she argued, "There's only one way to address this justice crisis: we need to reframe migration—as an integral part of life, fresh momentum for societies, a human right, and as an undeniable reality in a radically changing world."[8]

I cannot comprehend the strength it took to step onto that crowded ship with hundreds of strangers and maybe one or two loved ones. The bravery of the people on the *Adriana* far exceeds that of five rich men in a submersible bound for adventure, yet the world treated their lives as less valuable. Syrian refugees now have to risk their lives on ghost boats, ghost travelers along the borders, when once Syrians had sailed for the United States on the *Titanic*. Like the steerage-class passengers on that ship, they are denied rescue, the lifeboats reserved for those in first class.[9]

Matloob Hussein called his brother Adiil from the *Adriana*; Adiil was awaiting him in Greece, but Matloob said the boat was "very bad," that they had been loaded on "like cattle" and he was stuck below deck, in the belly of a boat made to hold a cargo of fish rather than live people. He turned his phone off for the journey. That was the last anyone heard from him.[10]

Donald Trump built his political career on the promise of a wall at the border, a wall that would somehow make impervious the US body politic.

The wall, journalist Daniel Denvir noted, "is a structure of political feeling."[11]

"Every time I talk about the border to people who are not from the Southwest, I say, my grandmother was alive when the border was drawn," Viktoria Zerda, now an immigration lawyer in Philadelphia but a child of the borderlands, told me. The border was drawn right through her family, which now exists on both sides of the line between Texas and Mexico. For many years, they crossed back and forth easily, and then slowly the border tightened, the journey became illegal and the family sliced in two. The United States had won Texas and surrounding lands from Mexico in a war sparked by settlers who opposed Mexico's decision to outlaw slavery. The enslavers won, and along the way tens of thousands of Mexicans became Americans. Or, as the protest chant goes, *the border crossed us.*[12]

What the changing nature of the border should remind us is that the border produces the migrant. Borders are anything but natural even when they are bodies of water, rivers and seas; countries negotiate and split hairs over which portion of a river is theirs, how far into the sea their territory extends. And the migrant constructs the nation in turn: their image is, as Robin D. G. Kelley wrote, used to define who belongs, to justify "inclusion, exclusion, and outright criminalization."[13]

The border is a process as much as a place, a decision to rescue a boat drifting at sea, or to slash a bottle left by volunteers in the desert, to crush and piss on stashes of food and clothing, to wave someone through and search another car, to ask a job applicant or a person stopped for speeding to produce citizenship documents. Policies change, politicians pound the table and pontificate, but day after day the processes at the border, of the border, go on. This posturing, like so much else, obscures the actual humans from the picture. "I don't think people understand just how violent border policies are," Zerda said. Thousands, tens of thousands die in the borderlands; mass graves have been uncovered across Texas. For those who survive the trek, violent assault, dehydration, heatstroke, injuries, and the looming threat of arrest and deportation, the trip having been all for nothing, await.[14]

"The border" as an imaginary space has room for none of that. But the border has a history, one of land grabs and skirmishes and wars, one of organized abandonment and criminalization, and most of all, one of great profit. Colonial powers imagined a world with no borders they were bound to respect beyond those that other colonial powers could enforce at the point of a gun. Nations like the Tohono O'odham, whose land was sliced through by the US border, had and have no power to keep out the forces of the bigger, better-armed state. Nearly eighty million Europeans colonized the Americas and Oceania, bringing indentured and enslaved laborers from Asia and Africa with them, and now as then imagined themselves besieged by the people they had overrun.[15]

The border is a global communications technology. It divides not just two places but people into hierarchies that are both strict and flowing, mobile, reshuffled at times. Today's world of passports was shaped by centuries-long processes of enclosure and seizure, the colonies a laboratory for experimentation and categorization.[16]

Colonized people are expected to stay at home unless they were picked up and moved by European ship to be slaves or indentured workers. Their goods and artworks would be taken back to Europe, but the people in the former colonial possessions today need visas to visit the treasures looted from them in shining museums.[17]

The passport, journalist Anna Lekas Miller explained, was from its beginnings a way to differentiate by status: Romans had documents to prove they were citizens and not enslaved. The name "passport" likely comes, she added, from documents used in medieval France "to keep vagrants and vagabonds from the countryside from coming into the cities, protecting the elite from who they saw as riff-raff and peasants." The modern passport, focused on nationality rather than class status, was formalized during and after World War I. There was a moment, Lekas Miller wrote, when, determining the shape of the peace in 1920, the European powers considered restoring freedom of movement. They decided against it.[18]

The United States linked citizenship and race from its earliest days. The institution of chattel slavery with its doctrine of *partus sequitur ventrem* (that which is brought forth follows the womb) required discrimination at the point of entry: Were you an immigrant or a slave? A "free white person" could be a citizen, according to the Naturalization Act of 1790; Chinese immigration was specifically banned in 1882, and national origin quotas would be imposed in the 1920s. Women, whose rights and labor status differed from that of men, could lose citizenship if they married the wrong immigrant, while men could more easily naturalize a foreign-born wife.[19]

The colonial lines on the map would not last, nor would the violence imposed on the colonized stay out of the metropole. By the Second World War, many Europeans had to flee invasion and occupation; the Nazis had, in the words of Frantz Fanon, turned Europe "into a genuine colony." Jews fleeing Nazi persecution were turned away at the US border: 908 refugees on the SS *St. Louis* were rejected, sent back to Europe because the quotas (for German and Austrian migrants) had already been filled. In the war's aftermath, the world's borders would be redrawn. The Cold War would come to shape a world split by the so-called Iron Curtain, and decolonizing nations would struggle to be free of the burdens of the so-called developed world. The United States would repeal the quota system, part of a broader political makeover, an embrace of the "nation of immigrants" ideal, never real—the southern border tightened at the same time—but a nice story to tell that burnished the nation's public face.[20]

Colonialism might have been formally dismantled, but it left its power structures behind. A new form of plunder would take the place of the old; capitalism reorganized but did not depart. "Structural adjustment" would once again bend the economies of the Global South to the will of the North, but this time ostensibly they submitted of their own volition, to receive as a "loan" some of the wealth they had created. Migrants would leave to support families back home; they would leave to flee destabilization and war; they would leave behind lovers friends cousins parents and send money back each month, a flow of remittances to keep the economy going.[21]

Some 3.5 percent of the world's population are migrants or refugees, displaced from their homes by violence or financial need or love or some other loss. They are demonized in the rich countries where they go, where there is little interest in their stories beyond checking to see whether the details add up, where they pick and pack and serve food, nurse the sick, drive taxis and trucks, clean and care for children, pack purchases in warehouses, start businesses, write books. They are split into binaries: refugee or migrant, legal or illegal, good or bad. Black and brown or white. "The mass production and social organization of difference," Harsha Walia wrote, "is at the heart of border-craft."[22]

Only certain immigrants constitute a border threat: the US border where the wall was to be built was of course the southern one, not the one with Canada, where half my family crossed not all that long ago. Free movement within Europe is sustained by the patrols of Frontex and the countries' forces to keep out those who do not belong.

Borders, in other words, are relationships. They separate but also connect. They are one-way much of the time: Americans can drop into any number of countries for a beach holiday or an adventure, but the reverse is harder to do. People from the Global South are treated as suspects rather than adventurers, tourists, guests. The acceptable migrant determined by political currents—Zerda noted that Cuban exiles would find welcome in the States, while those fleeing violence often instigated by the United States in other parts of Latin America are pushed back, deported, detained. Borders are designed to keep people out, and the story they create in doing so is that what is inside is precious and magical and needs protecting from the unreasonable foreign hordes.[23]

But what the borders are mostly protecting is stolen wealth and stolen land and the insecurity that comes with knowing that the theft was unjust. "If you have to militarize a whole border with billions and billions of dollars, is this land really yours?" Zerda asked. The United States isn't the only place where the seduction of the wall holds sway: fences and walls have recently been built between Spain and Morocco, between Greece and Turkey, Turkey and Syria, Hungary and Serbia and Croatia. Israel has surrounded itself with walls that even reach underground. *The wall is a structure of political feeling*, so too is the border at all.[24]

Zerda recalled a young man from El Salvador she helped when he arrived in the United States. "He was crying and he was like, 'I didn't want to leave my home country. I miss it.' I said, 'You're really grieving the loss of a life. Of a home. Of your family and friends and it's not by your own doing.'" The conversation haunted her. "Here, everyone thinks immigrants come here on their own volition because it's wonderful and beautiful and they have all these opportunities. And it's the complete opposite."

"It's ugly here," he said, and she thought he did not know how right he was.

Mohamed Mire felt like he was always being tested. Growing up in Somalia, there were tests to take to get into university, tests that he was working to pass when the civil war began in 1990. He had already done two years in the armed forces as part of a required national service program, and he wanted nothing more to do with guns or war, so he set out from Mogadishu to Kenya and from there, eventually, on to Nashville, Tennessee. "That's where I met my beautiful wife," he said—every time he speaks of her he calls her beautiful—and where his three children, Abdullah, Deeqa, and Safa were born.

In Nashville he worked a variety of jobs, at rental car companies and driving a shuttle bus for airport parking, and from 2006 he was a taxi driver; he and some other members of Tennessee's Somali community banded together to start their own taxi company, Magic Taxi. They're still going, he told me proudly. "If you go to Nashville that's the taxi company you need to call."

He was tested again when he got to Minneapolis in 2017. The family decided to move to be reunited with his mother, who had come to the United States in 2010. "Everyone in Somali community, they spread all over the country, everywhere. Basically, we're all over the world," he said. Amazon was recruiting heavily for warehouse workers in the Somali community, drawing on recent immigrants, and the application process required an online form and then an in-person session, and then, he said, "when you think that you get the job, they say, 'You have a test.'"[25]

He passed the test and took on the hardest job he'd had. There were cameras everywhere and a scanner that "is like jail" attached to his wrist so that it was impossible to put down. The scanner and the cameras were designed to track his movements, to make sure he was making quota. "Every three seconds you have to stow one product," he said, products brought by robots to the workers to be packaged. He began to feel like a robot himself, alone in a warehouse where the only time he spoke to another human was if he'd done something wrong and a manager showed up to tell him off.[26]

Human bodies are fragile, and they break and wear down differently than robots; they have good and bad days and children at home waiting for them to return: "When the Amazon customer receives their package," Mire said, "they should appreciate that everyone working at Amazon, they donate their blood because they're working like never before." Every three hours he got a ten-minute break, but just walking to the break room across the massive building took up most of the time. Bathroom breaks were timed, the scanner angrily warning him of "time off task," the dreaded metric that resulted in write-ups and firings. "And it's risky for you to fight."

Fight he did, nevertheless, joining the Awood Center, a worker center based in the East African community—*awood* is the Somali word for "power," and the center built power among workers like Mire and Hibaq and Safiyo Mohamed and brought Amazon to the bargaining table, a feat not yet equaled in the United States by any of the attempts to organize Amazon workers, over prayer time and Ramadan observance. Amazon like many companies recruited workers who were new to America presuming they would be docile, easily managed, unaware of their rights. But within the Somali and East African community, solidarity is a core value, Mire said, and the workers looked out for one another, holding walkouts when one of them was disciplined, a wildcat action upholding the principle that an injury to one is an injury to all. In 2023, the workers celebrated the passage of a statewide warehouse worker safety bill, requiring companies like Amazon make public their quotas and submit to investigation of their injury rates.[27]

Mire worked at Amazon through the first years of the COVID-19 pandemic and recalled vividly his fear of bringing the virus home to his family. Amazon orders were up, and productivity seemed more important to the company than the safety of immigrant workers. "When I come home, my kids love me, they love me so much they have to come hug me," he said. "I have to stop them and say, 'No, no. Hold on, let me change my clothes and wash my hands.' They were so disappointed. But at the end, they get used to it. So they come, 'Daddy, you washed your hands?' It was heartbreaking."

The turnover at the warehouse was high—a leaked document dropped in 2022 found that the company's own executives feared that they might burn through so many people that they could actually run out of workers to hire. "They take advantage of the Middle East, Somali people, and the Africans," Mire said. "Because they're new in America and they just hear Amazon, Amazon, Amazon. They don't know that a lot of companies pay more than Amazon pays."[28]

"And those immigrant people they make Amazon great, that's how they make money. Blood from the newcomers."

Over and over, Mire told me, "you have to sacrifice for your family." Sacrifice his time with them, to work long hours to pay the bills. Sacrifice his home, moving from city to city, to care for his mother. Sacrifice his body on the job to make Amazon profits. And Amazon did not offer the same loyalty to him or its other workers. In 2023, the company closed one of its Minnesota facilities, shuffling some six hundred workers elsewhere around the city. To keep their jobs, the workers had to pass yet another test.[29]

Being treated like interchangeable cogs, like robots themselves, is not a work experience limited to immigrant workers or even to workers of color. It is, however, easier for companies to treat people like Mire, and indeed his whole community, as if they are a different kind of person, one more willing to bend and break and be grateful for the opportunity as if it were a gift. *Border-craft is the mass production and social organization of difference.* It is also the denial of what Avery Gordon called "complex personhood": refugees and migrants are treated as one big mass, a "flood" that appears at the border with no lives of their own, no individual dreams and needs and loves. If grief is specific, personal, idiosyncratic, how does a society that sees people as interchangeable grieve for any of them or imagine the grief they might have?[30]

Mire left Amazon in 2020 and shifted to another omnipresent US company. He drives for Uber now. Uber is not better, he said, but he can log out of the app when he wants to. "You can work as much you want, even though the money is not that great, but still . . ." The Uber algorithm is as impenetrable as the Amazon quotas; he doesn't know how much of each fare a rider pays is going to him or to Uber, or even how much the rider is charged. The day we last spoke, at 4 p.m., he had been driving since 9 a.m. and had not even made a hundred dollars. And sitting all day was no better for his body than the warehouse.

The platform companies too rely on the work of migrants, treating them as a flexible workforce that can be picked up and dropped at will. Uber and other such gig economy companies classify their workers not as employees but as independent contractors because of that ability Mire cited, to turn off the app, but they do not have the freedom that a real independent contractor might to set their own rates and to take work not doled out by the algorithm. The whole process is technically sophisticated, we are told, but it relies, as geographer Dalia Gebrial wrote, on old systems of racialization and organized abandonment, turning Mire and his coworkers into what Marx termed a "disposable industrial reserve army."[31]

It contrasts harshly with the taxi company Mire and his friends started in Nashville, where they owned the medallion, set their conditions, supported each other. In the United States and Britain and elsewhere, migrants are routinely denied access to what social supports might exist, leaving them even more dependent on the gig economy and other forms of temporary work, work that is, in the terms we learned during the COVID pandemic, "essential" but undesirable.[32]

The current rules and restrictions on migrants echo the long history of vagrancy laws, first designed in the wake of the bubonic plague to compel labor from the remaining population. Mass death had loosened the strictures of feudal society, and serfs were making demands; vagrancy laws were a way to curtail those protests. In the United States those laws were expanded, on their face race neutral but unevenly applied to press more labor from formerly enslaved people daring to enjoy their freedom. A vagrant was a thing you were, not a thing you did; it was unsettledness, defined as a refusal to work. A particularly cruel implication for so many migrants, who often come looking for work when their homes are disrupted or destroyed.[33]

Migrants so often wind up defined by that status, rather than as people with whole histories. But migration is a loss as much as a gain, a complicated decision even when the situation at home is as bleak as it was in Somalia in the early 1990s when Mire first left. "I love my country, it's so beautiful, by the Indian Ocean," he said dreamily. "People that only stay in America, they don't know what's going on." He left family behind in Somalia—sisters and brothers, his father, aunt, and uncle—whom he had not seen for thirty-two years; when we spoke, he'd just returned from his first visit since he fled in 1990.

Such movement leaves people like Mire with a complicated kind of grief, a cumulative grief, as MaryGrace DiMaria explained: "Say I am losing watching my daughters grow up. I am not able to see those milestones." she said. "I'm not able to be there when funerals happen or my family's grieving. I do not know the language where I am. I need to build a new community that I don't have. All these losses, I'm feeling scared all the time, but also it's complicated because I left for a reason and I know why I am here." The communities Mire built—in Nashville, with the Awood Center—served as an antidote to that, a place where he was welcomed as a whole person, Somali and American and migrant and worker and father brother husband son comrade.

Mire's children and his beautiful wife moved back to Mogadishu recently. The kids are in a private school, learning about the culture they came from and spending time with their extended families. "Anytime they want, they can come back, but right now they like it over there." When I ask how it is for him, being alone now in Minnesota so that he can send money back, he told me of crying when he left Somalia, his family crying with him, asking why he'd only come for one month. But, he said, "It's okay, it's okay. You do whatever you do for your family."

I asked him what Americans should know about Somalia, and he spoke of a culture of collective care, of opening one's home no questions asked to relatives and friends, living with family for an entire lifetime. He wished that companies like Amazon had the same concept of hospitality. "If you have one room, you may have four people, six people who can live in that home together. No hard feelings. I will share, they need to know about how sharing is. Because in America people, they just say mine. But there there's no word 'mine.'"

2.2 Hostile

I grew up seeing the story of what happened in Mohamed Mire's country on the news and the movie screen (*Black Hawk Down*, 2001). I watched the first war in Iraq begin on television in a fifth-grade classroom, 1991, as Mire was beginning his long journey.

The far-away wars are easy to forget as long as you are not close to anyone fighting in them (which fewer and fewer Americans are); they slip in and out of the news cycle and out of political debate so easily, we forget the death our country is regularly dealing and see little of the grief we leave behind.[34]

That is, until the people who have survived the fallout arrive on our shores.

If the wars and their effects are not perceived, Judith Butler observed, then it amounts to "an interdiction on mourning: there is no destruction, and there is no loss." Donald Trump made this idea only more visible, more obvious, took it to its logical conclusion when he referred to people from "shithole countries" migrating to the United States. As if the

United States had nothing to do with the destruction, the precarity left in its wake, and the need to move. Anti-war protests, movements, votes are attempts to make the loss visible, the grief broadly shared.[35]

The border is still imagined as one-way door, from which Western military adventures and before them colonizers and before them "explorers" can set out. But others may not follow them back. It is protected by political choices and militarized border police and vigilantes. The border itself is a war zone, in the words of historian Greg Grandin, "the place where all of history's wars become one war."[36]

In Central America, Indigenous people first colonized by the Spanish and subsumed into modern-day states make their way across borders they didn't draw to escape wars they didn't start and climate catastrophes they didn't create. Jakelin Amei Rosmery Caal Maquín, a seven-year-old Q'eqchi' Maya girl who died of septic shock and cardiac arrest in 2018 in the custody of US border police, came from the highlands of what is now Guatemala, where biofuel and sugar planting pushed her people off the land they had known for centuries, where a 1954 coup backed by the United States led to genocidal violence against Indigenous people like her, where capitalist exploitation was backed by military weapons. As Ruth Wilson Gilmore explained, "The very forces who are producing the vulnerability for people are then policing the people who have thus been made vulnerable."[37]

It was supposedly a cold war, but what that meant was that the violence was outsourced and the United States could pretend its hands were clean, and it can now wring those clean cold hands about Central American children at its border and pretend there is nothing to be done. Pretend it didn't (sometimes illegally) arm and train the mercenaries who murdered dissidents, radicals, union leaders, anyone. That it didn't ignore the protests of the grieving mothers.[38]

US deportations have even become an arm of that violence. The gang MS-13 was formed in Los Angeles, not El Salvador, in migrant communities, and it was deported back to that country, destabilized by Reagan-era arms and training for death squads. "The United States, twice over, created MS-13—and then an influx of refugees to be demonized by Trump,"

Daniel Denvir wrote. It is a vicious cycle that the US pretends to have no part in. But those migrants brought their traditions of resistance with them too, traditions that infused a generation of labor organizing in Los Angeles. Often I wonder whether that is the thing that the United States actually wants to keep out.[39]

The war on terror was and is at once imagined as a civilizational conflict, a never-ending battle between the West and Islam and also something that began immaculately on September 11, that had no history to speak of. The grief in the United States was somehow supposed to be unique, of a different class than anything that had happened elsewhere and come before. The conflict was described as inherent, racial, one to bind together the West and close borders to the Middle East and Africa because anyone over there after all could be one of Them. Hostility to immigrants (often imagined as Muslims) becomes an issue that binds together in turn the rising right wing across the world.[40]

That the thing we think of as race is slippery can perhaps best be understood by looking at the racialization of Jews and Muslims. Constructed as "Other," a religious identity attributed racial characteristics. Antisemitism is thick with the fear that Jews can "pass," the idea that Jews are sneaky, have divided loyalties, are generally getting one over on gentiles, an idea repeated in today's bogeyman, the (Muslim) "terrorist." Replete in both is the idea that you can't always tell and yet that there is an inherent difference to be rooted out. Borders and immigration restrictions have to do double duty, then. Britain's first modern immigration controls targeted Jewish migrants fleeing antisemitism in eastern Europe and Russia (the people I come from). Jewish immigrants were blamed for failing to assimilate, likewise a claim made today about refugees from Syria and Iraq. Today's far right imagines "the figures of the subversive Muslim and the subversive Jew, unified in their contempt of national borders," plotting together to bring down the white nation.[41]

The wars not only create refugees and migrants and blur whatever line might exist between the two. They also train the people who come home and attempt to take the border war into their own hands, and they provide the weapons with which they do so. Patrick Crusius explained that he had "targeted Mexicans" when he began shooting in a Walmart in El Paso, six hundred miles from where he lived and close to the border. He killed twenty-three people.[42]

The border is a war that produces racism, produces violence and suspicion and precarity and despair. Viktoria Zerda had helped another young person, whose friend had been one of fifty people who died in the back of a tractor-trailer found outside of San Antonio, smuggled across the border and abandoned. The young person, she said, had shrugged: such is life, what happens, happens. The mother of the dead boy had made a gamble on sending her child north for a better life, but such horrific possibilities—fifty dead and sixteen survived—were part of the calculation. This was the set of choices they had.[43]

The story too often told is that there is no history to those people who climbed in the back of that truck and that we owe them nothing because they are different to us. It's a soothing lie, that sixty-six people in the back of a truck are at best victims and at worst criminals, the authors of their own misfortune, while five rich people in a submarine are adventurers.[44]

All Idris wanted to do was play football when he was a kid, growing up in Iraqi Kurdistan. He played defense, and, he told me with a wide grin, "I was really good." But then the war came to his part of the world, and he and his mother and brothers had to flee to Turkey.[45]

When we met in Leeds, in Yorkshire, in the north of England, Idris had been in the country by himself for seven years. He was seventeen when he arrived, alone, to claim asylum, which should have been easier for someone still technically a child. His mother and brothers stayed behind in the refugee camp in Turkey, but they sent him onward, hoping that he could get to a safer place, a better future. He has found that safety now—an apartment, a job, a car, friends to play football with—and he grins when he talks about his life, finally. But for nearly the entire time he had been in England, he has had to prove himself.

I met Idris at Positive Action for Refugees and Asylum Seekers (PAFRAS) in Leeds and spent the day with him and others who came to Britain seeking safety, most of them young and many unaccompanied. It is important to the PAFRAS staff that people new to the country get a chance to be whole people. And so we talk about football and play pool and drink tea and tell jokes about the stereotypes of the places where we are from. I will wind up losing at pool to a few young men who speak little English and I almost no Arabic, but "laughing at the Yank when she scratches on the 8 ball" is a universal language.

Idris was working on getting a visa to go visit his mother and brothers, and his infectious grin returned when he thought of seeing them. They had been trying unsuccessfully to get visas of their own for resettlement, trying to do things the so-called right and safe ways, but there is no safe way. There is only the gamble that Idris took, cycling through detention in Huddersfield and Bradford, losing a home, being shuffled from Leeds to Newcastle and back, away from anyone he knew, and always always the endless retelling of his story to judges and lawyers and advocates who scrutinized it for lies, mistakes, any reason to send him back.

In 2015 when he arrived the Islamic State (ISIS) was roaring across his country. British and American headlines were filled with stories of front lines and the violence of ISIS, but Idris was nevertheless treated as a potential threat rather than someone fleeing a shared enemy.[46]

As a young person, Idris just wondered why everyone in the asylum system seemed to hate him. The first thing that happened was a judge telling him, "You are not seventeen, you are eighteen." The judge told him that he could go back to Iraq, that his family was there. He did not have proof otherwise, and so he went to his first detention facility. Of course, the judge also had no proof of his age or where his family was, but that didn't matter.

His family had to send proof that they were in Turkey, he had to repeatedly find proof that he was who he was—at one point even the Iraqi embassy questioned whether he was really from Iraq. He was told he could go back to Baghdad, where he had never been, when ISIS was in his hometown; he did not, he noted, even speak Arabic, just Kurdish and now English. To him, Baghdad was another country. He had left his home behind and then his family behind, and then in England even his history and his identity were being taken away from him.[47]

"Seven years I've been showing the Home Office that my story is real," he said. "My only job is to show them that this is my story, that I'm not lying."

Idris survived what is in Britain known as the "hostile environment." Maya Goodfellow, whose book goes by the same name, noted that it is an unusually honest name for policy that more often gets hidden behind euphemism and doublespeak. The hostile environment is a collection of policies designed to insert the border at every interaction that someone like Idris might have with the outside world. Papers must be presented to rent an apartment, to go to the hospital, to go to school. Doctors, landlords, teachers, and of course police officers are expected to ask for papers before providing the service that is nominally their job. The home secretary sent vans out around the country that read, "Go Home or Face Arrest."[48]

But the environment had been hostile for many years. Idris was not the only one to have his age questioned; children have had their teeth and wrists X-rayed to try to determine their age. It was New Labour, ostensibly the kinder, gentler party, that brought in the "forced dispersal" policies that sent Idris and people like him all over England on their own, often to substandard housing. New Labour also introduced biometric ID cards that marked asylum seekers as outsiders, unable to get either a job or public support. There was a plan briefly to give them paper vouchers, a form of scrip rather than real money that could only be used in certain shops, while they waited for their claims to be processed, but public outcry over the "degrading and inhuman" plan ended it. The whole system of holding migrants as separate and unequal both created vagrants and punished them for being so, even more so after the success of the deeply anti-migrant Leave EU campaign succeeded and Brexit sent EU migrants into limbo.[49]

Bordering can even be retroactive, as many British Caribbean immigrants learned when the hostile environment came for them in 2018. The HMT *Empire Windrush* gave its name to the generation of migrants who came after 1948, and it gave its name too to the scandal that unfolded when it turned out that the Home Office had failed to keep records of their arrival. Many elderly people found out that they were "illegal" when they were suddenly refused medical care or other public services, lost jobs or homes. They had come as citizens of the empire; when the countries they had come from declared independence, Britain took the liberty of severing their citizenship. More than 160 people who had lived almost their entire lives in Britain were deported. While the government would eventually apologize, compensation has been haphazard, and the hostile environment itself grows more hostile.[50]

"Hostile environment" is an appropriate term for the conditions that greet migrants across the Global North. Borders tightening, legal routes cut down, and if you manage to get inside, the country's stated goal is to make you so miserable you "self-deport," as US presidential candidate Mitt Romney suggested in 2012. Such conditions make a mockery of the idea of "pull factors" for immigration, that migrants like Idris come to Britain because it's wonderful and accessible and welcoming and they can stroll right on in and see a doctor in the National Health Service. The reality is that Idris, like so many migrants to Britain and the United States and Europe, would happily have lived the rest of his life in the part of the world where he was born, except a war he did not choose drove him out of his home and desperation kept him moving as step by step he left everything he had known and everyone he had loved behind.[51]

There is so little room in this conversation for what migrants leave behind, for the understanding that there is grief in every step away from home. Instead, the answer is always to make the hostile environment worse. A plan, first proposed by then–home secretary Priti Patel and backed by her successor Suella Braverman, to deport asylum seekers to Rwanda certainly would not save Britain any money—it is likely to cost £169,000 per person, if it ever goes forward, which as of this writing it has not. In January 2024, the *Guardian* reported that the Home Office had hired an airplane hangar in which "to train officials to carry out deportations, including how to handle people who physically resist." The program is designed to scare, another deterrent that itself relies on racist ideas of which countries are and are not desirable destinations and treats African nations as still somehow subservient to Britain. Zoran, like Idris a refugee from Iraqi Kurdistan and just a year older than him, was restrained and bundled onto what should have been the first Rwanda flight until it was halted last minute by European judges. "I felt like I was going to die," he told reporters.[52]

For Idris, finally getting regularized status has been life-changing, but the most important thing is that he can soon see his family again. "The people without the family is nothing," he said.

The hostile environment certainly made him feel that way: that alone, without papers, he was nobody. If you are treated as a problem rather than a person every time you ask for help, how do you avoid it getting to you? How do you hold on rather than lose yourself? When, all over, people are talking about saving your country, but you yourself are not worth saving?

2.3 Bridge

I met Edain Altamirano in the office that Inquilinxs Unidxs Por Justicia shares with CTUL on George Floyd Square in Minneapolis. I had been walking among symbolic graves, and she had been on Zoom court with tenants testifying against their landlords. We were both tired but her smile was infectious, and I could see why even her silent presence on a call could soothe.

Altamirano had called Minneapolis home since she was seventeen, and she spent her days helping people to find and stay in homes of their own. "I think I was an organizer since I was little, but I didn't recognize that until recently," she told me with a laugh. She had been a fiercely independent child in a Jehovah's Witness family in Mexico City, taking on caring responsibilities for younger siblings after her father died young and learning to organize them to win arguments with their mother. She got a job to pay for high school, fell in love, and got pregnant. At that age, she said, "I felt that I could conquer the world." Her partner—now her husband—had family in Minneapolis, and so she agreed to move with him. When they could finally afford a home of their own, after years with her husband's family, Altamirano was thrilled, but then her son started to get sick, wheezing and coughing from the mold and the cold in the building. Unscrupulous landlords, she realized, targeted recent immigrants and assumed, often correctly, that they would not cause trouble. The landlords would blame the tenants for bugs and mice, implying that immigrants were dirty, and living in those conditions bred shame and compounded the fear of speaking up. When a tenant organizer knocked on her door, she was ready to get involved.

IX was founded by two organizers, Jen Arnold and Roberto de la Riva, who met through Occupy Homes, an offshoot of Occupy Wall Street, where a lot of the work had been preventing evictions and dealing with crises, but as they worked alongside CTUL and other labor organizations, they became interested in a union-style model where they would deliberately organize tenants of particular large landlords in order to change the power dynamic. One of their targets, a partnership known publicly as Apartment Shop, was then Altamirano's landlord.[53]

The founders of IX encouraged Altamirano to apply for an open position, doing what she already did, bringing neighbors together to improve their conditions. She had always been a big dreamer, had always believed in transformation, had always believed that her community deserved more than low-wage jobs and to bow and scrape for inclusion in America. She believed too that the kinds of conservative beliefs she had been raised with could be challenged, that immigrants' best chance of gaining real power within the system was by working alongside other people marginalized by landlords and bosses and police. She joked about the "immigrant filter," the lens through which people learned to mistrust and fear and close themselves off from the city and their neighbors even as they struggled to assimilate to America.

"People look at me like a bridge," she explained. She had a foot in both worlds, as a migrant from Mexico and also someone who had learned English and beyond that learned about how "the system" worked: the courts and the landlords, local and national politics, but also "capitalism, racism, gender." This particular niche she occupied could help her make people feel welcome while also pushing them to learn more. "I started to work on trainings about popular education, about race, power, our own experiences," she said. She created a women's group within the cooperative, where women could talk about violence and create new kinds of safety together. "That's one of the biggest things that I feel that I've achieved."

The day-to-day struggles for survival can get in the way of experiencing life, in the way of feeling the good and the bad. Work two jobs, get the kids to school and fed and to bed, and then collapse yourself, and all you can touch of your emotions is the edges around your exhaustion. Organizers often talk about dignity—union organizers speak of dignity on the job, and tenant organizers the dignity of one's home—and when I think of dignity I think of the ability to feel your feelings without having to apologize or stifle them. To claim a space for yourself. Tenant organizers do that physically, demanding that housing be more than just a bare roof over your head, and in doing so they make space for a full life.

Altamirano's experience of immigration was one of synthesis; she left her home and her family and their particular beliefs behind but still carried with her the history of her country and a fierce love for her people, and she blended that with a new political edge she developed while organizing against her landlord. Rather than the eternal presentness, the kind of enforced melancholy of not really being at home anywhere, she built community by learning and teaching history and by sharing her dreams of a future. A long lineage of migrations, as Cristina Rivera Garza wrote, can bring strength as well as grief. "Could it be true that those who move frequently remember more?"[54]

Even after Altamirano and her husband finally purchased a home and left Apartment Shop behind, the fight continued, and she worked alongside her former neighbors through a combination of lawsuits and protests and rent strikes to put pressure on elected officials and on the landlords themselves. As a result of their organizing, the tenant organization was able to buy five buildings that had been owned by Apartment Shop, buildings that are now the Sky Without Limits housing cooperative. The Sky Without Limits buildings are decorated with colorful murals detailing the values of IX and the cooperative: unity, empathy, *lucha*, justice, community. A banner to the neighborhood: we can dream bigger.[55]

Precarity after all is not just the condition of recent immigrants; it is the condition of all of us in some way, vulnerable to the other people around us, the condition of the vast global majority in an economic system designed to exploit and extract. The kind of organizing that Altamirano and IX do is based in this idea that we do not get to choose the people we live next to but we can build with them across difference a world where, rather than subsumed, that linkage is celebrated. Where it becomes the root of co-governance, of community autonomy, of democracy. The murals on the buildings are a declaration of interdependence and an invitation: join us.[56]

For Altamirano the experience has been one of liberation, a kind of liberation that means she can do things even when she has limitations, that means she feels supported and can in turn show her children that support and allow them in turn to choose the path that suits them. Immigrant parents, MaryGrace DiMaria noted, often carry a complicated grief watching their children leave them behind with language fluency and a new culture that feels alien. Altamirano has been on both sides of this grief: her mother, she explained, was hurt and worried when she left, saw it as a rejection of her values, and she does not want to place those expectations on her children. But it was good for her heart to finally take her children to Mexico, to see them meet the rest of her family.

The work has been grueling even as it has freed her; it is constant crisis, and it is easy to lose herself and disconnect from her body and her own needs. But the community she has built as an organizer is one that can hold her too when she needs it, a place where she has friends and care beyond her immediate family. A home.

* * *

In May 2022 I was walking through Dalston, England, back to the flat I was living in for the week, and suddenly I was in the middle of a police riot. The street was flooded with people surrounding police cars and vans, and I saw a labor organizer I knew standing nose to nose with the front of a van. There were fists raised and chants flying and dozens of camera phones in the air recording what was happening. The whole street—a busy commercial strip—was blocked, and at one point a police car pushed through the crowd and knocked down a bicycle courier, pinning his bike beneath the vehicle, and the crowd actually held the car back to pull the courier free.

I would find out later that the Metropolitan Police were raiding a common hangout for the couriers who delivered food in the area. The official story was that it was a raid to "target e-scooters and moped-enabled crime," but the workers suspected immigration enforcement was at the heart of it. It is a strange circle: gentrification pushes immigrants out of an area, but the gentrifiers rely on that immigrant labor to maintain themselves while working long hours, even as the city marshals police to enforce the borders between neighborhoods. But in Ashwin Street that day in May, the gentrifiers and the workers fought together against the hostile environment.[57]

One of the unions organizing those gig workers, Independent Workers' Union of Great Britain, had been in communication with the Copwatch and anti-raids networks created through the Kill the Bill organizing around the Police, Crime, Sentencing, and Courts bill and helped raise the alarm about the police action, drawing neighbors to the streets to put their bodies in defense of the riders. The police and council cited "antisocial behavior" as the reason to move the riders off the street, but the community's defense of them implied rather that they were at the heart of society.

Bordering is designed keep workers docile and to separate them from those with more rights; the difference in Ashwin Street was that their neighbors crossed that border and refused the split.[58]

What is happening in moments like this one is the production of *deportability* rather than deportation. Some workers will be removed to teach a lesson to the rest, but mostly the threat is what matters. And so they are treated as vagrants when they try to work. Workers are expected to leave their pesky human needs at home, and when they are immigrant workers, their "home" is assumed to be their country of origin, as if their bodies move and their hearts and souls remain behind. "No recourse to public funds" in Britain created what Dalia Gebrial called "the institutional unrecognition of migrants as populations with embodied, social reproductive needs—people who get sick or old, need housing or have families with care needs." They must provide entirely for themselves, even while they do the work of caring for others—whether in the health services or delivering hot meals on demand.[59]

Deportation is the safety valve when labor demand ebbs, removing people marked as surplus without regard for the homes, ties, or families they have built. Employers and governments use it to remove particular troublemakers—from the Palmer Raids in the United States in 1919 and 1920, which rounded up anarchists and communists and deported them, to the 2019 raid at Koch Foods, which arrested 680 Latinx workers who had been agitating for a union and dared to sue the company for discrimination and harassment. "While workers are declared illegal," Harsha Walia noted, "the surplus value they create is never deemed illegal."[60]

Guest worker programs illustrate this process neatly. After the US-Mexico border was redrawn, the US recruited people from the Mexican side of the line to come work in the States part time, picking crops during harvest seasons and then returning home when the job was done. A congressional commission noted, "In the case of the Mexican, he is less desirable as a citizen than as a laborer," and a Los Angeles Chamber of Commerce official said that "the oriental and Mexican" were suited to farm work "due to their crouching and bending habits [to which they] are fully adapted." Certain work deemed naturally the province of certain workers, who did not have human needs like the white American.[61]

As had been done with Chinese immigrants, the Bracero program was limited to men, who could not bring their families. When the program was officially ended, the farms did not stop relying on migrant labor; it was just made more precarious, the workers given even fewer rights. The irony was that tightening the border made it more likely that the workers would stay, permanently, where the jobs were. *Borders have always separated families.*[62]

"The idea of free labor, not labor with freedom, but labor that does not cost anything but reaps all the benefits for their employers, that idea is as old as America," longtime organizer Saket Soni explained. But guest worker programs are not just a US configuration. Around the world, low-wage migrant workers are shuttled into temporary programs where they are tied to an employer and cannot bring family or make a permanent home. They have no path to permanent status and often have to pay for access to the jobs. Unions are often explicitly forbidden.[63]

Politicians promise to close the border to protect jobs, then panic when they run out of cheap workers. In Florida, Republicans had to scramble when an anti-immigration bill appeared to actually prevent immigration: "This bill is 100 percent supposed to scare you," state representatives told a crowd. "It does give more police state powers going forward to deal with immigration, but still this is mainly a political bill." Farmers, they noted, were "mad as hell," as workers were departing for less hostile states. They built a hostile environment and then got angry when it worked.[64]

The goal is never for it to work *too* well. It is for the border to expand and to empower employers and police and the state to crack down whenever and however they want, to push delivery couriers off the corner and farm workers out at the end of the season. The border is everywhere, and it serves as both carrot and stick, holding the offer of permanency tantalizingly out of reach and making the price ever stricter compliance. The price is super-exploitation.

And if you are deported, the exploitation does not end. Deportees in El Salvador, often young people who grew up in the United States and therefore speak its language and cultural references fluently, are now a perfect target workforce for the country's growing call center industry. Deported workers who learned English and facility with the culture, the sports and music references, as children can more easily convince American callers that they're speaking to someone just like them. Surplus workers recycled into outsourced work for a fraction of what they'd make within US borders.[65]

The Biden administration finally made a move to expand protections for undocumented workers who report their bosses for abuses, allowing them the legal right to stay while an investigation is conducted. Cal Soto from the National Day Laborer Organizing Network (NDLON) explained that this policy had the potential to flip labor law enforcement on its head—rather than being employer focused, it could be employee focused, assuming that workers deserve protection as soon as they make a claim, that speaking out about workplace abuse is something that should be encouraged. It is a challenge to the long history of bordered labor.

But the deeper problem remains, in a system that, in Harsha Walia's words, "treats immigrants as commodities to be traded in capitalist markets and discarded if deemed defective."

Fatima came to England when she was twelve, and she was nineteen when we spoke, in the same office at PAFRAS in Leeds where I met Idris. While he was quiet and still, she was bubbly and her story nearly poured out of her. Yet they both had the same aura of not practice or preparation, but almost resignation, a used-to-it air that only shifted when we shifted gears and spoke about the things they like, the things they value.[66]

Fatima came to England from Gambia with her mother on what she thought was a holiday. She had no idea that she was to be left behind when her mother went home. She stayed with her aunt and uncle in Nottingham until 2022 and then moved out, stayed with a community elder briefly and then in temporary housing while trying to refight her asylum claim. While she lived with her aunt and uncle, she said, "I had to be grateful for them, because I was staying with them. By the age of twelve I was cooking, cleaning, I was basically taking care of the kids, whereas they go to work." She remembered telling her mother, and her mother repeating: Be grateful. Behave.

In Gambia, her mother had worked for the government and traveled a lot. Her parents had separated before she was born, but when her mother traveled, she would stay with her father's family. At the age of six, she underwent female genital mutilation. She remembered being the one "that went to get the razor." She remembered being held down, being given little aftercare, being told not to tell her mother or else they would do it again. Remembered not wanting her mother to touch her when she came home.

Her mother figured out what had happened, but there was little she could do. Her father's family had legal rights. So when her mother found out they were planning to marry Fatima to her cousin, she got her out of the country and brought her to England. "When I came here I thought, okay, maybe this is a fresh start." It wasn't until she began to make close friends in school that she realized the amount of housework she was doing was not common. "I never had a social life; I couldn't do the normal teenage stuff. I couldn't just do everything because I had to be at home."

She was peripherally aware that there was an asylum claim with her name on it, that it had been filed and refused, that she could not go to university without papers. But during the pandemic, her uncle, who worked as a taxi driver, was struggling to pay the bills. "He woke up one day and then he just basically said 'You are going to go back to Gambia,' because he couldn't afford for me to be living there." She had been a happy kid, she said, but the combination of feeling unwanted at home and by the country, her inability to plan for a future that seemed entirely out of her hands, began to weigh her down.

Her teachers noticed her depression and sent her to a social worker, but she had little faith in their interest in helping her. The support she had in school would disappear as soon as she left sixth form, and despite her good grades, she would not be able to attend university without access to student finance. She couldn't afford a lawyer because she did not have a paid job, just the unpaid work she was doing for her aunt and uncle. When she turned eighteen, she was completely on her own. She found a legal aid lawyer but had to contact the Home Office to access her files and do her own research. One legal aid lawyer disappeared, and they reassigned her to a new one, and then yet another. She had to get a doctor to give evidence of FGM, and then another one to testify to her mental health. While her classmates were off to university, she was getting a degree in the hostile environment, one for which she would never be given credit.

"They just don't understand that time is ticking. This is my life. My life has been on pause," she said. Her friends were on their third year at university, doing apprenticeships, and she was chasing lawyers and doctors and government officials while living on twenty-five pounds a week. *Grief is about the future.*

It was not just that Fatima had to grow up before her time. She and many like her are part of what Arlie Russell Hochschild called "global care chains," reconfigured family and work structures whereby migrant workers leave one family behind and end up providing care for another. Most of the writing on this subject is about adult women who leave to do paid work, but the informal work that Fatima did can also be understood this way. It is a way of living in which too many people never get the care they need even as their own caring is exploited. Women leave their homes for many reasons; but the place they will be absorbed is very often into someone else's home, where they will at once be told they are one of the family and threatened with expulsion for any misbehavior.[67]

Immigrant women become the fix for a broader economic crisis: it is increasingly financially untenable to have a one-income family, but the housework still needs doing. Fatima's uncle made explicit the ongoing threat that so many immigrant workers live under: when you cost too much, when you are no longer useful to me, you can go back to whatever awaits you. Her work was unacknowledged—she remembered her aunt telling her that if anyone asked who looked after the baby, she was to say her aunt did—and thus invisible, uncountable, a step toward treating Fatima herself as uncountable.[68]

Fatima's own grief, over what had been done to her by her father's family, her separation from her mother, her precarious status in the country that she came to consider home, was less important to her aunt and uncle than her ability to work. But as MaryGrace DiMaria noted, grief will come out in the body when it is not given space; it does not have a time line or operate according to will. "It just keeps on knocking," she said, showing up in the stomach, the chest, the guts.

The counselor Fatima had been seeing in school gave her a little diary to write about her feelings and to record how the stress and hurt had begun affecting her body. "I stopped eating because of stress," she said. "My body started just showing that I was not eating." She woke up one day to find bleeding that wasn't her period and went to emergency services, where the doctors asked her questions about her mental health and sent her to her GP. While she was at the doctor, though, her aunt and uncle went through her room. "They ripped out my diary and they put it on the table. And then they asked me, 'Why are you writing these things in the diary?'"

What stuck with her afterward was that most of her diary was about her own pain, sadness, and self-harm. There was very little about their treatment of her in particular, yet they seemed unconcerned with the demonstration that she was clearly not well. "They're like, 'You're so ungrateful. We put you here. God knows that you're a wicked girl.'"

But finally she had had enough, and their shouting at her drove her to stand up for herself. "I've been quiet for so long," she said, and told them that she was tired of cleaning up after their children, after them. Her uncle nearly slapped her, but her aunt held his arm back.

She called a helpline—one she had relied on before when she had panic attacks—and then called a friend, who then reached out to a community elder in Leeds, who took her in for a while. The family soon seemed to resent her and ended up kicking her out, her things in garbage bags. "You just have to learn not to put your trust in everything, in anyone, or just don't get too comfortable. You just never know." She worried she'd be sleeping in the street. "I was like, I might be the problem. Because it's a pattern. What is wrong with me?"

She had come across PAFRAS in her research for her asylum claim, and they helped her to find a place to stay once again, after a couple of weeks staying in a friend's university apartment. But all the moving exhausted her, and she felt lonely. "Sometimes you do need family, you need supportive family. I have no one," she said. "And I just don't know, because I don't control my future now." If her asylum case was rejected again, she could lose her housing. She could be deported.

Like Idris, she felt disconnected from her own story. Without an ID she could not go out with her friends; she couldn't order things online without a bank card. "We are restricted to do nothing. You can't work. If you're an asylum seeker in this country, they make it so difficult for you," she said. She found herself lying awake at night, her brain always working. When people were nice to her, she wondered when they would change their minds, or she would push them away. "I'm just like, don't get too close to me because if you get too close something bad might happen to you."

She sought ways to feel like a full human, even as she struggled to maintain relationships. Her mother, she thought, did not believe her side of the story, and romantic relationships were hard when she had no idea where she would be or what rights she might have. But she threw herself into the PAFRAS community, attending their café night every Thursday and making friends and then beginning to do volunteer work there as well, helping other people in her situation. She dreamed of studying law if she was able to remain.

She spent some of her volunteer time making social media stories for other young people in her situation, to make them feel less alone, to do what she wished someone had done for her. This too is caring work, but it is work she chose, work that brought her back to herself, that brought her comfort. Staff and volunteers and lawyers, she said, "can help you, but they have never experienced it." With the people who have been through the system, she can be angry and sad, and also she can laugh about it, she can express all the feelings that she has had to hold back.

"I just hate the words 'asylum seekers,'" she said. "That's what I'm going through right now. But that's not who I am."

2.4 Home

The Esperanza Community Center—*esperanza* is Spanish for "hope"—is in West Palm Beach, Florida, the city where my grandparents lived their final years and died within a couple of months of each other. I had been there before, but it didn't feel familiar other than the way every place made up of hotels and beaches and nice restaurants feels familiar. My father chose one vacation town and my grandparents another to live in and I went to Palm Beach to meet people who chose it for different and also for the same reasons.

Esperanza is in a lovely low building beneath matching palm trees, red flowers that I could not identify growing along the front. Inside I met Maricela Torres and Yirna Buitrago, the director and manager, respectively, and they gave me a tour of the building; the room with the diapers they distribute to the community, the room where meetings were held, and within it the little separate room for children, with toys and colorful posters on the walls and snacks and juice boxes piled high.

Buitrago was working on her English and I on my Spanish, and so our conversation happened in the space between the two languages; I understood more than I could formulate into words and so did she, so we muddled through with a lot of laughs. She is from Bogotá, Colombia, and she came to the United States in 2016 with her husband and children, fleeing death threats that came because she was a community worker and organizer, and her work challenged corrupt officials. Her father suggested she go to the US for a few months to relax and seek out other opportunities where she and her family would not be threatened.

Buitrago and her children stayed with relatives at first, and her husband, who worked in construction, moved around Florida to find work. She recalled arriving in a new apartment with only a suitcase, a plastic table, and two mattresses, thinking, *Oh my god, I want to go to Colombia.* It was lonely, but, she said, "for my children, all days I get up and continue." She missed her family in Colombia, and she missed her country itself: "It's beautiful, Colombia, it's absolutely beautiful, and the food, the cities, oh, my God, it's beautiful, but with the corruption it's hard."

Six months after she left Colombia, her father died, and she was unable to go back for the funeral to say goodbye without risking her asylum claim. Her mother was ill when we spoke, and Buitrago had only been able to see her once in seven years, when her mother and brother were able to get visas for a visit.

The process of applying for political asylum, she said, was long and complicated; like Fatima and Idris she went through lawyers and hoops and more hoops to jump through for years, having to produce proof that her life was threatened—as though when you pick up the phone in the middle of the night to hear a rough voice telling you how they'll kill you, you have a recorder just waiting nearby to capture it. For a long time she was studying English and working cleaning houses and driving for Uber and DoorDash and thinking, "I didn't study for this. I need other work. I need other work." For Latinx immigrants, she said, "people don't ask what you're trained in, you're cleaning, only cleaning, restaurants only." She longed for the kind of community work she had done in Colombia, connecting people to each other, supporting their needs, feeling supported in turn herself. She had worked under Gustavo Petro, then-mayor of Bogotá and now the first left-leaning president of Colombia in the country's history, doing conflict mediation and building harm reduction programs around drugs and alcohol and support for LGBTQ people in the city.[69]

It was only when she met Maricela Torres at Esperanza three years ago that she finally found her place. Together with Lenin Gomez and Andrea Gil, they started the Mujeres Fuertes (Strong Women) program. I joined them one morning, standing alongside Torres as she held a baby and offered juice to another child as the group of mothers, all with young children, talked actively about the experiences of migration, on their bodies, their lives. The mothers scooped babies from carriers and rocked them as they spoke, handing children treats and books and toys while they continued to talk, effortlessly multitasking.

The aim of the program, Gil said, was to help the women see their own strength and power. "People think that empowerment is success. An empowered woman is the one who has a good job, a good body, good aesthetics, a good job, a good house. We focus on, look, these women crossed the desert. It is an experience that makes them strong. Even if they don't believe it and don't know it. . . . We try to make them see their skills, their own abilities and their own strengths."

The language barrier is often the biggest obstacle, Gomez confirmed. When he and Gil and their oldest child came from Bogotá to Florida five years earlier, "I lost my words." His whole life, he had been working with words: he was a psychologist in Colombia and like Buitrago a community worker. He made theater and art. "All my life was building around words. So if I come to United States, I lose the words."

Gomez had family in West Palm Beach; first his uncle and then his mother had moved to the United States when he was younger. When his first son was born, he began to think about giving his family access to a different culture, a different country. "When you are driving, and you are stuck in traffic, you sometimes think the lane behind is faster than you. So you think, I'm in the wrong lane. I need to move."

It was an adventure, but it was also painful: "Grief is like a sensation, an emotion. It's something that you feel in your body," he said. "The grief in my body is, I need to restart with few words."

It was even harder for Gil, who had no family in Florida other than her husband. She had been a social worker in Colombia but spoke less English than Gomez. The first couple of years in the United States, she said, she had some symptoms of depression. "I cried a lot," she said. "In my country I have my apartment, and in this country my husband and me and my kids live in one room."

They had not sought the American dream, she said, and it wasn't money that drove them but rather wanting their children to experience something different, like Mohamed Mire wanting his children to know both cultures, languages, places. In Colombia, they had been professionals; in Florida Gomez worked in an IHOP washing dishes and driving for Uber, and Gil took on some cleaning work. To get recertified in their professions would require starting from scratch.

The family fractured further, Gomez said, because the immigration process for Gil was slow and difficult. They were still awaiting her papers when we spoke, five years after they had moved. It left her feeling helpless.

So they, like Buitrago, sought volunteer opportunities, to put their skills and training to use in their community, and they met one woman who decided to trust in them. "Trust is something that you receive," Gomez said. "It's like an egg. One egg can have a life inside, so it's very special. But it's fragile at the same time. Once you crush the trust, it's difficult to recover." That trust led them on a path that brought them to Esperanza that day, to Buitrago and to finding a way to use their skills and training and their personal experiences of movement and loss to support other people, newer arrivals with even less than they had.

Their second son was born in February 2020, right before COVID-19 made it to the United States, and when COVID hit, Gomez lost his job and turned to driving for UberEats to support the family. But that August he was hired to do community education around COVID safety. "It's good because it's something that had a relation with my career," he said, but at the same time, he worried that he could bring COVID home to his family. Still, it was the best job he'd been offered since they relocated, and he could do it while still working on the program at Esperanza.

In the time that Gomez and Gil had been in Florida, they had survived the Trump presidency and Governor Ron DeSantis's endless attempts to make the environment more hostile to immigrants; they had seen the Parkland school shooting and many other smaller acts of violence. Gil told me that much of her work in Colombia had been with people hurt and traumatized by the armed conflicts there, young people recruited into the wars, families displaced. "I worked in a project that sought to support these victims, and I traveled throughout the country, I coordinated a team of fifteen professionals including social workers and psychologists, and we made a strategy for the emotional recovery of the victims," Gil said. "I loved this job very much and it taught me the reality of the country, because I had always worked in Bogotá, in the capital. And I went out to very poor and vulnerable places, that gave me a broader look at what was happening around me."

Growing up in the '80s, the conflict was part of daily life, Gomez explained. "We can die in any street for a bomb or because you are in the wrong place with the wrong people." There were narco-traffickers and paramilitaries, leftist guerrillas and the government. His first real job was working with people who made the decision to put down their guns. He did art therapy and theater, sexual health programs and harm reduction, often with kids or young people, and said, "Part of my intention is to try to do the same here." Gomez had studied psychology in part because he wanted to find work that could not be replaced by computers, but he had not realized how hard it would be to keep doing it.

Gil and Gomez and Buitrago all had the kind of training and experience that Florida and the US more broadly desperately needed: conflict mediation and therapy and care, restorative justice and support for people living through trauma and trying to turn away from guns and violence. The country should be thrilled to welcome them. But the United States does not value, has never valued, such skills.

"Immigration is not a problem, it's a right," said Gil in Spanish. "It's a problem for the people who see us as immigrants with bad eyes." The translation has stuck with me. Bad eyes, *mal ojo* in Spanish: it recalls for me the Jewish idea of the *ayin hara*, the evil eye. The gaze that can cause harm where it falls, intentionally or unintentionally, out of jealousy, greed, hatred.[70]

Paul Gilroy suggested that there is something valuable in being able to see a culture from the outside, something valuable in a cosmopolitan eye that is in a way the inverse of the evil eye, carrying critical distance rather than blessing or curse. I heard that value in the calm appraisal of the hostile environment in the United States and Britain from Mohamed Mire with his thirty-two years of exile and nineteen-year-old Fatima learning to master the asylum system. The way they see that the culture of the Global North is hostile not only to outsiders but to life itself.[71]

The women in Mujeres Fuertes will bring the strength of desert crossers to the country they are learning to live in. "It turns out that no one has asked these women how they feel," Gil said. "That's why these questions are so important. That's why their voice is so important. Sometimes when they come here, they don't say anything. They just look at the floor. And little by little, over time, they start talking more. They express themselves more. The work we do here is very important."

Buitrago has been doing community work long enough that she has gotten good at drawing people out, learning what is important to them.

She looked after me for the days I was there, checking in on interviews and making sure I had what I needed. In addition to Mujeres Fuertes she also worked with day laborers and disaster relief workers, had traveled the state after hurricanes bringing information to the immigrant workers who picked up the mess left behind by the storms. While the women had their family, she noted, sometimes the men lived alone and failed to care for themselves; they needed different things from the center. "People all the time come here for help, for example, they need food stamps, Medicaid, they need passport appointments, need to change address, they register children in the school," she said. All the time, she wanted to create new programs, to address different needs, to improve her English so that she could help others learn, to make more money to send home to her family in Colombia, to get her legal situation and her papers sorted so that her daughter could go to university. "My daughter is an excellent student," she said proudly.

When I left Esperanza my heart was in my throat. I still hear Mohamed Mire as we hung up the phone for the second time, telling me he will pray for me, and I feel Yirna Buitrago's hug. I think of those moments of shared vulnerability, and I wish safety and an end to the evil eye for them and for everyone like them, crossing the desert or the sea.[72]

Break III

My father worked himself to death. I should not say that, but it is true. Even before the collapse of the small restaurant chain he ran, he had been obsessed with the value of work, though in sometimes contradictory ways. But after what he perceived as his failure (rather than the fate of something like half of all the small businesses out there), the only answer possible was to work more.

The bicycle shop was open seven days a week, and so he was there seven days a week, wringing more value out of his own sweat, his own lengthened working days. He obsessed over finding ways to improve, to promote, to make more efficient.

He blamed himself for not having worked hard enough to prevent failure, and then he kept on working until he could not do it anymore and I had to do it for him, I had to show up every day and try to make him leave, to take even a half day off. He wasn't doing anything anyway; he would let the phone ring and ring hoping someone else would get it. When people tell me that *people need to work, we need work to have meaning*, I think of him there and all the things he could have done that were not work. He liked to do things once, I want to scream, he played golf and liked good food and jokes and his convertible and sometimes playing tennis with me. He was interested once in what I did, what my sister did, what we thought. And then all of that stopped, and there was just work, and death.

When I was a child, I watched him do logic puzzles for fun; he saw making money as just one more puzzle. There never seemed to be anything he wanted from the money he made, other than maybe some time off to play golf. But once we lived in Hilton Head, with a golf course literally in our backyard, he rarely played, and if he did he had usually worked first. He did little for fun except watch more golf on TV and occasionally take my mother to a restaurant.

He was already not well when he started this schedule and not young either, and unlike at the restaurants he was actually doing the physical work, lifting rental bicycles onto a delivery truck and fixing, adjusting, in the South Carolina summer because summer was when the tourists were there and the money was made—three or four months when you had to cover your entire year and to make up for lost savings and to help two girls go to school. He was not big or strong at any point in his life, but there was no bit of physical work he was willing to delegate to the legions of young people who came through on summer jobs without doing it himself first. I wondered whether he was punishing himself or just genuinely convinced he had to have his hands on everything lest it fail again.

I learned from him to work two and three jobs at a time (once, for a brief period, four), to fill my hours with preparation and hope labor and to say no to days off, to spend an hour writing before work and more hours writing after, to always be looking for what is next because there was no net to catch me if I fell. Because when I did use that net—my parents' house, my teenage bed—it turned into just another form of work that was even harder to escape: running their business, looking after their needs, that was another job. I had to stay and watch my father.

And so there was another heart surgery, and the smoking, and I don't know what it cost him to admit he needed me to take care of everything but he could not despite my presence admit that what he needed most was to stop working. And then there was the bout of pneumonia and other things, and only then, finally, at seventy years old, was he maybe ready to retire.

When the business was finally handed over, nearly immediately he got sick. His "retirement" was a year in and out of hospitals, care homes, trundling an oxygen tank around, his dry humor gone. I wondered sometimes, lying awake those long awful nights when we did not know what would happen, whether he had held out to keep working, propelling himself through the days weeks months by force of will and his body finally gave out when he stopped. If he could not imagine a life without work.

I am enough my father's daughter that I thought I could work at grief. That I could apply that same force of will to *getting through it* faster or better or cleaner or something else. But as Judith Butler points out, you cannot Protestant ethic your way through grief the way my father did through his life; you cannot piously apply yourself to it, and there is no resolution to seek.[1]

Didn't stop me from trying.

I packed and went to the labor conference where I was due to present the weekend after I returned home from saying goodbye to my father, knowing that there would be people there who loved me. A conference organizer, a comrade I had only met on the internet previously, told me that they had set aside a spare room for me so I did not have to share one as I had planned and could have a silent place to retreat to in order to hold myself together. I moderated a panel on transit workers organizing and stared into space to try to keep from crying, and people I barely knew texted me to say, "Welcome to the dead dads club." It sounds awful but it wasn't; the people who had been there kept me going, as did the hugs from movement aunties and friends and past crushes.

And then my colleague's father died while we were there, and so I tried to show up for her as if I knew anything about grief, and we cried together and I tried to stop wondering why my partner hadn't called.

Work travel saved me but exhausted me. I tried to outrun my grief with assignments in strange-to-me places and in the connections I made in those places across an ocean I started to see a tiny glimpse of a future that wasn't a retread of my past, just a tiny crack through the fog, but I ran for it with everything I had and I was shocked when the path wasn't steady.

When I fell off cliffs again, each time, I was surprised.

Even when I began to repeat *grief isn't linear* like a mantra, when more friends lost more fathers and I wrote to them with what occasionally felt like hard-earned wisdom and also gifted wisdom, I still expected, somehow, to be on an upward path. I treasured those moments when I felt alive again, felt all the edges of my body and even something beyond it. I let people into my life who shouldn't have been there because at least they felt like something, anything, even when they disappointed me again.

But it would still come when I least expected it and least wanted it, and I would have to figure out how to hold myself together suddenly in a crowd. I did therapy and more therapy and wrote back and forth with the grievers, the ones who knew, and we shared readings and practices. I did yoga and wrote nearly illegible journals and all the things you are supposed to do but really what I needed to do was drift.

A tense I was not good at.

But how does one speak of being good at grief when *grief does you*?

I wrote a book about work being bad for you in the wake of my father working himself to death, and yes I felt the tension in my bones as I worked to keep from feeling, and yet the feelings made their way onto the page. And when the book was finished and it came out into a world turned upside down by a pandemic, I worked even more: I said yes to every request for my time, every podcast, every blogger, every question someone had. I worked so much on this little book in which the conclusion was that there are so many things more important than work, and I really did believe that, but I couldn't stop and couldn't say no.

I never learned how. So, slowly, I taught myself.

CHAPTER 3

Dig

Deindustrialization, work, and meaning

3.1 Don't Mourn

The adage "Don't mourn, organize!" is attributed to Joe Hill, the itinerant Industrial Workers of the World troubadour whose labor songs are still sung today. It's a slightly shortened version of what he wrote to Big Bill Haywood before his execution on trumped-up charges: "Goodbye Bill: I die like a true rebel. Don't waste any time mourning—organize!" Hill was not the only "Wobbly" to be killed while attempting to rouse the working class to rebellion, and mourn him they certainly did despite his admonishments.[1]

Another saying, "Pray for the dead and fight like hell for the living," comes from Mary Harris "Mother" Jones, also a Wobbly and best known for agitating during the mine wars. In her autobiography (which may have been, well, embellished) she described a visit to a miners' meeting in a church; she brought them outside, declaring the church an inappropriate place for such work, and then told them, "Your organization is not a praying institution. It's a fighting institution. It's an educational institution along industrial lines. Pray for the dead and fight like hell for the living!"[2]

Of the two, the first holds more weight, but I think I prefer the second. It offers the dead their due, rather than glossing over the grief that working people hold and have to carry around on the job with them, while no less of a demand for action, struggle, justice. In its juxtaposition perhaps it also leaves room for mourning that is not of a death, inevitable if oftentimes premature, but of other losses of the kinds that the miners of West Virginia and the workers of the world knew too intimately.

When I met him in Indianapolis in 2017, Chuck Jones was the outgoing president of United Steelworkers Local 1999, the kind of man your brain would conjure if you were told to think of a Rust Belt union leader: a whiskey-and-Marlboro-Reds rasp, a mustache and a smile and sad eyes. Likeable and abrasive at once. I sat in the union hall and listened to him tell stories about strikes from his younger days, about the lengths they'd go to prevent people from scabbing, the hell they'd raise.

I met Jones when the factory he'd worked at his entire adult life was closing down, when the president of the United States had called him out on Twitter, spawning micro-fame and death threats. Trump had promised to save the Carrier plant, had swept into the factory like George W. Bush on the aircraft carrier proclaiming, "mission accomplished," and Jones had the audacity to check his facts and call bullshit. To say the Rexnord plant around the corner from Carrier wasn't "saved" at all, and that like everything else the president pretended to give to the working class, the Carrier deal was a wad of tax breaks and underperformance. "It was sickening," Jones told me then. Carrier was still moving hundreds of jobs to a new plant just beneath the border in Mexico.[3]

Before the plants closed, conditions tended to deteriorate, I was told by Robert James, who would take over running the union from Jones and who had spent his adult life at Carrier. The companies brought in two-tier contracts, where the new hires would do the same job for less pay than the old hands, and workers were pushed for further concessions to keep the company open, a process that would continue right up until the announcement that the factory would shut down anyway.

Carrier was still open when I spoke to Chuck Jones again in 2020, as Trump was running for reelection, though it had been whiplash at the plant: layoffs, then rehires. Local news reported that the workers were "required to work eight- to 10-hour shifts, seven days a week. Many haven't had a single day off in more than a month." During the pandemic, the grinding schedule left them vulnerable to COVID-19, and workers told reporters that two or three of them had died. "We're tired and we're exhausted," said Jennifer Shanklin-Hawkins, who had worked at the plant for eighteen years. "They're not treating us right." The workers were skeptical that the company would stick around much longer, as companies around the state were still shutting down.[4]

The average salary at Rexnord, Jones explained, "was about twenty-five dollars an hour. They were working as much overtime, basically, as they wanted. A lot of them were working sixty hours a week and everything over forty was time and a half. They were bringing home pretty good paychecks." When the plant shut down, the jobs on offer were closer to sixteen dollars an hour, no overtime. "Some of them had to pull children out of college. Some of them, their wives went to work that maybe weren't working before and just made a whole lifestyle change. You saw a lot of people put property up for sale. Part of it was through foreclosures and some of it was they had to get rid of it and maybe cut back on their house payment."

There was something deeper to the job losses, though, that went beyond the financial. "They ain't got a clue if they never went through what it means to lose a job, especially due to no fault of your own," Jones said. "It really makes me bitter. I'm still bitter over this stuff and I don't think I'll ever get over it."[5]

Walter Benjamin, in the time of industrialized death better known as World War II, criticized the German working class for its uncritical belief in (capitalist) improvement, the "illusion that the factory work which was supposed to tend toward technological progress constituted a political achievement." Progress, he noted, could move forward in one way while being a retrogressive step for human life. The workers in Indiana were told that "progress" made them obsolete, that a faceless global capitalism (the "invisible hand," perhaps) had no use for them anymore, blamed them for their own human needs, wrote them off as the losers of history.[6]

Deindustrialization is a process of creating ghosts out of people who are still alive. But it is not dark magic that shuts down a factory and drains money from a town. The market is not a monster that must be appeased with blood sacrifice; it is a thing that humans made and can unmake just the same.[7]

Deindustrialization is a form of haunting.

The myth of the heroic (white) male worker, all made of muscles and pride, down in the bowels of the earth or the dark satanic mill or the superfactory, grease-smeared and skilled, tells us a lot about what is being grieved even if it is at the end of the day still a myth.[8]

The story of deindustrialization from ten thousand feet is one of collapsing profits and restive Global North workers and an international recomposition of the division of labor and of what "the working class" is. These are the long processes of capitalism: replacing workers with fixed capital, living labor with dead, turning to machines both to replace workers and to push them to move faster, to expand the workday and pay the workers less, to move around the world in search of both materials and cheap labor.[9]

The progress of the machines in particular is a subject of much hype today but has been overstated since the 1830s. Indeed, the automation hype is itself a form of labor discipline, the age-old threat to workers: you'd better behave or we'll replace you with machines. The machines are often designed as much to control workers as to replace them, the techniques of factory control themselves inherited from the slave plantation.[10]

Some workers found ways to rebel against the machine and the spying eye of the boss, to overcome their fragmentation. In those rebellions we can find the spark of solidarity, the building of a community, the composition of a class. From the machine breaking of the Luddites and the Swing rebellion to uprisings on slave plantations, early rebels destroyed the machinery of control and demanded to be seen as fully human rather than interchangeable cogs or inputs. These protests looked more like riots than an orderly present-day strike, legislated and regimented into near ineffectiveness, and this explosive potential had to be contained, routed into predictable if not fully controlled institutions: the union and the bargaining process.[11]

Skip forward a few hundred years, to the past century and the buildup for World War II, the prelude to the period of endless nostalgia. The war necessitated massive investment that could not be left to the capitalists, who had dug the hole of the Great Depression not two decades earlier. National defense spending built factories as well as military bases; governments intervened to (mostly) maintain labor peace; women and Black workers in the United States got unprecedented access to factory jobs at a decent wage as white men were sent to the front. The unions demanded and won steady wages and a settlement that would be expanded after the war was over, but when the white men came back, industry reshuffled again, and Black workers, last hired, first fired, lost out.[12]

The war solidified a concept that during the COVID-19 pandemic came to be known as "essential work." Coal miners were the exemplar—very aware that their countries' fortunes (and the war effort) relied on their willingness to put their lives on the line to dig coal. Miners would compare their wages and conditions to those of other industrial workers and act (strike) when they saw what they had as a raw deal. In Britain the mines were nationalized, as were many other major industries, so such "essential" work was directly done on behalf of the nation, and this arrangement heightened the workers' sense of ownership over their jobs.

Industrial workers were powerful, Marx and Engels argued, because of their ability to halt production, not because of some moral goodness or essential human value, and it is just because of that power that capital has never stopped trying to get rid of them as much as possible. We do those workers no favors by treating them as myths and legends or as creatures fixed in amber from another time.[13]

If you think of the entire history of industrial capitalism as the struggle over whether workers will work and for how long and how much, you can start to see the reasons why deindustrialization happened. The strike, a demonstration of workers' strength by the withdrawal of their labor, must stop production or circulation in order to have power. You cannot stop work in order to demand work; you cannot strike to keep a factory open. Joshua Clover called this the *affirmation trap*, "in which labor is locked into the position of affirming its own exploitation under the guise of survival." Once the proletariat had to be forced into the factories, now the industrial working class was desperate to hang on to them.[14]

From the 1970s, in the rich countries, the process of deindustrialization went from slow and sporadic to quick and brutal, changing the shapes of people's worlds. Cities bled people as they left in search of work, house prices collapsed, property taxes disappeared. Political anger over the process took a few shapes, and one of them was xenophobia, outrage at the workers perceived to be "taking our jobs" in Japan or Mexico or China as manufacturing moved and imports surged. Capital was moving more freely as borders were tightening: it was neither a coincidence nor a contradiction but two sides of the same process. Workers fixed in space or made deportable are more desperate and thus cheaper to exploit.[15]

The problem is bigger than one free trade agreement, and it certainly isn't Mexico's fault, a sentiment expressed over and over by the workers from Carrier and Rexnord even as the companies shipped workers from Mexico up to be trained by the people they would be replacing; they were, despite popular portrayals to the contrary, very aware that it was their bosses, not the workers across the border, who were making them redundant.

Industrial jobs were never the majority, but they set the pace and the standard for employment and created the broader structure of feeling that haunts us today. In 1970, 22 percent of US workers were in manufacturing; by 2017 that was just 8 percent. In France, the number fell by 50 percent from its postwar heights, and in Britain, 67 percent. The same process comes for everyone, though, eventually: Aaron Benanav wrote, "By the end of the twentieth century, it was possible to speak of a global wave of deindustrialization: worldwide manufacturing employment rose in absolute terms by 0.4 percent per year between 1991 and 2016, but that was much slower than the overall growth of the global labor force, with the result that the manufacturing share of total employment declined by 3 percentage points over the same period." Workers are cycled into the world system and made surplus by it without ever reaching the kind of (temporary) balance that the United States and Western Europe enjoyed after the wars.[16]

With the destruction of industrial work came the destruction of industrial unions. It was, after all, organization that helped make Global North labor expensive in the first place, not the generosity of a handful of bosses who looked at masses of workers and saw potential consumers. And the destruction of the unions meant the end of a whole world that the unions had built, a whole world that gave people not only meaning and stability but comfort, social spaces, something like love.[17]

Dave Green flopped onto the couch in the United Auto Workers Local 1112 hall with a half smile. The storied General Motors Lordstown plant had been idled, not technically closed—that would be a mandatory subject of bargaining—but rather "unallocated," a term that no one, even retired members who had been at Lordstown since it opened, had heard before. They were waiting for GM to tell them what it meant. The last Chevrolet Cruze had rolled off the assembly line on March 6, 2019, and the workers were hanging on to the thinnest thread of hope.[18]

"It's so stressful not knowing," Green, then president of Local 1112, said. "If they would just come and tell us they're gonna close the plant. . . . I don't want to say that's a good thing. But it would at least give people the ability to get some direction in their life.

"You ever lose somebody? You go through seven stages of grief. Well, a job's a pretty important thing like that too," he added. But the Lordstown workers couldn't grieve properly because they weren't sure; they didn't know whether to find new jobs or take the company's relocation offer or wait and hope.

Lordstown is a little town and a huge now-quiet automobile factory outside of Youngstown, Ohio, already a place full of stilled machinery and lost opportunity. But even in an area familiar with factory closures, the Lordstown story felt neverending. The plant, which had opened in 1966, was sold to a company called Lordstown Motors, which promised to build electric trucks there but declared bankruptcy in the summer of 2023. GM had partnered with LG Corporation to open a battery plant nearby, and the workers there voted overwhelmingly in 2022 to join the UAW, but the union had to fight to get the battery workers the same pay as mainline autoworkers.[19]

Tim O'Hara, then the local's vice president and a career Lordstown worker, had gotten used to the losses as a child of Youngstown. He remembered the day known as "Black Monday," when the closure of a steel mill at Youngstown Sheet & Tube put five thousand people immediately out of work and kicked off a spiral that led to fifty thousand job losses in the area. "I saw the grief, even back in the '70s," he said. "There were a lot of efforts to try to keep the mills open. The churches got involved, and there were a lot of attempts for employees to try to buy the mills. And of course, none of it worked." He was first hired at GM in 1977, the year the steel mill closed, his good fortune feeling oddly linked to the losses of his relatives and neighbors. He felt lucky to have a decent job. "I started at like $6.60 an hour. I was on top of the world. I had more money than I knew what to do with."[20]

But for his whole career, he lived with the awareness that it could all disappear at any time. "You're always waiting for the other shoe to drop. Is there going to be a layoff? So, while it was a good job, it was never really secure." He survived dozens of layoffs and recalls that the workers were simply expected to be elastic enough to be discarded and reclaimed over and over: "We were doing everything they were telling us we had to do, everything, and then they just came down and said, 'None of that matters.' I still remember when they built the last car, people crying, their tears are falling on the car as they did their job for the last time. I don't think that goes away. People just deal with it, just like they deal with any other kind of grief, losing a family member or whatever they're grieving. But I think it stays with you."

When, after a nationwide strike at General Motors in 2019, the union narrowly voted to approve a contract that accepted the end of Lordstown, O'Hara had enough seniority to retire, but his wife, also a Lordstown worker, did not, and so they moved with their teenage children to Bowling Green, Kentucky. "You had your family at home, and you had your family at work. And that was all lost when everybody had to move."[21]

"We had a strong local at Lordstown, obviously, which is probably part of the reason GM wanted to get rid of us," O'Hara said. When the workers transferred away, they often found themselves in less powerful and involved local unions, and that too was a loss, the solidarity and companionship on the shop floor and off broken up. "For me, on a personal level, it was a double-edged sword, because I was a worker, so I was an employee, and I was also a union official," he said. "They're taking away my plant that I spent over four decades at, I raised my kids, kept a roof over my head, drove nice cars, the whole middle-class lifestyle. And then, from the union aspect, I think 'Was I a failure? Was there something I could've done as vice president that could've convinced GM not to do this?'" Pictures of the plant still get him choked up, even years later. "We had a member that committed suicide shortly after. And I had a good friend that died from an aneurysm," he said, noting that stress and grief affect the body in different and untraceable ways. "I don't think it's ever going to go away."

Like the steel mills, the closure of Lordstown had ripple effects: more job losses, among union staff and restaurant workers and even teachers when students were pulled out of school to move elsewhere with their families. Youngstown had been filled with amusements for working people when the steel mills provided good pay if dangerous work. No more.

O'Hara came into American manufacturing just after its heyday; his parents and grandparents had been able to take or leave jobs, and even

O'Hara's older brother had been part of the wildcat strike wave in Lordstown's militant days. Lordstown was famous for its 1972 strike, when nearly eight thousand workers walked out over the speedup of work, the use of robots to hasten the pace of human labor and exhaust the workers. The workers at Lordstown were expected to make 101 cars an hour, or more than one a minute; one worker who remembered that time demonstrated for me how fast that would be, picking up a pen from his desk and noting that even doing that more than once a minute for a full day would be exhausting, let alone the hefting of tools and the observation the workers had to do as the cars rolled past. The workers in the plant rebelled against such treatment with the same kinds of walkouts that Mohamed Mire and the Amazon workers would use decades later, and then finally with an official strike that the leadership in Detroit did not seem to understand: The workers got paid well, so what were they so mad about? An article from the radical *Industrial Worker* newspaper at the time noted, "The average age of the work force at the plant . . . is 24. Most of the workers are sons and daughters of working-class people from the steel, auto, rubber and mining industries. They come mostly in old cars, many of them bearing peace symbols. But all we could perceive from many of the young black and white workers was confusion over the way the big union bureaucrats had taken over."[22]

Sometimes it seemed like the leadership of the UAW had detached from its workforce. Lordstown workers were not the only ones who were bluntly encouraged by union officials to behave and look grateful rather than raising hell. The UAW had in 1950 agreed to the "Treaty of Detroit," not an actual treaty but a five-year contract with GM where the union had officially given up what was euphemistically called "management rights" but in fact was the struggle for control over production itself. Bargaining would henceforth be about pay and conditions; workers lacked a say over things like the speedup, and perhaps more importantly over the companies' ability to close plants and discard workers as they wanted to. Such disposal would break up power centers for the radicals within the auto workforce over the years, and it would eventually come to Lordstown.[23]

The UAW elected new leadership in 2023, a slate of reformers who had used a corruption scandal at headquarters to demand "one worker, one vote" for union positions and then clean house. The corruption had overshadowed the 2019 strike; the new leadership promised militancy and delivered, with the union's first-ever strike at all three of the big US automakers at the same time later in 2023. The strike resulted in the best contract the UAW had seen in years, and perhaps most importantly for this story, the union won the right to strike in the future over plant closures—to strike across facilities, not only at the one being shuttered. It even managed to get a plant reopened: the Stellantis plant in Belvidere, Illinois. Matt Frantzen, president of the local union at Belvidere, said that the new leadership cared about his members' needs: "They want the reactions, the emotion, from the membership. They don't have a problem with the good, the bad, and the ugly."[24]

But the deal was bittersweet for the people of Lordstown. While GM agreed after the strike to include battery plant workers (including those at its Lordstown facility) in the main agreement, giving an immediate raise to the workers there, and giving some former Lordstown plant workers the opportunity to transfer back, it was too late for many, including O'Hara, who had already upended their lives. Some families had been separated by GM, paying for two homes, commuting long hours from Indiana or Michigan or seeing family once a month or so. "I call [GM CEO] Mary Barra 'Mary Appleseed' because she basically dropped a hammer on Local 1112, she sent our members all over the nation, but she planted seeds of Local 1112 in all these other states," O'Hara said. "Yes, they destroyed the Lordstown culture, but they've also sent Lordstown people all over the country to maybe start up a new version of what they call the 'culture.'"

Chuckie Denison, a third-generation Ohio GM worker, had signed on in Dayton, moved to Shreveport, Louisiana, when the Dayton plant closed, wound up at Lordstown right as the global economy imploded in 2008, transferred to Parma in 2015, and then took early retirement in 2018, having been with the company since he graduated high school. His fiancée was a Lordstown worker and took the transfer to Spring Hill, Tennessee, with a teenage daughter who had just one last year of high school left. But Denison stayed in Ohio: "Ultimately, I'm tired of chasing GM. I'm not letting GM dictate what I do for the rest of my life."[25]

3.2 Ruins

The strategy of organized abandonment that we now call neoliberalism was designed to splinter social solidarity, to crush not just labor unions and not just communism but any sort of collective action, to break us up into little individual market actors who compete, always, with each other. Such competition does not exclusively or even mostly break down along racial or gender lines, but it sure does make those lines seem brighter.[26]

Despite the lazy shorthands mostly coined in cities that have survived deindustrialization by turning to a service economy (finance for the wealthy, Uber and Deliveroo for the poor), working-class people mostly don't live their lives in concepts. Appending the term "white" to "working class" creates a division that existed less on the factory floor than off it, in the 1970s when the young workers at Lordstown made national news or in 2017 when Carrier did the same. As David Roediger wrote, "When the term is used, the accent will always fall on 'white' and the mumbling on 'working class.'" Solidarity on the shop floor and division in the voting booth is a story in itself, but the truth that any union organizer with half a day's experience will tell you is that if you can manage to bring together people who have not chosen each other but have been chosen by capital—hired into the same workforce, moved into the same apartment block, assembled not through affinity but through happenstance and a dab of profiling—almost any transformation is possible. The best way to transcend racism, sexism, and all the other -isms is to bring people together around shared interests and shared enemies.[27]

The white worker, W. E. B. Du Bois argued, was as much a creation of the slave system as its opposite, and the formal end of slavery did not erase the color line but drew it darker and drew it around the world. *Capitalism requires inequality and racism enshrines it.* The unions in the United States (and elsewhere) foundered on the color line over and over again, failing to organize Black workers or to represent them well when they did, failing to organize the former plantation South in a serious way, thus leaving it open as the first destination for capital flight out of the industrial North, that is, before capital packed up entirely and headed for the Global South to exploit Black and Latinx and Asian workers.[28]

The 1970s was a decade of crisis for capitalism broadly, and capital resolved the crisis by reorganizing itself far from the messy human needs of workers and their relationships and the gains they had won through decades and centuries of struggle. Deindustrialization was only one part of this process; slicing the social safety net to bits was another. Eliminate the good jobs and at the same time increase workers' dependency on a job by eliminating any support they might get outside of it, and watch those workers turn docile and even obsequious, begging for work. Increase punishment (prisons) for anyone who falls through the cracks.[29]

The cities crumbled too, from the destabilizing aftereffects of losing their industrial foundation. Those who could afford it might flee to the suburbs or the Sun Belt or to the few cities that had pivoted to serving a different form of capital, while those who could not were left behind. Unsurprisingly, the people who were left behind were often Black, but not exclusively, another blurring of the boundaries in which "Black poor" are counterposed to "white workers" even if both are mourning the loss of the same jobs.[30]

Outsourcing wasn't just a process of moving factories to Mexico; it was also a process of firing organized workers and bringing in the temps and subcontractors, temps who were also often people with precarious migration status and thus presumably harder to organize. The divide between "good" and "bad" workers mirrors the divide between "good" and "bad" migrants in its uselessness, yet the labor movement has bought into it too many times. The good workers being industrial, male, white, native born; the bad ones immigrant, temporary or service workers, women, Black, "willing" to work for less as if this is a choice they actively made and not a result of being twice abandoned, first by the state and then by a labor movement that ought to have struggled for them. That labor's gains since the crisis of the '70s have mostly been in these fields, caring and service workers, Black and Latinx, female dominated, is not a coincidence but a demonstration of how capital reorganized work toward those who were unorganized and how in response those workers decided to fight, sometimes with the help of traditional unions and sometimes in spite of them.[31]

The loss of industrial jobs, meanwhile, reminded industrial workers who had thought they were middle class that they were still the proletariat; proletariat in the original sense, which Joshua Clover reminded us is not those who work in production but those who have nothing but their labor to sell, those "without reserves."[32]

It is short-term work in warehouses or services or the modern piecework that is the gig economy that most abandoned workers are thrown into. If they are lucky they might have bought a piece of property that if they're even luckier hasn't lost value with the death of their town, a home that perhaps they can sell. On each side of the Carrier plant in Indianapolis are a Target and an Amazon distribution center, a stark reminder of the options that exist when the factory closes; in former mining towns in Britain, Craig Gent noted, the warehouses might be built right over the shuttered mines. "Mines, steelworks and docks went, but the people who worked and lived among them stayed. Entire towns subsequently endured a sort of drawn-out social mourning following a kind of civic death."[33]

Deindustrialization for some meant new jobs for others, in other parts of the world, and new risks with them. The workers at Rana Plaza, a factory complex home to five garment manufacturing companies in Savar, Bangladesh, just a bit north of Dhaka, had seen cracks throughout the building's eight stories, and reported them to a safety inspector, who ordered an evacuation. But the clothing factories decided to open the following day and threatened workers with the loss of their pay and their jobs if they did not come in. On April 24, 2013, the building collapsed, with thousands inside. More than 1,130 people died, another 2,500 were seriously injured. Most of them were women.[34]

"We cannot say that this is simply an accident. Rather than, we can say this is a kind of workers killing," Amirul Haque Amin, the president of the National Garment Workers Federation, told me, ten years on from the collapse of Rana Plaza. In 2016, thirty-eight people were charged with murder, but the trial process drags on. Some charges have been dropped; the owner of the building remains in custody.[35]

The grief was still raw ten years on. Eventually, Amin said, the victims' families received compensation, and the injured workers received medical treatment, but this was insufficient. "This was a massive victimization," he said. "Support, treatment, monitoring and rehabilitation, it actually needs to continue." Many of the survivors still work in the garment industry, he noted, while others are trying to piece together a living doing something, anything else. But it is hard to do that, as garment work is by far the country's largest industry. It brings in a lot of money to Bangladesh, but the workers' salaries remain quite low—some of them make about US$80 a month.

The NGWF had nearly four hundred members in the Rana Plaza building that day, and so the surviving members began the process of burying and mourning the dead, and fighting for the living. "In honoring, we also raise our voice," Amin said, and the union collaborated with other garment worker organizations and trade union federations within Bangladesh, and in the countries where the thirty-one brands made in the Rana Plaza factories were distributed, to demand compensation for survivors. Rana Plaza was part of the massive global "fast fashion" supply chain, where workers in factories are subcontracted by name-brand companies to produce quickly and cheaply. Companies with products made in Rana Plaza included Walmart, Primark, J. C. Penney, Benetton, and Carrefour.[36]

Kalpona Akter, one of the most prominent garment worker activists internationally, began working in a garment factory when she was twelve, supporting her sick parents and siblings. She described the work vividly in one interview: "I worked 14–15 hours per day, so that was barely one taka [about one cent] per hour. We would even work overnight, and catch a few hours of sleep on the factory floor before going back to work again. I remember I once spent 23 straight days at the factory, without going home even once. It was also common to be sworn at and slapped around there. There were a lot of us child labourers, and we had no idea about our rights. I still remember there was once a fire on the fifth floor, but they told us to keep working on the third and not evacuate. That is how little they valued our lives." This continued, until her coworkers organized to demand overtime pay; that day, she learned what a strike was.[37]

Akter recalled seeing an item of clothing made in Bangladesh retailing in US stores for seventy-five dollars. Workers like her were deliberately separated from the products of their labor; when they saw how much was made on their backs, they rebelled. Akter and others were arrested in New Jersey in 2015, demanding compensation from the Children's Place for Rana Plaza survivors. "We were there demanding the company pay $8 million in compensation," she said. "This seems like a large amount, until you realise the CEO alone receives around $12 million a year!"[38]

The sheer horror of the Rana Plaza collapse helped the workers' voices cut through internationally, and consumers helped pressure the companies to sign a landmark labor safety accord mandating inspections and supporting workers who spoke up about hazards. The unions insisted that the lost workers' lives were worth more than simply their earnings, that people should not risk their lives to operate a sewing machine so that companies could keep production out of sight.[39]

Ten years on, the NGWF rolled out a campaign targeting Walmart and the other companies that had refused to join the accord. Many of the brands, including Walmart, joined a voluntary accord rather than the legally binding one, but Amin stressed that the voluntary agreements did not work.[40]

Bangladeshi workers are not any more inherently exploitable than I am, but structural adjustment programs primed the country for international production, pushing people off the land and into the factories. And climate change too is destroying their livelihoods. Displacement is already happening: more than seven million people in 2022 alone moved, many of them within the country, to the capital and into the garment factories.[41]

Bangladeshi workers also left the country only to find themselves shoved into the same precarious conditions elsewhere. In England, they wound up in factories and then the service sector and the gig economy; in the Middle East, they are guest workers or undocumented manual laborers. In New York City, they helped lead the taxi workers' strike against Donald Trump's Muslim ban. Such exploitation at home and abroad reminds us that while capitalism devalues the lives of all workers, it especially relies on the ability to render certain groups of workers surplus.[42]

Yet the workers who survived Rana Plaza and the garment industry insist on the value of their lives and their grief, and they ask our solidarity. All of us, around the world: it is a cruel facet of the cheap clothing industry that it caters to people who are barely making ends meet as well as to those who want today's trends fast and discard them just as quickly. Cheap clothing requires cheap lives.

Across from Rana Plaza there is a monument built by garment workers: two giant raised fists, holding a hammer and sickle.[43]

The landscape of deindustrialization is artfully depicted in photograph after photograph, film after film, a new gothic landscape for the post-Fordist age. The smokestacks left outside the mall in Pittsburgh that used to be Homestead Steel, the bits of former factories as art galleries or playgrounds or just left behind. "Ruin porn," the lush portrayal of emptiness has been called. In consuming it, Leila Taylor wrote, "we become mourners at our own funeral."[44]

The photos are almost always stripped of their inhabitants, just as the factories and cities have been. Ruin porn is abstracted, haunting precisely because the people are no longer there.[45]

Part of the complicated grief that industrial workers feel when the industry departs is a grief for the generations of workers whose lives were lost on the job. They remembered disasters of generations earlier and disasters of personal experience. Chuckie Denison told me of watching a man next to him on an assembly line "have a heart attack and die right next to me. And we stopped the line. And management came and they actually moved him so they could start the line back up." The workers wished for stable employment for their children, but they wanted it to be anywhere but down the mines or in the factories.[46]

Marking and mourning industrial disasters, historian Ewan Gibbs explained, was a long tradition in British coal mining that intensified after the 1984–1985 strikes. "It actually has a synonymous nature with the struggle to preserve industrial employment," he said. The loss of the industry was being commemorated alongside these lost lives. Miners lived in the tension, as Trish Kahle wrote, between the professed idea that a human life was worth more than a ton of coal and the reality that those lives were regularly sacrificed for cheap energy, that mining was a "way of death" rather than life.[47]

Not all deaths in industry were catastrophic or quick. The work broke bodies down slowly too, coal dust and smoke gathered in the lungs, muscles and ligaments tore and strained, and repetitive motion ground joints down. Steel mills exposed workers to unbearable heat and burns. Younger miners, Gibbs noted, would sit alongside older men wheezing on the bus or the underground train and wonder how long until the black lung got them, until they breathed like that too. Workers and their unions fought for protections, for equipment that might save them if a mine collapsed and for regulations and the right to know what kinds of toxic chemicals they might be touching and inhaling. It is one of the many cruelties of deindustrialization that regulations began to kick in as the industries were dismantled, leaving the workers wondering: Had they just shut up and breathed poison, might they have at least been able to keep the house?[48]

Nate Holdren called workplace injury and social murder "a production of death, but also a huge production of suffering and misery." Some have used the term "industrial violence" to describe such things as the radium poisoning suffered by women hired to paint wristwatch faces with the radioactive substance or the deaths of 146 women in the Triangle

Shirtwaist fire in 1911 or the mines collapsing or indeed the individual injuries, the mangled hands or blinded eyes that happened every day. "Trapped in that machine was a human being with a name and a face and a life," Holdren wrote. And everyone who walked into the factory mine mill knew they could be next.[49]

The history of workers' compensation laws in the United States, Holdren showed, affixed a price to a worker's life and body parts. Compensation would come, according to actuarial tables, based on the price of one's labor—so if you lost a leg at work, and your boss lost the same leg, his compensation would be more. Such laws took away workers' right to demand justice in a courtroom, to tell their personal story and to have their loss heard and recorded, turning them instead into a mass, a proletariat, a people known only for the necessity of their work. "Payment for injury," he wrote, "would become as regular, brisk, and business-like as the ongoing maiming and killing of employees."[50]

The treatment of workers as machine parts was not even particularly subtle. Industrial physicians marketed themselves as repairmen of the "human machine," and one company argued, "The plant engineer, after passing upon the integrity of newly acquired equipment, periodically carries out an inspection to determine its efficiency, its rate of depreciation, and its relationship to the other portions of the plant with which it must coordinate its functions. The same logic applies to the human plant equipment. Hence the physical examination of the employee in all its phases." Substandard human equipment would be plucked out and disposed of, rendered surplus.[51]

The turning of human beings into "human plant equipment" is the ultimate logic of the system. *Capital is dead labor.* And when it has burned through the people, the entire town can be discarded. Daphne Carr wrote evocatively of Youngstown, where she grew up and later returned:

> The mills spewed out major pollutants, and working conditions became increasingly unsafe as machinery aged. The city's downtown went ghost as the suburbs' malls beckoned. Then came

> September 19, 1977. "Black Monday," when 4,100 workers at the Campbell Works plant of Youngstown Sheet and Tube lost their jobs. It was the first major steel-plant shutdown in the country. Brier Hill Works followed in 1978, then U.S. Steel-McDonald, Ohio, in 1980, and Republic Steel in 1981. Twenty-five thousand area jobs were lost. The community tried to fight back: workers and local clergy formed the Ecumenical Coalition of Youngstown to try to buy the mills and run them collectively. They failed. . . . Workers spoke of betrayal, of the moral economy of manufacturing, of corporate greed and decisions made by men in little rooms that affected the life and death of a city.[52]

The *Wall Street Journal*, Carr noted, dubbed the area a "necropolis." Its depression, addiction, divorce, and suicide rates all triple the national average; foreclosure, poverty, unemployment, arson, murder, all highest or near highest in the country.[53]

The opioid crisis, named such when it was suddenly recognized outside of the inner cities that had felt deindustrialization's bite first, is just one facet of all of this abandonment, but it makes for a useful synecdoche. Opioids used to numb the pain of working while injured, perhaps prescribed by a doctor in good faith or bought from the pill mills that popped up all over, became a way to numb the broader pain of being discarded.[54]

Opioid and other substance use can be and is a way that people deal with grief and loss, MaryGrace DiMaria said. "Working within these systems that don't allow you to talk about or name what's grief, what's trauma," people feel isolated, like something is wrong with them, and turn to a drug to cope.[55]

The world over, researchers find the same story in the places where manufacturing has disappeared. In one study, "automotive assembly plant closures were associated with increases in opioid overdose mortality"; another found "an obvious spatial association between deadly overdose and poverty, with the highest fatality rates clustered in the region's deindustrialized communities and Pittsburgh's inner-city neighborhoods." In

Eastern Europe, during the transition to capitalism, "deindustrialization was significantly associated with male mortality in both countries directly and indirectly mediated by adverse health behavior as a dysfunctional coping strategy." People discarded by capital are left to pick up the pieces however they can, even if it kills them. Economists Anne Case and Angus Deaton called these "deaths of despair."[56]

The crisis only got worse during the COVID-19 pandemic, when already-isolated people were further cut off from the world. Ninety-three thousand people died of an overdose the first year of the virus in the United States, a 29 percent increase from the previous year. Fentanyl, another synthetic opioid developed for medical use, was often to blame. "Essential" workers kept doing their jobs, while the newly laid off were introduced to the world of deindustrialization.[57]

I spoke to Tim O'Hara in 2020 before the presidential election, and he was haunted by the "back to normal" story being pushed on the campaign trail, the difference between corporate profits and the people he knew who were struggling. "Really, if you look at it, they're profiting off of death."

3.3 Mines

The first banner I saw in the center of Durham was in English and Arabic, reading, "Strength, Solidarity, Resistance," and the people holding it were singing along with a brass band playing Queen's "Fat Bottomed Girls," and even though this isn't my heritage at all I found myself crying. It was July 9, 2022, and the Miners Gala was back after COVID suspended it, and some two hundred thousand of England's workers were back in the streets.[58]

The Miners Gala is a daylong festival of labor where workers past and present gather to march from three corners of the city down to the racetrack where there are speeches, food and drinks, carnival rides and games, and much more brass band music. It was beautiful and that year it was dedicated to the essential workers and it was a reminder that while the coal pits are closed and not much has come to replace them, there is still exploitative and body-breaking work going on everywhere.[59]

The banners are one of my favorite things about British labor unions, they are gorgeous and lush and dramatic. They recall heroes of the movement and depict ideas and concepts and bring together threads of working people's struggles from around the world: I saw Irish revolutionary James Connolly over and over again; I saw Lenin and I saw American "miners' angel" Mother Jones, she who said, "Pray for the dead and fight like hell for the living." The banners are strung between poles and held by two people with leather harnesses and then ropes on either side to keep them upright so that even carrying the banner is a complicated collective endeavor. The Scottish hospitality workers carried their brand-new banner to Durham, at once the same as and different from the miners' banners, a painting in a gorgeous comic-book style of a service worker in a green apron like a Starbucks barista holding a tray with pints of beer, mounting a brick wall like *Liberty Leading the People* except they had a mop in their hand rather than a tricolore. The flag was in the background, and it said, "UNITE," a command and also the name of their union, Unite, "The Union Hospitality Sector" written along the bottom flanked by a smiling vacuum cleaner, a stack of dishes, and that familiar yellow "Caution: Wet Floor" sign.

The Durham gala is more than institutional memory; it is the working class telling a story of itself, how it fought, what it won, what it lost. It is a memorial, an act of grieving, and it is something else. The miners' slogan was repeated on hand-painted and stitched banner after banner: "The past we inherit, the future we build." Banners celebrating the education that mineworkers fought for (so our kids don't have to go down the mines to dig coal) made it explicit: "their future is built on our past." Even the anarchist bloc, dressed in black with red and black flags, carried a banner reading, "THE FUTURE WE BUILD."

The Lesbians and Gay Men Support the Miners banner made me tear up all over again. The miners union came to support queer people's rights and it didn't come to that understanding easily but came to it because solidarity was not about similarity of work or family or clothes or culture;

it was a repeated statement that *an injury to one is an injury to all*. Working class is not an identity so much as a collectivity, and you become part of it not by what you do for work but by choosing the right answer to one simple question: Which side are you on? Michael Jackson, one of the founders of LGSM, told me of the South Wales coalfield the campaign helped keep going during the strikes. "It's very isolated, out there, and yet it had a history of incredible internationalist and progressive thought. That's all due to the union," he said. "It provided a nascent health service, it built libraries, it built public swimming baths. The union was everything."

"Best days of my life, working down that mine," a man said behind me as we watched a samba band go by. Every time I have heard that said by a former miner, it seems to be immediately followed with and often preceded by stories of how awful the work was. This particular man was telling someone about the tunnels being so small and narrow that you had to lie on your back and if you brought your shovel in facing the wrong way you'd have to crawl back out to turn it around where there was more space. The former miner who'd led the tour of the National Coal Mining Museum had just finished telling us that the reason certain parts of the mine had been restricted to nine people was that an accident that killed ten or more was considered major but if it was only nine, no big deal. His life and those of his comrades were devalued by their bosses, but even so he said, "People always ask me did I like it, I say I loved it, best time of my life. Best people I ever worked with." The solidarity in the face of brutal, ugly work and the knowledge that though your boss didn't care if you died, your union did.

The essential work of making capitalism run has always been life threatening. It has not actually changed as much as we think since Marx wrote, "Capital comes dripping from head to foot, from every pore, with blood and dirt," just a few years before the first Durham gala was held in 1871.[60]

I expected to find melancholia in the Durham gala, a relentless clinging to something long past that would be deeply harmful to revive today. And there was plenty of melancholy and nostalgia to go around in the crowds. Yet I also found a labor movement that still had some life in it even as it marched behind banners of depopulated union branches.

"I think the main thing that we lost were the community spirit in the mining industry," Chris Kitchen, the general secretary of the National Union of Mineworkers told me a couple of months later. "Working down the pit where your safety depends on your mate and his safety depends on you, it's kind of a way of living, not just a job." The Miners' Welfare was, he said, more than just a pub; it was where you got married, celebrated birthdays, brought children, mourned the dead. The brass bands, of course, and the sports pitches. All of it paid for by the union.

Kitchen began working in the mines in 1982 in the Wheldale Colliery in Castleford and then when that one was closed transferred to Kellingley, seven miles away, a bigger, deeper mine and one of the last of that type in Britain, full of miners from other closed pits. "Most of us traveled, so the community spirit were watered down." Many of the workers were contractors brought in for short terms. "You couldn't really go out and advertise to a young lad like they did to me in '82, that this is a job for life and you'll have a career, because since '85, '86, we'd been on a permanent threat of closure."

Occasionally that spirit, long crushed, bursts back into life as it did that day in Durham. It was a remnant of something that had been much bigger and broader, and it perhaps papered over the differences that have grown up in communities since—communities that had been solidly Labour that, in 2019, shifted overwhelmingly to the Conservatives. Mining communities voting for the party of Margaret Thatcher. But in Durham that day I got to see a hint of what those communities had lost, why they might long for the days of dark and deadly work.[61]

The early 1970s were a period of pride for the National Union of Mineworkers. But deindustrialization had begun to bite even in the nationalized industry—coal is after all a finite resource, miners always recognized that when a pit was done it was done, no more to dig out of it—and in Britain it was about to be open war.

Kevin Horne, a longtime miner, and Kate Flannery, an activist who had grown up supporting the NUM, remembered the push from the bosses to build up coal stocks in preparation for the expected strike. "It's like digging your own grave," Flannery commented.[62]

Margaret Thatcher had brought in an American industrialist to make cuts to first steel jobs—nearly halved—and then coal. The announcement in March 1984 that five mines would be closed without the customary review kicked off the strike. For the coal communities it was all consuming; for the rest of the nation it was nightly news. Sustaining the strike meant keeping miners' families fed and picket lines strong, and that support came from wives and community members like Flannery and support organizations like LGSM and donations from cities and towns and even outside of Britain.[63]

It was clear that the government was treating the strike as a war; the miners were the "enemy within." But the miners were still not prepared for the level of violence the police would mete out. Kevin Horne and Chris Kitchen headed to the Orgreave coking plant in South Yorkshire on June 18, 1984, with hundreds and then thousands of others, and masses of police in turn, with horses and dogs, riot shields and truncheons.[64]

"We could see these police in the field marching up and down. There must have been three or four thousand," Horne recalled. A police officer asked him to help move some stones so that ambulances could get through, "and as soon as the road were clear, the horses came galloping through. Not the ambulances, it were the horses." The horses and the dogs and the men with shields and sticks. He fled down the field and across the road as the horses charged through the crowds of picketers, the mounted police swinging batons. When Horne turned to return to the front, he was arrested.[65]

Chris Kitchen was nineteen; he was there with his soon-to-be father-in-law, also a striking miner but one who seemed to be questioning whether the strike was worth it. "I'd said to him on a number of times, 'You need to come and see for yourself what's happening.' And ironically, the day that he did decide to go, we got sent to Orgreave." They lost each other at the first horse charge and never found each other again in the melee. Kitchen eventually found him at home, where they turned on the evening news, which seemed to show the miners instigating the police charge. "And he were sat there same as me, [saying,] 'That wasn't what happened,'" Kitchen said. "He never wavered for the rest of the strike."[66]

Footage and photos show galloping horses bearing down on miners in jeans and T-shirts, blood running down faces, police yanking men by their throats. In jail, Horne waited, scared and listening to "moaning and groaning and screaming and all sorts of things." He saw people dripping blood and handed over his sweater to wrap someone's wound with. They were brought to the magistrate's court and charged with riot in the middle of the night—a charge that could carry a life sentence.[67]

Horne was still awaiting trial when the first of the Orgreave arrestees had their day in court; he was in a pub and saw on the television that the charges had been dropped, the trial collapsing when it became clear that police statements had been dictated from the top, that they contradicted one another, that supposed confessions from the miners were false. The miners, who had insisted on going to trial and risking prison rather than admitting guilt of any kind, were free. Real justice, though, Horne still awaits.[68]

The narrative of the strike was set by the time the miners were acquitted. The headlines and the newsreels of "violent" miners—repeating the police story unquestioned—were impossible to take back. "It's very difficult to shift that," attorney Matt Foot, coauthor of a book on protest policing, told me. "Sometimes it's never shifted back."

As the mines were closed one by one, mining communities lost their livelihoods, and the ghosts of Orgreave came to loom larger and larger. "I still can't forgive and forget," Kitchen said. "I still don't trust the police like I should be able to." It seemed that Orgreave was the moment the police were let loose to crash through pit villages as brutally as they liked, arresting miners in workingmen's clubs and harassing people on the streets, and those tactics are still used today.[69]

The immediate violence compounded the slow brutality, Flannery said, of "losing your job, losing your dignity, losing your livelihood." Miners watched concrete poured down mine shafts, stacks destroyed, and knew that the government was now importing coal from abroad, from countries that did not have the health and safety protections that the NUM had wrung from a nationalized industry they had considered *theirs*. They mourned a lost sense of their importance to the country; they had gone from fueling industrial dominance to *the enemy within* to abandonment.[70]

Papers declassified in recent years have vindicated the miners' contention that the strike was deliberately planned for and provoked in order to privatize the industry. In the midst of an energy crisis, Kitchen told me, "it's ironic that whilst they've tried to greenwash it as closing the coal industry was for the benefit of the environment, there's no doubt it was never anything to do with the environment. It was a calculated political decision," Kitchen said. "Ironically now, we, the British public, are paying the price for that." They could have been further along in the fight against climate change, he argued, by controlling the coal industry and collaborating with the union rather than going to war. "They wanted to fragment people."[71]

"It was just gut wrenching for us all really, they fought so hard," Michael Jackson of LGSM remembered. "It's not that I ever thought that we were wrong. We were just beaten. It's as brutal as that. My anger is stronger because we were beaten, but there was nowhere to put that anger in a sense, which was the whole point. That's exactly what it was about: to demoralize people." He turned away from union work, buried himself in a new job, and grieved once again when his comrade Mark Ashton, a driving force in LGSM, died shortly thereafter.

Thatcher famously said, "Economics are the method; the object is to change the heart and soul." Perhaps the soul of Britain has changed, but more likely it was battered into submission and in some cases bought off. Privatization didn't just come to industry; publicly owned housing was sold off too, and in the coalfields that helped destroy the community. Kitchen noted that lots of people bought the coal board–built housing under the Right to Buy program. "But then, the village died." People were stuck with homes they owned and couldn't sell without a loss. They were less transformed into proud capitalist homeowners than trapped in isolation. Which will change your soul in a different way.[72]

There was something uniquely painful about deindustrialization at the business end of a truncheon. The longer, slower process of pit closures and consolidation, of negotiated displacement, had been ongoing, but the sudden shift from consultation to war haunts coal country. It was a sharp reminder that the process of transition was not inevitable, not a product of natural forces, but as Ewan Gibbs wrote, a product of human power relations.[73]

The moral economy of mining in Britain was not the same as in the United States, where the mines remained in private hands. Injury and death were common in both industries in the early years, but in the US the struggles to unionize the mines had often erupted into open armed conflict. A sort of inverse of the nationalized industry's moral economy developed in "company towns," privately owned fiefdoms in which miners lived and worked under a kind of martial law, sometimes paid in scrip for the company store rather than cash. The pay slip might feature deductions, Trish Kahle wrote, of "everything from rent to funeral costs." Rather than a sense of community ownership, the miners were constantly reminded that they owned nothing. Faced with such private tyranny and the prospect of death in the mine, it becomes understandable that miners took up arms. The famous Battle of Blair Mountain, just one of those armed struggles, consisted of white and Black workers (some of whom had been born enslaved) facing down police and private security, guns and gas and bombs dropped from planes.[74]

The upside, if it can be called that, of private mining in the States is that it was hard to crush the industry all at once. Battles in the Mine Wars continued into the 1970s, immortalized in Barbara Kopple's stunning documentary *Harlan County USA*. One former miner explained to Kopple, "I heard the boss man say one time, he said 'You be sure and don't get that mule no place where the rock'll fall in on him.' I said, 'What about me, if the rock fall in on me?' He said, 'We can always hire another man, you gotta buy that mule.'"[75]

The nationalized mines in Britain were safer, but not perfectly so. "None of us went down the pit naively," Kitchen said. "A lot of us were second-, third-, fourth-generation miners. My grandfather were a miner. He were killed underground when my dad were ten. We knew that regardless of how good the health and safety policies and procedures are, things can go wrong." Kitchen's job when we spoke, as the head of a union in an industry mostly gone, consisted of battling for compensation for industrial injuries and illnesses for his retired members, and attending memorials for those who had not survived the pits. Many of the monuments had been built, he noted, in the past fifteen or twenty years, "where people realized in the old pit villages what they've actually lost, and then want to commemorate it." *Mourning the dead and fighting like hell for the living.*

Politicians banging the drum of bringing back coal mining often mistakenly assume that it was the going down a tunnel and bringing back black mineral chunks that was intrinsically meaningful. What Ewan Gibbs found in the coalfields, though, and what I heard too was a kind of "critical nostalgia," an awareness that the jobs being mourned were brutal and killed you young, that people took them up because they were the best or more often only thing on offer, and yet they had built something that had value around the mines, something that is not found in abandoned coal towns and gentrified cities where service and gig work holds sway.[76]

In 2019, covering the general election in Yorkshire, I heard people at the door telling Labour canvassers, *It doesn't matter anyway, they won't change anything, there's no difference between the parties anymore.* But when I spoke to Kitchen in the summer of 2022, his wife, who worked for the Royal Mail, was on the eve of a nationwide strike; around the country the former nationalized industries were striking.

It was the strikes in the National Health Service that reminded Kitchen most of the miners' struggle, strikes of junior doctors and ambulance drivers and the first-ever strikes of nurses in the service's 106-year history. "We weren't fighting for better money. We weren't really fighting for better terms or conditions. We were fighting to preserve a way of life," he said. He saw managed decline in the health service as there had been in the mines, a push toward Thatcher's ultimate goal of privatization of the biggest and best-loved institution of the British welfare state. "I do fear that the same tactics that were used to destroy the mining industry have been deployed against the NHS."[77]

Michael Jackson laughed a lot when he told the stories of his youthful activism. He'd come to London, he told me, from a town called Accrington in the northwest of England when cotton was still milled there and coal still mined not far away. He left the north for university in West London in the 1970s, and, he said, "I came out as gay by calling up for help." He rang what was then called the Lesbian and Gay Switchboard in desperation: "I knew that I was queer and I just believed myself to be mad, sad, and bad."

The switchboard volunteers succeeded in convincing him that was not the case, and he went from being "this miserable, depressed, lonely, young closeted queer boy into this infinitely joyous and angry person." He'd come up with socialist politics and an affinity for the labor movement, but it was not at the time very often a welcoming place for queer people or even for women or men who weren't white, so he poured his energy into gay liberation instead, volunteering for the same switchboard that had supported his coming out. It was there that he met Mark Ashton, and when the miner's strike began, Ashton asked, "Do you fancy collecting for the miners?"

"By that stage I'm getting to know quite a lot of working-class, gay, left-wing men. So I'm beginning to kind of feel a bit more at home," he said. They formed Lesbians and Gays Support the Miners, which provided unconditional support for the strikers but insisted on being out as queer while doing it. "We were prepared to take on homophobia," he said. "That's how we were changing the world."

"We were careful not to see an LGBT community over here and a mining community over there," Jackson noted. "An astonishing number of people who were putting money in our buckets would say, my dad's a miner, my brother's a miner, my grandad's a miner." The reality was that the communities were intertwined, that as the saying goes, their liberation was bound up together. Which didn't mean that the interaction was smooth, that they didn't run up against homophobic jokes and fear. Mining is a brutal job and one which for many, many years had been exclusively male (women and children's labor was banned by law, for in the early days it would have been an entire family digging and lugging coal by candlelight). "Anybody who's got a physically brutal job will to some extent become brutalized by that," Jackson said. He and Ashton and the men and women of LGSM knew this well enough, and it prepared them to confront a certain kind of masculine pride and homophobic banter because they could see the love and real tenderness the miners also held for one another.[78]

When the government sequestered the NUM's funds, the mining communities were desperate for support, so supporters had to get creative about how to get it to them. LGSM wound up paired with a community in South Wales through one of its members, and they went for their first visit that October. Twenty-seven young queer people from London traipsed into the Miners' Welfare hall, and the conversations in progress fell quiet. They stood there uncomfortably for long seconds, "and then somebody started applauding us and we got a standing ovation from all two to three hundred people in there. It was just incredible. And that's before we'd even met them."

After that, Jackson laughed, there were a lot of questions, quite blunt questions about gay life and sex and all the rest of it, but questions that came from mutual respect. "It was the women who were really instrumental in persuading the men to stop having silly attitudes," he noted, as well as Dai Donovan, who was the first miner sent to meet them in London. A lifelong friendship began, even as the strike collapsed and the mines closed and Jackson turned away from organizing, only to be relaunched into activism when he met Stephen Beresford, who wanted to make a film about LGSM: *Pride*.[79]

Kate Flannery remembered the women against pit closures groups as having the same kind of effect on her. At first, she said, the women were expected to fundraise and to feed people, but they did not remain in the kitchen. It was the '80s, the prime minister trying to crush them was a woman, and also the men were being arrested and beaten and banned from pickets, so the women started to go on the pickets and leave their miner husbands home with the kids, daring the police to treat them as harshly as they had the men. (Often they did.)

"Some men didn't like it, did they?" she said, getting an affirmative nod from Kevin Horne. "But a lot of the men did. A lot of the men could see how amazing these women were, that the women became, in a way, the backbone of the strike." Horne recalled a lot of divorces for a variety of reasons during the strike—the tension of having no income for a year was brutalizing in a different way than mine work was—but he admired the way the women threw themselves into the fight.[80]

Industrial labor was built around the gendered division of labor that is often wrongly called "traditional." Henry Ford famously determined who would get the five-dollar-a-day wage in his car factories by sending inspectors into the homes of his workers to ensure that they were properly heterosexually married and procreating and therefore deserving of the family wage. Industrial jobs in the United States came with healthcare benefits for the whole family that incentivized heterosexual marriage. Women and men separated by space—women were banned from the mine—and time—steel mills and factories ran continuously—began to create a disconnect between men who worked night shifts and their families who had to adhere to the rest of the world's time rules. Such distance played havoc with personal relationships even as it reinforced gender roles.[81]

In the world of the mines and the factories cemented by many years of union struggle, men were to be the producers, the breadwinners, and women the homemakers, men drawing pride from their strength and willingness to endure grueling conditions to bring home the paycheck, women as Angela Davis wrote having "the special mission of being both reservoir and receptacle for a whole range of human emotions otherwise banished from society." The bourgeois family was a configuration for passing on property; for the proletariat, who had nothing to sell or hand down but their labor, it was something else entirely. For men, a consolation for the indignities of wage labor, a place where they could be the boss. But far from "traditional," this family had barely existed for a century and is too often romanticized: its realities included regular violence against women and children, tolerated much more than it is today. Nostalgia for this idealized period is much more common among men than among women.[82]

Working-class masculinity was something defined by both its difference from femininity and its difference from bourgeois masculinity. "Good" and "respectable" working-class men didn't complain or shirk; they did their duty even when it was rough and dangerous. They held in their emotions even when it was difficult: Sam, a former miner Gibbs interviewed, described the regular deaths in the mine and the expectation that the workers would "internalize their grief and carry on with their jobs." Men don't grieve: grief would require time that they did not have; grief would require *not being at work*. Yet the unspoken grief served to strengthen the miners' bonds and the community's sense that they owed something to the men who risked their lives, something that could not be defined by a wage or the price of a ton of coal.[83]

The bosses relied on the ideals of stoic and dedicated working-class masculinity even as those qualities posed a threat, too: the strike was also an example of manliness, the scab or strikebreaker often condemned in highly gendered terms. When Scottish shipbuilders resisted the shipyard closure on the Upper Clyde in 1971, they understood that they were reasserting "the dignity of working men." Collective power made them feel heroic, indestructible even while individual danger made them dream of escape.[84]

Organized labor had built its idea of the working class on white masculinity even if that was always an ideal that required you to squint and blur your vision sufficiently to ignore everyone else that was there, to ignore the young Black and white radicals organizing together in Lordstown and the moment when LGSM walked into that union hall in South Wales. In the face of crumbling security, many workers retreated to a fortress mentality, desperately protecting what they already had: masculinity and whiteness alongside the family home and the factory job.[85]

Failing to meet the terms of masculinity was and is heartbreaking, and the same masculinity mitigated against men dealing with their grief publicly or indeed at all. *Grief is not work.* The former industrial workers are stuck in a world that wants neither their labor nor their feelings. If they are unemployed, the world of today tells them, it is their own fault, and *they have failed as men*. They are not men, really, anymore, at all.[86]

The resentments conjured by these overlapping crises are easy to understand once you have traced them back. Men are angry at "a nation of women workers," as one of Gibbs's retired miner interlocutors put it, longing for the return of "industrial breadwinner masculinity," feeling besieged by so much change—change to their status most of all. Climate activism, feminism, migration, Black Lives Matter could all seem to be a part of an ongoing attack on their way of life.[87]

Such resentments can make a certain kind of sense, but they are misdirected, and the politics that have attempted to cater to them, right or left, have yet to solve the real problem. The right wing pushed to reopen mines to drum up culture-war differences, splitting the working class in deindustrial zones from workers in cities caricatured as cosmopolitan latte-drinking liberals. The center-left, meanwhile, promises green growth, a "Green Industrial Revolution" or "Green New Deal," implicitly selling what I often sarcastically call "manly man jobs for men" as part of the just transition that industrial workers have heard so much about but never seen.[88]

The men I spoke to were longing for a class identity defined by more than just oppression, a solidarity that meant something again. The lesson of Lesbians and Gays Support the Miners is that such solidarity can bring with it radically different understandings of family, care, and gender as long as it shows up to take your side.[89]

Kevin Horne went into care work after the mine closed, working with adult men with mental illness or learning disabilities: "It were very strange because I'd always been in industry. But I've always had this caring attitude, so I thought 'I'll give it a try.'" After beginning as a volunteer, the nurses suggested he apply for a job.

The work was grueling in a different way. He did in-home care in twenty-four-hour shifts, sleeping in his clients' homes, and the clients could be unpredictable, particularly when he was new to them. There were not many larger men like him in the field, which helped in working with clients who were also bigger men—he, like other workers, had been physically assaulted a couple of times on the job. He learned to deescalate conflict, to earn trust, to speak in "a nice voice that didn't rise or fall. Start shouting you'd get nothing done." He admired the women he worked with, who faced the same physical risks he did, and he became close with some of his clients, took them to football games and in one case had to help a man find his parents' graves.

Eventually, privatization came to his care work job as well. "We went on strike," he recalled. It was around 2011, he'd just turned sixty-five and could draw his pension, but he wanted to keep working part time. The nurses found it hard to be on strike; it was different from striking as a miner because the care workers felt guilty stepping away from their clients' needs. His coworkers accepted a deal that he and one friend couldn't abide, so he retired and his friend went to work at Doncaster Airport. "Which just closed, so she's being done again," he added.

He wanted to keep taking an ex-client to football matches—"I wanted to be his friend"—but he wasn't allowed.

Horne wasn't the only former miner to end up working in care. Matthew Higgs, a longtime nurse, recalled many former miners moving into hospital work: "On each ward there'd be one or two big Geordie men who'd lost jobs in the local pits in Durham. I can't think of a more dramatic change from work underground." Yet he too could see that the kind of teamwork and mutual care that the miners had underground were transferable skills, even if the miners themselves might not have recognized it. Like the women they now worked alongside, their caring skills were undervalued, and many of them had a hard time adjusting to taking orders "from a 20-year-old charge nurse."[90]

In *The Next Shift*, Gabriel Winant detailed the turn from industrial to healthcare labor in the Pittsburgh area: "The process of working-class decomposition was, at the same time, a process of working-class recomposition." Industrial workers were disorganized when the industry left; they scattered to retirement or relocation or new kinds of work, and new kinds of work came to dominate, symbolized by the University of Pittsburgh Medical Center taking over US Steel Tower, the letters UPMC literally replacing USS. This reorganization was happening across high-wage countries, where profit was increasingly being wrung not from production but from finance, while on the other end, industries that could not be relocated (like health care, which has to exist wherever people are) were often labor intensive yet underpaid.[91]

The care economy boomed *because* the people who had worked in the mill and the mine and the factory were worn down. Women were pushed into the paid workforce to support families that had lost a male breadwinner, and without formal training many of them ended up on the lower-paid end of the care economy. The growth of care intertwined with the decline of industrial work.[92]

Chris Kitchen's work as head of a mostly retiree union was its own kind of caring labor. In addition to commemorating loss and death, the union also ran a convalescent home at Scalby, which had once been run by the coal industry's social welfare organization. Now a holiday home rather than a medical care facility, it nonetheless was a place for miners to go and rest and spend time with their old work comrades. The union operated it at a loss, but, he said, "it's one of the few times that they get to talk to other ex-miners, and reminisce about the times when they were in the pit. It's nice to see them being able to get somewhere that's a decent standard, it's affordable, and it's the same kind of people that they used to work with." Many of the other welfare facilities around the mines were gone.[93]

During the dominance of the industrial worker (or the idea of him), other types of work were treated as peripheral. Retail and restaurant work, hospitals and schools, public transit and public service, these fields always existed and indeed always organized. Woolworth's workers, all of them young women, held a sit-down strike on the heels of the UAW, and Chicago's teachers had a militant union a hundred years before their 2012 strikes caught the world's attention. Jerry Wurf of the American Federation of State, County and Municipal Employees challenged organized labor in 1974 to "make ourselves more relevant to the needs of workers in a postindustrial society, and become an even more substantial voice in the shaping of the future than in the past."[94]

A stronger labor movement might have seen these other workers as necessary to building power for the entire class; a more perceptive one would have noticed that capital never stopped seeking profit, and profit never stopped being wrung from squeezed and whipsawed workers. The work now is not just in the hospital, it is in the restaurant, the hotel, the warehouses like those on either side of the Carrier plant, the street in Dalston where couriers were harassed by police. The workers losing their jobs at Carrier and Rexnord were certainly aware of their options, and that those jobs were "bad," but they were bad because they had been left unorganized.[95]

The workers in the Global North are now in competition with the workers in Bangladesh and China and everywhere else. Even the recent turn toward "reshoring" production has not and will not end global supply chains easily; capital has succeeded in many places in detaching profits from production—and from those messy humans attached to it. Capitalism faces a contradiction: the system requires workers even as it is constantly driven to eliminate them from the process. Workers in turn face their own contradiction: capital no longer wants them, but capitalism requires they work in order to eat. *Capital is dead labor.*[96]

The fragmentation of people that Chris Kitchen noted has transformed so many into gig workers dispatched by app or attached to a laptop doing piecework by the click, not simply because it is convenient for the upper classes to have a servant on demand but because keeping those people separate keeps them from figuring out their power. (Piecework is nothing new in manufacturing, of course; it dates back to Marx's day, when he wrote that it was "the form of wage most appropriate to the capitalist mode of production.") The app and its algorithmic managers leave workers feeling disembodied. The promise of gig and micro-work is "flexibility" that of course was impossible on the assembly line, but it is in fact just another kind of feeding the human into the machine. The cloud after all physically exists somewhere too, and somewhere there are workers tending to those machines, as demanding in their own way as the dark satanic mills of William Blake's time.[97]

Class traitor or class disintegration, machine or criminal. These are what the options for work in the present age feel like much of the time. It is no wonder that former industrial workers long for the stability of factory life. The paradox of today's discourse on work, though, is that the same workers who are so romanticized were thoroughly traduced when they made demands as a class. The miners who were "the enemy within" to Margaret Thatcher are to today's desperate Conservative Party the "Red Wall."[98]

The worker abandoned by deindustrialization is a real person, not a myth. There are many of them, and some likely do conform to the picture painted by Donald Trump or Boris Johnson of an angry white man tired of "woke" society. Others, though, are Kevin Horne looking after mentally unwell clients and enjoying the change, or Chuckie Denison raising hell with a Black Lives Matter sign. When I spoke to Denison in 2023, he was sick and tired and had nothing left to lose: "My house, my family, all my material shit, my job, my health. I've lost everything." Yet he was still looking for people to join him in trying to change the world, still thinking about what a mass strike would look like today, still reaching out to other workers in solidarity.

Nostalgia is melancholic; it is, in Peter Mitchell's words, "the refusal to accept that return is impossible—return to a home which has changed in our absence, or to a lost time"—a form of magical thinking, mistaking the best parts for the whole. We cannot actually grieve a thing we never had.[99]

The experience that people miss when the factory or the mine shuts down is a set of relationships that were built on the backs of necessity and struggle. Built out of turning grief into grievances but not letting those grievances curdle into resentment. Realizing grievances in collectivity is the first step toward politics, toward becoming a class, toward a demand for justice. Toward a shared burden—Judith Butler reminds us that the French *grèver*, to burden, gave us *grève*, the strike, the shared burden of grievance.[100]

It is impossible to summon back the era of industrial work to fix our planetary crises, and we should not want to, because the collateral damage of that system is killing us. It must be mourned because it is not returning. We must understand the past in order to make sense of and indeed to make the future—the miners' slogan, *the past we inherit, the future we build*. In the past we have inherited, there are clues to what a different future might be, one that does not require identities and communities built on brutalizing labor to have solidarity and communal luxuries.[101]

Thinkers from John Maynard Keynes to W. E. B. Du Bois have gestured toward a potential future in which we do much less work; Du Bois, following Marx, imagined a world where leisure was plentiful and miserable work scarce, in which we might "all be artists and all serve." Less often cited, though, is the history of such sentiment from within the labor movement itself. Yet within its culture there was and remains a tradition of learning and debate, reading and self-publishing that spawned radical ideas and challenges to the boss, the state, and often the union's own leadership. From the "lectors" who were paid to read to cigar makers while they rolled to dissident autoworkers' newsletters and email lists, workers have always had ways to ruthlessly criticize their own circumstances and imagine the future they might build.[102]

Autoworkers repeatedly expressed the desire to escape the industry, as did miners and steelworkers. When I asked the workers at Carrier and Rexnord what they'd *like* to do with their time, over and over again they would offer brief fantasies—of being a fishing guide, running a small business, winning the lottery and buying the plant themselves—before practicality reasserted itself. "Unfortunately, money *is* an issue." As Ruth Milkman noted in her classic study of autoworkers, the upheaval of deindustrialization wiped the classic questions of alienation and degradation from discussions of factory work. The affirmation trap demanded workers love their jobs or at least profess that they did as they fought to keep them, and it helped to erase the radical critiques that had been everywhere just a few short years before and had never gone away entirely.[103]

In Detroit, Black autoworkers who were aware they would be the first to be made surplus and also the first to have their bodies thrown against the machines built the Dodge Revolutionary Union Movement and the League of Revolutionary Black Workers. Like the Lordstown workers, they knew that industrial work was only "good" so long as the workers kept fighting every step of the way. Automation was central to their critique; like Mohamed Mire they realized that the robots were not there to take their jobs but to turn them into so much human plant equipment.[104]

Across the most dangerous industries, union leaders demanded free time, the right to be human, to enjoy life off the job. Edward Sadlowski Jr. of the United Steelworkers argued, "With technology, the ultimate goal of organized labor is for no man to have to go down into the bowels of the earth and dig coal. No man will have to be subjected to the blast furnace." Miners for Democracy put forth a vision of the future in which the lives of miners would matter more than coal; Tony Mazzocchi and his faction within the Oil, Chemical and Atomic Workers International Union fought alongside environmentalists and helped pass workplace safety regulations into law. Mazzocchi said, "It was the workers in these industries who taught me that there was a systematic conflict between profits and health."[105]

It is not an accident that workers' injuries and deaths were central to many of the struggles for justice and less work. The demand to be seen as fully human rather than human plant equipment contained within it so many demands to live a full life, free from black lung or chemical burns, a life that included grief and sorrow as well as joy and pleasure. Workers insisted on a "right to grieve" as part of some of these struggles; in Italy, Erik Baker wrote, within *operaismo*, workers saw funerals as political occasions and grief as a moment to rededicate themselves to struggle. In turn, they built a movement that understood individual freedom as stemming from the (still collective) refusal of work. In the 1990s, Italian workers formed the *tute bianchi* and protested neoliberalism in white overalls, linking the struggles of deindustrialization to those for decent homes, immigrants rights, and more. One worker explained the choice of garb as a way of making visible what haunted them: "White is the color of ghosts, it is a symbol of invisibility: the invisibility of the 'without'; without work, without papers, without guarantees, without appropriate citizenship, without rights."[106]

None of these spacious, gorgeous visions came to pass: we still labor long hours fragmented from one another. But the UAW brought shorter hours back as a demand in their 2023 strike, calling for a thirty-two-hour work week with no loss in pay. Shawn Fain, the union's new president, took to the podium in a shirt that read "EAT THE RICH" to announce victories, a return to the UAW of old in performance as well as in policy. "If we withhold our labor, no matter what industry it is, nothing's going to move. And the capitalist class can build all the factories they want or create all the businesses they want, but at the end of the day, if no one's there to work, they're not going to make any profits," he told me. "I think we really have to start valuing people's time, the greatest resource that we have on this earth." Working seven days a week, long hours, forced overtime, two or three jobs, he said, just to scrape by isn't good enough anymore: "When there's nothing left at the end of the week, you live check to check, you're missing out on life with your kids or time with your significant other or just pursuing things that you love doing." Time outside of work can bring unpleasant realizations: that community, as John Merrick wrote, "can be both freedom *and subordination*, often at the same time," that the thing we cling to can be the thing breaking us down. But it can also be time to create new forms of meaning for ourselves.

Chuckie Denison had promised himself and others to spend the rest of his life as an activist. But part of what he wanted to build was a world where working-class people's leisure time mattered. He longed for the days of Idora Park, an amusement park in the city that had closed down when he was little, and was haunted by crumbling playgrounds and basketball courts. When we spoke in 2023, he was helping to restore the Torch Club, a bar with a long history in Youngstown, where stars had once played. "I'm enjoying reviving that bar because it's so beautiful and like the history and—God, if the walls could talk," he said.[107]

It is not factory work, or work at all, that is central to the world he wanted to build. Rather, he and those refusing work in its various forms are realizing once again that they have nothing left to lose except, as Marx and Engels most famously wrote, their chains. The moments when proletarians come together are still potentially explosive, whether they be Amazon workers holding an unexpected sit-down strike or the Justice for Janitors campaign bringing together subcontracted and mostly immigrant workers across a city rather than a single workplace. The 2018 strike wave among US teachers began in West Virginia's mining country: locked out of the legal right to collective bargaining, the teachers organized across the entire state and kicked off a wave that went nationwide. Those workers, in factories or hospitals or warehouses or schools, built this world with the work of their hands and bodies and hearts, and thus they have the opportunity still to turn the whole damn thing upside down.[108]

Break IV

I turned forty during lockdown.

It was a time of suspended animation; the world had been plunged into grief time. I was waiting for updates on friends who had the virus or who had had it and were dealing with what we did not yet call long COVID, walking my dog with a cloth mask over my face and nodding at neighbors because my smile was covered as I crossed the street to avoid them. I was not ill in that first round of the virus, so I did what I usually do in a political crisis: I did journalism, cranked up to high volume, for less money. I emailed unions and put out calls on social media, and my podcast cohost and I talked to anyone who wanted to talk to us about what work was like during COVID, and we posted them and we kept going.

Work was all I had to do anyway, so I did it.

It began to get to me sometime in May, I think, the real ongoing awfulness of the whole thing. Not because I was unaware; I was hyperaware of the news, of every spike in death rates and every new bit of information, and I talked to grocery store workers nervously scanning food behind Plexiglas and sanitation workers picking up trash that might be contagious and an art worker who had been furloughed telling me that the world will need art on the other side of this and to so many nurses, public hospital nurses and private hospital nurses and Veterans Administration hospital nurses who all had their particular refrain of a story of not enough protective equipment not enough beds not enough information not enough support.

But all the knowing could not overshadow the not-knowing. The things we did not understand. The fear. The limbo. The world in grief time, unable to see through the fog, unable to imagine what a future might be or when we might begin to have one.

The second lockdown was worse for me than the first. I spent the first with housemates, which was bad, but I spent the second alone, which was torture. My fourteen-year-old dog died right as I moved into the sublet I'd be spending the winter in alone, and so I had no creature to touch day in and day out. I forgot what contact felt like.

The world had taught me that I was supposed to fix people, and my parents taught me that I was supposed to be perfect. But in the throes of lockdown, there was no one to see if I was perfect and no one to fix but myself. And as far as I could tell, I was doing the opposite of fixing myself. I was getting worse.

The physical loneliness and the flood tide of bad news blended into the return of my immediate, acute grief. My chest hurt again, and I lingered in bed holding my heart and then hovered around the mail room talking to the doormen from several feet away just to have some human interaction that wasn't mediated by a screen. I took to holding a stone in my hand while I did the Zoom calls, turning it over, rubbing it along my thighs, just to remember that I had a body, to overcome that disconnect of looking at the camera rather than directly at a face.

I knew what respiratory illness and an ICU looked like, smelled like, from when my father had been in the hospital with pneumonia and on oxygen, and I had been so exhausted with work and worry that was closer to the bone. I remember the cold.

I knew what respiratory illness felt like in my chest: childhood asthma sent me gasping to the hospital once, and I remember the taste of the oxygen mask and the breathing treatments sucked into lungs that felt like they'd gone on strike. I remember the constriction, and I replicated it later when my father died, a strange form of bodily solidarity that I had to shake out of. But it came back in those endless lockdown days, the feeling that I would eventually realize was actually just me holding my breath. Waiting for release that did not come nearly fast enough.

I began to study the lines appearing in my face each day, the weight of my forties suddenly showing up in my skin, the lines hashes clocking days weeks months passing by.

The Zoom funerals were the worst. I attended two that winter. One for Anne Marie, whose story I told in the book I had just launched when I learned that she had not survived COVID. On the call, Anne Marie's friends recalled her laugh and her love of fun, and her coworkers recalled her strength as an organizer demanding justice, and the organizers who had supported her held space over the goddamn internet so that even when we could not touch each other, we felt some sense of connection. Before the call ended and we were snapped back to alone reality.

The second one was for a friend from South Carolina, a friend who had not died of COVID but in a horrific car accident, leaving behind a young daughter. I had gone with her to get her first tattoo, a horseshoe: we were both horse girls. My sister called to tell me she was gone and then there was another godawful Zoom call and I felt so much more alone than ever.

The first time someone touched me was my ex; we went for a hike in the woods in the snow and he hugged me and I didn't know what to do with the sensations—it was too much. I would flinch when strangers passed too close for months after lockdown lifted, I would cry when we were finally freed and a friend lifted me off the ground bodily with his hug, and I would climb off the couch to sit on the floor next to him and demand more touch.

Voice notes got me through it. I was on Zoom all day every day, and so there was nothing left of me for the people I loved even as I desperately missed them. Just a little of my voice saying I love you I miss you tell me something what is happening with you. Tell me you are OK that you are breathing that you are walking your little walks every day moving your body reading something good tell me tell me tell me that you miss me. Tell me you love me too.

The first real funeral I went to was later, in London, in the summer, when Dawn Foster died. Dawn, a journalist like me, single, living alone, someone I had not known well but who had met me with generosity and humor. I remember crying into my mask and the surprising tightness of a friend's hug, a friend who had known her so much more deeply than I.

I cried in that church for everyone.

I cried in that church for my father and the funeral we didn't have for him and the distance I had deliberately put between myself and everyone who would have been at that funeral if it had happened.

I cried the next day when I said goodbye (for a while, not forever) to one person whose voice carried me through that horrific winter, and I got back in bed and held my chest together for a while and dreamed of hospital-white sheets and the taste of piped-in oxygen.

When I finally caught COVID, I had been vaccinated and I didn't get very sick, just raspy, but I panicked at the isolation again as I was sucked back into grief time that felt endless, those long days alone, untouched again. I was fine but I wasn't fine. Suspended, distant, stuck.

CHAPTER 4

Breathe

Pandemic, communities, and care

4.1 Lazaretto

On the train into the city of Bergamo in the north of Italy on a beautiful autumn day in 2022, I was remembering lockdown in my body somewhere. As the train slowed to roll into the station, I stared at tall, balconied apartment buildings, wondering whether they were the ones I had watched on blurry web videos of locked-down Italians singing to keep one another's spirits up. I could not remember the songs, only the feeling of watching them, knowing this was coming soon to me.

Bergamo is divided by a mountain, the old city at the top with spectacular views, tourist shops and medieval buildings and beautiful people eating ice cream in the streets. There were some wearing masks, at least indoors, but mostly you could forget that this city had been, in the words of Francesca Nava, the journalist who made connections for me here, "the lazaretto of Italy." "Lazaretto" is a term I had to look up: a quarantine space, a place where the infected are held, concentrated, kept away from others. Tybee Island, the next sea island south from where my mother lives, was once a quarantine station for people kidnapped from Africa and sold into slavery in Georgia, bounded on one side by what the enslavers named Lazaretto Creek. Nava would tell me later that she chose the term because it evokes Alessandro Manzoni's famous novel *The Betrothed*, set in Lombardy during the Great Plague. There was an implication, somehow, that the people contained within are suffering for others' sake, so that the rest of us should not have to.[1]

I tried to imagine Bergamo during lockdown, but of course had I been there then, I would not have seen the city at all, other than the interior walls of my home and the view from a balcony if I was lucky enough to have one. Unless I had been, like Pietro Brambillasca, working.

In the early days of March 2020 the Papa Giovanni XXIII Hospital was, to Brambillasca, a vortex of a kind. It seemed that he had been there since the beginning of time, working constantly but having no sense that anything he or any of the doctors and nurses and hospital staff did was having any effect on the strange virus. It felt like months or years were passing, when in truth the peak in Bergamo—which was the peak in Italy, which itself was the first country in Europe to really feel COVID-19—was just a few weeks. The second peak, experienced by the rest of the country, Brambillasca says, was not so bad in Bergamo, perhaps for the bleakest of reasons: because nearly a whole generation's worth of elderly people had already died. Perhaps because the virus had hit so hard, people in the city took precautions very seriously for a while.

Brambillasca and I met in Milan, where he lives and now also works, in a *pasteccheria* with the panettone cakes hung upside down overhead to age. It was loud, bustling, crowded again as if there had never been and was not still a virus circulating. Even though he had told his story many times, his anger still simmered at the things that could have been done differently, mingled with a frustration that there was so little he and the hospital could do at all. There was no medicine for the virus then, and treatments of any kind were a matter of guesswork. "You don't feel so important as you considered yourself before because you saw that your actions, you were basically pointless," he said.

At first, because he was an anesthesiologist, his time was spent putting the sickest patients on ventilators. Later, he worked in a COVID intensive care unit, when there were particular therapies, treatments that the brutal process of trial and error combined with the global scientific focus on the virus had brought. What happened in the hospitals, he said, was just the tip of the iceberg. Friends of his who worked in ambulances told him of the people they saw who died at home, before they even reached the hospital. "Most people never had any response from the health system at all," he said. "There have been some towns in the valleys up to the mountains that had eightfold to ninefold the mortality of the general population from the same period of the previous years. There was a generation of grandparents wiped away."

Ambulances queueing outside the hospital would send someone inside to ask for oxygen cylinders because the ambulance was running low and patients yet to be admitted were struggling for air. In the first weeks, whole families sometimes shared an ambulance and even an oxygen mask: older parents whose adult sons lived at home all got the virus, but not all of them would make it to the hospital. "He went in the ICU, they died."

But all this Brambillasca learned later. At the time, "I never put my nose outside the emergency department." He learned of the true size of the iceberg when he had time, finally, to take a deep breath of his own. He learned of the ease with which the virus spread through other hospitals, through buildings sometimes hundreds of years old. The region of Lombardy was in many places the most densely populated in Italy, and density fed contagion. Hospitals themselves, Brambillasca came to realize, were colossally unsuited to the problem of contagious illness. They acted, he said, like a dam, collecting all the sick people—and all the care workers—in one place. Hospitals are good for strokes, heart attacks, injuries. The concentration of patients in one place is exactly the opposite of what is needed in a pandemic.

In the midst of the crisis, despite their exhaustion, Brambillasca and several of his colleagues wrote an article calling for a reevaluation of health care and long-term planning for the next pandemic. "Western health care systems have been built around the concept of patient-centered care, but an epidemic requires a change of perspective toward a concept of community-centered care," they wrote. "Pandemic solutions are required for the entire population, not only for hospitals." The crisis required a different way of thinking about health care, a social understanding of care rather than an individual one.[2]

Lombardy, the doctors stressed, was one of the richest regions in Europe, yet people died in shocking numbers. Other regions in Italy, which had created a more distributed system of care, suffered less than Lombardy. Less than Bergamo.

Cristina Longhini has a young son, and so the metaphor she used for the COVID peak in Bergamo was from a Marvel movie. "The period was like the last film of Avengers, when a lot of people disappeared. Thanos for me is the COVID." She snapped her fingers. "Because immediately in a few days in a few hours in a few minutes people weren't there. A lot of people in that period called the hospital, and the hospital said oh there is no problem the parent stays well, is under the ventilator and after two hours or the day after the hospital called to say no, [your parent] is dead."

Longhini was a pharmacist in Milan, but her whole family lived in Bergamo, and her father was one of the many taken by the virus in those disconnected early days. For Longhini too, time warped and shifted, as she waited in Milan for updates that came too late. We met in Monza, outside of Milan, where she now worked, sitting outside at a mostly empty café during her midday work break, and she spilled her story, occasionally pausing to translate the word she was looking for into English with her phone. We were the same age, and I took her hand partway through the conversation because how could I not? I knew what she felt and also I had no idea what she felt. I was able to see my father in the hospital before he died, to say goodbye.

"Sometimes I look at my telephone and I want to call my father and it is not possible," she said. "I can't believe it, that it's true; I think that it was a dream, it's not possible that it is real."

The week that he was in the hospital was still a black hole for her. She did not see him, could not hold his hand, could not know how he was feeling, whether he was afraid. She called the nurses' station, but the swamped, exhausted nurses did not get back to her. "I reach my father with imagination," she said.

Claudio Longhini took sick on March 2 or 3. He was sixty-five, retired but very active, an involved grandfather with many hobbies, and it was unusual for him to be ill, to stay in bed. Cristina's mother, a pharmacist as well, called the doctor, who said he should stay home and take antibiotics. The first Cristina heard of it was several days in, when her mother and sister reached out to her. She spoke to her father—he called her Kiki, a nickname only he used, and admitted to her that he was worse. Her mother had tried to get a doctor to come, but they would not. The ambulance would not come because he was not in respiratory crisis. Her mother called a number that had been instituted for COVID cases, but that too proved little help. "After a lot, a lot, a lot of phone calls we found a doctor who came to my father," she said. That doctor saw that Claudio's blood oxygen was very low and sent for an ambulance, but there were no ambulances to be had in Bergamo. The ambulance that finally picked Claudio up came all the way from Monza. The Longhinis had to tell the ambulance driver how to find the Papa Giovanni hospital.

The songs on the balconies had begun by then, the singing adding to the sense of unreality. Cristina knew her father was in the hospital, knew he was on a ventilator, knew that he had COVID-19. Beyond that she knew nothing. She went out to her balcony while her neighbors sang, but all she could do was pray.

In Bergamo, there was quiet apart from the sirens.

After a week the Longhinis got a call from the hospital, asking the family to try to find a space in another hospital for Claudio, saying his situation was extremely grave. "I don't breathe in that moment, I didn't understand anything," Cristina said. She called everywhere she could think of, but reached no one. When she called the hospital back, they told her that her father had died. It was Father's Day in Italy.

The rest of Cristina's family—her mother, her sister, and her sister's husband—all had the virus at that point, and so it fell to her to drive from Milan to Bergamo. She was not supposed to be allowed into the hospital to see her father, but she accompanied the funeral home workers to the hospital anyway, and after waiting six hours, she snuck in with them to see her father for the last time. What she saw was shocking. "He had blood from his ears, from nose, from mouth," she said.

It took a month to get her father's ashes from the funeral home. Because Bergamo had seen so much death, army trucks were brought in to bring people's remains elsewhere for cremation, and so Claudio was sent on one to Ferrara, more than two hundred kilometers away. When Cristina spoke of this, the English words she landed on were the same ones she used to describe her father's love for travel. "He makes a lot of kilometers."

Even after they received the urn, the Longhinis could not have a real funeral. Cristina, her mother, and her sister had to get an appointment for a brief benediction at the cemetery, with other families lined up like in a doctor's waiting room, rushed in and out. Through all of this period, all three continued to work as pharmacists. With walk-in doctors' offices shut down and hospitals jammed with patients, pharmacists were often the only people worried Italians could reach. And there was nothing they could do. Like Pietro Brambillasca in the hospital, they felt powerless. They knew the ravages of the virus firsthand, but what could they advise? They didn't have enough masks for everyone, they feared for their own lives, and they were mourning Claudio.

It could have been otherwise.

That was the thing that became clear, to Francesca Nava, to Pietro Brambillasca, to Cristina Longhini. What happened in Bergamo did not have to happen. Longhini realized that even across Italy, the losses were not the same. Her mother saw travelers coming in and out of Bergamo before the lockdown, yet there was no "red zone" declared. "That they didn't make the red zone at that period was a massacre," she said.

She found a Facebook group called Noi Denunceremo (We Will Report/Testify), a group organizing for "truth and justice" for the victims of COVID-19. She posted a video that she made of a garbage bag she'd been given with her father's things in it, his pajamas covered in blood, and she watched some of the other videos, read other stories of people who'd also lost parents. There were many just like hers. "Because we don't have a psychologist or some person to help, we help with our stories," she said. "There is a sort of second family with some people that lost a father or mother or father and mother, because nobody else can feel what you feel." She became particular friends with a man named Diego, who had lost both his father and mother to the virus in just three days.[3]

The emergence of the COVID-19 vaccines gave her something useful to do with her pain. "For me it is a campaign for life," she said. When her mother, still also working as a pharmacist, was vaccinated, Longhini felt she could breathe properly for the first time since the beginning of the pandemic. She could feel hope again. When she administered the first injection to a patient, it brought her joy and relief. Vaccination became the most important part of her work, a battle that was medical, political, and deeply personal. "It is a piece of my heart in what I do every day."

It was hard, though, for her to watch the world go back to a superficial kind of normal, as if what happened to her, to her father, to so many others in Bergamo and around the world had been forgotten. Italy no longer felt like the place of the songs on the balconies. "The people are more aggressive. In that period people said that we will come out better—no, it's not true," she said. "The people forget very, very quickly." There were many who didn't want to hear what she had to say, her own story or even her call to get vaccinated. People have said to her that the photos of army trucks in Bergamo were photoshopped, were fake. This brought her to tears, she said, "because on the truck was my father."

People attacked her on social media because of her vocal public condemnations of the anti-vaccine movement, which had grown more and more aggressive throughout 2021, storming the headquarters of the Confederazione Generale Italiana del Lavoro, the Italian labor union confederation, in October. Water cannons were unleashed on crowds of protesters attempting to reach the prime minister's office. The far right and conspiracy theorists were particularly angry at Italy's "green pass" system, and anti-vaccine fervor helped inflate the ranks of the neofascists. Anti-vaxxers had even tossed Molotov cocktails at a vaccination center in Brescia, about fifty kilometers from Bergamo.[4]

Longhini took a job in Monza, leaving her old pharmacy in Milan, after the swell of anti-vaxx outbursts. She remained passionate about the work and believed that her experience helped her to guide people through the process, people who might be confused or frightened rather than outraged and thus might listen to a sympathetic voice and be sympathetic, in turn, to her story of her family's loss.

She reminded people that not everyone who succumbed to the virus was already ill. Her father was healthy, vibrant, athletic, feeling fine until he caught COVID. Her grief lingered, made worse by the persistent feeling that things could have been different. That yes, one day she would have said goodbye to her father, but she might have been able to be with him, to hold his hand and hear her nickname, Kiki, one more time. That her mother did not have to be left alone so soon, surrounded by reminders of her husband. That her young son did not have to try to comfort her. Even her father's dog mourned. It stopped eating and waited at the door for Claudio to return.

The conversation around the virus had become depersonalized, the lists of the dead just numbers, so it was a kind of therapy for her, she said, to tell her story, to know that her father's name would be in books and part of the history of the pandemic, to put a human face to the statistics. "People have to know, the new generation have to know what's happened in this period. This is how we will say that this situation will not happen another time." Like a world war, she said, people will forget, will want to forget.

"A lot of people live with the remembering, with the pain, with the feeling abandoned," she continued. "A lot of people survived the COVID. We are surviving people."

The practice of remembering is lonely. There are little reminders, all the time. Because there was no funeral, Claudio's friends sometimes found out on Facebook and messaged Cristina. Claudio, before his retirement, had worked for a company that made ice cream products and traveled widely for his job. In the summer of 2022, Cristina went to a gelateria in Crema, and a woman who worked there recognized her striking blue eyes—Claudio's eyes—and immediately embraced her.

What bothered Pietro Brambillasca the most was that there had been no time for reflection. "There's the sensation of uselessness," he said, "because we didn't have the time to calm down, to talk about it, to see what we should have done differently or better, and which are the lessons we learned about it. There was no idea about taking this time because there are new issues."

There was a sort of shame in Italy, because the virus was so bad there, but also an unwillingness to take responsibility for the crisis: "The idea is to forget." Brambillasca was less interested in blame for its own sake, but like Longhini, he wanted to have the time to create solutions for the future, to save other people the needless loss. Even among health workers it had become hard to speak of what happened. Doctors had to work harder; other illnesses were put on the back burner during the COVID peaks, and they had to pick up the slack when the virus subsided some. People were sicker because they had postponed necessary treatments for heart disease or cancer. New doctors and nurses were hired, but many also burned out, and rural doctors in particular were hard to replace.

Brambillasca himself took another job, moving closer to his Milan home, leaving ten years of professional relationships behind. The shorter commute, the ability to be home with his family more often, was worth it. The disappointment, the exhaustion led him to turn inward; he felt as though his suggestions for improving the health system, the work he was doing to try to make change on top of his long shifts making sure people could breathe, were rebuffed. Instead, he put his energy into his wife and his two daughters, seven and four. His frustration at how insufficient the system was—and remained—was palpable.

Health workers continue to try to change the system, though. Hospital workers tried to set up, in Bergamo, better communication between hospitals and general practitioners. "Hospitals can't mend social problems," Brambillasca said, but the community might. He wanted to see health centers that were "houses of community," that recognized that neighbors have an investment in one another's mental and physical and emotional safety and well-being, that focused on social health as well as physical, that would be better in a pandemic but also in supposedly normal times, because when is there not some kind of crisis, these days?

The health systems of late capitalism have no slack in them for reflection, for any time that is not "productive." There was no time for the kind of activity that was not precisely labor but allowed for human intelligence and care to operate, for healing to happen. There was no space to sit with loss. During the height of COVID, the doctors rarely had a moment to tell families that loved ones had died, beyond a brief video call, perhaps.

Work was a near religion in Bergamo, Francesca Nava stressed: "It's a place of hardworking people, and they have a very high sense of self-sacrifice." It had been, pre-COVID, very common for people to work sick. There was such pride in working, in never taking time off, that the region became first in the most horrifying of statistics: COVID deaths.

We were talking in Nava's Rome apartment, months later; the door was open to the terrace on a beautiful January day, and she held up the newspapers she'd saved from the early days of the virus. March 10, "Tutti in casa" (Everyone at home), "Ora è chiusa tutta l'Italia" (Now all of Italy is closed), March 11, "Non basta ancora" (It is still not enough), "La Lombardia: Più chiusure" (Lombardy: More closures), and then March 23, "Tutto chiuso, anzi no" (All closed, indeed no). March 11 saw all of Italy shutter so-called nonessential activities. "But a lot of factories could remain open," she said. "It is not enough. Eleventh of March is not enough."

Nava grew up in Bergamo, and when the pandemic hit she was inundated with calls from the city where her family still lived, where her cousin would keep going to work, where he would die of the virus. She saw two parallel realities happening: the world in Bergamo and the world outside of Bergamo. "It was us and them, and I was at the border of us and them."

"All the eyes of the world were on Bergamo, my city," she said, so she got in her car and drove north, alone on the highway, into a postapocalyptic world. She spent forty days in Bergamo, with factory workers, doctors and nurses, ordinary people and local politicians. "I felt like a pain collector," she said.

All the stories she absorbed, carried, put her into something that felt like a trance. She was writing articles daily, but when she was asked to write a book about what happened, at first she could not transform all her emotions into words. When she returned to her Rome apartment, her family was still in the south of Italy, and she spent two weeks crying, barely sleeping, barely eating, listening to the recordings she collected. She remembered telling her editor, "I cannot write this book, I'm not the right person," and the editor reassuring her that she just needed time, time to recover from the disaster.

"I felt the responsibility to give dignity to these stories. But I am an investigative journalist and an investigative journalist has to be cool and neutral. I was not neutral because this story, this tragedy, affected a part of my family. I lost a cousin, he was forty-eight, he had three sons. And he died because he was working. Because they didn't close the factories."

The grief had to take its course before she could write: "I let all the emotion go out without hurry, without pressure, and one morning, I woke up and I started writing and I never stopped. In less than two months, I wrote 240 pages."

Talking about Bergamo's work culture suggests blame lay with the victims, but Nava was clear where blame belonged: the regional leaders did not call for a red zone in the area. In Val Seriana, the industrial region of Bergamo, the politicians and the industrialists, the owners of the factories, refused to stop. "Bergamo is the area of Italy with the highest worker density due to the highest concentration of factories. We are talking about four companies, four factories per square kilometers against 1.6 as the national average. In Bergamo, there is one factory for every nine inhabitants. This area is worth about 10 percent of the national gross domestic product." In Val Seriana, there were 2,446 factories and six thousand service companies with an annual turnover of around €5 billion.[5]

"During the pandemic Agostino Miozzo was the coordinator of the scientific technical committee, this pool of experts who advised the government on decisions to be taken during the pandemic, he defined Lombardy and Val Seriana as one of the economic lungs of Italy. And as such, he reiterated that they could not close," Nava explained. Specifically, he said (translated from the Italian), "Closing that area meant stopping an economic lung of the country. Maybe we would have saved some lives, but it is easy to pronounce in hindsight." The head of the Lombardy industrialists said something similar.[6]

Production could not be stopped. The economic lungs of the country had to keep pumping, even if many workers' lungs would be stopped instead. Nava's cousin was one of those workers.

"This region is known for productivity and also for healthcare excellence, two areas that went into crisis in the pandemic," and now the region is left with "a collective scar," she said. There were no apologies from the officials who made the decision to keep the factories going. The political system, like the healthcare system, had no room for slack, for reflection. *Grief is anathema to capitalism.*

COVID saw a clash between the needs of capital and the needs of workers on the most basic level: the ability to breathe, to live. Decisions were made in something very like the fog of war, whether by Pietro Brambillasca in the hospital deciding when to put someone under to let a machine do their breathing for them, or a manager deciding to close a factory, or a politician deciding to call for red zones (full closure) or yellow (work continues).

Politicians feared that lockdown would lose them political support. They said they would put people's health first, but the support that came from industrialists was more important. "This is a story of hidden truth," Nava said.

One symbolic story took place at steel manufacturer Tenaris, which everyone, Nava says, refers to simply as "Dalmine" for the area where it is located in Bergamo. "During the pandemic, they continued producing because among the various activities they have, there was also the production of oxygen cylinders made of steel," Nava explained. "I was told by some trade union workers that with only two days of production, of activity, they could produce enough steel for making oxygen tanks for at least two months." Workers were pressured to come in "voluntarily," even after one of them, a man named Salvatore Occhineri, died. Companies could stay open by declaring that they were "essential," that they were part of the supply chain of necessary products, like oxygen to keep COVID patients breathing. "It has been calculated that during the toughest lockdown, when in all of Italy, no one could leave the house, in Val Seriana, more than 30,000 people could circulate for work reasons. In the whole province of Bergamo, which has 1,200,000 inhabitants, a quarter of them, 300,000 people were free to move. So this is a paradox. A lot of workers died in Dalmine.[7]

"A lot of factories were obliged to close because all the workers were sick," she continued. "A lot of little companies closed forever, like restaurants. But I think that the most important deep scar in this area was mental." People were depressed but reluctant to express it, to admit that they had a problem, that they need help. Instead, they turned to work.

It is the regional politicians whom Nava blamed first and foremost. It was their responsibility to run the health services, to make the decision to close or no, and those regional differences were vast. In Rome people simply did not experience the virus the way those in Lombardy did, so national politicians could conveniently ignore the subject.[8]

The Partito Democratico, the party of the social-democratic Left, missed its opportunity, Brambillasca and Nava both told me, to fight for accountability and a better healthcare system. A few months into Giorgia Meloni's "post-fascist" leadership, Nava said that the right wing had won because they provided some sort of opposition. "They campaigned against lockdown. So people just gave the vote to those politicians who guaranteed no more lockdown. [Because] you can't guarantee no more pandemic."

4.2 Isolation

COVID separated us into what I took to calling "Margaret Thatcher units": in lockdown, immediate families were allowed to remain together, and the rest of us were isolated. It echoed for me Thatcher's famous statement that "there is no such thing" as society; "there are individual men and women and there are families." Grief too shrank: those immediately touched by the virus were left to feel its ravages without the support we normally might have had. "It is impossible to grieve in the first-person singular," wrote Cristina Rivera Garza, and yet this is exactly what this pandemic left us to do.[9]

This isolation is not natural or normal. Our bodies, Dr. Rupa Marya and Raj Patel wrote, are badly tuned to all this solitude. Isolation is physically bad for us, associated with higher rates of cardiovascular disease and dementia. We were living in one of the loneliest times in human history before COVID hit, the destruction of neighborhoods and labor unions and faith communities and other organizations in which people came together and looked after one another contributing to a sense that we were on our own, and that lonesome feeling itself made us susceptible to all sorts of things, from conspiracy theories to viruses. I spent lockdown winter wrapped in blankets, staring into Zoom cameras, and longing for touch.[10]

Adam Kotsko reminded us that neoliberalism is a system that justifies its cruelty and isolation with the language of choice. We are encouraged to believe that we can choose every outcome that happens to us; the flip side of this dictum is that we must carry the blame for every bad result, every moment our choices go awry.[11]

Having health insurance is presented as a choice that responsible people make, rather than something rationed, as physician Adam Gaffney wrote, by ability to pay. COVID care had been universalized, at least to a degree mostly unknown in the United States, but rather than seeing that universal care as a model to move forward, COVID would come to be treated like every other illness in America: an individual problem.[12]

Health under capitalism is something you have to earn with sweat and strain, and yet it is necessary to be healthy in order to work to be able to pay in the first place. In the United States this is made obvious by the privatized system, but in Italy or in Britain where a public system provides most of the care, the private system nibbles around the edges, the wealthy able to buy better care as the public system buckles under years of austerity. A system that requires some people to be surplus is incapable of providing truly equal care. A system that treats health as an individual responsibility will wind up, as Beatrice Adler-Bolton and Artie Vierkant wrote, marking some people as permanently surplus, as expendable, valued only to the degree they pay for private care. This is what Adler-Bolton and Vierkant called "extractive abandonment": the process of finding profit in the breakdown of lives.[13]

Steven Thrasher used the term "viral underclass" to describe those so abandoned. He began by studying HIV and its stigma and then applied this understanding to COVID-19: "Marginalized people," he wrote, are made vulnerable to viruses, but "viruses are also used as justification for the policies and systems that marginalize people in the first place." The public response to COVID-19, he noted, made many people richer while making working people vulnerable; these were not coincidental results but inherent to the way capital accumulation happens. Viruses, Thrasher wrote, are transmitted in moments of connection, when lips and hands and bodies touch. They expose the truth of our interconnectedness; how, he asked, "can we declare war on where we meet?" And yet that was what lockdown felt like: a war on our connections.[14]

Lockdown living and its attendant longing for those we were not allowed to see was horrible but for some of us it was not new, exactly, to be kept artificially distant from the people we love. Anna Lekas Miller noted, "Our long conversations and glimpses into one another's lives through a computer screen mirrors the way that loved ones connect when they have been separated by borders for much longer."[15]

The pandemic forced us to depend on housemates, relationships of convenience that turned into sometimes-uncomfortable intimacies, or neighbors we'd previously not known. Any contact with a fellow human was suddenly precious. I memorized our mail carrier's face through the door, learned about a doorman's children through a mask. Parents suddenly realized how impossible a teacher's job is when they were left to manage Zoom classes and homework.[16]

Thatcher was wrong: there was such a thing as society, and we discovered it anew when we lost it.

"I remember, along with other nurses in my workplace, feeling like canaries in a coal mine," Elizabeth Lalasz said of the early days of COVID-19, when every shift was a scramble to figure out how to treat the new virus, protective equipment was scarce, and the world seemed to have ground to a halt except for so-called essential workers like her.[17]

Lalasz and I first spoke in the heat of the first COVID wave, when she and other nurses—Lalasz works at John H. Stroger, Jr. Hospital in Chicago and is a member of National Nurses United—had just held a national day of action demanding proper safety equipment for front-line healthcare workers. When we caught back up in March 2022, she was recently off her third stint on a COVID-only ward.

The nurses had their hard-won protective equipment and other safety precautions, but two years into the pandemic, she was feeling ground down. "My unit is one of the more stable units, but at least half of our nurses have left, retired, become traveling nurses, or have just quit altogether." New nurses who hadn't been on a COVID unit before needed to be trained, and then plenty of the hospital workers, despite being fully vaccinated, got sick with the newer, more transmissible variants.

There was a level of confidence in hospitals after a couple of years that wasn't there in the early days of the virus; at least they knew how to treat the patients, knew which protective gear was necessary, and mostly had access to the proper masks. They knew how to talk patients through it.

But each new variant brought some shifts, new things to figure out. And the rush to lift restrictions and push people back to work left Lalasz and her coworkers feeling even more invisible, as if no one with any power knew or cared what they still struggled with. "The whole idea of getting back to normal is an excuse for allowing people to continue to get sick without there being much of a discussion about it," she said. "[Management] knows how bad it is, but they want to remain mindless about it because it doesn't benefit them to actually acknowledge it."[18]

The call to declare COVID-19 over, to return to "normal," was compelling precisely because we all longed for normal. Normal has a soothing weight to it, a comforting blanket to slip back beneath, that might finally allow us to relax. Nobody wants to hear that normal is gone for good. Still less do we want to think about what our new normal might be.

When I called Lalasz that spring, the COVID-19 pandemic in the United States was approaching a grim, world-leading milestone—one million deaths. We are well past that now. Around the world, the number was over seven million at the time I wrote this. At that size, the numbers simply become statistics, detached from human bodies. It is the refusal to deal with the realities of the disease—to look the losses in the face, to take time to mourn—that haunts us now. This refusal is not simply an individual problem; it is a political decision.[19]

In part because of the very nature of the virus, its effects were hidden from most people. Hospitals at first banned visitors, so the workers were alone with the ill. "You connect with people and you carry their pain and their frustration and their anger and their joy and all that sadness, times four, times five, times six every day," Lalasz said. Without visitors, "you're their lifelines, and to have that level of responsibility is just so enormous. It shatters you at some point. Sometimes it's okay when the patient can go home and they're happy and they're like, 'I just want to tell you, thank you.' But when somebody dies, the sadness, it's profound in a way that I don't think any of us . . ." She trailed off, then picked up again: "We carry that, but it's been amplified a hundredfold with COVID. Because that person reveals everything about themselves to you when they're in the hospital."

Noah Cochrane is a counselor and one of the cofounders of the COVID Grief Network, an organization built to help young adults deal with the grief of the pandemic. "I just knew that there would be this mountain of grief coming," they said of the early days of the network, when they experimented with ways to support young people through the lockdown. "People are so uncomfortable with talking about death and dying and grief and at least in American culture, it's so private in this way that I think actually comes from a lot of discomfort."

The virus seemed to accelerate every form of isolation. As trusted coworkers left, Lalasz felt alone on the job, and when working with COVID patients, she intentionally avoided friends on the outside, not wanting to risk bringing them the virus. Yet every time anyone she knew contracted COVID or saw someone close to them get sick, she got a call. Elected officials promised that lockdown was over, but for the people still treating the sick, it never really ended. Without continued funding, continued support, continued attention from those in charge, would it ever?

The first memorial statue to the COVID victims and workers I saw was in Barnsley in northern England. A monument to essential workers risking their lives made sense, I think, in coal country, where the lives of the canaries taken down the mines, a former miner explained, were treasured: if the bird stopped singing, it was time to get yourself and the canary out too. Its life was connected to yours.

But by the time the memorial went up, the effusive gratitude of the early days—the claps for carers, the homemade signs in the windows thanking essential workers—was gone. Doctors and nurses faced threats of violence; fast food restaurants hung signs saying, "Nobody wants to work anymore." Those workers, over and over, told me that instead of "essential," what they felt was "expendable." It was those essential workers, along with the elderly, who got sick and who died, who lost family members and colleagues and friends and neighbors.[20]

The virus and lockdown rearranged the labor of the home while increasing our dependence on those outside of it. We ventured out rarely and put our lives in the hands of grocery store clerks; I was haunted by a piece written by Polly Smythe, who worked in a shop during the pre-vaccine days. "When I handed a customer his change through the small hole in the plexiglass divider, he reached out, took my hand, and clung to it. After about ten seconds, he let go, looked down at the floor and said: 'I'm very sorry. The thing is, I live alone.'"[21]

Service workers became both human shield and therapist, bearing an impossible emotional burden while risking—and sometimes losing—their lives. Those service workers were poorer and more likely to be people of color, people who were unable to refuse dangerous work because of lack of options. So many were undocumented and thus unable to access state benefits despite being part of an "essential critical infrastructure workforce."[22]

The deaths were racialized. Something like 70 percent of New York City's healthcare workforce is Black, Latinx, or Asian; Latinx people were some 60 percent of front-line cleaning workers. The workforce after deindustrialization is already concentrated in service work, and that work is cheap: 70 percent of essential workers, Tera Hunter wrote, "are paid minimum wages, less than fifteen dollars per hour, typically without health insurance, paid sick leave, or other benefits." The gig economy absorbed more workers during the pandemic: recall Yirna Buitrago and Lenin Gomez taking up delivery work, risking their safety to keep feeding their kids. The people who relied on those service workers also blamed them for spreading the virus. They were policed disproportionately, too, harassed for "social distancing" violations while moving through an otherwise locked-down world to bring us packages, food, alcohol, distractions.[23]

The CDC's charts breaking out US COVID deaths by race and ethnicity are breathtaking. I knew what the overarching story was, who had been ill, who had died, before I opened the page, but nonetheless the particular bar graphs in a gradient of purple, spiking above or plunging below the norm, had a kind of horrible beauty. Because race is, Stuart Hall reminded us, the modality through which class is lived, because we know that "essential workers" were disproportionately Black, Native, and Latinx, we saw that in the pattern of deaths. Because, too, the working class was more likely to live in multigenerational homes, to share more of their spaces with family or even friends, a virus that drove us apart would spread through their homes all the faster. Black, Native, and Latinx people died in every age group at higher levels than white people, and while the Kaiser Family Foundation noted that those disparities shrank over time, they fell from "almost 3 times as likely to die from COVID-19 and about 4 times as likely to be hospitalized" to merely twice as likely to die.[24]

That inequality contributed to the willingness of many people to throw off their masks and return to the streets and the shops. The perception shifted from "we're all in this together" in the early days of the virus to the slow realization that the spread would not only follow the circuits of capital, as Kim Moody wrote, but follow the bodies of those forced to keep working. It would follow Mohamed Mire home from the Amazon warehouse to his children running for hugs.[25]

Because "comorbidities"—that word does sound exactly like what it describes—are also distributed unequally, because the very air we breathe is unequal, because access to health care is rationed but also because the experience of racism itself, as Marya and Patel wrote, preconditions bodies to react differently "because of how the immune system has been toned over time, through lifetimes and ancestries of social oppression," essential workers died, and their coworkers scrubbed and worried and kept working. Exposure to death was itself another comorbidity, as Malkia Devich-Cyril wrote, and Black people disproportionately knew death, from COVID or violence or illnesses untreated by a vastly unequal health system.[26]

And so white Americans, a group of researchers found, became less likely to worry about COVID-19 the more they perceived the racial disparities in whom it killed. "Reading about the persistent inequalities that produced COVID-19 racial disparities reduced fear of COVID-19, empathy for those vulnerable to COVID-19, and support for safety precautions. These findings suggest that publicizing racial health disparities has the potential to create a vicious cycle wherein raising awareness reduces support for the very policies that could protect public health and reduce disparities."[27]

The hospital where Elizabeth Lalasz worked is a public safety net hospital in Chicago, which means that it treats people who don't have access to pricey privatized care. The hospital's patients are often poor, undocumented, incarcerated—she treated people who fell ill while in Cook County Jail, which was at one point the nation's largest-known source of COVID infections. They are the people whose lives, Lalasz noted, are not priorities for the rest of the world. But even the doctors and nurses, who are considered professionals and make good salaries, she said, felt as though their employers "don't care if we get sick and die. It's just a numbers game."[28]

Through the hospital and her union, she knows of several coworkers who died of the virus, and hundreds, including her, who have gotten sick, some more than once. She has coworkers who worked with long COVID symptoms, with breathing difficulties, kidney problems, a hard time walking.

Far from marking the beginning of the end, the existence of vaccines simply signaled more divisions: into the have-the-vaccines and have-nots. The first to get access were usually people with other forms of privilege or, as Steven Thrasher put it, prophylaxis: the ability to stay home and self-isolate. Vaccination became as politically polarized in the United States as it had in Italy, as COVID denial calcified into a new tenet of the new right-wing politics: real men don't get vaccinated, the cure is worse than the disease, or some other suspicion caused by a lack of trust in a system that mostly denies people life-sustaining care but was suddenly offering free medicine. In the Global South, meanwhile, people begged for access to what people in the North were turning down, but vaccinating them was less profitable. The vaccines, developed with public funding and unprecedented global cooperative effort, would nevertheless be the protected intellectual property of a few companies.[29]

4.3 Expendable

Mark Urquiza was an extrovert. "He was just like the king of the world within his tiny little piece of the universe," Kristin Urquiza, Mark's daughter, told me. He'd grown up working in the fields like his parents, his father born in Mexico, his mother in the United States to parents who had also come from Mexico. Kristin grew up in the shadow of Phoenix, Arizona, where her father had been all his life until COVID-19 took him in June 2020—when the state was reopening, when things were supposedly fine.

Kristin lives in San Francisco and was in her last semester of a mid-career public policy graduate program when COVID hit. During the first lockdown, she remembered, she and her parents were on the same page when it came to protecting themselves from the virus, despite their wildly different politics. "My dad was a Trump Republican," she said. "I think he came to Republicanism as a mechanism for assimilation. He was aggressively teased as a young person about being Mexican, about having a dad from Mexico, about having worked in the fields." Moving toward Trump was about moving toward whiteness, toward acceptance in the country he had after all lived all his life in, even as the community where he made his home celebrated its Mexican heritage. So when the governor of Arizona and Donald Trump declared victory over the pandemic, Kristin said, her father's reaction was, "Why would they be saying it's safe if it's not? Why would the governor say this? Why would the president say that?"[30]

It was of course an election year and Arizona would be a key battleground state, but the political polarization of the virus, Kristin said, had real effects in her family. "All of a sudden I was no longer a person who . . . my dad would say to anyone he knew is the smartest person that he ever knew and ever would know," she said. "I just became a liberal who was trying to tell him what to do."

Mark went back to his busy social life and attended a friend's birthday party at a favorite karaoke bar, which is where Kristin believed he caught the virus. He woke up June 11 with "the whole list of every COVID symptom." Kristin went into fix-it mode from San Francisco, because at the time there were thirteen-hour lines in her neighborhood just to get a COVID test. "I grew up in a neighborhood called Maryvale, which is 80 percent Latino, 40 percent at the poverty level, a very working-class neighborhood, and folks were all essential workers."

Kristin was able to find her dad a test, but while waiting to get results he was getting worse. He tried to go to the hospital but was told only to come back if he couldn't breathe; they eventually found an emergency room that would take him and give him oxygen, even if he didn't have a bed. (They never got his COVID test results back.) Kristin and her mother had a harder time finding a doctor or nurse who could talk to them and tell them what was really happening.

Mark died five days after being admitted to the ICU, on June 30, 2020. The governor of Arizona had issued an executive order pausing the reopening the day before. Kristin said, "When my dad died, it felt like a category 5 hurricane had been put in my body. And I was like, 'If I don't get this out, I am going to die.'"[31]

Kristin's mother had also tested positive for the virus while her father was in the hospital, and was terrified that with her diabetes she would die too. Kristin was left to manage her mother's illness and to communicate with the extended family and friends who loved her father, at the same moment that uprisings were breaking out in reaction to the killing of George Floyd. "The burden of that was all falling disproportionately on communities like mine," she said. "And I thought, how can I say I care about equity? How can I say I care about justice? How can I say I care about any of these things if I don't actually showcase how these policy failures and leadership failures are really impacting normal, everyday Americans? Because while my dad's story is tragic, it is not unique."[32]

The thing her father had taught her was that her potential was endless, and she had taken that belief forward into her political work. It seemed natural to turn that hurricane in her chest into political action. The situation reminded her of the HIV/AIDS pandemic in that little was done to help people who had been deemed disposable, expendable, surplus. "We decided to hold a political funeral and invited a reporter to my dad's funeral, invited the governor to come and wrote his obituary in such a way that we put the blame on politicians for his death."

The governor of course did not show up, and many of the family members were also not allowed to attend, to avoid spreading the virus.

Kristin felt like her rage could knock over buildings. "I wanted to make it known that this was wrong and that real people were dying as a result. And that it was okay to be upset and to demand better because we are the richest nation in the world with the best medical systems, supposedly—as long as you can pay for them."

She spoke to what felt like an endless stream of reporters and began to hear from families who had lost someone like Mark, who found her online and asked for help expressing themselves. Those connections became Marked By Covid, a political organization for justice and remembrance. She did everything from helping families write political obituaries and invite reporters to funerals to fighting for access to tests and treatments in low-income communities of color. "I didn't want to start an organization," she said with a laugh when we spoke in 2023. "I never wanted to start an organization. I've never wanted to be an executive director of a thing, that is not who I am." Yet it became a place for her to put the anger still roiling in her body.

Marked By Covid created a policy platform with demands for remembrance, for treatment and care, for ongoing support for the bereaved and those with long-term health effects and the care workers who carried the burden, for reparations for the damage done, for resilience and preparation for the next pandemic. Collective mourning, Kristin insisted, is a radical act: "Our communities are so often denied the ability to grieve and to mourn. This is something that I felt acutely during COVID because so many people didn't have whatever the ritual was. We did have a funeral, but it didn't feel like a funeral."

Once the push back to "normal" began, the COVID families felt forgotten, their needs and demands pushed aside. The abandonment made the pain all the worse. The fallout from the loss of a family member continued: "What happens now that 350,000 children have lost a parent?" Marked By Covid's call for acknowledgment is often treated as impossible, as though demanding a return to lockdown conditions and more isolation. But as Elizabeth Lalasz pointed out, there are many steps of commonsense care and precaution that come between "lift every single restriction as if the virus has been eradicated" and "complete lockdown once again." The very either/

or way this question is posed, as if there are only the two possibilities, is a symptom of the way pandemic grief has been distributed. Either you have been touched by death during COVID, or you have not.[33]

Our society, Lalasz says, simply hasn't been set up to understand collective decisions, collective care. Solidarity is a feeling and practice mostly pulverized in the neoliberal era. The early days of the pandemic broke from this logic because the virus had to be faced communally, but neoliberalism quickly rose from the dead yet again.[34]

At the height of the AIDS crisis, artist David Wojnarowicz and other activists demanded that their grief be seen, insisting that the impact of the virus not be quarantined in the part of the city where the queers and the weirdos and the poor and the dying found refuge. Rituals of grieving were necessary, he wrote in his memoir, but still they so often kept up the borders between us and them: AIDS activists were becoming "professional pallbearers" while everyone else was allowed to forget. He wrote, famously, "I imagine what it would be like if friends had a demonstration each time a lover or a friend or a stranger died of AIDS. I imagine what it would be like if, each time a lover, friend or stranger died of this disease, their friends, lovers or neighbors would take the dead body and drive with it in a car a hundred miles an hour to washington d.c. and blast through the gates of the white house and come to a screeching halt before the entrance and dump their lifeless form on the front steps."[35]

No complete bodies were thrown on the White House lawn, but inspired by Wojnarowicz a group of activists scattered the ashes of their loved ones felled by AIDS in 1992 in the famous Ashes Action. The flyer inviting participation read in part, "On October 11th, we will carry the actual ashes of people we love in funeral procession to the White House. In an act of grief and rage and love, we will deposit their ashes on the White House lawn. Join us to protest twelve years of genocidal AIDS policy." The ashes filled the air that day, invading the protesters' lungs as well as saturating the lawn, swirling around banners demanding universal health care and protesters chanting, "Act up fight back!" and wailing their grief as police horses approached. In 1996, Wojnarowicz's own ashes were also scattered there.[36]

The actions aimed to break down that border between us and them that Urquiza and Francesca Nava spoke of, to bring the reality of death to the people who were insulated from it—or thought they were. "The place where I think us who are grievers from COVID have come to is that we need to put that line in the sand because everything else comes from this," Urquiza said. "We're never going to fix the healthcare system. We're never going to address long COVID. We're never going to actually make sure the kids are okay if we don't get clear with the fact that this was a huge deal."

The commemorations even in the early days of the virus (though at the time we did not know just how early it was, how many more people we would lose) were held by political organizers. Nelini Stamp and Carinne Luck collaborated on Naming the Lost, a virtual memorial to read the names of the people who had died. Stamp herself had been ill and had lost two extended family members in those awful early days in New York City, and she said, "There was a weight lifted off of my own shoulders because I had the space to finally name the people I lost."[37]

Kelly Hayes also organized vigils for the dead, in Chicago where she lived and worked, both that May and then in October when the then-unthinkable milestone of one hundred thousand deaths in the United States was marked. She said, "Some losses are so severe that they rip apart the emotional landscape of a person's reality. To move on, you more or less have to construct a new world. Without others to bear witness with you, that process feels like a departure from sanity." Organizers hung art around the city, displaying their grief and solidarity publicly.[38]

Rituals for mourning can be a cornerstone of organizing, and yet COVID highlighted that many people did not have traditional rituals in their families or communities, that grief often happens haphazardly, as it did in my family. With the Poor People's Campaign, Ciara Taylor helped build a memorial during a 2022 mass march in Washington: "Folks were able to come and share their stories of loss, and not only how it had impacted them and their families, but to lift up the contradiction around this loss and the impact that it had on the community, versus the state's response to the loss." They made space for people to add their loved ones' names, to include the various reasons for their death, the virus and also the everyday lack of access to safety and care.

Such public grieving gave Kristin Urquiza hope. She remembered how her father loved to bring people together, how he always had the loudest laugh, and she insisted that no one forget.

"I'm in it for the history books," she said. "I want to make sure that COVID-19 is recorded as a modern tragedy in which the United States government abdicated its responsibility to keep people safe."

COVID grief is unequally distributed. Dealing with death and loss is hard enough, but for care workers like Lalasz and Deb Howze, it was exacerbated by underfunding and insufficient support. "Moral distress" was how Lalasz described the feeling the nurses experienced: they knew what they would need to care for COVID patients but were denied the equipment and staffing levels to do it. Others called it "moral injury."[39]

Their patients didn't seem to matter either. Deaths of the elderly in mass numbers were hand-waved away. Leaked messages showed British prime minister Boris Johnson opposing lockdown during the second COVID wave because the people dying tended to be elderly. "Hardly anyone under 60 goes into hospital (4 per cent) and of those virtually all survive. And I no longer buy all this NHS overwhelmed stuff. Folks I think we may need to recalibrate." A scientific adviser to Johnson recorded in his diary that the prime minister had said that his Conservative Party "thinks the whole thing is pathetic and Covid is just nature's way of dealing with old people—and I am not entirely sure I disagree with them." Texas lieutenant governor Dan Patrick speculated aloud: "Lots of grandparents" would be willing "to take a chance on [our] survival" in order for everyone to "get back to work."[40]

Deb Howze, a grandmother herself and a care worker for people a generation her senior, was haunted by the lack of concern for the lives of the old. "The elderly don't have choices about what they want to do," she said. Mary, one of her care clients, was in her early nineties but still mobile and had wanted, Howze says, to remain at home. But Mary was not allowed to make that decision: her family sent her to a nursing home, where she died.

The intimacy of home care is something Howze, who had worked in a variety of different positions during her long career in health care, preferred, even if it came with additional stresses and demands. Another of her clients, Polly, was one hundred years old when they both caught COVID-19, and Howze moved into Polly's South Minneapolis home to care for her while they quarantined. Polly had always had an evening drink with her neighbor Lee, but one day when Howze arrived for her evening shift, Polly told her, "Lee's not feeling well."

Lee died of COVID, and both Polly and Howze came down with the virus. Despite being high risk, they survived, together. Howze stayed in Polly's apartment for thirty days, helped throw a remote 101st birthday party for her, and then had to say goodbye when Polly's family moved her to California to be closer to them.

During that time, there was no one looking after Howze, who had after all continued to work while sick and quarantined. Nobody, she noted, was hired to take care of the front-line workers. The strange intimacy of their job was not, after all, reciprocal. Although Howze planned to go visit Polly in California, she was not actually treated as part of the family. In the moments when she grieved a lost client, she was still expected to behave as a professional, to not show emotion, even though it was her genuine care that employers paid for.

Howze came through her bout with COVID only to be blindsided by the suicide of her thirty-year-old son, Timothy, in April 2021. "He had everything going for him," and then he had a sudden mental health crisis, she said, her voice raw. While she would, like so many others, never be able to pinpoint one reason for her son's death, she held anger in her chest for the failures of care that the pandemic unveiled. "Look at the people that lost their parents, their children, their husbands, their wives, that went into the hospital, never saw them again, that's tragic," she said. "People's lives are upside down. People lose their houses, living in the car with their children because they lost their jobs, no fault of their own. Somebody's going to have a mental crisis, somebody's going to commit suicide."

Howze was giving voice to something real: addiction and binge drinking, drug overdoses and outward-facing violence spiked in the pandemic as people's support networks were suddenly cut away and we were left to marinate in our anger, rage, grief, and fear. The George Floyd uprisings expressed something beyond anger at police violence; intertwined in the rebellion was the feeling that the state had left us all to die alone: Floyd's last words, "I can't breathe," the same thing that so many patients were gasping.[41]

People's lives were upended in so many ways by the pandemic. Jazz Salm had spent most of her life in Florida and most of her adult life in the service industry—she liked the pace and flexibility of waiting tables. She'd just taken a new job when COVID hit; because she'd had precisely one day out of training when everything shut down, she wasn't eligible for any benefits.

"I was completely financially shut off. We spent all of our money moving. The only thing that I had to be connected to my family or even the internet, because we didn't have internet started yet at our house, was my phone." She needed to apply for unemployment—a nightmare in itself because the sheer volume of applications kept crashing Florida's system. The only way she was able to pay her phone bill was a $250 grant from the Restaurant Opportunities Center (ROC). "Your entire routine goes to crap. After that, then your mental health goes to crap. Everything just completely flipped."

The Walmart in her area was still open and hiring essential workers, so she applied to work there, but two weeks in, a routine temperature check at the door found that she had a fever. The only place she could get a COVID test was a specialized test site, where she waited in a five-hour line and saw three people pass out ahead of her. It still took fourteen days to get her result, and she couldn't go back to work without it. At that point, she was ready to give up on her home state, her relationship, and the shreds of what should have been a social safety net. A friend of hers in Valatie, New

York, offered her a place to stay, and she packed her clothes, her guitars, and got in her car and drove straight up. "It was absolutely horrendous. I can't even put into words how stressed and how scared everybody was."

Salm too became a home care worker, looking after her friend's grandfather-in-law. "It's completely a 180 from what my life used to be." She was happy to have landed on her feet but grieved her former life.

Somewhere on my travels I saw from a bus window a man wearing a black T-shirt that read, "COVID fucked my dreams." Young people who were not in the workforce yet lost the milestones they did not get to celebrate: missed high school graduations, proms, two years or more of freedom at universities. Young people lost parents and grandparents, as Kristin Urquiza noted, alongside their life experiences, and had fewer people around to help them through. They became breadwinners—I spoke to high school teachers who found their Zoom classes missing students regularly and when they reached out to the students, learned that they'd taken fast food or grocery store jobs because a parent was ill or had been laid off. They became caregivers for parents with long COVID.

Caregivers, Jess Kuttner noted, carry a kind of anticipatory grief particularly but not only when they are caring for family or loved ones. They mourn the loss before it comes; they live mourning every day. The work of care is so rarely supported anyway, but when the pandemic exacerbated everyone's needs at the same time as it cut us off from each other, the emotional and mental demands magnified. "Ideally we would live in a system where people doing that work would have a community of people around them to support them," Kuttner said, yet even if that had been true pre-pandemic it was almost impossible to maintain through it. Caregivers' needs get subsumed into their work.[42]

Because the damage has not been equally distributed, because it is concentrated in families and neighborhoods and communities and classes, there were many who had not been immediately touched by it, who, as Lalasz noted, "just want to move on." Precautions that would prevent more deaths, more grief are seen as a hindrance to the return to normal: "The individualizing means, hey, it's not so bad for me, so what are we so worried about?"[43]

Joe Biden began his presidency marking the four hundred thousand Americans (at the time) lost to the virus, saying, "To heal, we must remember. It's hard sometimes to remember. But that's how we heal." That number more than doubled since then, but there would be no more commemorations from the president. Instead, he and his press secretary emphasized the idea that COVID would soon be over. "A lot of people had a lot of hope with the Biden administration that they would do more than just push forward a vaccine only approach," Urquiza told me. "The biggest letdown was that Biden came into office being this emissary of grief." Yet he seemed unwilling to sit down with COVID families or to empower a commission to study the government's response.

When the powerful have decided to return to normal, those still grieving and still suffering find themselves suddenly the obstacle. As feminist scholar Sara Ahmed wrote, "*When you expose a problem, you pose a problem.*"[44]

The COVID pandemic hit us in a time of political polarization, a stretching and shifting of the sphere of legitimate political debate in both left and right directions, and the virus seemed to exacerbate these splits, too. Families like Kristin Urquiza's and indeed my own divided over how seriously to take the virus, and the battle took place in the public sphere and the workplace too.

Hospitals that had touted their healthcare heroes tried to shortchange them on wages and undercut their demands to hire more staff, despite public funding pouring in, and Lalasz was one of many hospital workers around the world who went on strike between 2020 and 2023. Instead of improving a system that buckled in the early days of a pandemic, it seemed to Lalasz that decision makers—politicians and hospital executives—let it continue to collapse. The $15 billion in COVID funding sliced from just one spending bill, when US spending on the virus was already insufficient, was another insult to those scrambling to hold the system together with duct tape, prayer, and their own bodies.[45]

The elderly, as Deb Howze noted, were mostly written off as acceptable losses, as "deaths pulled from the future," inevitable and maybe just accelerated by a couple of months. As Beatrice Adler-Bolton wrote, this idea that certain people's deaths were already happening and COVID just nudged them along, that they were preordained rather than preventable, is a politically manufactured one, part of a larger story of austerity. Some people were made expendable early on, and some people had been marked expendable before the pandemic began: the elderly and the disabled, the people unable to work.[46]

The virus tore through nursing homes and other long-term care facilities, killing residents and staff at astronomical rates—early in the pandemic, nearly half of all deaths were in such institutions. So many people died in nursing homes in appalling conditions that their state could no longer be completely ignored. In New York, Governor Andrew Cuomo's role in covering up nursing home deaths helped force him from office.[47]

The awful conditions in nursing homes, Howze said, made the case for home care even stronger, yet funding to pay people like her was scarce. Congress continued to stymie efforts by the Biden administration to budget more money for care and to require more of that money be paid directly to people like Howze, who noted that there would be no staffing crisis for home care or for nursing homes if the wages were better. She herself couldn't afford the health insurance she was offered through the agency that employed her. The labor of Black women like her, particularly their caring labor, was undervalued long before COVID. Her life didn't matter to anyone in power. Home care is a public responsibility, she argued, and if the country took those responsibilities seriously, we wouldn't have more than a million dead.[48]

Andrew Cuomo wasn't the only one to lose his political position because of his contempt for the living and the dead. In the UK, Boris Johnson and other highly placed government officials and staffers had thrown not one but sixteen parties while the rest of the country was locked down. Johnson had weathered many scandals in his time in politics, but the public outrage this time drove him from office. Those who loved the dead were briefly given the opportunity not just to talk about their anger at the departing prime minister but to remember their lost loved ones in public. Jean Adamson told reporters that her father, Aldrick, a Windrush-generation migrant to Britain, "died on his own, on a cold Covid ward without anyone there to hold his hand" while Johnson was having parties. Aldrick had been a member of his church choir and a devoted grandfather, and he was denied the funeral he would have wanted. Adamson said, "I am disgusted. It's a disgrace that we have a prime minister who, clearly, is not fit for office."[49]

Rivka Gottleib, who also lost her father to the virus, said that the stories of parties made her feel like the "wounds have been reopened." While her friends and family were forbidden to gather in their grief, to hold each other and provide comfort, the leaders' partying "confirms what we were suspecting at the time—that the people in charge don't care. They really didn't care. That was the culture in Downing Street; partying and boozing and self-interest and not taking it seriously."[50]

It was not simple callousness on the part of these top-level elected officials, though that is surely part of it, a political class largely insulated from the real-world problems of its constituents, uninterested in their pain. Underpinning that was a kind of contempt for the idea that the government should even try to make anyone's life better, an absolute refusal to change the way the world works even when it is more apparent than it has ever been that the way the world works is homicidal.

On March 2, 2023, Francesca Nava messaged to tell me that the Bergamo prosecutors had placed former Italian prime minister Giuseppe Conte, the former health minister Roberto Speranza, Lombardy region president Attilio Fontana, and others "under investigation on suspicion of 'aggravated culpable epidemic' and manslaughter in connection with the government's response at the start of the coronavirus pandemic." *Aggravated culpable epidemic.* Specifically, the investigation focused on the lack of stricter restrictions in Val Seriana, the closing and reopening of a hospital in Alzano, and the lack of a real national pandemic plan.[51]

Research carried out by scientist Andrea Crisanti—now a senator in Italy—and others suggested that between two thousand and four thousand deaths in Bergamo could have been prevented with earlier red zone–level lockdowns. Compared to the nearby Veneto region, which had the kind of decentralized healthcare system Pietro Brambillasca would have preferred as well as leadership willing to lock down and to test essential workers still going to their jobs, Lombardy had four times as many deaths per capita in those early days.[52]

The investigation began at the behest of family members who lost someone to COVID, part of the Noi Denunceremo group; they pressed for an investigation and filed a civil suit, in 2020, and the investigation took three years to complete. Cristina Longhini was one of many who testified before the investigators, the civil case, and the tribunal.[53]

"The work that the prosecutors in Bergamo are doing, they are going to rewrite the story. Because they listened to former prime minister, to ministers, to presidents of regions, to experts, medical doctors, victim parents and families," Nava said. "I'm not interested in condemnation, but me and a lot of people that have been affected, and also the public want to know what really happened during those weeks, those days. They want to know the truth. Because without truth, there is no future."

It was not about sending leaders to prison, Nava continued. Without an honest reckoning, she repeated what Cristina Longhini said: it will happen again. Yet an honest reckoning of COVID seemed like the last thing that anyone in power wanted, in Italy or anywhere else. "This is a kind of collective political responsibility. Not only the responsibility of this government, of this political ruling class, but as a question of a political responsibility that covers a lot of years, at least ten, twelve years of mismanagement. This is also a story of all the cuts they made, healthcare cuts, disaster recovery."

What is needed, she said, was a "collective recovery," but that still felt unlikely. Instead of collective healing, politicians offered individual denial and risk assessment. Despite the work that Nava and Brambillasca and Longhini did to make the pain public, and to demand real justice, a lot of people wanted to look away. What was a common destiny at one point, a global struggle, by 2023 had fractured into isolated stories. Some people carried the weight, and others pretended it had not touched them.

Nava still had untold stories on her recorder, in her notes. She had to choose which ones to include in her chronicle of COVID because there were so many. She dreamed of a healthy society, one that could come together. Instead, Italy elected the "post-fascists," though many people did not bother to vote at all.

To look at all the decisions, all the failures to act and all the counterproductive actions taken would necessitate a public, collective conversation about what has happened, one that truly grappled with all the losses suffered by people across the world. But one of the reasons such a conversation is terrifying is that it leads to a conclusion that feels too big, too impossible—that the entire capitalist system is responsible for exacerbating a disaster, from the conditions that led to zoonotic disease in the first place to the decision once again to toss mask mandates and invite the virus to spread.

The pandemic, Nate Holdren wrote, is a perfect example of capitalism's tendency toward social murder, toward violence that is not called violence, toward plausibly deniable death making. The suffering that comes with such denied murder is always disenfranchised, Holdren suggested when we spoke, because we cannot call it what it is. In the brief moments when Cuomo or Johnson or Conte were held accountable, the friends lovers daughters cousins of the dead received a brief acknowledgment that what happened to their loved one *did not have to happen.* That it was, in Engels's words, *murder just as surely as the deed of the single individual.*[54]

COVID, of course, did not always or even usually kill, but it left many people ill in ways that continue to confound, as its effects linger in organs, in exhaustion and debility that doctors struggle to cure. Those with disabilities found themselves doubly discounted in the conversation (or lack of one) around COVID: first their deaths were written off as "deaths pulled from the future," and then the way the virus produced more disability was ignored. More people rendered surplus. Debility itself, as Jasbir Puar has argued, is a way of life under capitalism and colonialism, leading to social and economic exclusion, which is another way of saying abandonment.[55]

The tendency of capitalism to create conditions that kill and maim, Holdren wrote, created problems for the government that it solved by depoliticizing its choices, pretending as if the paths it chose were inevitable, that there was no alternative. What could we have done differently? Many things, in fact: White House press secretary Jen Psaki scoffed at the idea of sending COVID tests to every American, shortly before the government decided it could indeed do just that, just as it had sent, multiple times, checks to every American. COVID allowed us to see the political choices behind the things we had been told were inescapable.[56]

4.4 Mutual Aid

A society that could not grieve so many of its deaths was always likely to respond to a pandemic badly.

One of the contradictions at the heart of capitalism is that it at once separates us from one another and also relies on our connections to keep us functioning well enough to keep working, to keep the economy purring. COVID, for a time, forced much work to stop, and it cut us off further from our other support systems, exacerbating our isolation. The reproductive labor—cooking and cleaning but also soothing and comforting, the work, in short, of care—that made so many of us fit to work in any way was stripped away, and we realized how feral we could become without it.

Grieving requires time and space, and this is precisely what neoliberal capitalism does not allow us. Nineteen-year-old Isabela Burrows, whose twelve-year-old little brother died suddenly during the pandemic, whose mother had called her manager at PetSmart to ask them to be gentle with her when she returned to work two days after his death, found herself called into the office and berated instead. The manager "said that my behavior was inappropriate. That it wasn't a big deal and that I needed to get over the fact that he died."

Grief doesn't happen on the clock of capitalism. If one young woman cannot take the time to mourn her brother because it might interfere with her retail job, it is no wonder that mourning for the toll of the pandemic is impossible. To fully acknowledge what we have lost—the million people in the United States, seven million around the world, and more than two years of life experiences, jobs, homes, relationships, sanity—would require a systemic change. It would demand we focus on collective care and cooperation, sacrificing profit in the name of public health, that we be willing to retreat from consumption in order to allow people to stay safe.

But such focus, such action is possible: it can be done because it was done. In the early days of COVID, when we still imagined that we were all in this together, we saw checks mailed to everyone and partly nationalized COVID health care, and temporary—all too temporary—hazard pay or bonuses. Expanded unemployment insurance (even if the systems crashed) and the billions poured into hospitals and healthcare systems, eviction bans and the suspension of student loan payments, and real shelter for the houseless were made real, and quickly. Convention centers became vaccination hubs; military personnel provided medicine. There were even some door-to-door vaccination programs that brought lifesaving care to those who could not easily travel for their dose. Furlough programs paid for working people not to work. People were let out of jails early to slow the spread of the virus. Even a year into the pandemic, the US government instituted child tax credit payments that would be mailed out as checks to every family, effectively a basic income for children. Capitalism doesn't like to admit that any of this is possible, and yet it was done.

Beyond the political decisions, too, there was a sense that communities were doing their best to pull together. Mutual aid networks sprang up, as people offered to get groceries or check in on vulnerable neighbors and tried to meet one another's needs in whatever small way they could. Existing worker organizations created formal mutual aid structures, like the ROC plan that helped Jazz Salm keep her phone on. There were "Thank you essential workers!" signs in windows, applause at night, and also healthcare workers received calls and messages from family and friends: *Could they send protective equipment? Could they do a fundraiser? Could they sew a mask?*

The isolation curiously flattened space even as it stretched out time: I was as far away, suddenly, from a friend who lived down the street as I was from dear friends on the other side of the Atlantic and, with the aid of Zoom and voice notes, could be as close, too (which is to say, not nearly close enough). Organizer Malkia Devich-Cyril took the pandemic time and created a virtual space for mourning and connection that they called Pandemic Joy. "What do you know about how a heavy song can lighten a load? My ancestors knew it: homegrown work songs torn from the diaphragm, pushed like a breath from the throat. And there it was, a song bleeding from the mic of my headphones," they wrote. "And we were somehow together, pandemic survivors, quarantined and huddled each around our own bright screens. . . . We moved, as escapees often do, through troubled terrain to arrive at one another."[57]

In those early days we saw just how quickly the world could change, and we saw that there was, in fact, money to make sure that people's needs were met. That health care could be free and we could be encouraged to use it. That we could be paid, regardless of whether we worked. That rather than looking out only for ourselves, we could both isolate as a form of collective care and still find ways, as Deb Howze said, to look after one another.

The turn back to "normal," then, was not primarily a push back to what we liked about our pre-pandemic lives, not a return to free and frictionless sociality, to live music and parties and restaurants. Work returned well before we were freed to have fun. No, the return to normal was a push back against the idea that the government could, let alone should, provide us what we need regardless of our income, that there are things more important than wage labor, that taking care of each other should come before making profits.

The neoliberal normal continued to crack, even after the pandemic was declared no longer to be an emergency. The so-called Great Resignation and the strike waves resisted the return to a pre-pandemic status quo: "When this started, they told us we wouldn't get more than 3% but now suddenly we've got 5%—they can afford to give us more," explained a London nurse, taking part in the first nursing strike in NHS history. Junior doctors across the NHS went on five strikes in a single year to demand that the government do something about the crumbling service. The basic hourly rate for junior doctors was just over fourteen pounds an hour.[58]

It wasn't just healthcare workers, either. Those deemed essential ranged from train drivers to processed food manufacturing workers. A Frito-Lay employee on strike in 2021 explained her reasoning in an op-ed: a coworker collapsed and died on shift, she wrote, and another simply subbed in to keep the line going. (A similar story to the one I heard from Chuckie Denison at GM.) Another coworker was denied bereavement leave when her father died because there was no funeral. "She had to take off two of her own days to grieve."[59]

Workers all over the world had uncovered a brutal truth: their bosses didn't care if they died. A young person who worked at Sephora in New York City put it this way: before the pandemic, they said, the job was pretty decent, if not particularly well paid. But when the stores were reopening after lockdown, it was a different matter: "I'm not going to risk my life for lipstick."[60]

Martin Olaya and Abraham Castañeda were working at the Mondi warehouse in Leonia, New Jersey, with a tight-knit group of colleagues, mostly immigrants who'd been with the facility through multiple owners and changes, when COVID first came to America. Warehouse work is grinding, high-turnover labor, and so it was unusual that this crew had hung together for so long. Castañeda had been there for twenty-six years and Olaya twenty years when the pandemic hit and their coworkers began to come down with the virus. On the night shift, which Castañeda worked, they were down to three people from the usual fifteen because so many were infected. Management, he told me, "said they couldn't close, and that we had to work, so we went to work like that for two weeks."

Then a coworker, Abundio García, died of the virus. García's brother also worked at the warehouse, and he told his colleagues that managers had called his brother in the hospital to ask when he was returning to work. Olaya asked for time off, and for the facility to be closed and disinfected, but he said it was not until a second coworker, Juan Romero, passed away that the Mondi premises was shut down and cleaned.

They continued to press the company for protections, until in June 2020, Olaya, Castañeda, and sixteen other workers, all immigrants, were simply told not to come back. The company that had employed them for decades now asked for proof of their immigration status. At a time when undocumented workers were being barred from COVID relief programs, this was especially painful. "That day that I got fired I couldn't sleep at night, because the brain starts working, starts assimilating what happened," Olaya said. "I started talking with my wife and kids about how it was not fair, that it was an injustice what they did to me and to all of my coworkers, the first thing that came into my mind was ask for help."

Martin Olaya and Abraham Castañeda decided that they would no longer accept being discarded by their bosses, and that they would use their grief to fight. Olaya ran into a friend in New Jersey shortly after he was fired and told him what had happened. That friend put him in touch with the Laundry Workers Center, an organization of primarily immigrant workers in New York and New Jersey known for its creative tactics and unlikely wins. The LWC supported Olaya and Castañeda and their colleagues as they began to realize that they could, in fact, bring the company to the negotiating table. They picketed the warehouse and brought public pressure on Mondi, even reaching out to workers in Spain where Mondi was headquartered. They spent months on the fight, even when it interfered with their attempts to find new work, their fight for justice bound up with their mourning for their colleagues.

In that first meeting with their bosses after they were fired, Olaya recalled, he noticed one of the managers shaking: "I guess they were nervous, because they never expected that we would get together to go to defend our rights."

What seemed, finally, to bring the company to a deal was a funeral march that the workers held through the town of Leonia, in remembrance of Abundio Garcia and Juan Romero. The marchers bore signs in English and Spanish with the names of their colleagues that asked, "Why have you forgotten those who died of COVID?" Nearly two hundred people marched, masked and distanced yet together, a community refusing to accept that they could be rendered surplus.

Simply giving time to grieve to Martin Olaya and Abraham Castañeda and the millions like them, who lost friends, family, coworkers was impossible for their bosses to imagine. Yet it would be a start, a start to valuing their lives while they are still here, and to imagining a future that would give all of us the care we need whenever we need it. Rest and care are antithetical to a capitalist system that requires constant labor and disposes of the unwell, and yet they are central to any post-COVID set of demands. The Marked By Covid policy platform includes a demand for "a universal care infrastructure, which includes child care, paid sick and bereavement leave, and support for family caregivers." Such a demand, they realize, is tantamount to totally reforming the political economy of the United States and indeed of the world. What if we stopped requiring people to risk their health in order to work, stopped defining health itself as the ability to perform labor?[61]

Their employers could not bring back Garcia and Romero, but the workers received compensation, and most importantly, conditions improved for those still in the warehouse. To Olaya the lesson was clear: "If the same thing happens to you, don't stay silent, don't remain with your arms crossed, go and knock on doors, and raise your voices, at the end there is going to be justice."

Break V

I was a vagrant for three and a half years, and then I moved to New Orleans. I lived in short- and long-term sublets and with housemates and back and forth, and then I finally signed a lease and took my things out of storage and moved into an apartment that is wholly mine, well, as mine as it can be without being able to buy property.

It is still a short-term decision, but it is as permanent as I can handle. New Orleans is sinking, is vulnerable, is doomed, depending on who you ask, to the looming climate crisis, and I missed it because it had made me who I am and I wanted to live here again, to experience it again before it is gone, to maybe help save it. I had felt like an exile, even if my exile was entirely self-imposed, and I decided I didn't need to be, even if I risked breaking my heart all over again by letting myself fall back in love with a city that it seemed inevitable we would lose.

I went down for six weeks, a vagrant still in my bones, assuming that there were two possibilities: either I would be swept back up and wonder why I had ever left or I would flee quickly, having run into one too many ghosts of myself. I stayed, I moved into a neighborhood that is a constant stop on the ever-present haunted history tours, I went to dance at the same clubs that I had gone to as a teenager, I kissed someone on top of a freight train on New Year's Eve. I didn't know what I wanted but New Orleans has plenty of wants to offer.

Living in grief time my desires seemed both muted and amplified, sometimes at the same time. It was hard to imagine anything because I did not want anything, and then when I did want something I wanted it so much and so hard that it seemed like it would kill me. I took to calling myself a grief monster, but really I was two different monsters, a wispy ghost and a devouring creature all gullet and appetite, occupying the space inside me.

Walking made it better, and I was grateful for the dog who needed walking when we were living again in a tiny apartment because I realized that just putting one foot in front of the other is a temporary cure to the futurelessness of it all. I walked and I made phone calls, walked and sent voice notes, but mostly I walked and listened to music and avoided eye contact with strangers. I walked and I felt normal until I saw something that tripped a switch somewhere inside me. I walked in the rain and the snow and the heat. When the dog died too I grieved him with more walking, pacing the streets of New York and London and New Orleans whenever the feelings threatened to be too much.

I felt impossibly young and also like my life was over. Like time had run out when I was not looking and there was so much I had not gotten to do.

Desire made me feel like a teenager again, and so I threw myself at it whenever it sparked within me. Between me and someone new, or someone I had known, in the space of a night or an hour or a moment on a couch when he touched my leg and I thought fuck it why not this one understands what grief feels like and for a while I was convinced that I could be the one who had healed with lessons to impart about all of this and how it hollows your chest out and I was so wrong because all I know for sure is that I cannot tell him or anyone else how it will go for them only that it will be a hurricane, that it will undo them.

Grief does not make us charming and sweet and wistful and lovable; it makes us monstrous and ugly and needy and desperate and angry and it makes us push everyone and everything we love away. It made him push me away. I knew it was coming and still it tore a hole in me.

This is I think why I cannot stomach the grief platitudes industry; grief is not joyful or peaceful. It is a war inside me, it is an alien chewing its way out, it is a tornado somewhere beneath my lungs, it is breaking me and people somehow can't see. I want them to see and I am terrified they will see and I am both of those things at the same time being pulled in opposite directions like there's a team of horses attached to each end except somehow unbelievably I am stronger than the teams of horses and I do not get torn apart.

Muna Mire wrote after the death of her brother about using makeup to construct a face for the public: "I found something resembling emotional equilibrium when my outsides matched my insides: both were freaky. My face, made up, created a self-invented balance to cling to in a world gone awry." The twin desires, the teams of horses: look at me, see me, help me, don't you fucking dare look at me, leave me alone. "When I left the house, people stared at me," she wrote. "I loved the attention. It felt amazing. I was in such a pained state that I wanted people—even strangers—to stop and pay attention. Look at me and acknowledge that things aren't OK, you coward. Is my face fucked up enough that you understand that? Grief gives you an unmatched confidence in blowing off the usual conventions about being polite in public. It became a game. Look at me, but don't even think about trying to talk to me. I've never ignored so many people in my life. It's funny how taken aback people are when you don't smile constantly to reassure them. I never noticed before how often I did that."[1]

I tried the same trick, smudging pink or red eyeshadow around my eyes to accentuate the look tears give me, sleeping in makeup and going out the next day, even though I could not imagine looking pretty, even as I was more desperate for love and touch than I had ever been. Out of exhaustion I was done forever trying to be anyone but myself. My patience thinned, my anger sharper, my standards growing higher.

My father never seemed to want anything. He was impossible to shop for at the holidays, I bought books he'd never read, CDs he would listen to briefly before returning to the same Neil Diamond or more often talk radio. My mother did the wanting and the spending for them both, and he seemed to enjoy that, giving her nice things, status symbols that signaled something about the type of man he was supposed to be, but for himself so little, no outward displays of anything. He wore the same clothes all the time, the same plain trousers and polo shirts year after year, finicky about fit but never style or quality. I always wondered why. I could find so many things to want, then and now.

Before he died I was careful not to want too much, to assume there would be a tradeoff to any gains, any success. I would make bargains in my head: *If I can have this thing I won't need that one*, imagining I could trade work success for love. When something good happens I still find myself waiting for the loss elsewhere, the balance to return. I am used to feeling like a tightrope walker making tiny adjustments to my desires lest they somehow be too much and anger the gods. *Life isn't fair*, I hear my father say, and yet I seem to have learned the opposite lesson from that particular platitude, that I can somehow make it fair by making myself smaller. I am always fascinated by the supposedly feminist quest to "have it all," which seems to mean a job and a husband and 2.5 kids and nice suits and an occasional vacation, and this seems both an unattainable list and like far too little, like a shrunken version of liberation.

When I was a child, my parents stressed, "You don't need a man, you can do anything you want to do, put your career first" (I was eight). They told me that I had to earn everything that I might get, even as they tried to pass on unearned privileges and pretend that there had never been disadvantages, either, that we didn't deserve. The idea of having it all always seemed impossible, a tangle of wishes that I'd implicitly been told were contradictory.

My version of having it all comes to me in an Italian hotel room, and I think in a moment of clarity that I have the life I dreamed of as a child, somehow I am an *author* and this is my *job* even if the near-stranger next to me doesn't love me (he will, someday), and the storm in my chest is quiet for a moment. I try to release the magical thinking, the bargains I make (with whom am I bargaining, anyway?) and the wishes that I know nobody will come to grant, and simply enjoy the good when it comes.

Now that I know loss will come regardless, I am freed somehow to want everything, to make decisions that seem impetuous but are things in fact I have wanted for decades. I know that I will survive this heartbreak and the next. I can fall in love with a city again, a man again, that will, I know, eventually be gone or worse, that I will have to leave. The impossibility of imagining a future, of planning, has become permission to try things I could never have imagined. There is no bargain I can make to stave off the worst, no sacrifice I can make of myself to prevent the people I love from hurting or dying. There is only now, and now again, and again.

CHAPTER 5

Weather

Climate catastrophe, the web of life, and salvage

I wrote this book the summer the orcas started to attack.

It was strange, the first time we heard about it, but then it kept happening, the sleek black-and-white whales crashing up against the yachts of the super-wealthy, tearing off rudders and in a couple of cases, sinking the boats completely. They acted in groups, coordinating their movements, and they clearly knew what they were doing.

I remember loving them as a kid, the creatures we then called "killer whales." Humans trained them to do tricks in captivity precisely because they were smart, but they suffered in captivity because they were social. They missed their comrades, their pods, their families. Of course I loved it when they seemed to be seeking revenge.

We don't know why the orcas began to charge boats, only that they had likely learned the behavior from one female, named Gladis Blanca or White Gladis. White Gladis, scientists theorized, had a traumatic interaction with a boat—maybe she'd been trapped or collided with one—and began to go after the boats in a form of self-defense. She brought her baby with her, and she taught others, who ranged from the Spanish coast all the way, perhaps, to the Shetland Islands. Orca society is matriarchal; orcas do all sorts of things for reasons that aren't strictly related to survival, like wearing salmon as hats.[1]

Orcas grieve: one female in a much-studied pod off the Pacific Northwest of the United States and Canada carried her calf for seventeen days after it died. "The first half of the killer whale's scientific name—*Orcinus orca*—comes from the Latin for 'of the realms of the dead,'" Ed Yong wrote. He spoke to Jay Julius, the chair of the Lummi Nation, who told him, "We've fished alongside them since time immemorial. They live for the same thing we live for: family."[2]

And why wouldn't the orcas come after humans, send a message to us that we weren't welcome? As Alexis Pauline Gumbs wrote, "Why should we be so arrogant as to assume marine mammals are telling us anything? The answer is in the question: *because it's our fault.*" The orcas' world was changing, the salmon overfished and the water heating, the boats plowing through their waters more and more often. They didn't have all the climate science, but it's not like I understand the science either: all I know is that my world is changing and who's at fault. The whales were easy to anthropomorphize and love—they seemed to have picked a side, after all.[3]

It's a mistake, of course, to attribute human motives to animals, but is it so far-fetched to think that loving, grieving, planning creatures might notice changes in their habitat and have some opinions about it? If orcas grieve, surely they can rage. Surely it is equally a mistake to assume that orcas and other creatures are too stupid to notice that humans have made a mess of things.[4]

5.1 Storm

The climate crisis became real for me in 2005, when I like most people watched Hurricane Katrina happen on TV. The difference was that I had lived in New Orleans not that long before. So I spent the days and then weeks trawling around for updates, calling and emailing people, scanning the news broadcasts for the faces of people that I didn't know how to reach—a neighbor whose name I was never quite sure of, the guy who fixed my car, a favorite bartender. All the little contacts that make up a life.

Before Katrina, no one in New Orleans really believed that the city could drown, that the rest of the country would let it. After Katrina, no one can ever forget. It was a clear and visible reminder that for some people, help does not come in times of need.

New Orleans made me, it made me "resilient," but also it made me look up and down as well as side to side before I cross the street, it taught me that the threats can be under your feet, that the terrain will shift, the street will not look the same month by month, that when the rain and the winds come everything can disappear. I learned to love and to let go there.

Sometimes it still, even nearly twenty years later, cracks me open, to think of all that happened then. I moved back to New Orleans in 2021, wanting to live there once again before the rest of the world lets it go for good. Wanting to be part of the place that shaped me again. I found it both exactly the same and entirely different, haunted with a new layer of ghosts.

When I was there the first time, when a hurricane approached us in the fall of 1998, I recall the rumors that abounded that the city had rigged the levees to blow along the poorer edges of the city, in order to spare the French Quarter and the tourist attractions. The stories were untrue but close enough to what had happened in 1927, when levees were dynamited during the Great Flood, to what did happen in 2005, that I understood why people believed them.[5]

Katrina killed almost two thousand people directly and destroyed the homes of many thousands more. Nearly a million people were displaced and many never came back. So much we know. We know too that so many of those who were displaced and killed were poor and Black, the same people who had made New Orleans the city that it was, created jazz and second lines and cooked the food that the tourists eat. We know there were vigilante killings and police killings, that Blackwater, the private security firm used to provide soldiers for the wars in Afghanistan and Iraq, patrolled New Orleans streets. Perhaps we recall that the first piece of "rebuilding" was the conversion of the Greyhound bus station into a jail, to hold those accused of "looting," as if everything they produced had not been looted for generations. As geographer and New Orleanian Lydia Pelot-Hobbs noted, the primary shelter the city offered so many survivors was a jail cell.[6]

Katrina taught us that disasters would not discriminate but the state sure would, that some buildings would withstand floodwaters and others would collapse, that Black people would be left to drown and some people would turn away precisely because the dying were not enough *like them*. That disasters last longer than the news cycle and leave scars that never fade. That grief lingers even after you think it has finished remaking you.

New Orleans is a city shaped by its grief, its traditions of mourning visible everywhere. The best and least known of them is the second line parade, rooted in Black working-class neighborhoods. The second line is many things at once; intertwined with funeral culture, it is a celebration that marks anniversaries and protests violence and claims the city's segregated streets for itself. Participants in the tradition often own very little, but during the parade they own the streets. The second line creates a safe space to cross boundaries real or imagined, to honor the dead and fight for the living, to insist on the value of an ordinary life lived in sometimes brutal circumstances and the joy in that life, in the areas of the city that the tourists don't visit, which the floodwaters overtook.[7]

Like the music that accompanies it, the second line blends cultures and histories together, creating different relationships than would otherwise be possible in the postindustrial city. It challenges ideas of respectability and the work ethic, offering up a different idea of a life well lived, one that treasures relationships and mutual aid rather than one that accumulates *stuff*. If you follow it, it will lead you somewhere you have never been and then leave you to find your own way home. You will find the real city beyond the disasters and the advertisements and the illusions of safety. New Orleans has made something beautiful out of hundreds of years of death and pain, colonization and slavery, wars and exploitation.[8]

It is easy to romanticize the city and to forget that sooner or later it will sink—there is even a record label, Sinking City Records, epitomizing the city's particular form of gallows humor.[9]

The people who make the decisions decided that New Orleans (and a thousand places like it in precarity and unique themselves in culture and meaning and beauty) could be sacrificed if it meant continued capital accumulation. Lahaina could burn and Hawaiians die, and developers eye the wreckage and see dollar signs. Even New York City would not be spared. In 2012 (appropriately enough, on Halloween) Michael Bloomberg, the billionaire then-mayor of New York, rang the bell at the New York Stock Exchange as it reopened just two days after it was shuttered due to Hurricane Sandy. The exchange was running on backup generators; all around it, the power was out. I got a tetchy reply on social media from Goldman Sachs when I pointed out that the bank's headquarters in lower Manhattan was lit up, wanting me to know that the bank had opened up a charging station for its less wealthy neighbors to plug in their phones while they waited for power to return.[10]

But in Red Hook and Sunset Park and Far Rockaway, activists and community organizers were mobilizing too, inspired by the mutual aid that had taken place in New Orleans after Katrina, to bring food and chargers and medical care to the people who were trapped in high-rises or whose homes had flooded, to channel donations and volunteers to help repair water-damaged homes. People who had been part of the Occupy Wall Street movement, challenging the power of finance, were cooking hot meals in a church basement while Bloomberg was ringing the opening bell for capital.

The people of New Orleans and New York and Lahaina and so many other places still live in the wake of disaster. In New Orleans the organized abandonment is ongoing, the destruction fresh when I moved back just months after Hurricane Ida, the knowledge that there will be more and bigger storms now part of the humid air. Yet still, the people dance.[11]

* * *

Disasters can hit in an instant, but in the aftermath it will take weeks and months and years to rebuild. Katrina left a desperate need for hands to perform the labor of gutting and tearing down and cleaning and rebuilding homes and businesses. The people who came to do the work were migrant workers, skilled tradespeople and general laborers, coming from within and without the Gulf Coast and within and without the United States itself, living in whatever dwellings they could cobble together, and creating a makeshift hiring hall at the base of the pillar on which stood, at the time, a towering statue of Confederate general Robert E. Lee.[12]

There is a statue to the migrant workers now, along the river on a manicured walking trail. It was put up in 2018. There was a monument on the I-10 overpass at the floodwaters' high mark for the first year, but it was painted over.[13]

Salvage, as the editorial collective of the magazine by the same name noted, happens between salvation and garbage. It is the work of sifting through rubble to make something livable again. It is a way of living that the workers standing beneath Lee's feet and commemorated with a statue after their departure knew well, having come already through wreckage and faced down borders and cops with nothing to sell but their labor.[14]

This story plays out around the world: disaster strikes, workers come to help, many of them migrants, many of them perhaps undocumented, day laborers, short-term workers. Disasters are growing more frequent as the planet heats and the weather changes: floods and fires, tornadoes and droughts. "Resilience" in this moment requires work, and that work is outsourced often to the most exploitable, a mobile workforce of second responders.

After Hurricane Ida hit New Orleans in 2021—not as bad as Katrina but a Category 4 storm that did billions of dollars of damage and left unquantifiable psychological scars—the National Day Laborer Organizing Network surveyed workers who came in the aftermath. They work for private households and formal businesses, some of them "storm chasers" who move in crews on their own, specializing in climate disasters, others mobilized by labor brokers who take a cut of their money. The money paid in the wreckage is often better than they could make elsewhere or at another time because the need is immediate and widespread. Yet workers experienced wage theft and other forms of abuse that exploited their irregular status. Mobile workers often don't know the area they are in and can be especially vulnerable to such scams. Workers are often denied protective equipment when dealing with mold and toxins, and many of them become ill.[15]

Employers had little incentive to protect the physical health and safety of their temporary workforce, let alone their mental and emotional health. Workers had almost no idea where to report any health and safety violations; they were vulnerable to abuses and cut off from any emergency support that might be offered by the federal government to others in the disaster area.[16]

Julio Robledo traveled from West Palm Beach with Esperanza and NDLON to support those salvage workers after Hurricane Ian struck Florida. He'd come to the United States from Guatemala and worked in construction all over the country and told me, "the Spanish community, they are scared," scared that they have no one to call, that they can't trust Americans, that they came to help but were met with threats. That they called lawyers who also demanded money to help them. That contractors handed the work to subcontractors who picked day laborers up from the streets and then refused to pay them. "My experience when I come to this country too, it's the same, we don't know nothing about this country."

Broad shouldered with big hands, Robledo looked like someone who had spent seven years doing construction work. The industry had been good for him and he'd never lacked work, but he missed his country and dreamed of returning home. Supporting other workers from Central America helped him feel connected to his community. Immigrant workers felt pressured to work all day with no breaks, no lunch, no safety precautions, afraid to tell anyone about their conditions; Sarasota felt like a police state compared to West Palm Beach. He and the Esperanza team distributed helmets and gloves and COVID tests and information on legal rights and mental health care and surveyed the workers on their conditions and needs.[17]

Around the country the story was the same even if the disasters were different. Workers who had perhaps fled hurricanes or drought or fire in their home countries too filled sandbags or doused flames or gutted basements and then returned to their own destroyed homes. Essential one moment then discarded the next, they moved on to salvage what they could somewhere else.

It is no surprise that the world requires super-exploitable workers to clean up after its crises, or that it continues to treat them as surplus, to consign them to vagrancy, when the cleanup is done. The system has been planetary from the start, and so the crisis it has created for the climate will further intertwine people across the planet.[18]

The exploitation of nature was also part of the capitalist system from its beginnings, the tendency to look on trees and land, water and minerals and see only commodities. Scientists have taken to calling our present geological era the Anthropocene, the time on the planet when its climate has been pushed and stretched by human action, not intentionally and yet deliberately just the same. They tend to date the period to the beginning of the Industrial Revolution, the fossil-fueled mechanized period of production and proletarianization. But Jason W. Moore and others have another suggestion: they call it the "Capitalocene," and so shall I. It is a clunky word, but it points the finger where it belongs. Moore, with Raj Patel, explained, "The root, anthropos (Greek for 'human') suggests that it's just humans being humans, in the way that kids will be kids or snakes will be snakes, that has caused climate change and the planet's sixth mass extinction." But the steam engine and the processes of mining and eventually drilling that would fuel it were not natural inevitable results of being human. They were innovations to speed the process of accumulation into the hands of a few, while the rest of us were so much interchangeable labor.[19]

Moore dated the Capitalocene to the 1400s, the dawn of European exploration and conquest, to Columbus landing in the Americas, claiming land and forcing the people who had been on it to work it. Hand in hand with the treatment of purportedly lesser peoples was the treatment of nature as a "free gift" to be used however seemed necessary. Nature was made expendable.[20]

Exploitation is the process of taking more than you give back, and the more that a thing can be cheapened—whether that thing be a human worker or a mountain under which runs a seam of coal—the more value can be wrung from it. It is a process of creating an us and a them: the people who get to do the exploiting and everyone and everything else.[21]

Capitalism required massive energy inputs to get going, and human labor is a form of energy. Enslaved people were not just workers but a form of capital that had been accumulated to turn the wheel of production. It can be hard to remember this, because we have spent a hundred and fifty-ish years living instead with the idea that humans cannot and should not be property, that the slave system was monstrous, that it is far better to dig coal and oil and gas (themselves the remnants of dead things) from the depths of the earth and burn them to power the things we have been told we need. But the two systems were not as separable as we might think. A plantation owner fanned by an enslaved child in the New Orleans heat, and then the quietly expensive air conditioners running now in that same French Quarter building are both luxuries that have far-reaching effects.[22]

Fossil fuels prevailed because they were a thing that couldn't fight back, because they were both free gifts of nature and easily claimed as private property. Because they amplified the power of human labor while supplanting it. Because once dug up they were supremely portable, particularly oil, which could be pumped into tankers and sent flowing through pipelines with little human help. Energy consumption improved our lives in the short term, but the fossil-fired social contract took its toll not just in regional destruction and coal dust in miners' lungs but climate crises that could turn coastal cities like New York and New Orleans into so many more sacrifice zones.[23]

The 1970s oil shock galvanized a shift in global capitalism that kicked off a new process of globalization. It could have been a moment for renewable energy—Jimmy Carter put solar panels on the White House in 1979—but "the environment" was never a priority for capital in general. Rather, the priority was to get profits rising again, even if that meant remaking the world. Wars were fought for oil, political calculations made to support death-making regimes as long as they kept the supply going, because oil kept the machines running. Spills like the Deepwater Horizon disaster off the coast of Louisiana in 2010 brought the costs of oil home to Americans, but the oil industry fuels Louisiana and so the deaths of eleven workers did not stop it.[24]

Renewable energy is not outside the dimensions of capitalism. Investments in solar and wind and the rest are not costless in terms of either human labor and lives or environmental destruction; we cannot, in other words, dodge the planetary crisis with more and different energy.[25]

Yet it often seems impossible to get people to see beyond a world in which they drive their own car to a certain kind of job that pays the bills for a certain kind of family. For every Kevin Horne who moves relatively easily from mining into care work, there is another worker who resists the idea that his work should in any way change, and often the unions themselves demand that the fossil fuel work continue. They are not wrong, after all, that as United Mine Workers of America leader Cecil Roberts argued, "There's never been a just transition in the history of the United States." And so industrial breadwinner masculinity clings to fossil fuels as the backbone of a system that once created well-paid jobs. Perhaps, as Andreas Malm and the Zetkin Collective suggested, it goes beyond the simple desire for jobs: there at times seems to be a deeply felt bond between fossil fuels, cars, planes, and (masculine) national identity, which can take the place of a missing class solidarity.[26]

Naomi Klein pointed out that the climate catastrophe changes everything. Those who double and triple down on a kind of violent (white) masculinity that sees the right to destroy as inseparable from freedom are reacting to the same fears that keep me awake at night when it is unseasonably warm or a tropical depression has been sighted in the gulf. It is a fear that this time capitalism will not come up with a solution, that our faith, as Rodrigo Nunes wrote, "in humankind's demiurgic powers" has been misplaced, that we are not gods after all but just creatures among other creatures that the weather can kill.[27]

"What capitalism will do is it will move the death and destruction around," Nate Holdren said. "We're not locked into one specific mode of ecocide." Emissions can be outsourced for a while, but the atmosphere, like capitalism, is global, and the poisoning felt first by now-far-away workers will eventually come home, too.[28]

We have had neither justice for workers nor a rapid enough transition to clean energy to stave off catastrophe. If a just transition has never happened in the United States, what are the odds that it will happen in a world still driven by US consumption? In Bangladesh, the overwhelming majority of foreign income comes from the garment sector; if that money disappears, how does the country deal with the coming climate disasters? If capitalism cannot save the country from the collateral damage of capitalism, it is equally true that the country cannot simply withdraw from the world system either. Bangladesh already sends climate migrants across the world. For them climate change is not some far-off future but is here now, before the benefits, such as they are, of industrialization have even reached them.[29]

The climate crisis is not a problem for the future; it is a problem that is here now but unevenly distributed. The planet is on fire, and some of the fires are set in protest, in outrage at what the world we have been born into looks like. The world is killing us; in 2012, Rupa Marya and Raj Patel wrote, "A quarter of all human deaths were traceable to environmental factors in the air, water, and soil."[30]

Capitalism is a system that relies on the possibility of infinite growth, but it has hit limits all around. We are almost certainly stuck with the planet we have and the finite lives we have too, and thus we fight here with the tools that we have against a system that is killing us. Vague calls for a just transition will not be enough; we need an end to all of the systems of division and inequality. To resist the lure of a bad utopia offered by titans of accumulation like Jeff Bezos and Elon Musk, ploughing their spare dollars into space travel in an effort to abandon this planet with those who can afford to join them. Those of us stuck here must learn to see beyond doom.[31]

The small office of Taller Salud in Loiza, Puerto Rico, was tucked next to a dentist's, the signs faded to off-white but still legible. And then a hand-printed banner on the gate on purple fabric: "Juntas Somos Poderosas." Together we are powerful. Jenifer De Jesús, the director of community and leadership initiatives at the organization, greeted me in makeup coordinated with her purple Taller Salud polo shirt and her turquoise cat-eye glasses and brought me inside to talk about the storms.

Hurricane Irma didn't devastate all of Puerto Rico, but it hit Loiza in September 2017 and left a hundred families without livable homes. María came two weeks later, collapsing everything: the power system, communications, transport, health care. Three thousand homes were completely or partially destroyed in the area that Taller Salud called home. The Carraizo Dam nearby caused more flooding when its reservoir overflowed, and the entire island was left vulnerable. Across the island, the storm set off mudslides and washed out roads, destroying tens of thousands of homes and causing the largest blackout in US history. The electrical grid was still spotty when I visited more than five years later.[32]

Taller Salud is a feminist community organization created in 1979 to respond to the sexual and reproductive health of the women in Puerto Rico, that had branched out over the years to include parental education and family support, prevention of domestic violence and community violence between men. As soon as Hurricane María happened, De Jesús knew "we had to attend our community."

De Jesús and her small staff organized the town into zones and zone by zone reached out to their members to find out what they needed. They found people sleeping in shelters without bathrooms or showers, and sometimes women were in the same shelter as their aggressors. Based on what they heard from the people of Loiza, they created a variety of programs: community kitchens, community censuses, in-home care for the ill and elderly, orientation processes, sexual and reproductive health services. They brought in doctors, mental health providers, midwives, and many of the people they helped then joined in the recovery work.

"As time went on we realized that the government wasn't getting there. At the beginning we thought we were attending the immediate to help sustain the people with the basics before the government came, . . . but we noticed that they were not going to come," De Jesús continued. Taller Salud would have to try to fill the "void from the government." She and her colleagues trained local women to be community health promoters, to study health needs and provide education, and to be leaders and spokespeople for the rights of the community, to demand the government actually step up.

De Jesús thought that the lack of response was intentional, a plan to displace local people "so they cannot recover, and they leave the country. That's what we have seen, how the people with the greatest need—Black people with low resources, mainly women, elderly women—they are denied the help of all the programs there are." Watching the organized abandonment of their community, the women of Taller Salud transformed their work over the longer-term recovery and created strategies around the idea of justice for the people in Puerto Rico: justice, for them, meant allowing people to stay.[33]

Because the island is a paradise, lush and green with gleaming beaches, and because it is a colonial possession still of the United States, there is plenty of demand for Puerto Rico's limited space, plenty of people who would love to move there and enjoy the low taxes and beautiful beaches and preferential treatment handed to those who come with capital. Puerto Rico, Naomi Klein wrote, has long been treated as a "blank canvas, a safe place to test one's boldest ideas," a laboratory for bombs and eugenic experiments and economic prototypes like the special economic zone, where manufacturing could be done at Global South costs while technically staying within the United States. Juan E. Rosario, a community organizer in Puerto Rico whose own mother was a thalidomide test subject, told Klein, "It's an island, isolated, with a lot of nonvaluable people. Expendable people."[34]

As if to prove the point, the numbers of the dead from María were wildly undercounted for months after the storm. The government's official number was 64, but months later a Harvard study placed the number at 4,645, possibly more—three times the death toll of Katrina. Getting the numbers right matters; the authors of the study wrote, "The timely estimation of the death toll after a natural disaster is critical to defining the scale and severity of the crisis and to targeting interventions for recovery." After Hurricane Fiona in the fall of 2022, the deaths were undercounted again: the health secretary eliminated the requirement that doctors be trained in identifying deaths due to disaster—the requirement that had been in place since María. "We have an elderly population with a lot of chronic health conditions, and a month after a hurricane they start to have heart attacks, they start to have problems with diabetes, they start to have asthma and so they are not counted as a situation related to the hurricane," De Jesús said.[35]

Puerto Rico has been a colonial experiment since Columbus landed there on his second expedition in 1493 and claimed the island for Spain. The Taíno people who had lived there for centuries received a letter they could not read from the king of Spain telling them they were now Spanish subjects, and the Spanish built settlements to search for gold, enslaving the Taínos, who when they fought back were brutally subdued. Slavery did not end in Puerto Rico until 1873; enslaved people had to purchase their own freedom. The United States won Puerto Rico along with Guam, Cuba, and the Philippines in the Spanish-American War in 1898, and the island's residents have occupied a space "somewhere between citizen and alien" (according to a Supreme Court decision) ever since, though they are technically US citizens. They are forced to import all their goods through US vessels, dependent on food and fossil fuels shipped in from elsewhere, trapped in a cycle of debt that has only worsened in recent decades, as a state of "fiscal emergency" has imposed austerity on the island. The year before María struck, Barack Obama signed the Puerto Rico Oversight,

Management, and Economic Stability Act (PROMESA) into law, restructuring its debt and establishing the Financial Oversight and Management Board, a body with final say on all economic decisions. The year María hit, Puerto Rico filed for bankruptcy.[36]

Puerto Ricans have been fighting colonial control for centuries, and PROMESA was just its latest cruelly named face. In 2019, they forced the governor to resign through massive protests, demanding better for the storm-battered people than more corruption and insults. The protests, like so many in recent years, were expressions of anger but also joyous, with dancing in the streets, singing, banging pots and pans, taking to the water and riding horseback to the capitol, demonstrating what the storm and austerity could not crush.[37]

The federal government's response to María was insulting to begin with. Donald Trump visited Puerto Rico and tossed paper towels into the crowd, a move that San Juan mayor Carmen Yulin Cruz called "terrible and abominable." While the US Navy had deployed a massive military contingent to its former colony in the Philippines in 2013 after Typhoon Haiyan, far less help was sent to Puerto Rico, and foreign help was banned. Trump told his administration that "he did not want a single dollar going to Puerto Rico," that "he wanted more of the money to go to Texas and Florida." In Puerto Rico, meanwhile, incompetence and corruption ruled: a no-bid $300 million contract to oversee restoration of the electric grid was awarded to a company with no prior experience and just two employees.[38]

Puerto Rico was filled once again with tourists by the time I visited, and shiny new private construction was evident across San Juan. Even so blue tarps on roofs were visible everywhere outside the capital, and even in San Juan the power flickered regularly.

The blue tarps haunt De Jesús. They were given out as temporary fixes by the US Army Corps of Engineers and FEMA immediately after the storm, designed to let people stay in damaged homes for a month or so. De Jesús and her colleagues counted the tarps themselves and watched as three different programs were announced with great fanfare to fix the homes with tarp roofs. But nothing happened. Even seeing a tarp in a store left a weight in her chest.[39]

Around the island, community groups like Taller Salud were stepping up where the government had failed. They faced the same challenge that the people in New Orleans and New York had: the capitalist state was willing to abandon them to themselves, to let them fill in the gaps and to toast their "resilience." The work that Taller Salud and other organizations like Casa Pueblo and the Centros de Apoyo Mutuo did, the strategies they discovered, happened against a backdrop of yet more austerity, where not only did the government not give but it took away. In 2018 I met Mercedes Martinez, president of the teachers' union Federación de Maestros de Puerto Rico, and teacher Liza Fournier at a labor conference; they told me of going into school buildings with machetes and hand tools to clean out all the garbage and welcome students back, only to have the government announce they would close more schools. After a disaster, Martinez told me, "you need to come to some type of normalcy again, and the Department of Education was denying our children their right to an education." The same thing happened in New Orleans after Katrina, when the public school system was ravaged by the sharks of school privatization.[40]

Many people express sadness in the wake of a disaster that happens far from them, particularly when that disaster hits a popular vacation destination like Puerto Rico, like New Orleans, like Maui. But there is a different kind of grief when you live there, when it is your home. De Jesús likened it to "an open wound as a town."

De Jesús had traveled to New Jersey for a meeting to commemorate the anniversaries of Hurricane Sandy, Irma, Ida, and María and to share strategies of resistance. What can make it better, make disasters more survivable, was a stronger, more connected community, social structures that could outlast the storm, and they built those structures from Loiza to New Orleans to New Jersey and New York. The women of Loiza wanted what all the survivors wanted: to fight coastal erosion and gendered violence; they wanted community kitchens and better jobs and care for the elderly. They wanted to stay in Loiza and to prosper.

Taller Salud created programs of care for employees as well as the community; it offered time off for rest and workshops on how to deal with grief and trauma, creative projects and support from social workers and psychologists and nutritionists, acupuncture and massage. When Hurricane Fiona hit just a couple of months before I visited Puerto Rico, the government left Loiza out of its disaster declaration at first. "That day, the only thing we could do was cry because we knew that the government didn't care about us," De Jesús said, but then she and her colleagues picked themselves up and campaigned for a change, sharing videos of the destruction, and in forty-eight hours they were included in the declaration. They created a community protection guide, adding the ideas and suggestions of their members, brightly colored pages showing what to have on hand in case of an emergency, how to do basic physical and emotional care. They had to combat despair and hopelessness at every turn: they distributed care packages in bright orange bags, bags that themselves became symbols. "When the people saw those bags, it was as if you gave them love, as if you hugged them."

But sometimes the despair or the material lack was too much, and people left, departing for Florida or New York or elsewhere in the mainland United States. Loiza was one of five towns with the largest population loss according to the 2020 census.[41]

De Jesús understood why people left. She recalled sitting down crying in a supermarket days after María, seeing the seed shelf empty. "Every time it rains it makes us sad because we know that every time it rains there is danger, a road can get damaged, you know that you are not going to have power, you know that somebody that you know is getting wet inside their house." The work was hard and tiring, she said, but they had learned to find in the midst of disaster bits of happiness. She wanted people to know "that we are maroon women and that we stay, we defend our country because this land belongs to us, and we must build the future that we want."[42]

Puerto Rico is one of the world's oldest colonies, and its story reveals much about the way humans have treated the world, particularly how certain humans have treated it in the pursuit of gold and profits. Puerto Rico, "rich port," a place to land and extract things. The Indigenous people of the island call it Borikén.[43]

From Columbus's time, from the Doctrine of Discovery—issued from the Catholic Church, declaring that all lands uninhabited by Christians were free to be claimed as property—the planet was divided up into chunks of exploitable turf, and people moved around like chess pieces, in various states of freedom and unfreedom, to do the work of exploiting it. Plants and animals were moved too, claimed or destroyed or both in the process.[44]

Dispossessed of their land (though "possession" is probably the wrong word for relations to land that don't involve enclosure) and of the other aspects of the web of life they relied on (animals and plants and bodies of water), Indigenous societies were broken up, forced to move, forced to learn to live in the ways the Christians thought were appropriate. Required to work, to marry, to see the world as so much property to be divided up.[45]

Spices and gold, exotic animals and new foods, wood and eventually rubber would be shipped around the world. Tomatoes, so essential to what we now think of as Italian food, came from the Americas; a cup of tea, so quintessentially English, came to England from its colonies in India and Sri Lanka; the sugar in it, as Stuart Hall famously noted, brought from slave plantations in Jamaica. Hall arrived in England to study at Oxford as part of the Windrush generation of migrants from the colonies; he wrote, "I am the sugar at the bottom of the English cup of tea. I am the sweet tooth, the sugar plantations that rotted generations of English children's teeth." The colonizers too brought new organisms with them as they moved: new animals and plants, and viruses and bacteria. Disease.[46]

The violence that was unleashed upon Indigenous people by Columbus and the flow of colonists who came afterward was justified by that doctrine from the church, that the heathen, the devil worshipper, the witch, or even the Muslim or Jew had no rights that a Christian was bound to respect. The witch hunts in Europe, Silvia Federici explained, were growing as colonization sped up, the persecution used at home and in the colonies was a way to signal "that the rule of the old gods was over." The old forms of knowledge, which predated Western invasion and Enlightenment, were to be subsumed or eradicated.[47]

It was on the bodies of women that much of the violence that shaped the modern world was enacted. The violence of the witch hunts alongside more quotidian brutalities used to change women from being human in our own right into "a natural source of wealth and services," our labor and the birthing of children—as many as possible—something else to be subsumed under the control of men. This division came alongside the other primary distinctions of that age of expansion, the distinctions that still shape our own: white men and Other, land and property, vagrant and worker. Man and Nature.[48]

Witch hunting had as much to do with spiritual belief then as the Doctrine of Discovery did. But it did its part to crush lifeways that valued the world as a place of relationships and interdependency, that interfered with the race to profit. A belief system that understood the world as alive and populated perhaps by spirits and unseen forces that needed to be appeased, appreciated, respected taught values that conflicted with wage work and land ownership. A belief in magic could be an end run around the kind of work that newly global capitalism required, a threat to the ruling class.[49]

The world of the witch-hunters and the slave ship and the colonization of Puerto Rico did not occur in some backward Dark Ages that we can comfortably disavow. The Capitalocene had already begun; indeed, these relations were how it began. The world, Federici wrote, "had to be 'disenchanted' in order to be dominated."[50]

Who was the savage and who was civilized, then? We are still fighting, hundreds of years later, battles over the statues of conquistadors and enslavers and colonial overlords from Columbus to Cecil Rhodes. But it is the system of domination they left behind, spread to all points on the globe, that we must grapple with, because its material legacies are killing us. The originators of modern philosophy and science spoke of Nature as female, with her secrets locked in her "bosom" and "womb," only to be loosed by pressure or violence; they wrote that humans are meant to be "the masters and possessors of nature." Nature included women, Black and Indigenous people, non-Christians, anyone who could not work. *Capitalism has always been racial* but also has always been gendered, always global, always expanding.[51]

Engels criticized the habit of viewing Nature as pieces and parts to be moved and manipulated: "This method of work has also left us as legacy the habit of observing natural objects and processes in isolation, apart from their connection with the vast whole; of observing them in repose, not in motion; as constraints, not as essentially variables; in their death, not in their life." He continued, "In the contemplation of individual things, it forgets the connection between them; in the contemplation of their existence, it forgets the beginning and end of that existence; of their repose, it forgets their motion. It cannot see the woods for the trees."[52]

It is too easy to justify the destruction of those who are deemed categorically Other, to render so much of the world ungrievable. Federici argued for a political "re-enchanting" of the world, a challenging of the capitalist logics that treat all the world like so much dead labor or so many commodities for extraction. Struggles to save air and water, to stop tearing the tops off mountains and cutting down old growth forests (the lungs of the earth), and to value human reproduction properly, she argued, are central to this process because "they reconnect what capitalism has divided: our relation with nature, with others, and with our bodies."[53]

Frantz Fanon, the revolutionary psychiatrist, wrote of the struggle to break free of the colonizer in Algeria and elsewhere as a process of reclaiming, of revolt against the totalizing regime of occupation. The colonial regime, he wrote, went beyond simple domination and rendered its people part of the landscape, part of "a hostile, ungovernable, and fundamentally rebellious Nature." Colonization is the attempt to tame all this Nature, from humans to mosquitos; "cutting railroads through the bush, draining swamps, and ignoring the political and economic existence of the native population are in fact one and the same thing."[54]

Those colonial landscapes still exist. Asad Rehman told me over a cup of tea a story that echoed eerily the ones I heard in New Orleans:

during the 2022 floods in Pakistan, "the Pakistan authority broke certain dams to protect certain affluent areas, which inundated the poorest; the landless were the hardest hit." The dams and levees in Pakistan, he noted, were built in the days of British colonial domination, structured to move commodities and people toward their destinations, a system that shaped who lived where and which parts of the landscape were considered valuable. It is a similar story in Latin America, where dams holding back tailings—the waste from mining—will be broken in certain directions in case of flooding. Whose lives and land matter will be decided based on centuries-old geographies of power.[55]

Because the land grabs have not stopped. Colonies liberated themselves but were then subjected to a different kind of domination, structural adjustment and debt (which Puerto Rico has aplenty even as it remains a US possession) and forced integration into the new regime of globalized capitalism. Forced to produce crops for the market while the people had to pay cash for things they used to grow themselves. Africa has seen a new scramble for its resources, resources that now include the rare minerals used to make batteries and solar panels at the same time the land itself has been grabbed for planting trees for carbon offsets, a process that many have called green colonialism.[56]

When we talk about climate change these days, we often talk of climate refugees, less often of reparations for the nations, like Pakistan, that were integrated into a global capitalist system against their will, that bear so little responsibility yet so much vulnerability to the storms fires floods that are coming. What this conversation should include, Rehman, the director of War on Want, told me, is a right to stay: a right not to have your home destroyed in the first place, a right to declare that your life is valuable whether or not it produces profits or absorbs waste for the North. A right not to be displaced by settlers or wars or rising seas or winds. A right not to have to move to the city and become cheap labor or to have to trek across international borders to become a refugee in the first place.

The UN Human Rights Committee issued a ruling in 2019 that climate-related threats should give displaced people a right to claim asylum, but that ruling was not legally binding, and it is not always possible to disentangle climate damage from any of the other reasons that people might move. Tens of millions of people are already displaced, with projections for the near future ranging even higher, up to a billion. I may myself become one of them; every time I leave New Orleans during hurricane season, friends remind me to take everything I cannot afford to have swept away in a flood. But I, a modern vagrant anyway, can relocate more easily than so many. Julio Robledo's family and friends in Guatemala face some of the highest risk for environmental catastrophe; farmers in his country are already being displaced by drought, yet in America they are hardly welcomed. The tightening of borders is climate policy as much as the speedup of renewable energy production.[57]

Climate disasters are already here, and thus so is climate grief. For people like me it is often an anticipatory grief, an anxiety fizzing in your chest or your bones, a sense of dread and doom and hopelessness. But for people who survived Katrina and María, the floods in Pakistan or the droughts in Guatemala, it is a very real loss that has happened already. It is grief that Jenifer De Jesús carried with her every day when she went to work caring for her community, and it is grief handed down through generations whose homes were taken away, whose worlds ended when Columbus landed in 1493, when the slave ship came ashore, when the land was enclosed. Such grief has been fuel for rebellion for centuries.[58]

5.2 Sacrifice

When I arrived at the Oceti Sakowin Camp on the banks of the Cannonball River in North Dakota in September 2016, the Obama administration had temporarily halted the construction of the Dakota Access Pipeline (DAPL), the oil pipeline that was the cause for the massive encampment spreading across the hills north of the Standing Rock Reservation, holding at its peak perhaps ten or even fifteen thousand people calling themselves Water Protectors.

Oceti Sakowin was the name of the camp, but it is also the name of the Seven Council Fires, seven nations of Dakota-, Nakota-, and Lakota-speaking people across the Great Plains, seven nations that had not come together in at least seven generations. "Mni Wiconi"—water is life—was the slogan, and it was something more than a slogan; it was an incantation, it was a statement of truth. The camp then was not a protest space but a reunification and a synthesis, a return to an earlier tradition and a world where new technologies and new ideas mixed, where communal meals were served with donated food from all over (the first night I was there, moose was on the menu, brought from Maine) and where wide-ranging debates about the future between elders mixed with a school for young people to learn the history that the colonizers tried to erase. Historically, Lakota scholar Nick Estes wrote, the Oceti Sakowin would reunite in times of celebration, trade, and hunts but also in times of threat and resistance. The camp was all of those things and more.[59]

Faith Spotted Eagle, an Ihanktonwan elder and member of the Seven Council Fires, told me that she had always been raised "to operate on a foundation of respect for all living things, Mother Earth, animals, and people, in that order." Water was one of those living things: "The outer world has lost sight of the fact that the water has a spirit," she said. "That is why we use water in all of our ceremonies. It is the first medicine. I think having grown up along the Missouri River, I know the power of the river. It can take lives and it can give life."

Spotted Eagle had come to Standing Rock when the first camp began, the Sacred Stone Camp on land owned by LaDonna BraveBull Allard, in April 2016. The Sacred Stone Camp filled, and then a second camp began across the river, swelling in size as the news got out, as water protectors marched and put their bodies in front of construction equipment day after day. The movement at Standing Rock, Spotted Eagle said, was fed by the international fight against the Keystone XL Pipeline, led too by Indigenous people in Canada and the United States. During that struggle she had reached out to other nations, the Pawnee and the Ponca and then others who signed on to the new treaty they made to come together to stop the destruction the pipelines would bring to the land and the water. White farmers joined them too, in a Cowboy-Indian Alliance that had ridden horseback down Washington, DC's Independence Avenue in 2014. "We had the farmers and landowners come up and they cried and we were teasing them about being the new Indians, because they were losing their land and now they could feel what we felt," Spotted Eagle said.[60]

The pipeline was the present incarnation of hundreds of years of settler history in which the land was enclosed and claimed and polluted, in which treaties were made and broken as the Native nations were driven into smaller and smaller reservations often far from their homes. In which lands were traded for health care and education and welfare guarantees that were routinely violated before the ink on the treaties was dry. The KXL pipeline and then DAPL were to cross unceded lands of the 1868 Fort Laramie Treaty, lands where generations of ancestors were buried. During the construction process of the DAPL, twenty-seven burials were discovered in the path of the machines and the Standing Rock people went to court to protect them. In response, the company sent in private security with dogs, and the water protectors attempting to stop their ancestors' graves from being upturned were beaten and bitten and tear gassed. Leaked emails later showed security contractors discussing the use of "skunk spray" often used against Palestinians by Israeli forces.[61]

The Native people, Spotted Eagle said, had historical trauma from so much loss, so much violence, but so did the settlers: "They still live in the fear that we are going to take their land back. A lot of their behavior is fear-based."[62]

Against the capitalism imposed on tribal governments, the camp was a space of decolonization. "Be sure you put decolonization," Spotted Eagle told me. The experiments of day-to-day living and of fighting off the external threat went hand in hand. The fight against climate catastrophe and against the immediate destruction threatened by the pipelines and the struggle to remain sovereign nations against the onslaught of settler colonization hundreds of years in the past were all one process. The destruction of the land and the water and the animals had been crucial ways that local climates were changed and Native people killed or driven out since the arrival of the first settlers. Food stocks were burned, trees cut down, buffalo killed in vast numbers, smallpox and cholera deliberately passed on. Native people's bodies were treated not as human remains but as waste or even as adornment: their body parts were made into jewelry and souvenirs. The Native nations have survived, though, through apocalypse and climate catastrophe; as Estes's book reminds us, *their history is the future we face.*[63]

That history includes periods of revolt, like the Ghost Dance, a revolutionary practice that swept across the land in the late 1800s, a "comprehensive challenge to the colonial order of things." The Ghost Dancers resisted the boarding schools and Indian agents, they danced and built camps and spoke their own languages rather than English; they prefigured a decolonized world, and they resisted the ongoing military incursions. The history books mostly suggest that the Ghost Dance ended with the 1890 Wounded Knee Massacre, when more than three hundred Ghost Dancers—more than two-thirds of them women and children—were massacred by the Seventh Cavalry. But the movement's practices and spirit were part of the long history of resistance to colonialism that bloomed back into view of the settler world at Standing Rock.[64]

It should be shocking but not surprising to us that the destruction of the land brought with it the destruction of the bodies of Native ancestors, turned up with the turning up of the ground to lay the pipeline. *Even the dead will not be safe.* There were the militarized police and private contractors who used dogs and gas on the water protectors, but there is also the more insidious violence perpetrated around the "man camps" of construction and fossil fuel extraction, the murders and disappearance of Indigenous women. This is why women's leadership was so important to Faith Spotted Eagle and others.[65]

Life in the camps restored a different understanding of gender and of reproductive work, the reproduction of the community both as it had been and as it would be in the future. Rather than centralized leadership, they prioritized dissent and discussion, the contributions of all.

Queer and transgender Native youth, many who use the umbrella term "two-spirit" for a multitude of gender and sexual possibilities beyond the settler-imposed nuclear family, held leadership roles at the Oceti Sakowin camp, a challenge to the binary worldview of settler-colonial capitalism.[66]

The pipeline, in the end, was built. The Army Corps of Engineers temporarily halted it under Barack Obama, but Donald Trump reversed the decision, and despite continued protests and court battles, oil has flowed through the DAPL since 2017. Oil drilling and moving and burning goes on even as capital turns to lithium mining and electric vehicle construction, wind turbines and solar panels. But something was born—or reborn, in Spotted Eagle's words—at Standing Rock that rattled the nation.[67]

There was much to mourn when the camps came down, but a flame keeps burning in everyone who experienced that place. Seven years later, I can remember the smell of the campfire and the air and the flapping flags and hoofbeats. I remember sitting with Faith Spotted Eagle as she told me that the goal of the conqueror was continuing control over humans and the Earth. "And if we don't decolonize, if we don't stop and every single day examine how I have become like the colonizer . . ." She paused, then continued. "I asked my daughter this, I said, 'My girl, what is going to happen someday if we lose our songs, if we lose our language and we no longer think like Natives?' She looked at me and it was just chilling. She said, 'Then, the colonization process is complete.' That just gave me chills."[68]

But someday, she told me, "when Mother Earth really shakes herself, those property lines are going to dissolve."

The Dakota Access Pipeline was originally drawn to snake along near Bismarck, the capital of North Dakota and the second-largest city in the state, one that is 90 percent white. But it was rerouted to a place that would cross the river instead by Standing Rock, an 84 percent Native area.[69]

The strategy has been obvious for decades. In 1983, the State of California hired a fancy public relations firm to help it decide where to locate a new garbage incinerator. The company was asked to help decide where the people were the least likely to fight and if they did fight, the least likely to win. The answer was, of course, to target the poor. To target the less educated, the elderly, to keep middle-class people well away from the sites. Aim for rural areas, though South Central Los Angeles was also on the target list. "All socioeconomic groupings tend to resent the nearby siting of major facilities, but the middle and upper-socioeconomic strata possess better resources to effectuate their opposition," the report read; as China Miéville wrote, "The poor should be targeted, in other words, not because they will not fight, but because, being poor, they will not win."[70]

What is now called environmental justice is the struggle to value the lives and homes and air of poor and working class people. It is an uphill battle even today, even as the US government has an Office of Environmental Justice, which explains its job as "to protect overburdened and underserved communities from the harm caused by environmental crimes, pollution, and climate change." But how does one office fix all the harms of generations of broken treaties, slavery, and violence? And what happens when the harms are outside US borders, as so many are?[71]

The UN's special rapporteur on extreme poverty Philip Alston put out a report in 2019 that suggested the world was on track for "climate apartheid," pointing to that moment after Hurricane Sandy: Lower Manhattan blacked out except for the Goldman Sachs building lit up by generators. "An over-reliance on the private sector could lead to a climate apartheid scenario in which the wealthy pay to escape overheating, hunger, and conflict, while the rest of the world is left to suffer," he wrote. Or, as Asad Rehman put it, "basically the rich will use wealth, seek safety, and leave the poor to burn or drown."[72]

People in what are designated by capital as the sacrifice zones have been made expendable for hundreds of years and have no choice but to fight, and fight now. While the leaders of rich countries dither and talk about their grandchildren, the grandmothers of the South (and grandmothers of the spaces relegated to waste in the North, like Faith Spotted Eagle) are suffering now. “Way back in 2009 in the climate justice movement, we were arguing for temperature limits to be limited to less than one degree. And the Global North was arguing for two degrees,” Rehman said. Only now do bodies like the Intergovernmental Panel on Climate Change point to colonialism as one of the “historical and ongoing patterns of inequity” that leave certain people vulnerable to storms. And so climate justice requires more than storm-proofing buildings or even cutting emissions: it requires social protections, livable wages, public services, the kinds of things that construct resilient communities rather than scatter people to the winds after the storms.[73]

Part of the politics of the sacrifice zone is that it is whenever possible constructed out of sight: it keeps the realities, or as economists call them the externalities, of the system out of view. But the sacrifice zone, Nate Holdren noted, is as old as capitalism, as old as the slums clustered around factories that Engels visited in England. “There’s a long-standing history of processes that essentially localize a political problem, split a group off from us, and then, hey, the big picture problem got solved for most people, so now this local population is out of sight, out of mind.”[74]

One of the lessons of Hurricane Sandy and indeed of Katrina was that even within the zone of destruction, there will be parts and people who are marked for abandonment and others who will be saved. As Mike Davis long ago pointed out, Malibu, California, was built to burn and was repeatedly saved from destruction because the wealthy found it beautiful. The richest and poorest places in Southern California, he wrote, “are comparable in the frequency with which they experience incendiary disaster.” Yet the history of Malibu is one of public subsidy for private catastrophe; tax breaks and a panoply of subsidies helped rebuild it time and again, while slumlords let their tenants burn in tenements in Westlake. “If enormous resources have been allocated, quixotically, to fight irresistible forces of nature on the Malibu coast, then scandalously little attention has been paid to the man-made and remediable fire crisis of the inner city,” Davis wrote.[75]

What happened in the fireplains of California is what happened in New York's outer boroughs during Sandy: two kinds of people lived in the flood zones, the wealthy who wanted luxurious beach views, and the poor in halfway houses, rehab facilities, and rickety public housing. When the latter are washed away, there is just more beachfront property for the rich, the ones who can afford to rebuild. These are the politics of heat waves, too: the poor have no air conditioning, the already-ill more likely to succumb. Even in the same heat, people experience it differently. Workers have been dying of the heat faster and faster in recent years, and workers of color—undocumented workers in the fields picking food—die more often.[76]

The strategy of shoving crises out of sight has worked. In the same way that many white people were fine with mass COVID death as long as they were reassured that it was mostly Black and brown people doing the dying, those same people believe that they will muscle through the climate crisis and those who die will probably deserve it. But the floodwaters, like the virus, do not discriminate so surgically. The rich are better able to bear the costs, but increasingly the middle classes are feeling the pinch.[77]

During carnival season in 2023 I went out to Norco, Louisiana, for a bicycle tour of the communities wedged between oil refineries and chemical plants, in what is known as "Cancer Alley," just about a forty-minute drive from my front door. I've lived in New Orleans off and on for years but had never really seen the plants up close, just passed them a few times driving west on I-10. But as I breathed in that air, my throat tickled, my eyes burned, and I wondered, Was it the high wind off the river as a storm blew our way, or was it the air itself? I didn't want to breathe too deeply.[78]

We rode along the levee, stopping at key locations in historic struggles: the 1811 slave rebellion as well as more recent fights for environmental justice. Sheila Tahir, the host and a staff member at Louisiana Bucket Brigade, told us that the first refinery there was built on what had been the Trepagnier plantation, the land before that enclosed away from the many

Native nations that had used the Mississippi's mouth as a trading village (its name, Tahir said, was Bulbancha, a Choctaw word meaning "place of many languages"; it had a language of its own so that the many peoples who met there could communicate).[79]

The Bucket Brigade began distributing air-sampling buckets to communities in Cancer Alley so they could test their own air, rather than rely on the corporations to tell them whether what they were breathing was toxic. The companies site their facilities in places where people are already considered disposable, so of course those people are not listened to when they complain. *Target the poor.* Jo Banner, the cofounder, with her twin sister Joy, of the Descendants Project, grew up in nearby Wallace. Her ancestors were enslaved on Whitney and Laura and Evergreen Plantations, and she joined the ride to tell us about the fights she'd been in for her right to breathe and for their homes since she was ten.[80]

Banner and her sister grew up learning the stories of the uprisings and of a man named San Malo, who was the leader of a maroon colony in the area. (I hear an echo of Jenifer De Jesús in Puerto Rico: *we are maroon women, and we stay.*) Louisiana, Tahir added, had the largest number of maroon colonies in the United States, places where enslaved people had liberated themselves and built shadow societies with Indigenous people. Their understanding of the land gave them power, but they were never acknowledged as having the right to it. When the refineries came in, later, the story was the same.

Those ancestors built community on the land they had been forced to work and then were displaced when Shell bought the plantation to build on, yet they still wanted to stay close to one another, to the river and the land. They bought land themselves and formed the community of Diamond, and in the 1990s and early 2000s Margie Richard and her neighbors began to see illness everywhere. Asthma, cancer, sarcoidosis, miscarriages, and stillbirths. Richard, Tahir said, "first saw the parallel between plantations of the past and the petrochemical oil and gas company of today. She said, 'If my ancestors can stand up to slavery, I can surely stand up to Shell.'"

They could not force Shell to move, not when oil made up such a huge part of Louisiana's revenues, so they fought it for the money they needed to move themselves. And they won, but even in their winning they lost: "They had to choose between the health of them and their loved ones or staying connected to their community," Tahir said. "Despite being rooted to the land and this culture, people felt they had no choice but to leave. It was a matter of life or death." The unique cultures built in these places were scattered to the winds.[81]

The town of Norco was named for NORCO the company, now owned by Shell but originally the New Orleans Refinery Company. When the refinery was built, Tahir explained, it mimicked the old settler-colonial practices of declaring the land empty and then displacing the people who were on it. Erasing the history that had already been erased so many times. The towns around Norco were what Ruth Wilson Gilmore called "forgotten places," but they were right there for the visiting. The forgetting was done deliberately as Louisiana doubled and tripled down on the petrochemical industry, Lydia Pelot-Hobbs wrote, becoming the third-largest producer of crude oil in the United States and using the oil money to fund all sorts of projects, what there was of a welfare state as well as the prisons to hold the people deemed surplus, a surplus that expanded when the oil market crashed. The industry's dredging of canals and digging to lay pipelines and drilling everywhere helped make the area more vulnerable to the storms that burning oil made more frequent.[82]

Louisianans loved and hated the oil industry, relied on it for jobs even as it poisoned their air and flooded their cities. They made excuses for it as their neighbors fought it. *When you expose a problem, you pose a problem.* Fishing communities as well as the people who lived alongside the refineries and plants (often called "fenceline communities") had their lives shattered by spills and storms but stoically kept going. They mourned but few imagined a Louisiana without oil money even as it made up a shrinking slice of the state budget. Shrinking faster were coastal towns, some of which disappeared entirely. "Gone is Yellow Cotton Bay, once a prime fishing settlement in Plaquemines Parish," Arlie Russell Hochschild wrote. "The church in Grand Bayou stands on stilts; a small cemetery is accessible only by boat. Thirty-one communities are now listed only in the historical record."[83]

A few weeks after the bike ride, I joined Jo and Joy Banner for another event in Cancer Alley, this one something Jo described as "grief work." The Banner sisters and the Descendants Project helped organize a "listening pilgrimage" called Born by the River. It began at Whitney Plantation, which unlike most of the nostalgia tours in the area focuses its work on educating people about the realities of slavery.

Thirty years before Formosa Plastics had attempted to buy the land where we stood to build a plant. "We were told we had four months to move. Formosa was about to do what not even slavery had done, which was move us from this land," Jo said. The community fought and won, but "not one time did the parish apologize or ask us what the ramifications were. So many times we are forced to be strong, to be resilient," she said. "I'm tired, sometimes I just need to grieve."

The pilgrimage brought us to a little cemetery in the Willow Grove community that had been, in the plantation's heyday, where enslaved people had lived. The area had been hard hit by Hurricane Ida, and many of the little houses still had blue tarp roofs. The woman playing the violin wore a long black dress in the heat as she played over the graves. A local minister stepped forward with some of the elders from the community. "How can we allow those who are greedy for money and have nothing else in their minds determine what our community looks like?" he said. "I don't believe these people are worthy of being deserted."

We ended up at the Banners' property, a former plantation building they bought to restore and make their headquarters, cooled by the shade of a sprawling tree. The performers, a mother-daughter duo, sang Sam Cooke's classic "A Change Is Gonna Come," and its first words, "I was born by the river," brought tears to my eyes. I looked down at the Stop the Wallace Grain Elevator yard signs and up at the people around me and let the music do its work.

Weeks after that event I returned to that building and sat in the shade with Jo Banner as she told me her family's story. "We hear a lot in this conversation about petrochemicals and business and economic development and investment, but I think back to my ancestors, who came through slavery, fought a war, and then started investing into the community way back then. It's a shame that they come here and they tell us what economic development is and what it is not, because we've been doing it for a very long time."

They were still fighting for their home. The grain elevator was being sold as green development by a company called Greenfield Louisiana; its CEO told reporters in 2021 that it would help the community by "diversifying the tax base and creating 100 jobs," praising his company's "great care to engage the community on this project." Jo Banner disagreed. "Certain structures on the facility would be as tall as three hundred feet. That's as tall as the Statue of Liberty and Big Ben. Eighty large trucks a day is what they would average, and also over a hundred thousand tons of particulate matter per year will come from this facility. This is what they mean by 'green.'"[84]

To Banner, "the system of exploitation is the real enemy." It had begun by exploiting the enslaved to produce sugar, then free labor and petrochemicals, and now grain. Exploitation shapeshifts, she said, and I thought of Nate Holdren's explanation of the way social murder gets rearranged but does not stop.

From the time she was a child, Banner remembered getting sick from chemical leaks on the river, the smells that would waft through the air. When Formosa Plastics sent real estate agents into the town to buy them out, her grandmother was the first to feel the pressure. The agents told her, "If you don't cooperate, they're going to take your land anyway." Of course, they didn't say it quite so bluntly, but they implied heavily that the deal they were offering was the best the Banners could hope for. Her family would not have fought it, except for a man named Wilford Green, one of their neighbors, who decided to challenge the company. Through that battle, the residents discovered that the president of St. John the Baptist Parish had been paid off to rezone the area from agricultural to industrial. The parish president went to jail, the plant was never built, and the

Banner sisters stayed in Wallace and dedicated themselves to learning and telling the stories of their community. The process still haunted them, emotionally and materially: the grain elevator company wanted to use the same rezoning ordinance to build, and the Banner sisters filed suit citing that decades-old corruption.[85]

Sitting by the levee with the breeze washing over me, I could see why the Banners fought so hard. We were far enough from the plants that the air smelled of nothing but grass and trees, and it was a beautiful day, a beautiful home. I wondered what it would be like to have family go back ten generations in one place, what it would be like to have grandmothers and great-grandmothers who remembered when the chemical plants came in, to have a family member partially blinded by an explosion at the bauxite plant where he worked and to be blamed for taking payouts from the companies that did the destroying. "What other retribution do communities have?" Banner asked. The workers and the communities faced the same awful calculus of money for a limb, for an eye, for their lungs, for a house.

The Banner twins went into Louisiana's other big industry: tourism, which relies on the work and talents and histories of Black people, as musicians and as ghosts and as living workers. "This is something that's common for Creole people," she said. "Death was not the final . . . it didn't end relationships." Her grandparents told stories as if they were happening in the present, made their ancestors live. She gestured to the posts around us, a little walking trail of Louisiana folklore, each post with a sign explaining a different creature or spirit or bit of magic, the Loup Garou and the Fifolet and healing hands. "The folk tales and the stories, all of that combined to make us really love our community and the history and the weirdness and the strangeness." The Banners were re-enchanting their world.[86]

The tourism industry was where they could use that history, but the industry kept them on the outside. "We were getting pushed out of our own history." The Descendants Project began as a challenge to the tourism industry, to allow them to talk about their ancestors, to challenge the nostalgia for the plantation. "We knew it was radical, but we weren't afraid to claim our identities as descendants and move forward in that direction. And we did not care who we pissed off." They hadn't intended to be an environmental justice organization, but then they heard about the plans for the grain terminal, and they realized that historic preservation and climate justice overlapped.

The parish had the highest death rate per capita in the country when COVID first hit, the virus pairing with other forms of damage to be deadlier than ever. Jo Banner pointed to the police killings of Eric Garner and George Floyd: If your breathing is already compromised, how hard do you have to fight to survive? Grain dust, she noted, is one of the oldest kinds of pollution, dating back to ancient Egypt. "I just feel like everyone wants to choke us out one way or the other. They're trying to choke the life out of us."[87]

In the midst of all of these fights, Hurricane Ida arrived, right on Katrina's anniversary, August 29, and the power went out and the storms destroyed buildings and damaged the home where Jo lived with her sister. And then her brother died, a week after the storm. "I still am not going through the grieving process the way one is supposed to," she said. "It's a luxury to grieve, the way I see it, because we just take for granted that a person dies, [you get] time and space to just properly mourn. But that's not given to everybody. Collectively, it doesn't happen to this community. They weren't given the time post-slavery, even during slavery."[88]

Capital counts on the exhaustion of people like Jo and Joy Banner. It counts on the piling up of hurt and loss to make them give up, move away, stop fighting. The climate divide is not really between those who "believe science" and those who do not, as Ajay Singh Chaudhary pointed out. It is between "those who stand to gain—both in this moment and in the future as traditionally conceived—from fundamental system preservation . . . , and those whose current exhaustion is part of the fuel for that system as much as any petro-chemical or industrial agricultural practice."[89]

Jo Banner is determined to stay where she is surrounded by her ancestors, the people in the cemeteries and the people whose graves were never marked. "Everywhere there's a plantation, there's at least one burial ground," she said. She had been thinking about what a real environmentally friendly development might look like in Wallace, not towering grain elevators and not even the growing of sugar cane. In her research she learned that lavender is a plant that grows well in Louisiana and might even help to clean contaminated soil. It would smell lovely, it would honor the dead, it might even be profitable. "The decision was made long ago to make the ground sacred," she said, by the people who buried the dead without marker or mourning. "And now the country has to deal with the ramifications of that. That was out of our control, but hopefully it's in our control now."[90]

Māori climate justice activist Tina Ngata put forth an explanation of indigeneity that has resonated with me, with Jo Banner's story, and so many of the stories I have told here. While many people assume being Indigenous is simply having been somewhere before colonization, she said, there is another understanding: "That is a way of knowing, being, doing, and relating that grows out of the soils and the waters and the ecologies upon which you are standing. It is inherently a localized notion of being." The knowledge systems are in the language, the kinship structures, architectures, and economies, in the relationships that you have with place and living things: "That relationship brings value into how you live your life and the decisions that you make and how you arrange yourselves and relate to the challenges that are going on around you as well."[91]

Ngata's articulation seemed to echo a Jewish concept that is almost the opposite of indigeneity: that of *doikayt*, "hereness," a Yiddish word for a diaspora principle that means that where we stand is our home and we fight there, alongside others, for our lives. It was a concept opposed to Zionism, opposed to the idea that Jewish safety would come from having our own state, our own walls, our own army. What it has in common with Ngata's definition, with what I heard from Faith Spotted Eagle and Jenifer De Jesús and from Jo Banner, is a stress on relationships and practice, in how we behave rather than who we inherently are, in our teachings and language embodying concepts of justice. Jo Banner's ancestors had been brought to Louisiana against their will, but she was working still to heal the land as well as her people.[92]

5.3 Salvage

I've lived through hurricanes and tornadoes and once had to drive three states to avoid a forest fire, but it was drought in London that brought me a sense of existential fear that wouldn't go away. London, not home but a place I love, dry as bone and cracking, haunted me. The parks like so much straw, the only green in hardier patches of weeds and the tops of trees. The yellow dead grass worn away to rough brown dirt paths and patches like scars. The spectacular disasters continue, as they will continue, but the everyday heat can kill you too.[93]

The term that many people offered me for that feeling of pervasive looming loss, of anticipatory grief, was "solastalgia," a portmanteau of the words "solace" and "nostalgia" coined by Australian philosopher Glenn Albrecht. "Solastalgia is when your endemic sense of place is being violated," Albrecht told the BBC in 2015. It is a feeling of "dis-ease," according to one report, "a lack of ease due to a hostile environment that a person is powerless to do anything about."[94]

There is a sense that pervades the post-Enlightenment world that all it will take is telling people the truth often enough, loudly enough, to make them change. That people will "believe the science" and join a movement to fight the planetary crisis, that they will see news reports of "fire-induced storms" or mass flooding or hurricanes where they shouldn't be and be moved to act. The Enlightenment narrative tells us that the experts and our leaders will figure things out and we should let them do it; our experience of the world tells us that the system those people and their ideas have built relies on super-exploitation and death and is in no way equipped to save us. That even if they did change right now, "committed warming," the cumulative effects of the past carbon-fueled centuries, would continue: "'Committed warming' is our history literally haunting us," Ajay Singh Chaudhary wrote. "The ghost of dead labor living on not only in commodities, but in 'externalities.'"[95]

But our leaders are not listening to the panicked demands of the climate movement. The people who make the decisions are approving more drilling for oil and squabbling over air quality policies. We are haunted not just by the actual disasters but by the hopelessness of being led by people stuck in a kind of death-drive "realism" that feels more unhinged with every day that passes. People who tell us that they are the reasonable ones while our homes burn.[96]

It is the people who work on climate crises every day to whom I turn when I feel despondent, and so I reached out to Xiomara Caro Díaz, director of the María Fund in Puerto Rico. "It feels like in Puerto Rico, our job, probably in the next couple of years, is being doulas of grief," she said. For her, there has been grief in abandoning one project to focus entirely on disaster relief; grief for María and then Fiona came, and all the old panic resurfaced. In those rapid-response moments, she noted, "it's much easier to reproduce patriarchy, colonialism, white supremacy, because in moments of deep fear and deep loss and deep grief, it's so much easier to put someone on a pedestal, to suddenly depend on one leader."

At the María Fund, she said, they've worked to change their culture, "so that we can be in relationship to take more risk, to be bigger in our visions, to be able to make more mistakes together." There is so little space to be OK with failure, she said, in part because the stakes are just so high. And yet grappling with that failure is part of the struggle.

In April 2023 I visited Camille Barbagallo and Nicholas Beuret on the farm where they live an hour-ish from London, and we ate home-grown vegetables while I quizzed them on the climate crisis. Longtime climate campaigners as well as partners, they were wary of so many of the common frameworks for discussing the planetary crisis: "I've really railed against the doom," Barbagallo said. She pointed to three emotions or, perhaps better, emotional states that drive climate politics: guilt, anxiety, and grief. People move among the three in ways that are difficult to articulate, and they are probably impossible states to transcend entirely. Rather, they are states we learn to manage, to live with, and to use.

Accepting that you are grieving, Barbagallo and Beuret suggested, is a part of accepting the situation, the planetary crisis. But acceptance, Barbagallo said, has to mean a refusal to give up rather than giving up. We do not,

Beuret said, grieve the climate as a whole: we grieve the people we lose, the place that is destroyed, the creatures killed. We grieve in horrible specificity. Yet social movements could be a collection point for all those horrible specificities, where we care for one another. *Grief is a (collective) becoming.*

It's guilt, Barbagallo suggested, rather than grief or anxiety, that prevents action and connection. Guilt that is individualizing, that tells us we have to personally expiate sin and results in us judging others who are insufficiently active, or acting but doing it wrong. "Neoliberal capitalism gives you huge amounts of boxes to tick. It enables you to offset your carbon this way. It enables you to think about all of the individual lifestyle solutions," she said. "And that's what's breeding the working-class rage. Because I don't think a huge amount of the working class feel much guilt in relation to the climate. They're like, 'We weren't in charge. We were in the mines having our kids grow up with fucking lung disease.'"

We have seen considerable backlash against climate policies that are built on the idea that we are all equally responsible for climate change. The Gilets Jaunes in France, sparked by an increase in fuel taxes, were a politically incoherent assemblage of people struggling with the spiking costs of everything and precisely that kind of rage that the crisis is not their goddamn fault. The movement spawned the catchphrase, "The elites talk about the end of the world, but we worry about the end of the month."[97]

Climate organizers responded with the slogan, "End of the world, end of the month, same fight!" The people who set the world on fire are the same ones who make money from your fuel costs skyrocketing. In 2022, British campaigners, including Barbagallo, kicked off the Don't Pay campaign with a pledge to refuse to pay energy bills if a million people signed up. Two hundred thousand did, an energy company called it an "existential" threat, and the government extended an energy price guarantee through the winter. But how much more power will be necessary to actually produce change? The Gilets Jaunes set cars afire and dropped them in tollbooths, riots have circled the globe, fuel protests erupted in Haiti and Mexico, and still the oil companies reported their "biggest annual profits ever" in the fourth quarter of 2022.[98]

Anxiety is anticipatory; the thing hasn't happened yet and maybe never will. It is different from the living-through. In the weeks and months and years after Hurricane Katrina, as Lydia Pelot-Hobbs wrote, time felt different. There was a constant feeling of emergency, that to rest was to miss opportunities or to lose people for good to the floodwaters, to exile, to the jails being built. Yet people needed rest and time to heal, as well.[99]

Without time to pause, we miss some of the catastrophes happening around us. We can miss the mass destruction of billions of creatures and plants all over the world. Sometimes we rely on them for food, for pollination, for ecosystem maintenance, and sometimes we think they're expendable. Wild things that know nothing of wage labor are still a part of our lives, Alyssa Battistoni argued: "Human beings need not just human care, but a lot of other kinds of beings and life and things to survive. The biospheric functions to keep the planet habitable for us—thus far—are comprised of all of these other kinds of creatures/beings. It is not a human-only, social-only enterprise, the work of keeping people alive." We owe these creatures some work of our own, some repair and regeneration of their worlds.[100]

We can care for the world around us, care as a practice and care as an emotional relationship. Many environmental activists, Nic Beuret suggested, are already motivated by a deep attachment to things that are not people. This can result in a kind of misanthropy, but it can also result in a deeper sense of interrelatedness, which poses a challenge to traditional politics, he said. Yet for the city dweller unused to sublime encounters with nature, can the grief be the same? Can you grieve something, he asked, "that you don't even know exists?"[101]

Unsurprisingly it is the people who live closest to the forms of nature being destroyed who wind up fighting the hardest to save them. The people of Standing Rock who started the fight for Mni Sose, the river; the women of the Niger Delta who have been fighting to save mangrove trees since 1984; the Indigenous nations who came together to win a historic and binding vote against oil drilling in the Yasuní biosphere reserve in Ecuador. In Oaxaca, Mexico, Meztli Yoalli Rodríguez Aguilera wrote of the slow death of the Chacahua lagoons, being destroyed by pollution and construction.

The people of the lagoons took care of the water and the land as they would a relation: "And it's very painful to see a loved one in front of your eyes that smells bad, that you cannot touch," Rodríguez explained.[102]

It was the loss of Rodríguez's mother and its attendant grief that led them to see what was happening as a form of grieving. Grief time led Rodríguez to pause, to understand that the people of the Chacahua lagoons were also grieving the loss of a form of home: "My mother meant home for me, for them, the lagoons mean home."[103]

Rodríguez's description of *slow life*, the way grief made them move differently, resonated with my own experience; it also brought me back to Bronislaw Szerszynski's description of drift, the middle voice, and the slow time of the world. Drift, Szerszynski wrote, built the world over billions of years, slowly settling and flowing into the shape we know. We need, he suggested, "to learn how to use drift without taming it—to drift in the middle voice, not always to subordinate it to our active-voice tendencies. We also need to learn how to drift well—which also means living in a way that makes the world safe for drifting things." In doing so, we will see more of the things around us as worth grieving in the first place. This is what Szerszynski called "a planetary ethic."[104]

Nature is at best a place to visit on holiday for so many humans; at worst, it's a site of value extraction for capitalists. It is an instrument for use, either for recreation or for production, always separated, always soulless, always inert. Yet we have never quite succeeded in getting rid of animism; it haunts us, the belief that the world itself might take revenge on us.[105]

Climate grief, Camille Barbagallo noted, is particularly uncomfortable for people just coming to terms with the idea that "mastering" nature might not just have been the wrong path but might have been genuinely impossible. And yet people across the climate movement in its various permutations have begun to turn away from Enlightenment dualism. The relentlessly rational Barbara Ehrenreich, in *Living with a Wild God* and again in *Natural Causes*, refused religion but defended the idea of a "world which seethes with life, with agency other than our own, and, at the very least, with endless possibility."[106]

And so I return to the orcas. I love them, but the idea that wild creatures were going to do the work of stopping the Capitalocene for us was always fanciful. And anyway I remain invested in a world with humans in it; we are not a virus to be eliminated, not inherently the problem just for being people. As I write this a fifth friend has just told me she is pregnant, and I am mentally scanning my yarn stash for things to make baby gifts for five babies that while not biologically mine are nevertheless my kin. I do not dream of a humanless planet or of leaving this one behind to terraform another. My life, those I love, human and nonhuman, are here.[107]

Climate chaos is something we will live with and that will change us but that will also be part of our everyday existence. It will be brutally normal punctuated with moments of calamity. It already is. And thus we need to learn to live sustainably in apocalyptic times. We need space for rest and care; we cannot wait until we have "won" for joy and love and life because there is no winning, there is just a dial to shift a little bit one way or the other. The reason we cannot stop, Josh Cohen stressed, is precisely the reason we must have pauses, breaks.[108]

"Do more" is the logic of capitalism, of endless growth. It is hard to escape it precisely because it has structured our world. But sometimes the solution is "do less," it is in fact "work less" and "consume less" and "produce less," it is Walter Benjamin's emergency brake on the voracious turning of the cycle. I think of the power produced by stopping. I think of the strike, always, of the workers in Flint sitting down in the GM plant and refusing to work, of the little social worlds produced on the picket line, of the pizza being reheated over an open fire outside the GM plant in New Jersey. Of Greta Thunberg and her school strike.[109]

Because in those strikes there is pleasure and joy produced at the same time as power. There is camaraderie and dancing and new forms of trust and desire and love that requires so little to sustain it other than a willingness to show up. There is a space created that you can leave and return to again. In the seizing back time from capital, there is time for everything else that has been denied us.

Break VI

I was never a child; I was always something different. A little construction of flash cards and expectations shuttled between preschool and art class and gymnastics and the local TV that came to film me reading a book at age three. Superbaby. Not a baby at all. A social experiment with twin ponytails and a squeaky voice.

The books helped though. I was reading adult books at nine and latching on to the wrong lessons. Turning the stories around and around in my head. Living in my head. My friends would get angry because I wanted two things from visiting their homes: their books and, if they had one, to play with their dog.

Animals made sense to me because of their big sweet guileless eyes. People were harder; they expected things of me but it wasn't always clear what. The flash cards and classes were easy enough: learn the right answer, repeat it. Figure out what's on the page and say it out loud; win praise. Animals too had rules of a sort, or they followed them anyway, trained like I had been for good behavior.

Horses were the thing I was best at, that made sense to me; riding was a team sport but teamed up with a creature that didn't need me to talk, rather than with kids my age who expected me to kid properly. Weird kid. Spooky kid. Queer (which was just schoolkid for *you're not like us* in the 1990s). Nerd. There was no more money for horses by the time I got really good at them, and so I scraped by and learned to hustle, ingratiate myself, perform differently. The world wasn't fair—my father's answer for everything when he changed the rules or the world did.

My first love looked at me like a horse did, like I might have had a treat for him.

We moved south and I left everything behind except my boxes of books and my taste for boys who knew how to play. *Life isn't fair.* My father drawing house plans and doing logic puzzles and paying our bills on credit. Me turning my energy back to being good at things, mostly at school, something I could control. That would help me to have control over my future, or at least that was the story I believed at the time. No longer desperate, just exhausted and alone. My family a thing I would never quite feel safe in though I still struggle to explain why.

I left home after home again and again and again in order to learn what I wanted to be.

But I got to be good at loving people somewhere along the way, turning outward to people as I had once to four-legged creatures, realizing that most of us feel odd in our skins and need someone to see our struggles. I learned to be a good friend and a good lover and a good partner and yes then again a good daughter, to anticipate needs when there weren't rules. To figure out which demands were too much.

What is it, really, to fall in love with someone? To be excited at their every message (letter/call/text/goddamn heart on a goddamn social media site), to navigate the space between thrilling unsure-ness, insecurity, and the absolute comfort of their presence. To fall asleep immediately next to them or to lie awake, alternately, to watch them and enjoy the pleasure of their warmth. What is it like to accept as Judith Butler wrote, that "we're undone by each other. And if we're not, we're missing something. If this seems so clearly the case with grief, it is only because it was already the case with desire"? To roll over and offer up yourself for the unmaking and the remaking.[1]

"It's like having your heart running around outside your body," a friend once joked about loving their dog, and their joke made me wonder how impossible loving a child must feel on top of that. But maybe the heart is always a thing constructed outside the body with those who are willing to join in. That, rather than a silly sentimental thing or an immaterial wish at best, love is, in Avery Gordon's words, "not mystical or a mystification; it is the intimacy of a contact with another, often asymmetrical, usually fragile and fraught with the strains of mastery. It is a prerequisite to sensuous knowledge."[2]

What does it mean to love and to stay? I had left so much all I wanted was someone who wouldn't leave me, and when my father got sick the first (no, second, really third) time, I clung to someone whose body felt deceptively solid but who did not actually see me, was always trying to give me gifts that I didn't want that he bought with my money. I left him when I realized there was more to love than staying.

And when my father got sick the last time, I realized that someone could be there and gone at the same time, that there are people in the world who can go through life without learning how to love the same way I had. That I would have to go through grieving alone, too.

The contradictions of grief: no one was able to go through it with me, and yet if I let them, the people who loved me would hold me as best they could as I was transformed. A lover whom I could not fix would help me see finally that I didn't need to fix him for him to love me. He taught me that staying could look many different ways, that he could still be there for me across an ocean, in ways that did not look like what I had thought love would be. He taught me to trust. Taught me that maybe I had never had to earn anyone's love in the first place, even my father's. That I could believe in the presence of care even when I could not see it.

To write about grief is to write about love, a thing I have accepted even though I am repulsed by so many of the cliches about grief and love. It is so easy to write insincerely about love because love like grief is something that defies the parts of speech we have, the tenses for action and the existence of a thing that one can touch and define. To love as to grieve is to drift. It is to learn to believe that beneath you is something that will hold you and carry you, something that cannot be constructed by labor or destroyed by it. Something that can and will undo you.

Everyone you love will fail you, and also everyone you love will die. In between are the moments when we can see and know and surprise each other, when we show up and we hold on and ease one another's hurts. But there is no love without pain or loss; this is what grief taught me.

Maybe the thing that grief taught me above all is that I never had anything but the slimmest illusion of control. Yet strength is something different from control and the power to do things; to survive the inevitable departures and shifts and losses comes from strength rather than control. Because we are always going to be undone by one another, this understanding could be the foundation of a different world.

To have hope for the future is to believe people and the world can change and yet that we will have no direct control over it, that we can only open ourselves to the process of loving and being undone by one another, that changing the world is a process that will require many of us imagining and struggling together. Like grief it is unending, an ongoing creation and tending and bringing together. It is only ever possible with others. It is a risk and it comes from the spaces between people, and it is the only way we will survive the ruins.

Conclusion

Walking with Ghosts

I do not remember what year it was that I first heard this particular chant, but I remember the room and the face of the organizer who taught it to us; he had learned it from Mexican comrades who dated it perhaps back to Mexico's revolution, to Emiliano Zapata and his fight for *tierra y libertad*, land and freedom. The organizer at the front of the room asked us all in turn to call out the name of someone from the various movements that had taught us, who had gone before us—he chose Ella Baker—and the rest of us would respond with the rest of the chant. *Ella Baker vive! La lucha sigue sigue!* We went around the room, invoking the dead to be with us as the struggle continued.[1]

Elsewhere, the call is simpler but the meaning the same: *presente!* I saw it repeated across the internet when the police shot young forest defender Manuel Esteban Paez Terán, known to most people as Tortuguita. Tortuguita was part of the movement to stop what has become known as Cop City, to protect the Weelaunee Forest from those who would destroy it to build a $90 million police training facility.[2]

We walk with ghosts of those who came before, and we hold a special place for those killed while fighting for justice, those whose deaths remind us what we are up against but whose lives remind us of the kind of world we want to live in. Mark Fisher—*presente!*—wrote that all the visored cops and tear gas (and bullets) were designed to prevent us from seeing the kind of world we could live in, the kind of world where care and joy were the products that mattered. If, Fisher suggested, following Herbert Marcuse, the brutalities of the past forty years, or indeed the past four hundred, have been about the "exorcising of 'the spectre of a world which could be free,'" then holding our ghosts close is an act of "unforgetting," a counter-exorcism, a bit of magic that opens us up to possibilities.[3]

So we learn to live with ghosts. We learn to live in these contradictions because they are the basic contradictions of modern life and perhaps even of life itself. We live, every day, with the unlivable.[4]

To write is always, I think, to write ghost stories. Certainly, to write history is. To write this book was to excavate graves and filter through dust and reopen my wounds, and it was to sit with people while they reopened their own wounds in the hopes that the bleeding would help still others to understand what they had lost.[5]

Writing is also the process of breathing life back into that which has been rendered inert, commodified. It is an attempt at re-enchanting one part of the world. It is an attempt to create what has barely existed before, which is to say justice. What would justice for Tortuguita look like? What kind of justice are your ghosts asking of you?[6]

Grieving is a kind of sensuous knowledge, a materialist grappling with the immaterial. It is something inevitable that nevertheless often results from a great harm, a great wrong done, the making-surplus of so many lives to keep the machines of growth chugging along. We must both let grief happen to us and recommit ourselves, if possible, to righting that injustice. Let it welcome us to the struggle. Because *even the dead will not be safe from the enemy if he wins.*[7]

We live in a time of collapse, of ecosystems, political parties and orthodoxies that had held for decades or even centuries.

One collapse triggers another. The COVID pandemic set off not only shock waves in supply chains but also strikes and worker organizing, demands once again to have a say in the production process and not to be treated as machine parts but as breathing humans who want to keep one another safe. Collapsing countries send migrants across the world, who bring new stories and new ideas to the places they land. The collapsing industrial job helped destabilize the gender roles that so many people had come to believe were natural, making space for an efflorescence of experiments with gender and sexuality to happen in public. And each of these movements has its backlash, which clings to fear and to denial and to a violent hope that things might simply stay the same.[8]

"Sometimes it feels like we are just a generation of grief," Xiomara Caro Díaz told me. "We are sitting in the rubble of so many things." The struggle to survive amid the wreckage leaves us little time, after all, for imaginings of any type. Human lives feel so fragile against the monsters we face.[9]

But it is our very fragility, our vulnerability in the midst of collapse, that can show us a different way. Our grief and rage can inspire motion; our pain and loss can bind us together. Our very lack of control over our lives, our bodies, is the thing that reminds us what is at stake. If we accept that our lives are precarious, that we are all surplus and all ghosts, we can build spaces and lives around this fact rather than around disposal.[10]

We can, looking at the multiple states of emergency all around us, drive ourselves to exhaustion, to a kind of martyrdom that sees working ourselves to death as heroic, as long as it is "for the cause." But a system that cares nothing for our individual lives will not be put down by our heroic deaths.[11]

It is here where grief time can teach us something. Because grief time is stretched and squeezed, because it is circular and shifting rather than linear, it provides a challenge to the straight-ahead modes of progress, standardized and clock bound, that capitalism brought to our lives. It requires us to think and move in the rhythms of human vulnerability and limits, to understand that we need other people to cover the gaps when we need a pause, to look out for one another as we step up and step back.[12]

It is those collectivities that provide consolation in moments of setback and defeat, of loss. Ciara Taylor told me that she returns, with comrades, to Frederick Douglass's speech after the Supreme Court's *Dred Scott* decision upholding yet again chattel slavery as the law of the land. Douglass argued that rather than "settling" the question of slavery once and for all, the decision signaled opportunity for the abolitionists: "The fact is, the more the question has been settled, the more it has needed settling. The space between the different settlements has been strikingly on the decrease." Over and over, and in increasingly, uneasily strident terms, the issue was declared dead precisely because the movement was growing. "We have to understand these setbacks as the ruling class pushing back against us because we are gaining ground," Taylor said.[13]

Antonio Gramsci wrote from a fascist prison at a similar moment of interregnum, when the power, the right, of the rulers to rule was in question yet people everywhere struggled to see through the fog. The old common sense—what we now might call capitalist realism—was fractured, the powerful holding onto their power through brutality more than consent. We know what happened in Gramsci's Italy and across Europe and the world, but the results of our own time have yet to be determined. We reach back over and over again for Gramsci's words: "The crisis consists precisely in the fact that the old is dying and the new cannot be born; in this interregnum a great variety of morbid symptoms appear."[14]

Sometimes, this is mistranslated as "now is the time of monsters."[15]

Gramsci was sent to prison for having been the leader of the Communist Party, locked up not simply for opposing fascism but for advocating an entirely different world and for laying out strategies for how to get there. At the trial that would send him to the prison that would destroy his health and kill him shortly after his release, the prosecutor famously insisted, "We must stop this brain working for twenty years!" When I first heard this I got choked up; today, again, writing it, it makes me want to cry. They did and did not succeed in stopping him. His *Prison Notebooks* are widely read and quoted today, yet he died before those twenty years were up.[16]

Fascism required blood sacrifice, thrived and thrives on a romanticized view of brutality and death of which Gramsci's was not by far the worst. Fascism is the process of not only rendering certain lives ungrievable but in fact making their ending something to celebrate. And so it recurs, in greater or lesser proportions, wherever the deaths that a capitalist society requires cannot be fully moved out of sight. And so it is coming back now.[17]

It is, of course, not often called fascism when it returns. It may not look exactly like the thing that came before. It comes wrapped in nostalgia for past glory and a thing that looks like grief. It longs for sovereignty (as death) and the power of ethnic purity and masculinity, which is to say it longs for domination that is both imagined as natural and also must be reinscribed with violence. It grows out of collapse and offers to alleviate the fears that collapse brings. As Peter Mitchell wrote, "We escape the trauma of the history we happen to be living through by entering the mythic time of the history we didn't."[18]

It is a fantasy but one that is compelling because at least on some level it acknowledges grief before shrinking it into grievance. Fascists, too, I learned in writing this book, memorialized their dead with *presente*, the word the same in Italian and Spanish. If grief is unruly, undisciplined, unmanageable, and sometimes unintelligible—if sometimes we do not know precisely what it is we are grieving—the energies that can be harvested are enormous. They can be turned toward justice or brutality.[19]

In a society where grief has been foreclosed so much of the time, which cannot deal with loss, a lot of people confuse a feeling of discomfort for unsafety and exercise their power to put other people in an actual position of unsafety. Because their discomfort is the worst they can imagine feeling. They rage: at Black people demanding justice, at migrants asking admittance at the border, at the loss of jobs that upheld a certain kind of masculinity, at the request that they wear masks to avoid the spread of COVID, at the idea that fossil-fueled consumption might have to change to avoid planetary catastrophe. Sometimes they turn to conspiracy theories to justify this rage, other times just outright denial.[20]

The first time I went to Indiana, in 2016, I met Tom Lewandowski, a longtime organizer who had watched his community tilt further and further right. "Bad bosses and totalitarians create spaces between people. Donald Trump is probably both," he told me. Trumpism and other right-wing movements offered emotional representation rather than material, they gave resentments a name and a shape. Resentment, Mark Fisher suggested, "is a form of anti-solidarity," or negative solidarity, an anger solely at the fact that someone else is getting what we think we should get. It divides, as Lewandowski said.[21]

Apocalypse and utopia, China Miéville reminded us, have always been intertwined. The good life for some made possible by the immiseration of others. Death for the grunts, the foot soldiers, while those at the commanding heights of power aim to conquer mortality itself. The obsession of not a few of today's tech titans (and right-wing power funders), is to render death obsolete. Peter Thiel and Jeff Bezos, Sergey Brin and Jack Dorsey all pour their wealth into technologies that promise to reverse or halt aging; the hot new ideology is "longtermism," which suggests that humans can in fact become "posthuman," digital beings rather than biological. The ultimate separation of human from nature: the body just another programmable machine. Where this overlaps with fascisms old is the idea that any kind of brutality might be justifiable in the present to ensure that this future utopia might come about.[22]

Perhaps it was not a coincidence that one of the blockbuster films of the summer of 2023 was *Oppenheimer*, the story of the Jewish physicist with communist leanings who shepherded the nuclear bomb into existence to defeat the Nazis. Much was made, in the film, of Oppenheimer's invocation of the Bhagavad Gita, the line "I am become death, destroyer of worlds." Onscreen, the words haunt him. Offscreen, the billionaires continue world destroying, confident that they or their digital ghosts will be able to shoot off to another world when they're done. In 2021, Jeff Bezos brought *Star Trek* star William Shatner to the edge of space in his *Blue Origin* rocket, and when they landed, as Shatner began to speak to cameras about what he'd felt, Bezos interrupted him to shake up and spray a bottle of champagne everywhere.[23]

Shatner later wrote of his trip, "I discovered that the beauty isn't out there, it's down here, with all of us. Leaving that behind made my connection to our tiny planet even more profound. It was among the strongest feelings of grief I have ever encountered. The contrast between the vicious coldness of space and the warm nurturing of Earth below filled me with overwhelming sadness. Every day, we are confronted with the knowledge of further destruction of Earth at our hands: the extinction of animal species, of flora and fauna . . . things that took 5bn years to evolve, and suddenly we will never see them again because of the interference of mankind. It filled me with dread."[24]

Mutual aid practices kept people alive during COVID lockdowns and uprisings and in the Weelaunee Forest. Street medics trained in protest movements treated wounds from police batons and pepper spray and the normal bumps and bruises of collective life; they mediated conflicts and protected one another. Those skills transferred to disaster relief, in the wake of Hurricane Sandy and elsewhere, as medics worked in tandem with professional nurses going door to door to meet people's health needs while they were stuck inside. "Medicing is not just physical care. The quiet emotional work matters just as much," medic Riley Clare Valentine wrote. "Effectively responding to authoritarianism requires a form of care that is informed by the past to build a radical future." Street medics, they noted, trace their history back to the civil rights movement, to healthcare networks built by the Black Panthers to provide care to their communities, for survival pending revolution.[25]

Mutual aid also keeps people alive when crossing deserts and oceans to find a new home. People provide care in a recognition of common humanity in moments of need. It is a recognition of our obligation to each other and to the world.[26]

I like to think of solidarity as a form of care. In a chapbook I wrote with Melissa Gira Grant, she defined it as "power and love, directed," and I still believe that, but I would add that it is relational, it requires a showing up, it requires a doing rather than just saying or being. It is a continuous practice that makes our care powerful, that allows the direction that makes it political.[27]

Care is difficult. It is risky. At times, yes, it is work. It is also an emotion that drifts. It has its middle voice. We may have many words for the activities and feelings that fall under the umbrella of care.

The distance between what the capitalist system promises and what it provides is most obvious, I think, when we discuss care because it is not so easily defined and confined. It leaks. Nurses and doctors develop relationships that go beyond billable hours. Care requires time that expands. A radical care practice is one that recognizes in these challenges a place to expand precisely where the demands of the working world would have us contract. It understands all of us as kin.[28]

Care and its attendant obligations trouble our ideas of identity. Our boundaries. We cannot be wholly individual, wholly on our own. We can try to draw lines around the people we owe care to, but those lines too are easily traversed. Care is not biologically determined; often our supposed blood family fails us, and we rely on others: we make kith, not kin. We cannot care equally about everyone in the world, but it is possible, potentially, to care intensely, desperately, for anyone.[29]

Against a world that would splinter us into groups and make those groups unequally vulnerable, radical care crosses borders. The Black Panthers' ambulances picked up poor white people who were also neglected by the formal healthcare system. Rescue ships in the Mediterranean save people from the waters without asking where they are from or why they are there. Antiracist practices of care refuse the distinction between people while also recognizing that there are reasons why Black and brown people have been left needing more.[30]

Making new structures of care is a process of building relationships and networks and practices and spaces that can deal with all the contradictory messiness of life. The people who have cared for me in my worst moments have been part of something ugly and rough and terrifying; the care I have given in someone else's worst moments has made them push me away, embarrassed or ashamed at what I had seen. We care sometimes for the ungrateful and the cruel, we witness the awful and the shocking. I held a basin under my father's mouth as he vomited, as he was unable to hold it himself and wished like anything—I could see it in his eyes—that he had never needed that. I held a lover while he panicked and reassured him over and over that he was not *work*. It was hard and it was ugly and it was the only thing worth doing.[31]

Witnessing grief, Sophie Lewis wrote, "is an ancient form of mutual aid" based on the understanding that we will all grieve someday. Our world, though, has so few infrastructures for grieving; in community, we must and do make our own. We demand the right to grieve, which is a right to our time, but it goes beyond that. It is a demand that labor not subordinate life and love to work. A society that makes room for grief, its ebbs and flows, is a society that makes room for all the uneven messiness of life. It is one that has room for care and for falling in love as well as the heartbreak of loss.[32]

The most powerful organizing happens not amid small groups of friends, though those small groups are often how something is sparked; the real strength comes when we are able to reach across distance and difference to stand together anyway. Care-driven organizing requires us to provide for people's needs whether we agree with or love or even like them; it requires getting to the root causes of the thing that caused them harm. It requires us to hold one another as we fight.[33]

Cultures of political organizing have changed in recent years to center care, to be more welcoming and holistic. Mariame Kaba noted that at the mosque she attended, new people are greeted by name, welcomed in: their losses are acknowledged, their successes celebrated. Movement spaces that take this into account, that consider what is now called "healing justice," are stronger for the long haul.

The miners' union halls provided such a space for everyone. The union was where you did everything—birthdays, holiday celebrations, football. Gramsci studied the Catholic Church not because he was a believer (he was not) but because it was a structure that accompanied people their whole lives; he wanted the Communist Party to emulate that, to be not just a political home but a place of support for people in their times of need. Such accompaniment is what matters too to Kaba: "What I can offer people anytime, doesn't matter if it's good or bad, but I could accompany them."[34]

Can social movements then build spaces that hold those cycles of rest and celebrations of life, commemoration of loss, spaces that are connected to the struggle but not the place where it happens? Can the movement hold the moments that are not work? Donna Haraway suggested, "Our task is to make trouble, to stir up potent response to devastating events, as well as to settle troubled waters and rebuild quiet places." A movement must, I think, be able to do all of the above, but to discern where and when each reaction is called for. Because those moments of grief are messy and often not a good place to begin strategizing; they are a car on fire, a necessary expression, a primal scream. They can bring great power, can inspire, but grief demands tending before it can be harnessed.[35]

Work—even movement work—can be a place where we drown our feelings, but grief refuses to be drowned. It is too much like water itself, flowing around and over the obstacles we place in its way.[36]

Capitalist society has pathologized grief in order to shrink it, to insinuate that it is a problem and that if we insist on feeling it, we are the problem. Jess Kuttner, a therapist, nonetheless told me that she thinks that grief doesn't belong in therapy but in community: "People need support and care and tending, and that's normal." If we construe the world along lines of diagnoses and pathology versus "normal" life, we are missing something profound about being human. "We're communal beings. We should be heartbroken for each other."[37]

Ritual was something that was growing increasingly important to Ciara Taylor's work at the time we spoke. "Ritual is this expression of consciousness, which is undergirded by our conditions," she said. Some rituals are unconscious, habits, structures of feeling we've inherited; others, like saying the Pledge of Allegiance in a classroom, pushed on us. "We've been thinking a lot about alternate ways. What are the rituals that actually benefit us? That lift up the values and the principles of those who are hurting, which is most of us." Rituals of grief that can be incorporated into protest but that are also necessary on a more personal level. That are mutual aid, that build relationships, that strengthen us for living through collapse, because we do not know yet where we are in the struggle, how much more disappointment we must survive.

Rituals that celebrate, that lift up values and principles, that build and strengthen relationships have an essential place in a disenchanted world, where people are seeking meaning that can be separated from the ordinary processes of getting by. They can provide a kind of abundance amid scarcity, a kind of spirituality that is rooted in the here and now rather than what the Industrial Workers of the World used to call "pie in the sky when you die."

The change we want to see in the world begins in the spaces where we claim for ourselves the right to care and be cared for outside of the boundaries of the workplace, the demands of paying the rent. It is in those spaces that we keep alive the possibility of a better world.

What I mean here, I think, is a kind of fugitive care, fugitive grieving, salvaged from the wreckage. It is imperfect, rugged, at times chaotic, a living experiment. It is the process of even temporarily abolishing the present state of the world to hold possibilities.[38]

Love and grief and care show us the power of the middle voice, of the intertwined-ness of object and subject. Of the power of the things we don't understand and will never control. Of how intimacy and connection are resistant to structures of power and knowledge that insist on such order. How vulnerability to one another is a form of strength.[39]

One of the things that grief taught me is that no care, no love, is exactly reciprocal. The way I showed up for my father before his death is not the way that he took care of me as a child; I could not care for the people who looked after me when grief was new to me the way they cared for me so I paid it forward; I held others the way I had not been but had wanted to be held. When someone apologized to me for needing such care I told him, "Let me do for you what no one did for me." Because pain and life chances are not equally distributed, neither is our need for care—*to each according to their needs*. I return to philosopher Eva Kittay's concept of *doulia*, a play on the word "doula" and a concept of interdependence rather than pure reciprocity. It is an ideal for a society in which caregivers are cared for in turn, because the work they do benefits us all.[40]

Rupa Marya and Raj Patel noted that the English word "care" "has its origins in the Gothic *karôn*, 'to lament, to grieve.'" This root should remind us that care is not fluffy and soft, though it is sometimes beautiful and always necessary. Because as I have written, grief contains within it more than sadness, just as care contains within it more than kindness. And so for a moment I want to return to rage and even to hate. It is not simply that if we love one another enough, capitalism will wither and die, or that we must simply turn the other cheek and forgive all wrongs in order to desire the end of prisons and police. There are structures that need to be torn down and people who uphold those structures, and anger as much as love needs to be directed. Anger, someone once told me, is self-respect. Rage is not always strategic, but it can be, still, life giving.[41]

The car on fire with which I opened this book reminds us that there is destruction necessary to build the world we want. After the emergency brake is pulled, the train and its tracks must be dismantled. I think here too grief has something to teach us about the complicated feelings that come with letting go, about releasing that which has hurt us. Confrontation is necessary, to clear space for justice.[42]

I have argued here that grief is a necessary part of life, a painful yet transformative experience that deserves its space and time and respect and care.

But the amount of misery, the violence and cruelty of this world, the premature death all around us—this is not necessary. This, I think, we can change. The radical project is to accept that death and grief are inevitable but not let that be an excuse to ignore all the preventable horrors, or rather to be motivated to tell the difference between the inevitability of mortality and the brutality of racial capitalism.

A transformative politics, then, a socialism or communism worth the name, would be interested in expanding the range of "emotional freedom" alongside the material, because it would recognize the two as intertwined. The realm of emotional freedom begins where the realm of necessity ends; we must have time and our needs met in order to experience the rich spectrum of emotions that come with a full and connected life. We could protect one another's vulnerability while accepting the inevitability of that vulnerability, able to risk more emotional entanglements precisely because our bodily survival is assured.[43]

Caring for one another is part of this process. Becoming a caregiver teaches us that there is something desperately wrong with the way capitalist society allocates value and time. It insists that we make friends with our mortality.[44]

I cannot honestly write here that I have made peace with mine. At times it leaves me breathless, panicked, still. I have the ordinary vanities of a woman in her forties, aware that the world around me places different value on an aging woman. Grief still tears me apart at times. But it has taught me patience that I never had and acceptance of a strange kind; it has allowed me to see the way the people around me show up for me, to recognize the ways I am loved. To let go of my desire for control. Grief has taught me to live with the knowledge that I can be undone at any moment, and to live alongside the fear.[45]

As I have aged I have had to become comfortable with the idea that I may not live to see the better world I work to bring about. That the struggle does not depend on any one person is something I have long known; it is a knowledge that has brought me a kind of peace. On my bedroom wall hangs a print that reads, "Do not be daunted by the enormity of the world's grief. You are not obligated to complete the work, but neither are you free to abandon it." It is a line from Jewish rabbinical teachings, and it reminds me that I am one of many, that the struggle continues without me.[46]

The value of all the lives around me, before me and after me—not in some hypothetical calculable way but the connections that I can see, my young niece as she sings at the top of her lungs the words of musicians who are her grandmother's age—this is what keeps me going. We are always, in one sense or another, salvaging something from the brief time that we have. People will always get sick and die. We will break each other's hearts; we will move and change. Grief is inevitable. It is part of what it means to be human. Only in a society that makes no room for this reality does grief become revolutionary.[47]

Because we live in a time when the gap between promise and fulfillment is so large, when the state offers nothing but cruelty and walls and closes its eyes to our illness, rationalizes mass death, and capital picks up shop and leaves us unable to pay our way, when the natural world itself seems to be seeking revenge, we are, I think, feeling particularly vulnerable. We are constantly imagining the end of the world and worrying about the end of the month. In this time we have a choice: to cling to crumbling structures that will collapse and bury us, or to hold on to each other while we pick our way through the rubble. We can mourn as we build something else.[48]

I think of Palestinian people in Gaza, pulling one another from the rubble left by Israeli bombs. I am haunted, like, I think, everyone who saw it, by a video of a young girl on a stretcher carried by several men. She asks them, "Am I being taken to the cemetery?" and one of the men replies, "No, love, here you are, you're alive, and beautiful like the moon!" I return again and again to the defiant insistence on life, on beauty amid the ruins, the word so many of us learned as we counted days and then weeks and then months of destruction: *sumud*, steadfastness, through horrors that most of my readers will never suffer. Hala Alyan explained, "The idea of *sumud* has become a multifaceted cultural concept among Palestinians: it means steadfastness, a derivative of 'arranging' or 'saving up', even 'adorning.' It implies composure braided with rootedness, a posture that might bend but will not break."[49]

The people we meet amid the ruins may not be the ones we would have chosen. I do not know if the man in the video knew the girl he comforted, only that he did it with practiced care. We may be hailed by our neighbors, coworkers, the person we pass on the street who asks for a favor, a coin, a hand. One of the challenges of building a politics for collapse is that working across difference is hard. It requires patience and forgiveness and generosity and learning. It requires care for the immediate needs of others and also for the needs that span generations. It requires this kind of composure amid destruction, to salvage what we can.[50]

After this kind of rupture the future is uncertain, as is the map from here to there. But people have done it before, risked everything to make a better world, and sometimes they have even succeeded.[51]

I think our struggles will be about homes and care and the thing we call "supply chains" but that are in fact people doing work. They will be about removing bottlenecks in access to basic needs and about surviving the floods and fires and bombs. They will be about who will pay for capitalist destruction. They will be about forcing the powerful to concede something to the rest of us.[52]

The struggles will generate fierce opposition: fascists and the rest of the far right and even ordinary neoliberalism will resist giving up their resource hoards as fiercely as any fairy-tale dragon, even when those hoards are fairy tales as well.[53]

There are way stations being built in the ruins right now. In Minneapolis, Inquilinxs Unidxs Por Justicia has its housing cooperative and its office building on George Floyd Square, shared with CTUL. Their work is a process, Jen Arnold told me, of building pieces of the world they want to see along the way, of building material infrastructures of resistance that then can expand. Sisters Uncut occupied an empty council flat in Hackney, East London, bringing together the community to work on collective solutions to "Islamophobic street attacks, harassment by transphobes, beatings by abusive partners, assaults by cops, and violent evictions," all the everyday dehumanizations of life at this point on the clock of capitalism. It was messy and confrontational, but it built something new. This is the everyday making of abolition, of making the world in the conditions we were given, not the ones we chose.[54]

In Puerto Rico, Xiomara Caro Díaz was also thinking about the kinds of organizations that could hold failure and loss and grief. The kinds of movements that have space to dance and that have support for people to step away when they need to mourn. She dreamed, she told me, of organizing a march of the dead. To let go of the idea that you can solve everything by endless work, she suggested, might make it more likely that you figure out how to change something. Working in the ruins requires an ability to admit when things are not working, when they have failed. In a world full of expectations of endless progress, it can feel impossible to admit to setbacks and disappointments, but learning from loss is necessary. An organization that holds space for people to just be people is more likely not to lose its members when they face loss.[55]

The work that I saw in Puerto Rico, in London, in Minneapolis, and elsewhere was taking place in what Rodrigo Nunes called a movement ecology. Each group had in different ways accepted a version of Caro's insight, acting on a piece of the problem and thereby expanding the possibilities for others, in their neighborhoods and in the world. In Minneapolis, tenant organizers and labor organizers shared space and joined the street uprising and the precinct occupation; unions financially supported community organizations, and teachers joined their students in protests. Thinking ecologically is not only thinking about the needs of the planet but also thinking about the relationships we already have and the ones we want to build, the way our political and economic actions affect one another. Thinking of ourselves and others not as leaders and followers but as people who at any time might lead and always have something to learn.[56]

Admitting we do not know the answers—that I certainly do not—we can nevertheless make what Nunes called "strategic wagers," educated guesses as to what types of action will connect with the most people, where the pressure points can be.[57]

The path ahead is bumpy and full of twists around which we cannot see and events we cannot control. In moments of uprising, of mass strikes and rebellions, we construct new paths and new connections, new forms of consciousness, even that nebulous thing called "class consciousness." If you have come this far with me and still flinch at this word, consider that the week I wrote this, before the United Auto Workers went on strike, an Australian capitalist called publicly for "pain in the economy" to "remind people that they work for the employer, not the other way around." What he called "arrogance" in the labor market was only the earliest sprout, post-pandemic, of a real class consciousness, but he was determined to root it out. (He later apologized, but his is not a rare view, only rare in how bluntly and publicly he expressed it.) The capitalists already have class consciousness; they always have. Because capital requires a group that is subjugated, a lesser caste. Their vision of the world is the world as it is, only we grovel more.[58]

So let's dream of a world otherwise. Such dreams are born in moments of rupture; they are inspired by loss. They are emotional as well as intellectual, irrational in their beauty. They come amid the flames and floodwaters, in conversations in police vans. They come, as Saidiya Hartman wrote, from "waywardness and the refusal to be governed." From moments of excess and overwhelm, from insisting on living in the ruins. Grief is excessive; so is revolution. It is a defiant *yes* when the rest of the world would say no. It is a refusal of the foreclosing of our time, an overflowing of humanity into the places where it is forbidden. We will not be machines anymore.[59]

That such visions are born from ruin is, I think, what makes them possible. It is a salvage communism we can imagine now (a term that I take from the *Salvage* magazine collective). It is a project of worldmaking from the pieces that we have been left.[60]

Walter Benjamin at his most messianic understood that what I have called grief time is a pause that contains endless possibility. Our time is filled with so much bullshit, but grief time, in my experience, while it enveloped me in fog also seemed to tear away the spell that made bullshit seem worthwhile. I wanted, rather than to rebuild the cracked foundations, to blast the whole thing to hell.[61]

* * *

I want to return to love as I close. I want to return to the people I found in the wreckage of my life and the people who held out their scarred hands to me from my past. After I finished writing I went for a walk and bought supplies for Rosh Hashanah—because it was, that evening, the Jewish New Year—and had a wander through the parts of South London I love the most. I paused in a park where I had gone first with a person who has been picking up pieces of me since he met me, and I sat on a bench and hit shuffle on the playlist that I made for this book, and the song that came up was called "Be and Bring Me Home," and I thought of what it means to be home, what it means to miss someone, the difference between heartache and heartbreak and grief. And because the universe is perverse and sometimes magic, I looked at my phone as I left the park, and he had texted me a heart and an apology for something infinitesimally small in the scale of the rubble we have walked through together.[62]

That night I poured honey on apples sliced sideways to show the star in their heart and toasted with pomegranate seeds in wine and tore bread and tossed it in the river alongside people I love, and I said goodbye to the old year and made wishes for the new. Because every new year brings with it endless possibility for love and loss, for heartbreak and mourning. For the opportunity to live otherwise, to know in our bones that alternatives exist.[63]

The rituals of the New Year are always in their way grief rituals. One of the phrases that Jewish people use at times of mourning is "May their memory be for a blessing," an acknowledgment that the dead are gone but they are also with us. In recent years in the streets I have heard a permutation on this ancient wish, one that has come back to me over and over again. And so I say here, to close, remembering all the people we have lost, the names too numerous to say here, the fathers sisters cousins lovers brothers friends, the ancestors we claim for ourselves: may their memory be for a revolution.

Acknowledgments

Writing a book is never really a solitary endeavor, but this one felt more solitary than most. And yet as I read back through it and work through edits, I could see on every page the conversations, the arguments, the support, and the losses that shaped it. And so it is not an exaggeration to say that writing the acknowledgments is my favorite part of the process.

Let me begin with all the wonderful people at Bold Type Books, some of whom have been with me since that very first meeting that became my very first book. Clive Priddle, who took over the daunting task of editing me and wrangling my prose into shape: thank you for your eagle eye and years of support. Jaime Leifer, Jocelynn Pedro, and Lindsay Fradkoff have also been with me for years of this journey and have remained excited about my work even when I wasn't. Pete Garceau made my cover pretty, and Miguel Cervantes made sure everyone saw it. Thanks to Annie Chatham for shepherding me through production, and Carrie Watterson provided thoughtful copy edits that were a pleasure (a rarity in this industry). Work may never love any of us back, but working with all of you is as good as it gets.

Sarah Burnes, gem of agents, brought me much needed cool mom energy, reminded me to rest rather than force myself to work, and talked me off many a ledge. Katy O'Donnell taught me how to write a book and though no longer my editor remains a dear friend.

The Type Media Center too supported me from that first meeting that led to that first book: thank you endlessly to Taya McCormick-Grobow and everyone who works and has worked there over the years. Thank you to the Lannan Foundation for so many of those years.

Alissa Quart and the Economic Hardship Reporting Project also gave me crucial backing for reporting that gave me the idea for this book. Rosie Warren first asked me if I wanted to write something about grief and John McDonald followed up and *Salvage* published that first piece, a thousand thank-yous to both of you and to the entire *Salvage* collective, and I hope you forgive me for making "salvage" also a cornerstone of this book. Matt Seaton too commissioned my thinking on grief, and the folks at the *Progressive*, who have given me a regular outlet, have published several pieces that dealt with this theme: thanks to Norman Stockwell, David Boddiger, Emilio Leanza, Bill Lueders, Allie Tempus.

To other editors who continue to commission and support and improve my reporting and writing: Ari Bloomekatz, David Dayen, Paula Finn, Don Guttenplan, David Marcus, Laura Marsh, David O'Neill, Lizzy Ratner, and Jessica Stites. A special thanks to Natasha Lewis and everyone at *Dissent* for backing *Belabored* for so long and continuing to let me run wild in your pages with pieces that no one else would understand.

Namwali Serpell sent me an article on "drift" that helped me crystallize my thinking on grief, as well as writing one of the most beautiful novels on the subject I've ever read.

To the friends and comrades I'm still grieving: Dan Clawson, Niema Ross-Ferguson, Jessica Munyon, Kacie New, Anne Marie Reinhart, Dawn Foster.

Barbara Ehrenreich and Mike Davis passed while I was writing this book; one I knew slightly, the other not at all, but both led the kinds of lives and did the kind of work I aspire to.

And to the people who worked with my father and me way back when: Fred, Armando, Tony, Jonathan, Travis, Sean, everyone who made it bearable.

Dr. Melanie McKay introduced me to Hélène Cixous and Judith Butler way back in 2001.

I am deeply grateful to everyone who spoke to me for this book, more so perhaps than any before because what I asked of all of you was so personal. But some of you were more than just interlocutors, you were fixers, comrades, and friends. Yirna Buitrago, Chuckie Denison, Kate Flannery, Nate Holdren, Francesca Nava, Tim O'Hara, Cat Salonek, Cal Soto, Ciara Taylor, Maricela Torres, Kristin Urquiza, and last but very much not least Viktoria Zerda. Others who didn't make it into the pages by name but who made invaluable connections both intellectual and personal: Daphne Carr, Andrea Dehlendorf, Sofia Gualandi, Josh Keller, Ally Swadling and everyone at PAFRAS, Chris Newman at NDLON. Carinne Luck, Nelini Stamp, and Kelly Hayes for talking early pandemic grief with me and the rituals you made. Trish Kahle and Ewan Gibbs for helping me think through coal. MaryGrace DiMaria, Josh Cohen, and Jess Kuttner (and Robert Kuttner for making the introduction) were my guides to thinking about Freud, psychotherapy, and grief. Malkia Devich-Cyril for inviting me to Pandemic Joy and sharing your own grief journey with me, and Maria Poblet for introducing us. Camille Barbagallo and Nic Beuret (and Azadi and Bastian!) for hosting me and my questions. Alice Pettit for opening your home to me without question and introducing me to your entire community, and Amira, for sharing your mom with me. Francesca Coin for continuing to give me reasons to come back to Italy.

And a special thank-you to Mariame Kaba for being a friend, a comrade, sounding board, moral compass, and beacon of clarity at the darkest times. Like everyone who has the good fortune of knowing you, I have a set of Mariame-isms that I repeat to myself when I'm stressed and share with others, little kernels of gold. I'm so glad you're in this book and in my life.

Terry Cramer, for keeping me sane.

I have, I think, the best group(s) of friends and comrades in the entire damn world, and as always I am probably not even mentioning everyone I could. This is not a brag, it's the deepest gratitude. For a start, thank you to Nihal Al-Aasar, Anthony Arnove, Kate Bahn, Alyssa Battistoni, Stella Beccaril, Gargi Bhattacharyya, K. Biswas, Grace Blakeley, Edna Bonhomme, Matt Bors, Maurice BP-Weeks, Sarah Brouillette, Mary Clinton, Arielle Cohen, Brenda Coughlin, Molly Crabapple, Stacy Dobrinsky, Veena Dubal, Sarah Feld, Helen G., Yoni Golijov, Malcolm Harris, Amelia Horgan, Clare Hymer, Mindy Isser, Sarah Jones, Laleh Khalili, Zack Lerner, Sophie Lewis, Odette Lindsay, Max Loizo, Geo Maher, Sally Mercedes, Joanne McNeil, Kate O'Shea, Eleanor Penny, Kareem Rabie, Rebecca Rojer, Ryley Rubin, Stuart Schrader, Eleni Schirmer, Charlotte Shane, Susan Shepard, Nikhil Pal Singh, Quinn Slobodian, s. e. smith, Ben Smoke, Astra Taylor, Christy Thornton, Ronald Wimberly, Todd Wolfson, and Sarah Woolley.

Zoe Samudzi, thanks for always being up for talking about fascism. Janice Cable for the road trip. Laura Flanders for encouraging me at every turn. Ashon Crawley always reminds me to think otherwise (and makes me laugh). Colin Smith, it's good to know you again. Kieron Gillen, it's good to be so well known for so long—you remind me who I am. Ajay Chaudhary for all the Walter Benjamin; John Paetsch for advice on Deleuze that I promptly ignored; Dan Denvir and Thea Riofrancos for years of comradeship and good advice; Patrick Blanchfield and Abby Kluchin for all the Freud (and evidence to back up my suspicions); Adelaide and the *Season of the Bitch* podcast coven for making me think about gothic Marxism; Gareth Forest for conferences and very good wine because nothing is too good for the working class; Nica Siegel for talking through exhaustion, grief, and losing; Shaun Harkin and Becca Barnes for welcoming me to Derry over and over again, and Aodhan and Ronan too; Ray Malone for theater and local hags and Venice; the Planet B productions crew for indulging me; Philip Proudfoot and Mahdi Zaidan for always having a spare room for me and the best secret gift ever; Adam Elliott-Cooper for thinking through Gramsci; Gary McQuiggin for the gators; Rodrigo Nunes for whatever the opposite of left melancholia is; Joshua Clover, for pushing me to better adjectives and sharper thinking; Michelle Chen for many many years of *Belabored* and for not giving up; and Jane McAlevey for being a force of nature and embodying so many struggles I write about in this book.

To the New Orleans crew, who welcomed me back with open arms: Michael Belt, Aaron Grant, Jess Issachar, Nicole Washington, Drew Christopher Joy, Hannah Pepper, Thomas Adams, Debbie Goldgaber, and Lula the Dog. Nicole Manganelli for invaluable design advice and thoughts on grief. Cassady Fendlay, for always letting me yell about justice and being the best costume-making buddy. Lydia Pelot-Hobbs for all the introductions political and personal, yelling about the tendency of the rate of profit to fall at odd hours, and at a critical juncture, suggesting I read *The London Hanged.*

Cortney Harding, for the rock 'n' roll and your home when I needed one.

Brandy Jensen, the most compassionate person I know and also the funniest, thanks for always taking my heartaches seriously.

Raj Patel for pulling me out of a grief hole with wit and grace and making me feel like my work has value when I doubt it.

Elle Hardy, for the orcas, the submarine, the vagrant solidarity, and Brixton.

To Robin D. G. Kelley for consistently inspiring my writing—it's an honor to realize we're thinking along the same lines.

To Adam Kotsko, for the demons; Jessie Kindig, for the witches; Nathalie Olah and Raechel Jolie, for the ghosts; China Miéville, for the monsters.

Lawson McClure and Julian Siravo, for reminding me that deep care is definitely not gendered, no matter what the whole world thinks.

Connor Lewis, collaborator and occasional sender of cringe, your friendship is a gift.

The people who remember my early days of grieving: Holly Wood, for telling me what was happening to me. Melissa Gira Grant for the chapbook and taking me in. Nicole Aro for telling me "that's what friends are *for*," which I still hear in your voice. Nantina Vgontzas, Isham Christie, Kevin Prosen, Chris Brooks, Rory Fanning, Barbara Madeloni: you all held me together at an extraordinarily vulnerable moment, and I will never forget that.

Freddie Stuart, Matt Cole, Frankie Mace, Kulsoom Jafri, and Polly Smythe for picking me up off the floor again when the world conspired to throw me back into mourning. James Meadway, for keeping me sharp and a friendship I can relax in. Archie Woodrow, for the collaborative overlapping. Claire English, for always being willing to talk about care and more importantly, to practice it. Joe Guinan, who excels at hosting and will know what I mean when I just say: the armadillo. To Maev McDaid, four countries and counting. To the people who have opened their homes to me over my summers in London: Nathalie Olah, again, and Homer the cat. Joana Ramiro: never change, I need your humor and your warmth always. Dalia Gebrial, who always knows the right snack to go with a crisis; Nancy Hitzig, karaoke, dance breaks, and night swimming don't begin to sum it up; and Anna Lekas Miller and Salem Rizk: you're my family.

The grievers, to whom this book is dedicated: Angelica Sgouros, thank you for all the suggested reading and for seeing me in hell. Antonia Jennings, for a description of grief I have used many times. Ethan Earle, for sangria at Spain bar and for seeing me, always. Joshua Eaton, for the best advice I got, which I have branded on my heart now. Laura Clawson, thank you for sharing your dad with me, it was an honor to share a corner of your grief. Natasha Lewis, you get thanked twice, this time as a dear friend and Robyn dance buddy. Samhita Mukhopadyay, in addition to talking through loss, you have made me feel so much more comfortable in our godawful industry.

Stephen Lerner and Marilyn Sneiderman, my labor family, for taking me in, feeding me well, lighting Shabbat candles, and continuing to teach me.

Peter Mitchell, you were never work.

Michael Whitney, no one knows me like you do, and I wouldn't have it any other way.

To Amanda, John, and most of all Agnes, who make actual family fun.

To my father, who wouldn't like this book because it's about him, but isn't here any more to stop me, and was proud of me anyway. I miss you every day.

To my mother, I love you for making me who I am.

Peter Frase: thank you for trusting me, and for five and a half years that were not a failure. Sometimes things end, and other times they change, and I am eternally grateful for the friendship we have salvaged.

Craig Gent, the word "friend" doesn't begin to describe the support you have given me over the past several years, and yet maybe it does, because maybe this is the friendship to which all others aspire.

Brett Scott, you taught me things about repair, trust, and patience that have made me a better person and kept me tethered to this world when I thought I would explode more times now than I can count. I love you.

Dania Rajendra. More than anyone else, this book is for you.

Notes

Introduction: Haunted

1. Sharpe quotes Hartman thus: "The 'autobiographical example,' says Saidiya Hartman, 'is not a personal story that folds onto itself; it's not about navel gazing, it's really about trying to look at historical and social process and one's own formation as a window onto social and historical processes, as an example of them' (Saunders 2008b, 7). Like Hartman I include the personal here, 'to tell a story capable of engaging and countering the violence of abstraction' (Hartman 2008, 7)." Christina Sharpe, *In the Wake: On Blackness and Being* (Durham, NC: Duke University Press, 2016), loc. 348, Kindle.

2. Janet Malcolm, "The Journalist and the Murderer-I," *New Yorker*, March 5, 1989, www.newyorker.com/magazine/1989/03/13/the-journalist-and-the-murderer-i.

3. Cristina Rivera Garza, *Grieving: Dispatches from a Wounded Country* (New York: Feminist Press, 2020), 8–9.

4. In *Undoing Gender*, Butler seemed to capture precisely what I was feeling; they wrote:

> I think one is hit by waves, and that one starts out the day with an aim, a project, a plan, and one finds oneself foiled. One finds oneself fallen. One is exhausted but does not know why. Something is larger than one's own deliberate plan or project, larger than one's own knowing. Something takes hold, but is this something coming from the self, from the outside, or from some region where the difference between the two is indeterminable? What is it that claims us at such moments, such that we are not the masters of ourselves? To what are we tied? And by what are we seized?
>
> It may seem that one is undergoing something temporary, but it could be that in this experience something about who we are is revealed, something that delineates the ties we have to others, that shows us that those ties constitute a sense of self, compose who we are, and that when we lose them, we lose our composure in some fundamental sense: we do not know who we are or what to do.

Judith Butler, *Undoing Gender* (New York: Routledge, 2004), loc. 57–58, 323–329, Kindle; Judith Butler, *Precarious Life: The Powers of Mourning and Violence* (New York: Verso, 2006), loc. 512–523, 547–549, Kindle.

5. Jennifer Senior, "What Bobby McIlvaine Left Behind," *Atlantic*, September 2021, www.theatlantic.com/magazine/archive/2021/09/twenty-years-gone-911-bobby-mcilvaine/619490/; Jackson Rainier, "The Blindside Wipeout of Grief," NextAvenue, June 1, 2020, www.nextavenue.org/the-blindside-wipeout-of-grief/.

6. Rupa Marya and Raj Patel, *Inflamed: Deep Medicine and the Anatomy of Injustice* (New York: Farrar, Straus and Giroux, 2021), loc. 309, Kindle; Senior, "What Bobby McIlvaine Left"; Litsa Williams, "64 Examples of Disenfranchised Grief," WhatsYourGrief, April 2, 2018, https://whatsyourgrief.com/64-examples-of-disenfranchised-grief/; "Ambiguous Loss / Non-death Loss," Care Counseling, https://care-clinics.com/grief-and-families/; Emily Kenway, *Who Cares: The Hidden Crisis of Caregiving, and How We Solve It* (London: Wildfire, 2023), 33; Graison Dangor, "When Facing Loss, Embrace Change and Don't Force Closure, a Therapist Urges," NPR, January 5, 2022, www.npr.org/sections/health-shots/2022/01/05/1068368442/when-facing-loss-embrace-change-and-dont-force-closure-a-therapist-urges; Gargi Bhattacharyya, *We, the Heartbroken* (London: Hajar Press, 2023), loc. 56–84, Kindle.

7. Hannah Arendt, introduction to Walter Benjamin, *Illuminations: Essays and Reflections*, ed. Hannah Arendt (New York: Mariner Books Classics, 2019), loc. 299–318, Kindle; Walter Benjamin, *One Way Street*, ed. Michael W. Jennings, trans. Edmund Jephcott, preface by Greil Marcus (Cambridge, MA: Harvard University Press, 2016), loc. 520–522, 1102–1106, 1118, Kindle; Butler, *Precarious Life*, loc. 462–463, 483–491, 574–580; Butler, *Undoing Gender*, loc. 281–282, 315–316; Garza, *Grieving*, 99, 136–137.

8. China Miéville, *A Spectre, Haunting* (Chicago: Haymarket Books, 2022), loc. 404–405, 1174–1177, Kindle; Ashon Crawley, *The Lonely Letters* (Durham, NC: Duke University Press, 2020), loc. 169–170, 216, Kindle.

9. Peter Mitchell, *Imperial Nostalgia: How the British Conquered Themselves* (Manchester: Manchester University Press, 2021), 3, 18; Adam Kotsko, *Neoliberalism's Demons: On the Political Theology of Late Capital* (Stanford, CA: Stanford University Press, 2018), loc. 492–499, Kindle.

10. Miéville, *A Spectre, Haunting*, loc. 40–41; Jeremy Gilbert, "Microdose: A Ghost Story for Christmas," *ACFM* (podcast), Novara Media, December 22, 2022, https://novaramedia.com/2022/12/22/acfm-microdose-a-ghost-story-for-christmas/; Avery Gordon, *Ghostly Matters: Haunting and the Sociological Imagination* (Minneapolis: University of Minnesota Press, 2008), loc. 8, 63, Kindle; Jacques Derrida, *Specters of Marx: The State of the Debt, the Work of Mourning & the New International* (New York: Routledge Classics, 2006), loc. 122, Kindle; Mark Fisher, *Ghosts of My Life: Writings on Depression, Hauntology and Lost Futures* (London: Zero Books, 2014), loc. 17–18, Kindle.

11. Gordon, *Ghostly Matters*, loc. 182–198; Derrida, *Specters of Marx*, loc. 126.

12. Being haunted, Gordon argued, "draws us affectively, sometimes against our will and always a bit magically, into the structure of feeling of a reality we come to experience, not as cold knowledge, but as a transformative recognition." Gordon, *Ghostly Matters*, loc. 8, 19–22, 50, 65–66, 98, 193–194, 198–200; Walter Benjamin, "Theses on the Philosophy of History," in *Illuminations*, loc. 197–198; Theodor Adorno and Max Horkheimer, *Dialectic of Enlightenment* (London: Verso 2016); Mitchell, *Imperial Nostalgia*, 18; Derrida, *Specters of Marx*, loc. 9.

13. Raymond Williams, *Marxism and Literature* (Oxford: Oxford University Press, 1978), 132–133; Gordon, *Ghostly Matters*, loc. 18, 132; Antonio Gramsci, *Selections from the Prison Notebooks*, ed. Quintin Hoare and Geoffrey Nowell Smith (New York: International, 1971), loc. 8299–8655, Kindle; Nate Holdren, *Injury Impoverished: Workplace Accidents, Capitalism and Law in the Progressive Era* (Cambridge: Cambridge University Press, 2021), loc. 4256, Kindle; Bhattacharyya, *We, the Heartbroken*, loc. 115–151, 200–271; Eva Illouz, *Cold Intimacies: The Making of Emotional Capitalism* (New York: Polity Press, 2013), loc. 73, Kindle.

14. Lynsey Hanley, "Remembering Dawn Foster," *Tribune*, July 20, 2021, https://tribune mag.co.uk/2021/07/in-memory-of-dawn-foster.

15. Sigmund Freud, "Mourning and Melancholia," in *The Penguin Freud Reader*, ed. Adam Phillips (New York: Penguin, 2006), 310–312, 317–319, 322–324; Judith Butler, *Frames of War: When Is Life Grievable?* (New York: Verso, 2016), loc. 2984–2989, Kindle.

16. Fiona Maccallum and Richard A. Bryant, "Imagining the Future in Complicated Grief," *Depression and Anxiety* 28 (2011): 658–665, https://doi.org/10.1002/da.20866; Donald J. Robinaugh and Richard J. McNally, "Remembering the Past and Envisioning the Future in Bereaved Adults with and Without Complicated Grief," *Clinical Psychological Science* 1, no. 3 (2013): 290–300, doi: 10.1177/2167702613476027.

17. Mark Fisher suggested, "Haunting, then, can be construed as a failed mourning. It is about refusing to give up the ghost or—and this can sometimes amount to the same thing—the refusal of the ghost to give up on us." Fisher, *Ghosts of My Life*, 22; Butler, *Precarious Life*, loc. 465–471; Derrida, *Specters of Marx*, loc. 121, 217; Gordon, *Ghostly Matters*, loc. 52–54; 64–65; Margaret Cohen, *Profane Illumination: Walter Benjamin and the Paris of Surrealist Revolution* (Berkeley: University of California Press, 1995); Mark Fisher, *Postcapitalist Desire: The Final Lectures*, ed. Matt Colquhoun (London: Repeater Books, 2020), loc. 83–123, Kindle.

18. Marx, in *The Eighteenth Brumaire of Louis Bonaparte*, wrote, "The social revolution of the nineteenth century cannot take its poetry from the past but only from the future. It cannot begin with itself before it has stripped away all superstition about the past. The former revolutions required recollections of past world history in order to smother their own content. The revolution of the nineteenth century must let the dead bury their dead in order to arrive at its own content. There the phrase went beyond the content—here the content goes beyond the phrase." Karl Marx, *The Eighteenth Brumaire of Louis Bonaparte* (Mumbai: Sanage, 2022), loc. 6, Kindle; Rodrigo Nunes, *Neither Vertical nor Horizontal: A Theory of Political Organization* (London: Verso, 2021), loc. 4963–4964, Kindle; Franco "Bifo" Berardi, *After the Future*, ed. Gary Genosko and Nicholas Thoburn (Chico, CA: AK Press, 2011), loc. 17, 24–25, 52, 55, 59, Kindle; John Berger, *Hold Everything Dear* (New York: Vintage, 2008), 6; Ajay Singh Chaudhary, "The Long Now," *Late Light*, November 2022, https://late-light.com/issues /issue-1/the-long-now; Fisher, *Ghosts of My Life*, 14–15.

19. I first read the phrase "slow cancellation of the future" in the writing of Mark Fisher, where he credited it to Franco Berardi, but later I learned that Raymond Williams had used it first in his novel *Border Country*. Fisher, *Ghosts of My Life*, 6–8, 23–24, 27; Lynsey Hanley, "I Learned What It Was to Love and Leave a Place After Reading Raymond Williams," *Guardian*, June 15, 2020, www.theguardian.com/commentisfree/2020/jun/15/border-country-raymond-williams-book -changed-me; Benjamin, "Philosophy of History," loc. 204; Gordon, *Ghostly Matters*, loc. 64. There has been much written about "left melancholia," from Walter Benjamin through Wendy Brown and Jodi Dean and Rodrigo Nunes and many more besides, about the attachment to failed tactics and past revolutions, the thing Marx wrote about above. Walter Benjamin, "Left-Wing Melancholy (On Erich Kästner's New Book of Poems)," *Screen* 15, no. 2 (Summer 1974): 28–32, https://doi.org/10.1093 /screen/15.2.28; Nunes, *Neither Vertical nor Horizontal*, loc. 924–927, 941–956, 995–1004, 1016–1027, 1063–1064, 4936–4944; Wendy Brown, "Resisting Left Melancholia," first published in boundary 2 in 1999, available at Verso, February 12, 2017, www.versobooks.com/en-gb/blogs /news/3092-resisting-left-melancholia.

20. Sara Marcus, *Political Disappointment: A Cultural History from Reconstruction to the AIDS Crisis* (Cambridge, MA: Harvard University Press, 2023), 19; Nunes, *Neither Vertical nor Horizontal*, loc. 5025–5035; Fisher, *Ghosts of My Life*, 8–9, 11.

21. Sarah Jaffe, "Mourning Routine: Namwali Serpell's Novel of Family, Grief, and Storytelling," Bookforum, September–November 2022, www.bookforum.com/print/2903/namwali-serpell-s-novel-of-family-grief-and-storytelling-25058; Bronislaw Szerszynski, "Drift as a Planetary Phenomenon," *Performance Research* 23, no. 7 (2018): 136–144, doi: 10.1080/13528165.2018.1558436; Emerson Malone, "We Need to Abolish the 'Exonerative Tense' of Headlines," *Buzzfeed News*, May 4, 2023, www.buzzfeednews.com/article/emersonmalone/police-traffic-safety-headline-language-exoneration.

22. Szerszynski, "Drift as a Planetary Phenomenon."

23. Butler, *Precarious Life*, loc. 474–476.

24. Szerszynski, "Drift as a Planetary Phenomenon."

25. Josh Cohen, *Not Working: Why We Have to Stop* (London: Granta Books, 2019); Melanie Klein, cited in Marcus, *Political Disappointment*, 18–19.

26. Erik Baker, "The Right to Grieve," *Jewish Currents*, March 13, 2023, https://jewishcurrents.org/the-right-to-grieve.

27. Michelle Honig, "The Forward Guide to Sitting Shiva," *Forward*, January 28, 2019, https://forward.com/life/414979/forward-guide-sitting-shiva-jewish-mourning/; Kevyn Burger,"Bereavement Researcher: We Must Do Better for the Grief-Stricken," Next Avenue, February 18, 2019, www.nextavenue.org/bereavement-researcher-grief-stricken/; Sita Balani, "Without Mourning," *FiveDials*, Spring 2021, https://fivedials.com/reportage/without-mourning-sita-balani/.

28. Balani, "Without Mourning."

29. Walter Benjamin, "The Storyteller," in *Illuminations*, loc. 37–39. Modern science, Rupa Marya and Raj Patel tell us, backs up the logic of crying and lamenting, of vocalizing grief. Such vocalizing stimulates the vagus nerve:

> The vagus nerve is the longest in the human body. Starting in the brainstem, it gets its name from the Latin vagus, "wandering," and like a vagabond, it travels to and innervates most of our internal organs, influencing how fast the heart beats and when digestive juices are secreted into the intestines.
>
> When the vagus nerve is well toned through regular stimulation, it creates greater resilience in the face of stress. (*Inflamed*, loc. 171–172, 315–316)

Quinn Terry, "Irish Keens, Modern Grief, and the Digital Landscape of Mourning," *Nursing Clio*, January 13, 2021, https://nursingclio.org/2021/01/13/irish-keens-modern-grief-and-the-digital-landscape-of-mourning/; Elizabeth Catte, *What You Are Getting Wrong About Appalachia* (Cleveland: Belt, 2018), 54.

30. Ann Braude, *Radical Spirits: Spiritualism and Women's Rights in Nineteenth-Century America* (Bloomington: University of Indiana Press, May 25, 2020), loc. 398–400, 535, 701, 742, 813–816, 927, 944, 1378–1381, 1402–1405, Kindle; Rhae-Lynn Barnes, "Man of Means by No Means," in *After Life: A Collective History of Loss and Redemption in Pandemic America*, ed. Rhae Lynn Barnes, Keri Leigh Merritt, and Yohuru Williams (Chicago: Haymarket Books, 2022), loc. 1926–1944, 1949–1957, Kindle; Leila Taylor, *Darkly: Black History and America's Gothic Soul* (London: Repeater Books, 2019), loc. 873–875, 894–903, Kindle.

31. If you would like to read at length my exploration of this subject, the book I was writing is Sarah Jaffe, *Work Won't Love You Back: How Devotion to Our Jobs Leaves Us Exploited, Exhausted, and Alone* (New York: Bold Type Books, 2021). See also Silvia Federici, "From Crisis to Commons: Reproductive Work, Affective Labor and Technology, and the Transformation of Everyday Life," in *Re-enchanting the World: Feminism and the Politics of the Commons* (Binghamton, NY: PM Press, 2018), loc. 3584–3587, 3664–3692, Kindle; Kenway, *Who Cares*,

165–170, 176; Illouz, *Cold Intimacies*, loc. 120–129, 145; Raj Patel, *The Value of Nothing: How to Reshape Market Society and Redefine Democracy* (New York: Picador, 2010), 68; Alva Gotby, "A Capitalism of Feeling: Emotional Reproduction, Work and Gender," Autonomy, April 14, 2021, https://autonomy.work/portfolio/gotby-emotional-repro/; Silvia Federici, *Caliban and the Witch: Women, the Body, and Primitive Accumulation* (New York: Autonomedia, 2004), 14–16; Premilla Nadasen, *Care: The Highest Stage of Capitalism* (Chicago: Haymarket Books, 2023), loc. 440–441, Kindle.

32. For those of you who have never seen *Love, Actually*, it's a sprawling and often schmaltzy British comedy about one family and its various members' attempts at falling in love over the holidays, starring some of the best actors of various generations—Emma Thompson, Alan Rickman, Keira Knightley—alongside Hugh Grant as the prime minister who actually stands up to American pressure to invade Iraq, though Iraq is never mentioned. Yes, it's convoluted. No, grief and doves don't have much of a role, though Liam Neeson does play a grieving widower whose son sets him up with Claudia Schiffer. Andrew Male, "Are puns quite what you want at a time like this?," Twitter, August 2, 2022, https://twitter.com/Andr6wMale/status/1554406053458153472.

33. Sociologist William Davies wrote in 2015, "One of the last remaining checks on the neurochemical understanding of depression was the exemption attached to people who were grieving: this, at the very least, was still considered a not unhealthy reason to be unhappy. But in the face of a new drug, Wellbutrin, promising to alleviate 'major depressive symptoms occurring shortly after the loss of a loved one,' the APA caved in and removed this exemption from the DSM-V. To be unhappy for more than two weeks after the death of another human being can now be considered a medical illness." William Davies, *The Happiness Industry: How the Government and Big Business Sold Us Well-Being* (London: Verso, 2015), loc. 2399–2760, Kindle; Ellen Barry, "How Long Should It Take to Grieve? Psychiatry Has Come Up with an Answer," *New York Times*, March 18, 2022, www.nytimes.com/2022/03/18/health/prolonged-grief-disorder.html.

34. Freud, "Mourning and Melancholia," 310–312, 317–319, 322–324; Baker, "Right to Grieve."

35. Peter Frase, "The Garage Sale, and Other Utopias," in *Garage Sale Standard*, issue 1 of 2, published by Martha Rosler on the occasion of the Meta-Monumental Garage Sale, at MoMA November 17–30, 2012; Wallace Shawn, *The Fever* (London: Faber, 2009); Federici, *Re-enchanting the World*, loc. 2226.

36. Marx explained it thus:

> A commodity is therefore a mysterious thing, simply because in it the social character of men's labour appears to them as an objective character stamped upon the product of that labour; because the relation of the producers to the sum total of their own labour is presented to them as a social relation, existing not between themselves, but between the products of their labour. This is the reason why the products of labour become commodities, social things whose qualities are at the same time perceptible and imperceptible by the senses. . . . There it is a definite social relation between men, that assumes, in their eyes, the fantastic form of a relation between things. . . . This I call the Fetishism which attaches itself to the products of labour, so soon as they are produced as commodities, and which is therefore inseparable from the production of commodities.
>
> This Fetishism of commodities has its origin, as the foregoing analysis has already shown, in the peculiar social character of the labour that produces them.

Karl Marx, *Capital*, vol. 1: *A Critique of Political Economy* (Digireads.com, 2011), loc. 22–25, 29, 31, 44–45; Derrida, *Specters of Marx*, loc. 209; Holdren, *Injury Impoverished*, loc. 101–104, 5329–5339; Playwright Wallace Shawn explained this concept in *The Fever*: "What really determines the value of a coat? The coat's price comes from its history, the history of all the people involved in making it and selling it and all the particular relationships they had. And if we buy the coat, we, too, form relationships with all those people, and yet we hide those relationships from our own awareness by pretending we live in a world where coats have no history but just fall down from heaven with prices marked inside." Shawn, *The Fever*; Frase, "The Garage Sale, and Other Utopias"; Anna Lowenhaupt Tsing, *The Mushroom at the End of the World: On the Possibility of Life in Capitalist Ruins* (Princeton, NJ: Princeton University Press, 2015), 62; Silvia Federici, "Re-enchanting the World, Feminism and the Politics of the Commons in an Era of Primitive Accumulation," in Federici, *Re-Enchanting the World*, loc. 2226; Gordon, *Ghostly Matters*, 169; Patel, *Value of Nothing*, 67.

37. Holdren, *Injury Impoverished*, loc. 333–341, 377–378, 484–497, 504, 603–614, 631, 666, 717, 1121–1130, 2300–2336, 2864, 3612, 4046; Butler, *Undoing Gender*, loc. 423–424.

38. Fisher, *Postcapitalist Desire*, 141, Gillian Rose, *Love's Work* (New York: NYRB Classics, 2011), loc. 1423, Kindle.

39. Anna Lowenhaupt Tsing explained, "Just as in factories workers are alienated from the things they make, allowing those things to be sold without reference to their makers, so too, things are alienated from the people who make and exchange them. Things become stand-alone objects, to be used or exchanged; they bear no relation to the personal networks in which they are made and deployed." Tsing, *The Mushroom at the End of the World*, 5, 110, 121–122, 133; Max Weber, *Charisma and Disenchantment: The Vocation Lectures*, introduction by Paul Reitter and Chad Wellmon, trans. Damion Searls (New York: New York Review Books, 2020), loc. 132–140 (introduction), Kindle, 549–567, 576, 621–628, 734–737, 750–753, 868–876; Mark Fisher, *Capitalist Realism: Is There No Alternative?* (London: Zero Books, 2009), 4; Marx, *Capital*, loc. 95; Illouz, *Cold Intimacies*, 79–81; Jaffe, *Work Won't Love You Back*, 10.

40. Federici, *Caliban and the Witch*, 40–44, 135; Leila Taylor, *Darkly*, loc. 865–872; Barbara Ehrenreich, *Natural Causes: An Epidemic of Wellness, the Certainty of Dying, and Killing Ourselves to Live Longer* (New York: Twelve, 2018), 186.

41. Ehrenreich, *Natural Causes*, 199–200; Berardi, *After the Future*, 17; Braude, *Radical Spirits*, loc. 429–465, 1320–1321, 1349–1373, 1410; Marya and Patel, *Inflamed*, loc. 17; see Max Weber, *The Protestant Ethic and the Spirit of Capitalism* (New York: Simon and Schuster Digital, 2013).

42. Some other examples of Marx at his most gothic: "We have hitherto considered the tendency to the extension of the working-day, the were-wolf's hunger for surplus-labour" (*Capital*, loc. 132). "In fact the vampire will not lose its hold on him 'so long as there is a muscle, a nerve, a drop of blood to be exploited'" (159). "The whole mystery of commodities, all the magic and necromancy that surrounds the products of labour as long as they take the form of commodities, vanishes therefore, so soon as we come to other forms of production" (47). And of course the famous "Capital is dead labour" line (127). See also Miéville, *A Spectre, Haunting*, loc. 192–195, 222–223; Tyler Malone, "The Zombies of Karl Marx: Horror in Capitalism's Wake," *LitHub*, October 31, 2018, https://lithub.com/the-zombies-of-karl-marx-horror-in-capitalisms-wake/.

43. Miéville, *A Spectre, Haunting*, loc. 592–597; Derrida, *Specters of Marx*, loc. 122–123, 126, 132–136; Fisher, *Ghosts of My Life*, 18–19.

44. The full line is, "But, if constructing the future and settling everything for all times are not our affair, it is all the more clear what we have to accomplish at present: I am referring to *ruthless criticism* of all that exists, ruthless both in the sense of not being afraid of the results it arrives at and in the sense of being just as little afraid of conflict with the powers that be." Karl Marx, "Marx to Ruge, Kreuznach, September 1843," in Letters from the Deutsch-Französische Jahrbücher, www.marxists.org/archive/marx/works/1843/letters/43_09.htm; Critic Margaret Cohen called Benjamin's work a kind of "Gothic Marxism," pointing to "the valorization of the realm of a culture's ghosts and phantasms as a significant and rich field of social production rather than a mirage to be dispelled." Margaret Cohen, *Profane Illumination: Walter Benjamin and the Paris of Surrealist Revolution* (Berkeley: University of California Press, 1995), 1–2, 4, 11–12; "Episode 150: Gothic Marxism," *Season of the Bitch* (podcast), October 2020, https://open.spotify.com/episode/1gWg9jryQMZVY5cgSGbnB9?si=9aa275d8d79e4f73&nd=1; Adam Turl, "A Thousand Lost Worlds: Notes on Gothic Marxism," *Red Wedge*, June 4, 2015, www.redwedgemagazine.com/evicted-art-blog/a-thousand-lost-worlds-notes-on-gothic-marxism; Fisher, *Ghosts of My Life*, 19.

45. Lydia Pelot-Hobbs, *Prison Capital: Mass Incarceration and Struggles for Abolition Democracy in Louisiana* (Raleigh: University of North Carolina Press, 2023), 19.

46. That's why each consecutive crisis of capitalism is a crisis of social reproduction. Crisis itself is, following Ruth Wilson Gilmore and Lydia Pelot-Hobbs, "the accumulation of contradictions in the social formation so that it can no longer reproduce itself." The contradictions require change, but whether that change will be an improvement for most working people depends on the outcome of struggle. Pelot-Hobbs, *Prison Capital*, 19; Federici, *Caliban and the Witch*, 64, 80, 84, 136, 141, 146; Peter Linebaugh, *The London Hanged: Crime and Civil Society in the Eighteenth Century* (New York: Verso, 2006), loc. 188–287, 1203–1237, 3214, 3784–3796, 4793, 4955–4968, Kindle; Silvia Federici, "Marxism, Feminism, and the Commons," in *Re-enchanting the World*, loc. 3206–3219, 3878; Ewan Gibbs, *Coal Country: The Meaning and Memory of Deindustrialization in Postwar Scotland* (London: University of London Press, 2021), loc. 226–236, Kindle; Davies, *Happiness Industry*, loc. 677; Joshua Clover, *Riot. Strike. Riot: The New Era of Uprisings* (New York: Verso, 2016), loc. 515–520, Kindle; Patel, *Value of Nothing*, 82, 94, 112; Nate Holdren, "Social Murder: Capitalism's Systematic and State-Organised Killing," in *Marxism and the Capitalist State: Towards a New Debate*, ed. Rob Hunter, Rafael Khachaturian, and Eva Nanopoulos (New York: Palgrave Macmillan, 2023), 185–208; Kotsko, *Neoliberalism's Demons*, loc. 1622.

47. Marx, *Capital*, loc. 1:84; Garza, *Grieving*, 22–23, 157; Berardi, *After the Future*, 140–141, 145–146; Nancy Leinfuss, "Wall Street Plays Death Card in Securitization Market," Reuters, July 31, 2009, www.reuters.com/article/us-abs-securities-death-analysis-idUSTRE56U5UX20090731; Benjamin, *One Way Street*, loc. 557–559; Patel, *Value of Nothing*, 174; Ruth Wilson Gilmore, *Golden Gulag: Prisons, Surplus, Crisis, and Opposition in Globalizing California* (Berkeley: University of California Press, 2007), loc. 58, 60, 63, Kindle; Nadasen, *Care*, loc. 1039–1043, 1060–1061, 1067–1090, 2388–2389, 2441–2444, 3436–3437; Federici, "From Crisis to Commons," loc. 3704; Julian Knowlton Siravo, "Elder Liberation and a Future Beyond Wage Slavery: The Role of an Ageing Population in Shaping a Future Beyond Work" (unpublished paper, Royal College of Art MA City Design, London, 2018); Miéville, *A Spectre, Haunting*, loc. 1178–1183, 2143–2143; Patel, *Value of Nothing*, 88–89.

48. J.-A. Mbembé and Libby Meintjes, "Necropolitics," *Public Culture* 15, no. 1 (2003): 11–40, Project MUSE, muse.jhu.edu/article/39984; Linebaugh, *The London Hanged*, loc.

1126–1157; Steven Thrasher, *The Viral Underclass: The Human Toll When Inequality and Disease Collide* (New York: Celadon Press, August 2, 2022), 191–192.

49. Holdren, *Injury Impoverished*, loc. 3584, 4166, 5058–5059; Marx, *Capital*, loc. 1:142–143; Federici, *Caliban and the Witch*, 17.

50. Marya and Patel, *Inflamed*, loc. 35; Nate Holdren, "Depoliticizing Social Murder in the COVID-19 Pandemic," *Bill of Health* (blog at Harvard Law School Petrie-From Center), March 21, 2022, https://blog.petrieflom.law.harvard.edu/2022/03/21/depoliticizing-social-murder-covid-pandemic/; Holdren, "Social Murder."

51. Friedrich Engels, *Condition of the Working Class in England* (written September 1844–March 1845; source: Panther Edition, 1969, from text provided by the Institute of Marxism-Leninism, Moscow; first published: Leipzig in 1845; English edition (authorized by Engels) published in 1887 in New York and in London in 1891; transcription/markup: Zodiac Tim Delaney in 1998; proofed and corrected by Mark Harris, 2010), www.marxists.org/archive/marx/works/download/pdf/condition-working-class-england.pdf.

52. Dawn Foster wrote of Grenfell:

> In the richest borough of one of the wealthiest countries in the world, people in social housing, many on low incomes, were killed and injured in a fire that could have been prevented or contained. Rather than diverting blame from those responsible, or treating it as an act of nature, our responsibility is to ask why it occurred.
>
> Time and again, residents reported serious concerns about the safety of the building to the management organization, the local council, and the member of parliament (recently unseated in the general election). They were met with silence, and several told me on the scene they were convinced it was because they were poor, living in a rich borough that was determined to socially cleanse the area as part of a gentrifying project.

Dawn Foster, "A Very Political Tragedy," *Jacobin*, June 14, 2017, https://jacobin.com/2017/06/grenfell-tower-fire-inequality-housing; Holdren, "Social Murder"; Robert Booth, "Cost of Grenfell Tower Disaster Soars to Nearly £1.2bn," *Guardian*, July 30, 2023, www.theguardian.com/uk-news/2023/jul/30/grenfell-tower-disaster-cost-soars.

53. Taylor Telford, "COVID Cases and Deaths Grossly Underestimated Among Meatpackers, House Investigation Finds," *Washington Post*, October 27, 2021, www.washingtonpost.com/business/2021/10/27/meatpacking-house-report/; see Erik Loomis, *Out of Sight: The Long and Disturbing History of Corporations Outsourcing Catastrophe* (New York: New Press, 2016); Sarah Jaffe, "Work Won't Love You Back: We Were Warned," *Progressive*, May 5, 2023, https://progressive.org/magazine/work-wont-love-you-back-we-were-warned-jaffe/; Holdren, *Injury Impoverished*, loc. 41–42, 147, 239; Beatrice Adler-Bolton and Artie Vierkant, *Health Communism: A Surplus Manifesto* (New York: Verso, 2022), loc. 184–191, Kindle; Lauren Berlant, "Slow Death (Sovereignty, Obesity, Lateral Agency)," *Critical Inquiry* 33, no. 4 (Summer 2007): 754; Richard Fuller, Philip J. Landrigan, Kalpana Balakrishnan, Glynda Bathan, Stephan Bose-O'Reilly, Michael Brauer, et al., "Pollution and Health: A Progress Update," *Lancet* 6, no. 6 (May 17, 2022): E535–E547, https://doi.org/10.1016/S2542-5196(22)00090-0; Tom Garris, "Some 7 Months After East Palestine Derailment, Neighbors Raise New Contamination Concerns," WTAE, August 29, 2023, www.wtae.com/article/east-palestine-train-derailment-contamination-concerns-august/44928717#.

54. Nadasen, *Care*, loc. 59; Kotsko, *Neoliberalism's Demons*, loc. 63–65, 71, 125–130, 170, 649.

55. Melinda Cooper, *Family Values: Between Neoliberalism and the New Social Conservatism* (Brooklyn, NY: Zone Books, 2019), loc. 57–60, Kindle; Davies, *Happiness Industry*, loc. 66, 76–78,

88, 99; William Davies, "The New Neoliberalism," *New Left Review* 101, (September/October 2016), https://newleftreview.org/issues/ii101/articles/william-davies-the-new-neoliberalism; Kotsko, *Neoliberalism's Demons*, loc. 1891, 2116.

56. Kotsko, *Neoliberalism's Demons*, loc. 1483, 1611–1723, 1811–1834; Cooper, *Family Values*, loc. 439–441, 2684–2687, 2774–2777, 3257–3259; Butler, *Precarious Life*, loc. 96, 678; Thrasher, *Viral Underclass*, 192.

57. Butler, *Undoing Gender*, loc. 433–447; Butler, *Precarious Life*, loc. 97–99, 156–158, 631–634, 654–656, 1111–1133.

58. Political economist Paul Baran put it thus:

> The cancerous malaise of the system which renders it a formidable obstacle to human advancement, is that all this is not an assortment of fortuitously appearing attributes of the capitalist order, but the very basis of its existence and viability. And such being the case, bigger and better Food and Drug Administrations, a comprehensive network of Distinguished Citizens Committees, and the like can merely spread a veil over the existing mess rather than clean up the mess itself. To use an earlier comparison once more: building sumptuous cemeteries and expensive monuments for the victims of war does not reduce their number. The best—and the worst—that such seemingly humanitarian efforts can accomplish is to dull people's sensitivity to brutality and cruelty, to reduce their horror of war.

Paul Baran, *The Political Economy of Growth* (New York: Monthly Review Press, 1957), xvii; Butler, *Precarious Life*, loc. 658, 714–717, 844; Butler, *Frames of War*, loc. 1806–1810.

59. Nunes, *Neither Vertical nor Horizontal*, loc. 1653–1654; Butler, *Precarious Life*, loc. 580; Garza, *Grieving*, 138.

60. Gordon, *Ghostly Matters*, loc. 2.

61. Angela Y. Davis, "Women and Capitalism: Dialectics of Oppression and Liberation," in *The Angela Y. Davis Reader*, ed. Joy James (Hoboken, NJ: Blackwell, 1998), 179; Andrea Long Chu, "My New Vagina Won't Make Me Happy," *New York Times*, November 24, 2018, www.nytimes.com/2018/11/24/opinion/sunday/vaginoplasty-transgender-medicine.html.

62. Olúfẹ́mi O. Táíwò, *Elite Capture: How the Powerful Took Over Identity Politics (and Everything Else)* (Chicago: Haymarket Books, 2022), loc. 1363–1393, Kindle; Butler, *Precarious Life*, loc. 495–507, 584–595, 608–618; Kelly Hayes and Mariame Kaba, *Let This Radicalize You: Organizing and the Revolution of Reciprocal Care* (Chicago: Haymarket Books, 2023), 151.

63. Donna Haraway, *Staying with the Trouble: Making Kin in the Chthulucene* (Durham, NC: Duke University Press, 2016), loc. 1050–1058, Kindle.

64. Hélène Cixous, *Three Steps on the Ladder of Writing* (New York: Columbia University Press, 1994), 11–12.

65. Hayes and Kaba, *Let This Radicalize You*, 23.

66. Butler, *Undoing Gender*, loc. 444–447; Garza, *Grieving*, 137.

67. Benjamin, "Philosophy of History," loc. 199–200; Nunes, *Neither Vertical nor Horizontal*, loc. 3440–3445.

68. Walter Benjamin, "Paralipomena to 'On the Concept of History,'" in *Walter Benjamin: Selected Writings*, vol. 4: *1938–1940*, paperback ed. (Cambridge, MA: Harvard University Press, 2006), 402; Butler, *Frames of War*, loc. 3121–3124; Miéville, *A Spectre, Haunting*, loc. 1258–1259.

69. Donna Haraway offers a word that gets partway there: "sympoiesis," a making-with, an evolving together. Haraway, *Staying with the Trouble*, loc. 443, 947; Jason W. Moore and

Raj Patel list a series of those words from other languages: "The Anishinaabeg, whose original lands extended widely across northeastern North America, have Minobimaatisiiwin, which means 'the good life' but also 'a continuous rebirth' of reciprocal and cyclical relations between humans and other life. Southern African Bantu languages have ubuntu, human fulfillment through togetherness, and the Shona language has the further idea of ukama, a 'relatedness to the entire cosmos,' including the biophysical world." Raj Patel and Jason W. Moore, *A History of the World in Seven Cheap Things: A Guide to Capitalism, Nature, and the Future of the Planet* (Berkeley: University of California Press, 2018), 19.

70. Balani, "Without Mourning."

Chapter 1: Burn: State violence, solidarity, and rebellion

1. Kelly Hayes and Mariame Kaba wrote of the protests:

> While public gatherings were generally discouraged, 1,200 doctors signed a public letter expressing support for the protests, describing them as "vital to the national public health and to the threatened health specifically of Black people in the United States." Doctors and other clinicians suggested best practices for safer demonstrations, and a culture of care sprung up at protests; the distribution of masks and hand sanitizer became standard features of marches and rallies. Through signage, outreach, rhetoric, and artwork, protesters reminded each other that masking and preventing the spread of COVID-19 were manifestations of their larger concern for their communities and each other. The phrase "we keep us safe" became both a mantra and a call to action. Protesters' safety efforts were successful: a study conducted by the National Bureau of Economic Research in the summer of 2020 ultimately found "no evidence that urban protests reignited COVID-19 case growth during the more than three weeks following protest onset." The study further indicated that "cities which had protests saw an increase in social distancing behavior for the overall population relative to cities that did not." (*Let This Radicalize You*, 62)

2. In the words of *Newsweek*:

> A majority of Americans, 54 percent, believe that burning down a Minneapolis police precinct building following the death of George Floyd was justified, according to a new poll.
>
> The survey, which was conducted by Monmouth University, surveyed 807 U.S. adults from May 28 to June 1. It asked respondents if they thought the actions taken by protesters, including the burning of the precinct building, was fully justified, partially justified or not at all justified.
>
> According to the poll, 17 percent said the actions were fully justified and 37 percent said partially justified, for a total of 54 percent. In comparison, 38 percent said that the action was not at all justified. The poll has a margin of error of plus or minus 3.5 percentage points.

Matthew Impelli, "54 Percent of Americans Think Burning Down Minneapolis Police Precinct Was Justified After George Floyd's Death," *Newsweek*, June 3, 2020, www.newsweek.com/54-americans-think-burning-down-minneapolis-police-precinct-was-justified-after-george-floyds-1508452.

On the "largest movement in American history," the *New York Times* reported, alongside its protest map, "the recent Black Lives Matter protests peaked on June 6, when half a million people turned out in nearly 550 places across the United States. That was a single day in more than a month of protests that still continue to today." Larry Buchanan, Quoctrung Bui, and

Jugal K. Patel, "Black Lives Matter May Be the Largest Movement in U.S. History," *New York Times*, July 3, 2020, www.nytimes.com/interactive/2020/07/03/us/george-floyd-protests-crowd-size.html.

3. Ruth Wilson Gilmore, "Race and Globalization," in *Abolition Geography: Essays Toward Liberation* (New York: Verso, 2022), loc. 229–234, Kindle; see also Gilmore, *Golden Gulag*, loc. 28.

4. Gilmore, many essays in *Abolition Geography*, including "Race and Globalization," loc. 1561; "Terror Austerity Race Gender Excess Theater," loc. 2344; and "Forgotten Places and the Seeds of Grassroots Planning," loc. 5435. Gilmore herself follows her fellow geographer David Harvey in the use of the term, though she has greatly expanded it; for more, see David Harvey, *The Limits to Capital* (Chicago: University of Chicago Press / Midway Reprints, 1989), 303.

5. Gilmore, "Race and Globalization," loc. 1537–1596.

6. Richard A. Oppel Jr., Derrick Bryson Taylor, and Nicholas Bogel-Burroughs, "What to Know About Breonna Taylor's Death," *New York Times*, March 9, 2023, www.nytimes.com/article/breonna-taylor-police.html; Nicholas Bogel-Burroughs and Will Wright, "Little Has Been Said About the $20 Bill That Brought Officers to the Scene," *New York Times*, April 19, 2021, www.nytimes.com/2021/04/19/us/george-floyd-bill-counterfeit.html; US Department of Justice Office of Public Affairs, "Former Minneapolis Police Officer Derek Chauvin Sentenced to More Than 20 Years in Prison for Depriving George Floyd and a Minor Victim of Their Constitutional Rights," press release, July 7, 2022, www.justice.gov/opa/pr/former-minneapolis-police-officer-derek-chauvin-sentenced-more-20-years-prison-depriving.

7. I stole the "clock of capitalism" line from organizer, educator, and poet Dania Rajendra. Following Stuart Hall and colleagues, Aviah Sarah Day and Shanice Octavia McBean wrote, "In the 1970s, 'mugging' wasn't itself its own category of crime. Its 'rise' was statistically manufactured by police taking a pic 'n' mix approach to what counted as a mugging: bashing together different categories of crime and projecting a new crime—'muggings'—into existence." Aviah Sarah Day and Shanice Octavia McBean, *Abolition Revolution* (London: Pluto Press, 2022), loc. 765, Kindle; see also Stuart Hall, Chas Critcher, Tony Jefferson, John Clarke, and Brian Roberts, *Policing the Crisis: Mugging, the State, and Law and Order* (London: Red Globe Press, 2013). Historian Donna Murch noted that the Omnibus Crime Control and Safe Streets Act of 1968 "provided $400 million in 'seed money' to expand law enforcement efforts across the country. It established the Law Enforcement Assistance Administration, which became the 'fastest-growing federal agency' of the 1970s, with a budget that mushroomed from $10 million at its inception to $850 million in 1973." Donna Murch, *Assata Taught Me: State Violence, Racial Capitalism, and the Movement for Black Lives* (Chicago: Haymarket Books, 2022), loc. 499, Kindle. In a conversation in *Jewish Currents* magazine, Osterweil and Samudzi noted:

> VO: The enslaved—who were not only excluded from property ownership, but were themselves defined as property—understood innately that the concept of property made no sense. They would call just having a meeting "stealing" the meeting, and they would call escaping "stealing away." Once you have been made into property by a society, then you recognize that any freedom you're going to have has to be stolen.
>
> ZS: You write, "This specter of slaves freeing themselves is American history's first image of black looters." I really love the way you play with time, retroactively applying the word "looters" and connecting it to contemporary usage. It really allows us to connect the sheer magnitude of the state's theft, trafficking, and enslavement of African people to its present fear of the black looter destroying and stealing in return.

Zoé Samudzi, "Stealing Away in America," *Jewish Currents*, June 10, 2020, https://jewishcurrents.org/stealing-away-in-america.

8. At the beginning of capitalism, Peter Linebaugh showed, criminalization was a process of gradually making illegal—and punishing with the noose—all the former ways that the poor had pieced together a living. As they resisted the pressure to work in various ways, the law and the workplace were reshaped to discipline them once again. Such changes in the law, he wrote, "may be seen then less as an attack on 'crime' than as an intensification of the exploitation of [the] workers." *The London Hanged*, loc. 291–356, 1533–1679, 1723, 3152–3155; Jon Swaine, "Ferguson Protester Faces Four Years' Jail over Charges of Kicking SUV," *Guardian*, August 15, 2015, www.theguardian.com/us-news/2015/aug/13/ferguson-protester-faces-four-years-jail-over-charges-of-attacking-suv-and-driver; Ann O'Neil, "Who Was Arrested in Ferguson?," CNN, August 22, 2014, https://edition.cnn.com/2014/08/22/us/ferguson-arrests/index.html; Gilmore, "Public Enemies and Private Intellectuals: Apartheid USA," in *Abolition Geography*, loc. 1284–1319; Gilmore, "Race and Globalization," loc. 1650; Gilmore, *Golden Gulag*, loc. 13, 58.

9. Gilmore wrote that the prison boom, specifically in California, where her study took place, but also elsewhere, resulted from the surpluses created by neoliberal restructuring: surplus land, surplus finance capital, surplus state capacity, and surplus labor (people). "Make no mistake: prison building was and is not the inevitable outcome of these surpluses. It did, however, put certain state capacities into motion, make use of a lot of idle land, get capital invested via public debt, and take more than 160,000 low-wage workers off the streets." Gilmore, *Golden Gulag*, loc. 54–56, 63, 73–82, 88; Ruth Wilson Gilmore, "Abolition Geography and the Problem of Innocence," in *Abolition Geography*, loc. 6307; Hettie Judah, "Diamond Reynolds: The Woman Who Streamed a Police Shooting Becomes a Renaissance Madonna," *Guardian*, June 26, 2017, www.theguardian.com/artanddesign/2017/jun/26/luke-willis-thompson-philando-castile-autoportrait. Legal scholar Nadine El-Enany wrote, "Slow, or structural, violence is more difficult to identify than the sudden violent spectacle. It is an opaque kind of violence in part because it is excluded from investigation and interrogation by the law." In the case of prisons, it is not simply excluded from investigation; it is what the law produces when it produces criminals—people who can be removed and who, it is implied, deserve whatever they get while locked up. Nadine El-Enany, "From Love to Justice: Families' Interrogation of Racial State Violence," *Social & Legal Studies* 32, no. 1 (2023): 55–74, https://doi.org/10.1177/09646639221094149; Gilmore, *Golden Gulag*, loc. 14, 26, 214.

10. "Today's prisons are extractive. What does that mean? It means prisons enable money to move because of the enforced inactivity of people locked in them. It means people extracted from communities, and people returned to communities but not entitled to be of them, enable the circulation of money on rapid cycles. What's extracted from the extracted is the resource of life—time." Gilmore, "Abolition Geography and the Problem of Innocence," loc. 6302–6354; Ruth Wilson Gilmore and Craig Gilmore, "Beyond Bratton," in Gilmore, *Abolition Geography*, loc. 3877. In an essay considering a prison newsletter written by incarcerated women a hundred years ago, Molly Hagan pointed to "an intentionally absurd thought experiment" from social scientist and criminologist J. C. Oleson: "What if instead of incarcerating people, we put them in a 'punitive coma' for the duration of their sentence? Prisoners would simply wake to find themselves older, their time, or rather their punishment, having been painlessly extracted. Oleson's Swiftian proposal reveals what we really want from punishment: not the time itself, but the prisoner's awareness of its loss." Molly Hagan, "The Meaning of Time in *The Hour Glass*," *JSTOR Daily*, October 13, 2022, https://daily.jstor.org/the-meaning-of-time-in-the-hour-glass/.

11. George Zimmerman, for those who do not remember, killed seventeen-year-old Trayvon Martin in 2012 and was acquitted. Timothy Bella, "How George Zimmerman Stretched 15 Minutes of Infamy into a Decade of Disgust," *Washington Post*, February 26, 2022, www.washingtonpost.com/nation/2022/02/26/george-zimmerman-trayvon-martin-10-years/. Daniel Penny was the man who choked Jordan Neely to death on a New York City subway car in 2023, and we will get to that subject shortly. Penny was originally let go by police at the scene, and then later arrested and charged with manslaughter after protests. Alex Woodward, "Daniel Penny: Everything We Know About Ex-Marine Filmed Choking Jordan Neely in Fatal Subway Incident," *Independent*, June 8, 2023, www.independent.co.uk/news/world/americas/crime/daniel-penny-marine-chokehold-video-jordan-neely-b2333853.html; Gilmore, "Abolition Geography and the Problem of Innocence," loc. 6497–6503; see also Eleanor Penny, "Abolition Geography: Ruth Wilson Gilmore & Dalia Gebrial on the Verso Podcast," *Verso* (blog), May 18, 2023, www.versobooks.com/blogs/news/abolition-geography-ruth-wilson-gilmore-dalia-gebrial-on-the-verso-podcast; the article that described Brown as "no angel" was John Eligon, "Michael Brown Spent Last Weeks Grappling with Problems and Promise," *New York Times*, August 24, 2014, www.nytimes.com/2014/08/25/us/michael-brown-spent-last-weeks-grappling-with-lifes-mysteries.html.

12. Cedric Robinson, *Black Marxism: The Making of the Black Radical Tradition*, rev. and updated 3rd ed. (Chapel Hill: University of North Carolina Press, 2020); Robin D. G. Kelley noted that Robinson took the term from South African activist intellectuals, who "used the phrase 'racial capitalism' to refer to South Africa's economy under apartheid. [Robinson] developed it from a description of a *specific* system to a way of understanding the *general* history of modern capitalism." Robin D. G. Kelley, "What Did Cedric Robinson Mean by Racial Capitalism?," *Boston Review*, January 12, 2017, www.bostonreview.net/articles/robin-d-g-kelley-introduction-race-capitalism-justice/; see also Zachary Levenson and Marcel Paret, "The South African Tradition of Racial Capitalism," *Ethnic and Racial Studies* 46, no. 16 (2023): 3403–3424, DOI: 10.1080/01419870.2023.2219300. Rationalize in both senses of the word: to "attempt to explain or justify (behavior or an attitude) with logical reasons, even if these are not appropriate" and also to "make (a company, process, or industry) more efficient, especially by dispensing with superfluous personnel or equipment." *Oxford English Dictionary* (2016), www.oed.com/search/advanced/Meanings?q=rationalize. Linebaugh, *The London Hanged*, loc. 9213–9341; In Olúfẹ́mi O. Táíwò's words:

> You don't need to be sold on the phrase "racial capitalism" to understand it. Use it or don't; the world will be what it is, whether we subtract a word or add several to any term. What matters about racism, capitalism, racial capitalism, and any other options are the ideas underneath and what we do with them. Racial capitalism offers us a clue: If it is true that racism and capitalism are in a mutually supporting relationship, then we should expect that any potentially effective anti-racist and anti-capitalist struggles will also be mutually supporting. Our ultimate goal isn't to understand the origins of a term or even its lineage, but to understand the workings of a world we are trying to change.

Olúfẹ́mi O. Táíwò, "A Framework to Help Us Understand the World," *Hammer and Hope*, Winter 2023, https://hammerandhope.org/article/issue-1-article-8.

Dalia Gebrial said:

> I think for me the usefulness of a term like racial capitalism is to essentially give us the tools to think about how social differentiation and class composition happen through and alongside one another and how these are very integral processes in shaping the kind of inequalities and exploitation that we see today. I often think of

> racialisation as like a resource and an organising principle, in the same way that you can think of oil as a central resource of capitalism. I feel like racialisation can almost operate in that it's this kind of endless, often material resource from which capitalism can draw the tools from which it is able to reproduce itself. (Penny, "Abolition Geography")

Sharpe, *In The Wake*, loc. 474; Gilmore wrote, "Human sacrifice rather than innocence is the central problem that organizes the carceral geographies of the prison-industrial complex. Indeed, for abolition, to insist on innocence is to surrender politically because 'innocence' evades a problem abolition is compelled to confront: how to diminish and remedy harm as against finding better forms of punishment." Gilmore, "Abolition Geography and the Problem of Innocence," loc. 6509–6510, 6610; Melinda Cooper, "Infinite Regress: Virginia School Neoliberalism and the Tax Revolt," *Capitalism: A Journal of History and Economics* 2, no. 1 (Winter 2021): 41–87; Tobi Haslett, "Magic Actions," *n+1*, Summer 2021, www.nplusonemag.com/issue-40/politics/magic-actions-2/.

13. Bhattacharyya, *We, the Heartbroken*, loc. 429–439, 952; Amanda Barroso and Rachel Minkin, "Recent Protest Attendees Are More Racially and Ethnically Diverse, Younger Than Americans Overall," Pew Research Center, June 24, 2020, www.pewresearch.org/short reads/2020/06/24/recent-protest-attendees-are-more-racially-and-ethnically-diverse-younger-than-americans-overall/.

14. Jamiles Lartey and Ciara McCarthy, "Memphis Teen 'Was Running Away' When Shot Dead by Police, Witnesses Say," *Guardian*, December 16, 2015, www.theguardian.com/us-news/2015/dec/16/memphis-darrius-stewart-moving-away-from-police-officer-shooting-witnesses.

15. Nick Valencia, "Memphis Leaders Pass Measure That Ends Police Stops for Minor Infractions, Three Months After Tyre Nichols' Death," CNN.com, April 12, 2023, https://edition.cnn.com/2023/04/12/us/memphis-pretext-stops-tyre-nichols/; Edwin Rios, "Calls to 'Demolish and Rebuild' Police as Memphis Mourns Tyre Nichols," *Guardian*, January 28, 2023, www.theguardian.com/us-news/2023/jan/28/tyre-nichols-memphis-protest-police.

16. "I-40 Bridge Reopens Following Hours-Long Protest," Action News 5, July 11, 2016, www.actionnews5.com/story/32411896/protesters-blocking-i-40–bridge/.

17. Sharpe, *In the Wake*, loc. 1525–1537; Imani Perry, "Stop Hustling Black Death," *Cut*, May 24, 2021, www.thecut.com/article/samaria-rice-profile.html; Pelot-Hobbs, *Prison Capital*, loc. 278.

18. Derecka Purnell writes, "Lezley McSpadden said of her son, Michael Brown: 'I just want them to know who Michael Brown was. That's my purpose. My son was not a bad person, he was not a thug, he didn't have a rap sheet, he didn't tote a pistol, he was not like that at all.'" Derecka Purnell, *Becoming Abolitionists: Police, Protests and the Pursuit of Freedom* (New York: Astra House, 2021), loc. 4100, Kindle; Claudia Rankine, "The Condition of Black Life Is One of Mourning," *New York Times*, June 22, 2015, www.nytimes.com/2015/06/22/magazine/the-condition-of-black-life-is-one-of-mourning.html.

19. Rankine, "Mourning." Sharpe, *In the Wake*, loc. 2025; W. E. B. Du Bois, *Black Reconstruction in America: An Essay Toward a History of the Part Which Black Folk Played in the Attempt to Reconstruct Democracy in America, 1860–1880*, ed. Henry Louis Gates Jr., introduction by David Levering Lewis (Oxford: Oxford University Press, 2014), loc. 1835–1848, Kindle; Nadine El-Enany puts it this way: "Settler colonial authorities destroyed indigenous families, stealing children and exposing them to extreme physical and mental abuse, depriving them of their language and culture. Slavery annihilated kinship for black Americans . . . entailing the tearing apart of families." El-Enany, "From Love to Justice."

20. Adam Elliott-Cooper, "'Our Life Is a Struggle': Respectable Gender Norms and Black Resistance to Policing," *Antipode* 51, issue 2 (March 2019): 539–557, doi: 10.1111/anti.12497; Adam Elliott-Cooper, *Black Resistance to British Policing* (Manchester: Manchester University Press, 2021); El-Enany, "From Love to Justice"; Purnell, *Becoming Abolitionists*, loc. 1396–1401; Fleming Smith, "'Remarkable' Judy Scott, Mother of Walter Scott, Dies at 76," *Post and Courier*, January 30, 2020, www.postandcourier.com/news/remarkable-judy-scott-mother-of-walter-scott-dies-at-76/article_ede47cee-4365-11ea-a487-ab876ede6039.html.

21. Gilmore, "You Have Dislodged a Boulder: Mothers and Prisoners in the Post-Keynesian California Landscape," in *Abolition Geography*, loc. 5383–5415; Gilmore, "Abolition Geography and the Problem of Innocence," loc. 7690; El-Enany, "From Love to Justice."

22. Perry, "Stop Hustling Black Death"; Da'Shaun Harrison, "Updated Statement from Samaria Rice, Lisa Simpson, and the Collective," *Medium*, March 31, 2021, https://dashaunlh.medium.com/official-statement-from-samaria-rice-lisa-simpson-and-the-collective-b466399bcd2f.

23. Elsewhere, James wrote indelibly, "What we are witnessing before our very eyes is the process whereby women's struggle is hidden from history and transformed into an industry, jobs for the girls." Selma James, *Sex, Race and Class: The Perspective of Winning; A Selection of Writings 1952–2011* (Binghamton, NY: PM Press, 2012), 128, 212.

24. Andreas Malm and the Zetkin Collective noted in *White Skin, Black Fuel* that "the Oxford Dictionary gives two definitions of the term 'extraction': 'the action of extracting something, especially using effort or force' and 'the ethnic origin of someone's family,' as in being of German extraction." Like capital punishment / the punishment of capital, the contrast is telling when we consider the construction of race. Andreas Malm and the Zetkin Collective, *White Skin, Black Fuel: On the Dangers of Fossil Fascism* (London: Verso, 2021), loc. 4286, Kindle. Táíwò, *Elite Capture*, loc. 154–181, 832–841.

25. Perry, "Stop Hustling Black Death"; Táíwò, *Elite Capture*, loc. 947–948.

26. Butler, *Precarious Life*, loc. 462; Butler, *Undoing Gender*, loc. 405–407; Clover, *Riot. Strike. Riot*, loc. 1570–1621, 2411–2417.

27. OaklandMurals.com, "All Mothers Were Summoned," photograph, artists @sheandsampaguita, @shocktheworld, Gina Lau, painted June 2020, photographed June 2020 by Kris Diede, https://oaklandmurals.com/all-mothers-were-summoned/; Twitter, @uche_blackstock, "all mothers were summoned when he called out for his mama." March 31, 2021, credited to Instagram @privtoprog, https://twitter.com/uche_blackstock/status/1377220946889748483; Urban Art Mapping, "All Mothers Were Summoned When He Called Out for His," artists Mibaron, jmz, axz, photograph by Froukje Akkerman, https://georgefloydstreetart.omeka.net/items/show/1124.

28. In *Wayward Lives, Beautiful Experiments*, Saidiya Hartman wrote of the lives that Black women carved out of a freedom that was always threatened, noting that "flexible and elastic kinship were not 'plantation holdover,' but a resource of black survival, a practice that documented the generosity and mutuality of the poor." Saidiya Hartman, *Wayward Lives, Beautiful Experiments: Intimate Histories of Riotous Black Girls, Troublesome Women, and Queer Radicals* (New York: W. W. Norton, 2020), loc. 1189, Kindle.

29. Amanda Rivkin and Jeremy Borden, "Darrell Cannon," Chicago Police Torture Archive, https://chicagopolicetorturearchive.com/darrell-cannon.

30. Joey Mogul, another attorney with the People's Law Office, presented the evidence to the UN committee, saying in part, "For the past 30 years, the United States has failed to comply with Article 2 of the Convention Against Torture. Back in 1982, Mayor Richard M. Daley was informed of specific torture allegations made by Andrew Wilson when he was Cook County state's attorney. As state's attorney and as mayor, he has not only failed to investigate, but

has continued to suppress evidence of this documented pattern of torture. We have exhausted all remedies locally." Natalie Y. Moore, "Payback," Marshall Project, October 30, 2018, www.themarshallproject.org/2018/10/30/payback.

31. Adam Sege, "Man Dies After Chicago Police Use Taser During Arrest," *Chicago Tribune*, May 21, 2014, www.chicagotribune.com/news/breaking/chi-man-tased-by-police-while-resisting-arrest-dies-20140521-story.html; Mariame Kaba, "Damo's Dead & Other Reasons to Fight," *Prison Culture* (blog), May 26, 2014, www.usprisonculture.com/blog/2014/05/26/damos-dead-other-reasons-to-fight/.

32. Civil Rights Movement Archive, "Dec. 17, 1951: 'We Charge Genocide' Petition Submitted to United Nations," Zinn Education Project, accessed January 30, 2024, www.zinnedproject.org/news/tdih/we_charge_genocide_petition; William L. Patterson, *We Charge Genocide: The Historic Petition to the United Nations for Relief from a Crime of the United States Government Against the Negro People* (New York: International, 1970).

33. *We Charge Genocide: Police Violence Against Chicago's Youth of Color: A Report Prepared for the United Nations Committee Against Torture on the Occasion of Its Review of the United States of America's Third Periodic Report to the Committee Against Torture*, http://report.wechargegenocide.org/.

34. Moore, "Payback."

35. Judith Butler, "Between Grief and Grievance, a New Sense of Justice," in *Grief and Grievance*, ed. Okwui Enwezor, Naomi Beckwith, and Massimiliano Gioni (Phaidon Press, 2020), 12–14.

36. Murch, *Assata Taught Me*, loc. 1803–2053; see also Jason E. Smith, "Abolition After the George Floyd Rebellion: On Jarrod Shanahan and Zhandarka Kurti's 'States of Incarceration,'" *Los Angeles Review of Books*, January 4, 2023, https://lareviewofbooks.org/article/abolition-after-the-george-floyd-rebellion-on-jarrod-shanahan-and-zhandarka-kurtis-states-of-incarceration/.

37. As Rodrigo Nunes wrote, "The best one can hope for is that most participants of an ecology embody an ethos of acting ecologically, non-competitively, without a narcissistic investment in their own protagonism, placing the health and the interests of the ecology as a whole above their own or their organisation's; and that the ecology retain a capacity for diffuse control that can ensure that 'evil' opportunists (those who exploit opportunities for their own ends) will also be 'bad' ones (quickly found out and isolated)." Nunes, *Neither Vertical nor Horizontal*, loc. 767–768, 2028–2685, 3249–3252.

38. Marcus Rediker, *The Slave Ship: A Human History* (New York: Penguin, 2007), loc. 5763, Kindle; Gilmore, "Abolition Geography and the Problem of Innocence," loc. 6322–6354. Rediker quotes a letter from a financier to a slave ship captain in 1700: "The whole benefitt of the Voyage lyes in your care in Preserving negroes lives" (Rediker, *Slave Ship*, loc. 138–156, 1130, 4319, 4467–4474); Sharpe, *In the Wake*, loc. 1998; Guy Faulconbridge and Kate Holton, "Update: Lloyd's of London Apologizes for Its 'Shameful' Role in Atlantic Slave Trade," *Insurance Journal*, June 18, 2020, www.insurancejournal.com/news/international/2020/06/18/572696.htm.

39. "Protestors March Along I-55 Bridge Following Release of Tyre Nichols Traffic Stop Footage," Action News 5, January 28, 2023, www.actionnews5.com/2023/01/28/i-55-bridge-shut-down-due-protestors/.

40. Doreen St. Felix, "The Memphis Police Are Not Bystanders to the Death of Tyre Nichols," *New Yorker*, February 1, 2023, www.newyorker.com/culture/cultural-comment/the-memphis-police-are-not-bystanders-to-the-death-of-tyre-nichols; Marcus, *Political Disappointment*, 106.

41. Leila Taylor, *Darkly*, loc. 1147–1149, Kindle; Joy James and Rebecca Wilcox, "How the University De-radicalizes Students, Professors, and Social Movements," Villanova University, YouTube, February 18, 2022, www.youtube.com/watch?v=IjeWk4VGNGk&ab_channel=villanovauniversity; Murch, *Assata Taught Me*, loc. 1091–1093; Marcus, *Political Disappointment*, 146–147.

42. Avery Gordon wrote: "Complex personhood means that the stories people tell about themselves, about their troubles, about their social worlds, and about their society's problems are entangled and weave between what is immediately available as a story and what their imaginations are reaching toward." Gordon, *Ghostly Matters*, loc. 4; Tyre Nichols, "T. Nichols Photography" (2023), https://thiscaliforniakid2.wixsite.com/tnicholsphotography/about.

43. L. J. Abraham Facebook page, www.facebook.com/watch/live/?ref=watch_permalink&v=1015661522735601.

44. Decarcerate Memphis, "Driving While BIPOC Summary" (2022), https://emma-assets.s3.amazonaws.com/dzubb/47ef855ecaa40bbb8ed08fe66aaa5862/Driving_while_BIPOC__Summary.pdf; Brittany Brown, "Tyre Nichols' Death Began with a Traffic Stop: Now, Organizers Want to Rethink Public Safety," MLK50, February 6, 2023, https://mlk50.com/2023/02/06/tyre-nichols-death-began-with-a-traffic-stop-now-organizers-want-to-rethink-public-safety/.

45. Sydney Gray, "Black and Low-Income Drivers Impacted Most by Traffic Stops in Memphis," Action News 5, December 12, 2022, www.actionnews5.com/2022/12/12/black-low-income-drivers-impacted-most-by-traffic-stops-memphis/.

46. Statement from the Wells family (Tyre Nichols's family), Decarcerate Memphis Instagram post, www.instagram.com/p/CpgSktFPXix/; Brittany Brown, "Tyre Nichols Family, Organizers Mistrustful of Council's Police Reform Ordinance," MLK50, April 6, 2023, https://mlk50.com/2023/04/06/seeing-the-mpd-language-nichols-family-organizers-skeptical-of-city-councils-police-reform-ordinance/.

47. Vicky Osterweil, *In Defense of Looting* (New York: Bold Type Books, 2019), loc. 3450–3468, Kindle.

48. Keith Magee, "The Remarkable Response of RowVaughn Wells After Her Son Tyre Nichols' Death," *Time*, January 30, 2023, https://time.com/6251186/rowvaughn-wells-response-tyre-nichols-death/.

49. Al Lewis is not the only one to focus on the economic power behind the police. As Robin D. G. Kelley noted, part of the municipal debt that many cities carry comes from payouts from wrongful death lawsuits—Tyre Nichols's mother, RowVaughn Wells, sued the city for $550 million—and those debts in turn make money for bondholders. The banks, Kelley noted, "are making money off of death." That money moves from taxpayers to the city to the banks rather than to schools, services, streets. Christina Heatherton, Robin D. G. Kelley, and Peter Linebaugh, "Robin D.G. Kelley and Peter Linebaugh on American Thanatocracy," *Conjuncture* (podcast), January 24, 2024, https://open.spotify.com/episode/6gBQEtKlTxUeQKUpfhmQhn?si=0796cf8676ce4c7b; Alyxandra Goodwin, Whitney Shepard, and Carrie Sloan, "Police Brutality Bonds: How Wall Street Profits from Police Violence," Action Center on Race and the Economy, June 24, 2020, https://acrecampaigns.org/research_post/police-brutality-bonds/; David Royer, "Trial Date Set for Tyre Nichols Family's $550M Lawsuit Against Memphis," WREG News Channel 3, January 25, 2024, https://wreg.com/news/local/tyre-nichols/trial-date-set-for-tyre-nichols-familys-550m-lawsuit-against-memphis/.

50. Shortly before I visited Memphis, a shooter killed six people, including three children, at a Nashville school, and yet in the state a federal judge "quietly cleared the way to drop the minimum age for Tennesseans to carry handguns publicly without a permit to 18—just two years

after a new law set the age at 21." Kimberlee Kruesi and Jonathan Mattise, "After School Shooting, Tenn. Gun Laws Likely to Remain Lax," Associated Press, March 29, 2023, https://apnews.com/article/gun-laws-tennessee-shooting-6192267a5ef5791416adda36667d287b.

51. Purnell, *Becoming Abolitionists*, loc. 1571–1602.

52. Day and McBean, *Abolition Revolution*, loc. 257; Matt Foot and Morag Livingstone, *Charged: How the Police Try to Suppress Protest* (London: Verso 2022), loc. 165–188, Kindle.

53. Daniel De Simone, "Stephen Lawrence: BBC Names New Suspect in UK's Most Notorious Racist Murder," BBC News, June 26, 2023, www.bbc.co.uk/news/uk-65989993; Foot and Livingstone, *Charged*, loc. 2076–2355; see also Elliott-Cooper, *Black Resistance*; Day and McBean, *Abolition Revolution*, loc. 299–525, 612–625, 1808–1823.

54. Day and McBean, *Abolition Revolution*, loc. 379–553; Angela Y. Davis, Gina Dent, Erica R. Meiners, and Beth E. Richie, *Abolition. Feminism. Now.* (Chicago: Haymarket Books, 2022), 19–20.

55. Day and McBean, *Abolition Revolution*, loc. 553–555.

56. Megan Specia, "Sarah Everard's Death Set Off a Movement, but for Friends the Grief Is Personal," *New York Times*, March 17, 2021, www.nytimes.com/2021/03/17/world/europe/sarah-everard-uk.html; Day and McBean, *Abolition Revolution*, loc. 556–656; Molly Blackall, "Sarah Everard: Reclaim These Streets Cancels Its South London Vigil," *Guardian*, March 13, 2021, www.theguardian.com/uk-news/2021/mar/13/sarah-everard-vigil-in-south-london-cancelled-organisers-say.

57. Day and McBean, *Abolition Revolution*, loc. 879–896, 1139–1142; Foot and Livingstone, *Charged*, loc. 4041–4063.

58. Day and McBean, *Abolition Revolution*, loc. 1466; Kate Kellaway, "Patsy Stevenson: 'We Were Angry at Being Told We Couldn't Mourn the Death of a Woman,'" *Observer*, December 7, 2021, www.theguardian.com/uk-news/2021/dec/07/patsy-stevenson-interview-everard-vigil-arrest-faces-of-year.

59. Day and McBean, *Abolition Revolution*, loc. 562, 1139–1142.

60. Day and McBean, *Abolition Revolution*, loc. 1476–1488.

61. Day and McBean, *Abolition Revolution*, loc. 866–983, 1022–1034, 2576–2582, 4025; Foot and Livingstone, *Charged*, loc. 4035.

62. Day and McBean wrote, "As Abolitionist Futures have noted—from the 1981 Scarman Report (on the Brixton riots) and the 1999 Macpherson Report (which examined the murder of Stephen Lawrence), and right up to the present day—police emphasis during a crisis is never on how to eliminate racism or sexism from policing and society; but focuses squarely on how to placate public sentiment." Day and McBean, *Abolition Revolution*, loc. 828–839, 1028–1034; Amy Walker and Molly Blackall, "Why Did Cressida Dick Resign? The Failings Which Left the Met Police Commissioner 'No Choice' but to Quit," iNews, February 11, 2022, https://inews.co.uk/news/cressida-dick-resign-why-met-police-commissioner-quit-failings-explained-1455269; for more on Cressida Dick, I highly recommend the two-part episode of the *Bad Gays* podcast on Dick, the Metropolitan Police, and queer and lesbian identity: Huw Lemmey and Ben Miller, "S5E8&9: Cressida Dick," *Bad Gays* (podcast), February 2022, https://badgayspod.com/episode-archive/s5e8-cressida-dick-part-one.

63. Gilmore and Gilmore, "Beyond Bratton," loc. 4224.

64. Becky Z. Dernbach, "Valerie Castile Says the State's New School-Meals Law Is an Investment in Minnesota's Kids—and a Tribute to Her Son, Philando," *Sahan Journal*, March 17, 2023, https://sahanjournal.com/education/free-school-meals-bill-minnesota-valerie-philando-castile/.

65. Dana Ferguson and Brian Bakst, "Minnesota Legislature Passes $72 Billion Budget; Ends Session," MPR News, May 22, 2023, www.mprnews.org/story/2023/05/22/minnesota-legislature-poised-to-wrap-up-72-billion-budget-before-deadline.

66. Eliott C. McLaughlin and Ray Sanchez, "Minneapolis Police Clear Officers in Fatal Shooting of Jamar Clark," CNN, October 21, 2016, https://edition.cnn.com/2016/10/21/us/jamar-clark-shooting/index.html; Murch, *Assata Taught Me*, loc. 139; Rebecca McCray, "Jamar Clark Protests Persist as Community Demands Answers in Shooting Death," TakePart, November 19, 2015, www.takepart.com.s3-website-us-east-1.amazonaws.com/article/2015/11/18/jamar-clark-minneapolis/; Steven W. Thrasher, "The Men Who Shot at the Minneapolis Protesters Want to Scare All Black People," *Guardian*, November 25, 2015, www.theguardian.com/commentisfree/2015/nov/24/minneapolis-protesters-shot-terrorize-black-people. Cameron Clark told reporters, "It's like a dream, but it's really true though," he said. "Because I never thought a white supremacist, or anybody, would have come in and caused harm to us, at a nonviolent protest, so it kind of shocked me. What was the reason, or who sent you down here to cause this harm? You shot five black people. What was the reason, and why? Me, waking up every day, looking at my wound, and the pain that I go through, it's really crazy." Doualy Xaykaothao, "On Eve of Scarsella's Sentence, Victim Still Feels Wounds," MPR News, April 26, 2017, www.mprnews.org/story/2017/04/26/on-eve-of-scarsellas-sentence-victim-still-feels-wounds.

67. While modern abolitionist politics is building deliberately to counter hundreds of years of common sense about the need for police and prisons, it is also true that there have been those who fought them from their inception. In London in 1780, a mob burned Newgate Prison. When brought to trial, one of those men, asked why he did it, replied, "The Cause." Asked to elaborate, he said, "There should not be a prison standing on the morrow in London." His cause, of course, did not succeed. The first police force would be formed eighteen years later, in 1798. Linebaugh, *The London Hanged*, loc. 5972–5975, 7314–7484.

68. "Minneapolis Police Fire Teargas at Protesters After Death of George Floyd—Video," *Guardian*, May 27, 2020, www.theguardian.com/us-news/video/2020/may/27/minneapolis-police-fire-teargas-at-protesters-after-death-of-george-floyd-video; Nunes, *Neither Vertical nor Horizontal*, loc. 2028–2122.

69. "Minneapolis, Minnesota, Question 2, Replace Police Department with Department of Public Safety Initiative (November 2021)," Ballotpedia, https://ballotpedia.org/Minneapolis,_Minnesota,_Question_2,_Replace_Police_Department_with_Department_of_Public_Safety_Initiative_(November_2021); US Department of Justice Civil Rights Division and US Attorney's Office District of Minnesota Civil Division, "Investigation of the City of Minneapolis and the Minneapolis Police Department," press release, June 16, 2023, www.justice.gov/opa/press-release/file/1587661/download.

70. Associated Press in New Orleans, "Death of Man Shot by Police After Hurricane Katrina Ruled as Homicide," *Guardian*, April 1, 2015, www.theguardian.com/us-news/2015/apr/01/new-orleans-death-police-hurricane-katrina-homicide.

71. Tobi Haslett, "Magic Actions," *n+1*, Summer 2021, www.nplusonemag.com/issue-40/politics/magic-actions-2/.

72. Sara Marcus wrote of Reconstruction, "But in the history of this country, the experience of a possible transformation's failure to arrive becomes particularly salient beginning with the failure of Reconstruction and its aftermath. From that point forward, the experience of outdated and unfulfilled desire predominates throughout the twentieth century." Marcus, *Political Disappointment*, 2, 24; Du Bois, *Black Reconstruction in America*, loc. 2531–2534; Rhae Lynn Barnes and Keri Leigh Merritt, "Introduction: The Present Crisis,"

in Barnes, Merritt, and Williams, *After Life*, loc. 429–430; Peniel E. Joseph, "The Afterlife of Black Political Radicalism," in Barnes, Merritt, and Williams, *After Life*, loc. 2039–2067; Keri Leigh Merritt and Yohuru Williams, conclusion to Barnes, Merritt, and Williams, *After Life*, loc. 3606–3613; see also Sarah Jaffe, *Necessary Trouble: Americans in Revolt* (New York: Nation Books, 2016), 159–187; Brian Schwartz, "Joe Biden Sees Fundraising Surge in Wake of George Floyd's Death and Trump's Response to Protests," CNBC, June 2, 2020, www.cnbc.com/2020/06/02/biden-sees-fundraising-surge-in-wake-of-george-floyd-death-trump-response.html; Ruth Igielnik, Scott Keeter, and Hannah Hartig, "Behind Biden's 2020 Victory," Pew Research, June 30, 2021, www.pewresearch.org/politics/2021/06/30/behind-bidens-2020-victory/; Akela Lacy, "Democratic Backlash to 'Defund the Police' Jeopardizes Popular Reforms," *Intercept*, December 7, 2020, https://theintercept.com/2020/12/07/defund-police-qualified-immunity/.

73. Day and McBean, *Abolition Revolution*, loc. 205.

74. Sharpe, *In the Wake*, loc. 2501.

75. Aviah Sarah Day [@Aviah_Sarah_Day], #waterloositin, Twitter.com, October 28, 2023, https://twitter.com/Aviah_Sarah_Day/status/1718311867020431521; Sisters Uncut [@SistersUncut], Waterloo Station Sit-In, October 28, 2023, https://twitter.com/SistersUncut/status/1718262061086425532.

76. Adam Shatz, "Vengeful Pathologies," *London Review of Books*, November 2, 2023, www.lrb.co.uk/the-paper/v45/n21/adam-shatz/vengeful-pathologies.

77. Jewish Voice for Peace, "The Root of Violence Is Oppression," October 7, 2023, www.jewishvoiceforpeace.org/2023/10/07/statement23-10-07/. "Gaza: Forced and protracted displacement of Palestinians would constitute a serious breach of international law and an atrocity crime," Norwegian Refugee Council, December 26, 2023, www.nrc.no/news/2023/december/gaza-displacement/.

78. Eyewitness News, "300+ Arrested After Peace Activists Hold Protests in Grand Central Calling for Cease-Fire," ABC 7 New York, October 28, 2023, https://abc7ny.com/grand-central-pro-israel-rally-mta-metro-north/13982013/; "Thousands Protest in Rome in Support of Palestine," YouTube video, posted by Middle East Eye, October 29, 2023, www.youtube.com/watch?v=G4prwzqSmNQ&ab_channel=MiddleEastEye; Black Jewish Alliance [@BlackJewishA], "Police are attempting to arrest Jews in prayer," Twitter, November 2, 2023, https://twitter.com/BlackJewishA/status/1720008869051617644.

79. According to the military website for Pine Bluff, "Pine Bluff Arsenal is a world leader in the design, manufacture and refurbishment of smoke, riot control and incendiary munitions, as well as chemical/biological defense operations items. It serves as the group technology center for illuminating and infrared munitions and is also the only place in the Northern Hemisphere where white phosphorus munitions are filled." Pine Bluff Arsenal, "Home," accessed November 22, 2023, www.pba.army.mil/command/info.htm; Amnesty International, "Lebanon: Evidence of Israel's Unlawful Use of White Phosphorus in Southern Lebanon as Cross-Border Hostilities Escalate," Amnesty International, October 31, 2023, www.amnesty.org/en/latest/news/2023/10/lebanon-evidence-of-israels-unlawful-use-of-white-phosphorus-in-southern-lebanon-as-cross-border-hostilities-escalate/.

80. Bisan Owda, a Gazan filmmaker, is twenty-five. Plestia Alaqad, a journalist and recent graduate, twenty-two. Motaz Azaiza, twenty-five, celebrated his birthday on Instagram in January shortly after evacuating from Gaza. Bisan Owda on Instagram, www.instagram.com/stories/wizard_bisan1/; Plestia Alaqad on Instagram, www.instagram.com/byplestia/; Motaz

Azaiza, on Instagram (his birthday post), www.instagram.com/p/C2uNFskLO3Q/; Zaina Arafat, "Witnessing Gaza Through Instagram," *New York Magazine*, November 20, 2023, https://nymag.com/intelligencer/article/bisan-plestia-motaz-gaza-through-my-instagram-feed.html.

81. The statement of the Statue of Liberty activists read in part:

> After shutting down Grand Central Station last week, HUNDREDS of us are taking over the Statue of Liberty and risking arrest, including rabbis, elected officials, celebrities, descendants of Holocaust survivors, elders and children—because we will not be silent while the Israeli military wages a genocidal war in our name, with our tax dollars. The famous words of our Sephardi Jewish ancestor Emma Lazarus etched into this very monument compel us to take action supporting the Palestinians of Gaza yearning to breathe free.
>
> As Jews in the US, many of our families were greeted by the Statue of Liberty while escaping violence and pogroms. Some were let in, but others were turned away. Our government has a long history of complicity in genocidal violence. This time, we call on our political leaders to make a different choice. Call for a ceasefire. Stop funding Israeli airstrikes on Palestinians. From Ellis Island to Gaza, never again means never again—for anyone.

Jewish Voice for Peace, Instagram, November 6, 2023, www.instagram.com/p/CzUHeN4AQTx/; Hoda Katebi, "HAPPENING NOW: We have blocked EVERY SINGLE DAMN ENTRANCE to Boeing Factory 598 outside St. Louis, the facility that manufactures Joint Direct Attack Munition (JDAM) systems and Small Diameter Bombs (SDBs) for Israel to drop on Gaza, RIGHT before the first rush of workers come in to assemble and ship bombs," Instagram, November 6, 2023, www.instagram.com/p/CzTo8QtrWzS/?img_index=6; Bassem Masri died in 2018. Cori Bush, the congressperson from St. Louis and the coauthor of the ceasefire resolution in Congress, paid tribute to him on the floor of the House in 2021: "Bassem was one of us. Bassem showed up ready to resist, to rebel, to rise up as St. Louis mourned Michael Brown Jr.'s state-sanctioned murder. . . . I remember Bassem putting his life on the line for us." David Warren, "Rep. Cori Bush's Impact on the US Israel-Palestine Debate," Mondoweiss, May 28, 2021, https://mondoweiss.net/2021/05/rep-cori-bushs-impact-on-the-us-israel-palestine-debate/.

82. If Not Now Movement, "Why We Organize," IfNotNowmovement.org, accessed November 22, 2023, www.ifnotnowmovement.org/why-we-organize.

83. Motaz Azaiza [@motaz_azaiza], "Gazans in their way evacuating the city toward south of Gaza strip," Instagram, November 10, 2023, www.instagram.com/p/CzdvaKnsFvt/; Motaz Azaiza [@motaz_azaiza], "The super mom," Instagram, November 10, 2023, www.instagram.com/p/Czd2z_ZMjWz/; Motaz Azaiza [@motaz_azaiza], "Palestinians evacuating Gaza city and the north of the strip towards the south of the strip due to the Israeli heavy bombing and the military orders to leave the city," www.instagram.com/p/CzhAxJeLdoT/; "London November 11: One Million March for Palestine," YouTube video, posted by ReelNews, November 12, 2023, www.youtube.com/watch?v=Cqk6VXiFm6c&ab_channel=ReelNews.

84. Rabbis for Ceasefire [@rabbis4ceasefire], "HAPPENING NOW: Prayers for a Ceasefire Ring Out at the Capitol," Instagram, November 13, 2023, www.instagram.com/p/Czl3ltauQSQ/; Rabbis for Ceasefire [@Rabbis4ceasefire], "In the face of loss, Jewish tradition recognizes our profound need to mourn," Instagram, November 5, 2023, www.instagram.com/p/CzRvo13O7if/.

85. Hisham Awartani, no title, *College Hill Independent*, December 1, 2023, https://theindy.org/article/3137; Reuters, "One of the Three Palestinian-American Students Shot in Vermont Is

Paralyzed," *Guardian*, December 3, 2023, www.theguardian.com/us-news/2023/dec/03/vermont-one-of-three-palestinian-american-students-shot-paralyzed.

86. Jacqueline Rose, *The Question of Zion* (Princeton, NJ: Princeton University Press, 2007), loc. 89–94, Kindle; Nicki Kattoura and Geo Maher, "Israel-Palestine War: Why Must Palestinians Condemn Themselves for Daring to Fight Back?," *Middle East Eye*, November 9, 2023, www.middleeasteye.net/opinion/israel-palestine-war-why-condemnation-trap; Heatherton, Kelley, and Linebaugh, "American Thanatocracy."

87. Jacqueline Rose, *The Last Resistance* (New York: Verso, 2017), loc. 916–917, 1640, Kindle; Rose, *The Question of Zion*, loc. 1063–1240.

88. Journalist Adam Shatz wrote:

> Israel's disregard for Palestinian life has never been more callous or more flagrant, and it's being fuelled by a discourse for which the adjective "genocidal" no longer seems like hyperbole. In just the first six days of air strikes, Israel dropped more than six thousand bombs, and more than twice as many civilians have already died under bombardment as were killed on 7 October. These atrocities are not excesses or "collateral damage": they occur by design. As Israel's defence minister, Yoav Gallant, puts it, "we are fighting human animals and we will act accordingly." (Fanon: "when the colonist speaks of the colonised he uses zoological terms" and "refers constantly to the bestiary.") Since Hamas's attack, the exterminationist rhetoric of the Israeli far right has reached a fever pitch and spread to the mainstream. "Zero Gazans," runs one Israeli slogan. A member of Likud, Netanyahu's party, declared that Israel's goal should be "a Nakba that will overshadow the Nakba of 1948." "Are you seriously asking me about Palestinian civilians?" the former Israeli prime minister Naftali Bennett said to a reporter on Sky News. "What is wrong with you? We're fighting Nazis." ("Vengeful Pathologies")

Omer Bartov, Christopher R. Browning, Jane Caplan, Debórah Dwork, Michael Rothberg, et al., "An Open Letter on the Misuse of Holocaust Memory," *New York Review of Books*, November 20, 2023, www.nybooks.com/online/2023/11/20/an-open-letter-on-the-misuse-of-holocaust-memory/; Rose, *The Last Resistance*, loc. 2756.

89. Rose, *The Last Resistance*, loc. 1774, 3141.

90. Rose, *The Question of Zion*, loc. 72, 1233–1245, 1752–1760, 1823, 1937; Rose, *The Last Resistance*, loc. 491, 920.

91. Scholar Josh Ruebner wrote in the *Hill* that the threat was not idle but in fact in process, quoting Israeli security cabinet member and agriculture minister Avi Dichter as saying, "We are now rolling out the Gaza Nakba. Gaza Nakba 2023. That's how it'll end." Josh Ruebner, "Israel Is Threatening a Second Nakba—but It's Already Happening," *Hill*, November 17, 2023, https://thehill.com/opinion/international/4313276-israel-is-threatening-a-second-nakba-but-its-already-happening/; Rose, *The Question of Zion*, loc. 35–66, 1803–1809.

92. Frantz Fanon, glossed by Malm and the Zetkin Collective, wrote of the experience of colonization as "not as a flowering or a development of an essential productiveness, but as a permanent struggle against an omnipresent death. This ever-menacing death is experienced as endemic famine, unemployment, a high death rate, an inferiority complex and the absence of any hope for the future." Malm and the Zetkin Collective, *White Skin, Black Fuel*, loc. 4846; Rose, *The Last Resistance*, loc. 979–993; Barnaby Raine, "Jewophobia," *Salvage*, January 7, 2019, https://salvage.zone/jewophobia-2/; Megan Wachspress, "The 'New Antisemitism' and the Logic of Whiteness," *Los Angeles Review of Books*, November 29, 2023, https://lareviewofbooks.org/article/the-new-antisemitism-and-the-logic-of-whiteness.

93. Gillian Rose, *Mourning Becomes the Law: Philosophy and Representation* (Cambridge: Cambridge University Press, 1997), 27, 30, 36, 41–43, 76, 100; Bartov et al., "Open Letter."

94. Anshel Pfeffer, "Why Israel Should Not Compare Hamas to the Nazis," *Ha'aretz*, October 31, 2023, https://www.haaretz.com/israel-news/2023-10-31/ty-article/.premium/why-israel-should-not-compare-hamas-to-the-nazis/0000018b8692-d055-afbf-b6b34f9e0000; Rose, *The Last Resistance*, loc. 1076; Rose, *The Question of Zion*, loc. 1971.

95. Rose, *The Question of Zion*, loc. 606–614, 1839–1881, 2019; Rose, *The Last Resistance*, loc. 1094, 1202, 2182–2188, 3751–3998, 4109–4249.

96. This making of Jewish pain into a biological fact, making of Jewishness into a biological trait discounts the very things that Jewish religion and history have so valued. As Dade Lemanski noted, an emphasis on "making Jewish babies," on reproduction, "teaches young Jews that Judaism and Jewish history are not, actually, something to be studied or learned, but rather something natural, essential, and inherited without any effort, which undermines a far more robust and multifaceted approach to Judaism and replaces it with biological essentialism." Dade Lemanski, "On Zionism, Sexual Coercion, and Biologically Essential Judaism," *Sinkhole/Gloryhole*, December 27, 2023, https://sinkhole-gloryhole.ghost.io/on-zionism-sexual-coercion-and-biologically-essential-judaism/; Shatz, "Vengeful Pathologies"; Elliot Kukla, "Opinion: I'm the Child of a Holocaust Survivor: I Know the Trauma Inflicted on Gaza Will Last for Generations," *Los Angeles Times*, November 17, 2023, www.latimes.com/opinion/story/2023-11-17/generational-trauma-gaza-children-holocaust-survivor.

97. Rose, *The Last Resistance*, loc. 281; Rose, *The Question of Zion*, loc. 1278.

98. Gabriel Winant, "On Mourning and Statehood: A Response to Joshua Leifer," *Dissent*, October 13, 2023, www.dissentmagazine.org/online_articles/a-response-to-joshua-leifer/; "Noy Katsman on CNN: 'My Call to My Government, Stop Killing Innocent People,'" YouTube video, posted by Breaking the Silence, October 10, 2023, www.youtube.com/watch?v=DeritmLPpBQ&ab_channel=BreakingtheSilence; Dan Berger, "The Abolitionist Logic of 'Everyone for Everyone,'" *Jewish Currents*, December 1, 2023, https://jewishcurrents.org/the-abolitionist-logic-of-everyone-for-everyone.

99. Maya Rosen wrote in *Jewish Currents*:

> As Lee Siegel, whose brother and sister-in-law Keith and Aviva are being held hostage, put it to me, "Every day that goes by and every further military action from both sides can only put the hostages more at risk." Amid these concerns, Israeli government officials have issued a string of strikingly callous statements. Gilad Erdan, Israel's ambassador to the United Nations, said in an interview that the hostages are "not going to stop us, prevent us from doing what we need to do in order to secure the future of Israel." Bezalel Smotrich, Israel's finance minister and head of the far-right Religious Zionism party, argued in a cabinet meeting, "We have to be cruel now and not think too much about the hostages." When an interviewer responded to Minister of Heritage Amichai Eliyahu's suggestion that Israel should drop an atomic bomb on Gaza by asking about the fate of the hostages in such a scenario, Eliyahu replied, "I hope and pray for their return, but there are costs in war."

She continued, "As Mairav Zonszein, senior analyst at the International Crisis Group, a research and policy think tank, told me: 'Netanyahu's seeming apathy towards the families of the hostages makes you wonder whether they would be more of a priority if they were among his base.' In a crass articulation of this point, which he now denies making, right-wing Member of Knesset Simcha Rotman said on November 1st that the blood of two religious settlers killed in February in the West Bank 'is redder than that of those killed on October 7th.'"

Maya Rosen, "Hostages' Families Fight to Be Heard," *Jewish Currents*, November 15, 2023, https://jewishcurrents.org/hostages-families-fight-to-be-heard; Berger, "The Abolitionist Logic of 'Everyone for Everyone.'"

100. Rivkah Brown, "The Israeli War Machine Runs on Jewish Fear," Novara Media, October 25, 2023, https://novaramedia.com/2023/10/25/the-israeli-war-machine-runs-on-jewish-fear/; Rose, *The Last Resistance*, loc. 833.

101. Sarah Jaffe, "A Long History of Antifascism Is Driving the Jewish Demand for Gaza Cease-Fire," *In These Times*, December 15, 2023, https://inthesetimes.com/article/chanukah-jewish-antifascism-israel-palestine-jvp-ifnotnow-gaza-ceasefire.

102. Hanno Hauenstein, "Why Is Germany Cracking Down on Pro-Palestine Protest?," *Nation*, October 30, 2023, www.thenation.com/article/politics/germany-palestine-protest/.

103. Nicki Kattoura and Nada Abuasi, "Grief Beyond Language," Institute for Palestine Studies, October 27, 2023, www.palestine-studies.org/en/node/1654517; Devin G. Atallah, "Beyond Grief: To Love and Stay with Those Who Die in Our Arms," Institute for Palestine Studies, October 24, 2023, www.palestine-studies.org/en/node/1654491.

104. Bisan Owda [@wizard_bisan1], "29/11/2023. It's getting darker," Instagram, November 29, 2023, www.instagram.com/p/C0PdsY_riMp/; Nadda Osman, "Israel-Palestine War: Israeli Forces Destroy Central Archive of Gaza City," *Middle East Eye*, December 7, 2023, www.middleeasteye.net/news/israel-palestine-war-israeli-forces-destroy-central-archive-gaza-city.

105. "Can You Tell Us Why This Is Happening? Testimonies from Gaza," *n+1*, November 23, 2023, www.nplusonemag.com/online-only/online-only-can-you-tell-us-why-this-is-happening/.

106. "Can You Tell Us Why This Is Happening?"

107. Hala Alyan, "The Palestine Double Standard," *New York Times*, October 25, 2023, www.nytimes.com/2023/10/25/opinion/palestine-war-empathy.html; Malm quoted in Hayes and Kaba, *Let This Radicalize You*, 172.

108. Ibrahim Husseini, Majed Abusalama, Aviah Sarah Day, and Shanice Octavia McBean, "Solidarity Under Siege: Palestine and the Criminalization of Protest," YouTube video, posted by Haymarket Books, November 20, 2023, www.youtube.com/watch?v=ttFcqjGHGz8&ab_channel=HaymarketBooks.

109. Raine, "Jewophobia"; Rachel Shabi, "To Understand Israel-Palestine, First Understand the History of Racism and Antisemitism," *Guardian*, November 13, 2023, www.theguardian.com/commentisfree/2023/nov/13/israel-palestine-racism-antisemitism?s=09; Rose, *The Question of Zion*, loc. 1561.

110. Day and McBean, *Abolition Revolution*, loc. 1701; Purnell, *Becoming Abolitionists*, 1706, 1945–1953; Murch, *Assata Taught Me*, loc. 1122; Táíwò, "A Framework"; Eli Day, "Finding a Path to an Enduring Black-Palestine Solidarity," *+972 Magazine*, September 30, 2019, www.972mag.com/black-palestine-solidarity-dream-defenders/; Edith Garwood, "With Whom Are Many U.S. Police Departments Training? With a Chronic Human Rights Violator—Israel," Amnesty International, August 25, 2016, www.amnestyusa.org/updates/with-whom-are-many-u-s-police-departments-training-with-a-chronic-human-rights-violator-israel/; Zaina Alsous and Sammy Hanf, "How Durham, North Carolina, Became the First US City to Ban Police Exchanges with Israel," *Scalawag*, May 18, 2021, https://scalawagmagazine.org/2021/05/israel-palestine-durham-police/; Alice Speri, "Israel Security Forces Are Training American Cops Despite History of Rights Abuses," *Intercept*, September 15, 2017, https://theintercept.com/2017/09/15/police-israel-cops-training-adl-human-rights-abuses-dc-washington/.

111. Mersiha Gadzo, "How the US and Israel Exchange Tactics in Violence and Control," Al Jazeera, June 12, 2020, www.aljazeera.com/news/2020/6/12/how-the-us-and-israel-exchange-tactics-in-violence-and-control.

112. Jonathan Guyer, "Most of Israel's Weapons Imports Come from the US: Now Biden Is Rushing Even More Arms," *Vox*, November 18, 2023, www.vox.com/world-politics/2023/11/18/23966137/us-weapons-israel-biden-package-explained; Annie Karni, "Senate Bogs Down on Ukraine and Israel Aid After G.O.P. Blocks Border Deal," *New York Times*, February 7, 2024, www.nytimes.com/2024/02/07/us/politics/congress-ukraine-israel-aid.html; Rose, *The Question of Zion*, loc. 1552–1560.

113. Rose, *The Question of Zion*, loc. 114–118.

114. Elle Hardy, "What Do Christian Zionists Think About Jews?," *Unherd*, December 4, 2023, https://unherd.com/2023/12/what-do-christian-zionists-think-about-jews/; Karen Attiah, "John Hagee at the March for Israel? Bad Choice," *Washington Post*, November 17, 2023, www.washingtonpost.com/opinions/2023/11/17/israel-gaza-march-john-hagee/; Bruce Wilson, "'Half-Breed Jew' Committed Holocaust, Claims Netanyahu Ally John Hagee," *HuffPost*, March 12, 2015, www.huffpost.com/entry/netanyahu-ally-john-hagee_b_6848226; Rose, *The Question of Zion*, loc. 470; Rose, *The Last Resistance*, loc. 1155.

115. Or, as Jacqueline Rose wrote, "Jewishness must find itself in the connections between peoples, whether in the Diaspora or in Palestine." Rose, *The Last Resistance*, loc. 296, 4000; Rose, *The Question of Zion*, loc. 2197.

116. Bassem Saad, "Palestine's Martyrdom Upends the World of Law," *Protean Magazine*, January 27, 2024, https://proteanmag.com/2024/01/27/palestines-martyrdom-upends-the-world-of-law/; Berger, *Hold Everything Dear*, 70; JustVision, "Shahid," Glossary, accessed February 8, 2024, https://justvision.org/glossary/shahid.

117. Li explained in detail:

> Legally, the most compelling aspect of South Africa's case is not its devastating recitation of the facts attesting to the scale of killing and destruction in Gaza but rather its meticulous reconstruction of genocidal intent. It begins with pages of brazen statements from the highest echelons of government and the military vowing to wipe out Gaza and then proceeds to demonstrate that those sentiments have trickled all the way down to rank-and-file conscripts. It also details how mass displacement, the systematic deprivation of food and water, and the widespread destruction of health-care infrastructure have set the stage for an entirely foreseeable public health emergency that may claim even more lives than the bombing.
>
> Beyond the legal arguments, the case has also resonated because of the country that brought it to the ICJ. For some Western liberals, South Africa's moral credibility as a symbol of multiracial reconciliation adds even more gravity to the charge of genocide—or at least makes it more difficult to dismiss. For Palestinians, the case harkens back to a long tradition of joint struggle between anti-colonial movements. And for international lawyers, it recalls earlier waves of Third Worldist litigation, especially the cases brought by Ethiopia and Liberia to challenge apartheid South Africa's hold over what is now Namibia.

Darryl Li, "The Charge of Genocide," *Dissent*, January 18, 2024, www.dissentmagazine.org/online_articles/the-charge-of-genocide/; Linah Alsaafin, Tamila Varshalomidze, and Brian Osgood, "Israel's War on Gaza Live: 300k at Risk of Famine in North Gaza—UN," Al Jazeera, February 8, 2024, www.aljazeera.com/news/liveblog/2024/2/8/israels-war-on-gaza-live-us-says-space-for-truce-deal-israel-vows-war; Saad, "Palestine's Martyrdom"; Fatima Al-Kassab, "A

Top U.N. Court Says Gaza Genocide Is 'Plausible' but Does Not Order Cease-Fire," NPR, January 26, 2024, www.npr.org/2024/01/26/1227078791/icj-israel-genocide-gaza-palestinians-south-africa; Emma Graham-Harrison, "Gaza Death Toll Set to Pass 30,000 as Israel Prepares Assault on Rafah," *Guardian*, February 25, 2024, https://www.theguardian.com/world/2024/feb/25/gaza-death-toll-set-to-pass-30000-as-israel-prepares-assault-on-rafah; Wafaa Shurafa and Kareem Chehayeb, "Palestinian deaths in Gaza pass 30,000 as witnesses say Israeli forces fire on crowd waiting for aid," Associated Press, February 29, 2024, https://news.yahoo.com/strike-palestinians-waiting-aid-gaza-085752518.html.

118. Husseini et al., "Solidarity Under Siege."

Chapter 2: Flow: Migration, home, and freedom

1. Nicholas Boni, "No Matter How Rich You Are, You Can't Own the Sea," *Jacobin*, June 23, 2023, https://jacobin.com/2023/06/titan-submersible-implosion-search-media-wealth-inequality; Moira Lavelle and Vedat Yeler, "Survivors: 'Greek Coastguard Was Next to Us When Boat Capsized,'" Al Jazeera, July 5, 2023, www.aljazeera.com/features/2023/7/5/survivors-greek-coastguard-was-next-to-us-when-boat-capsized; Human Rights Watch, "Greece: Disparities in Accounts of Pylos Shipwreck Underscore the Need for Human Rights Compliant Inquiry," Human Rights Watch, August 3, 2023, www.hrw.org/news/2023/08/03/greece-disparities-accounts-pylos-shipwreck-underscore-need-human-rights-compliant.

2. Christine Chung, "Extreme Travel Rescue Operations Are Vast in Scale and Cost: Who Foots the Bill Is Murky," *New York Times*, June 20, 2023, www.nytimes.com/2023/06/22/us/titanic-submersible-search-rescue-costs.html; Alex Horton and Dan Lamothe, "What the Titan Search Could Cost—and Who Will Pay for It," *Washington Post*, June 23, 2023, www.washingtonpost.com/national-security/2023/06/23/titan-search-cost/. Mohammed is a pseudonym for a survivor quoted in Lavelle and Yeler, "Survivors"; Louisa Loveluck, Elinda Labropoulou, Heba Farouk Mahfouz, Siobhán O'Grady, and Rick Noack, "They Knew the Boat Could Sink: Boarding It Didn't Feel like a Choice," *Washington Post*, June 24, 2023, www.washingtonpost.com/world/2023/06/24/greek-migrant-boat-victims/.

3. Nektaria Stamouli, "Questions Mount over Latest Migrant Tragedy in Mediterranean," *Politico*, June 18, 2023, www.politico.eu/article/migrant-boat-disaster-mediterranean-greece-tragedy-elections-hellenic-coast-guard/; Infolibre, "Action—Intervention in the Port of Thessaloniki for the Mass Murder of Immigrants off Pylos," June 18, 2023, https://infolibre.gr/2023/06/18/drasi-paremvasi-sto-limani-thessalonikis-gia-ti-maziki-dolofonia-metanast-ri-on-anoichta-tis-pyloy/; "Migrant Crisis Front and Center in Pope's Greece-Cyprus Trip," *Independent*, November 30, 2021, www.independent.co.uk/news/greece-pope-francis-cyprus-lesbos-iraq-b1966625.html; Carola Rackete with Anne Weiss, *The Time to Act Is Now: A Call to Combat Environmental Breakdown*, trans. Claire Wordley (Rosa Luxemburg Stiftung, 2021), loc. 123–127, Kindle, first published in 2019 by Verlagsgruppe Droemer Knaur, Munich, Germany, as *Handeln statt hoffen*.

4. Rackete with Weiss, *Time to Act*, loc. 63–131, 184–186, 205–209, 588–591.

5. Rackete with Weiss, *Time to Act*, loc. 137–138, 211–247, 708–709; Warsan Shire, "Home," Facing History & Ourselves, January 5, 2017, www.facinghistory.org/resource-library/home-warsan-shire.

6. Rackete with Weiss, *Time to Act*, loc. 421–422, 658–659, 1237–1241; Roland Hughes, "Carola Rackete: How a Ship Captain Took on Italy's Salvini," BBC News, July 6, 2019, www.bbc.co.uk/news/world-europe-48853050; "Italy Drops Carola Rackete Charges," *DW*,

December 23, 2021, www.dw.com/en/italy-drops-charges-against-sea-watch-captain-carola-rackete/a-60245299; Lorenzo Tondo, "Matteo Salvini Goes on Trial over Migrant Kidnapping Charges," *Guardian*, October 2, 2020, www.theguardian.com/world/2020/oct/02/matteo-salvini-set-to-be-tried-over-migrant-kidnapping-charges-italy.

7. Frontex's own website states:

> Cooperation with non-EU countries is an integral part of the Frontex mandate to ensure implementation of the European integrated border management (IBM) and one of the strategic priorities for the agency's work.
>
> Together with partners from outside of the EU, Frontex works to develop an increasingly connected global border management community that lives up to the highest standards for border management, coast guarding, law enforcement and return, guarantees the protection of fundamental rights and closely cooperates addressing irregular migration and cross-border crime.
>
> Frontex develops and maintains a reliable network of partnerships with the competent authorities of non-EU countries, particularly in countries neighbouring the EU, as well as in countries of origin and transit for irregular migration.

Frontex.europa.eu, "Other Partners and Projects" (2023), https://frontex.europa.eu/partners/other-partners-and-projects/non-eu-countries/; Marion MacGregor, "EU Report Reveals Systematic Cover-Up by Border Agency," InfoMigrants, October 14, 2022, www.infomigrants.net/en/post/43994/eu-report-reveals-systematic-coverup-by-border-agency.

8. Hayes and Kaba, *Let This Radicalize You*, 122–123; Sasha Ingber and Vanessa Romo, "Captain Who Rescued Migrants at Sea Refuses Paris Medal, Calling It Hypocritical," NPR, August 21, 2019, www.npr.org/2019/08/21/753107888/captain-who-rescued-migrants-at-sea-refuses-paris-medal-calling-it-hypocritical; Rackete with Weiss, *Time to Act*, loc. 712–714.

9. Anna Lekas Miller, *Love and Borders: Passports, Papers and Romance in a Divided World* (Chapel Hill, NC: Algonquin Books, 2023), 28.

10. Loveluck et al., "They Knew the Boat."

11. Greg Grandin, "American Extremism Has Always Flowed from the Border," *Boston Review*, January 9, 2019, www.bostonreview.net/articles/greg-grandin-american-extremism-has-always-flowed-border/; see also Greg Grandin, *The End of the Myth: From the Frontier to the Border Wall in the Mind of America* (Metropolitan Books, 2019); Zoé Samudzi, "Stealing Away in America," *Jewish Currents*, June 10, 2020, https://jewishcurrents.org/stealing-away-in-america; Daniel Denvir, *All-American Nativism, How the Bipartisan War on Immigrants Explains Politics as We Know It* (New York: Verso 2020), loc. 1182, 1584, 3582; Lee Sandusky, "Scenes from an Emergency Clinic in the Sonoran Desert," *LitHub*, September 7, 2017, https://lithub.com/scenes-from-an-emergency-clinic-in-the-sonoran-desert/; Francisco Cantú from *The Line Becomes a River*, quoted in Grandin, "American Extremism."

12. Denvir, *All-American Nativism*, loc. 962–971, 1765–1767; Harsha Walia, *Border and Rule: Global Migration, Capitalism, and the Rise of Racist Nationalism* (Chicago: Haymarket Books, 2021), loc. 590–597, 797–800, 1555–1564; Todd Miller, "How Border Patrol Occupied the Tohono O'odham Nation," *In These Times*, June 12, 2019, https://inthesetimes.com/article/us-mexico-border-surveillance-tohono-oodham-nation-border-patrol.

13. Walia, *Border and Rule*, loc. 345; Robin D. G. Kelley, foreword to Walia, *Border and Rule*, loc. 215.

14. John Carlos Frey, "Graves of Shame," *Texas Observer*, July 6, 2015, www.texasobserver.org/illegal-mass-graves-of-migrant-remains-found-in-south-texas/; Walia, *Border and Rule*, loc. 1131–1135.

15. Linebaugh reminded us that some of those sent to do the work of colonization went too as an alternative to a prison sentence: "transportation" to the colonies, first in America and then Australia, was used to break up solidarity and put the unruly to work. Linebaugh, *The London Hanged*, loc. 606–737; Grandin, "American Extremism"; Walia, *Border and Rule*, loc. 263–279, 341–246, 506, 614.

16. Walia, *Border and Rule*, loc. 2638; Táíwò, "A Framework"; Gilmore, "Abolition Geography and the Problem of Innocence," loc. 6273; Paul Gilroy, *Postcolonial Melancholia* (New York: Columbia University Press, 2004), loc. 2–5, 12, 15, 43, 51, Kindle.

17. Lekas Miller, *Love and Borders*, 172–173.

18. Lekas Miller, *Love and Borders*, loc. 29; Du Bois, *Black Reconstruction in America*, loc. 5746–5748; Marx quoted in Robin D. G. Kelley, *Freedom Dreams: The Black Radical Imagination* (New York: Penguin Random House, 2001), loc. 614–630, Kindle.

19. Sharpe, *In the Wake*, loc. 478; Denvir, *All-American Nativism*, loc. 257, 270–296, 1938; Walia, *Border and Rule*, loc. 777; Lekas Miller, *Love and Borders*, 84.

20. Denvir, *All-American Nativism*, loc. 297, 1878, 1949–1961, 1980; Lekas Miller, *Love and Borders*, 32–33; United States Holocaust Memorial Museum, "Voyage of the St Louis," *Holocaust Encyclopedia*, https://encyclopedia.ushmm.org/content/en/article/voyage-of-the-st-louis. In 2012, then–deputy secretary of state William Burns declared that the United States had been "wrong" and that it had "made a commitment that the next time the world confronts us with another M.S. Saint Louis—whether the warning signs are refugees in flight or ancient hatreds resurfacing—we will have learned the lessons of the M.S. Saint Louis and be ready to rise to the occasion." Rather than an apology, the statement feels self-congratulatory. William J. Burns, "The Legacy of the M.S. Saint Louis," US Department of State, September 24, 2012, https://2009-2017.state.gov/s/d/former/burns/remarks/2012/198190.htm; Rackete with Weiss, *Time to Act*, loc. 325–327; Frantz Fanon, *Wretched of the Earth* (New York: Grove Press, 2005), loc. 57, Kindle; Nunes, *Neither Vertical nor Horizontal*, loc. 1545–1547.

21. Walia, *Border and Rule*, loc. 1721; Fanon, *Wretched of the Earth*, loc. 57–58; Kelley, *Freedom Dreams*, loc. 2650–2652; Táíwò, *Elite Capture*, loc. 232–234, 356–359, 366; Aviah Sarah Day and Shanice Octavia McBean wrote: "You might wonder how much difference migrants sending a few pounds back home would make, but the World Bank estimates that remittances from the Global North to the Global South reached $ 440 billion in 2010, which is ten times more than the total amount of development aid flowing in the same direction." Day and McBean, *Abolition Revolution*, loc. 2074–2079.

22. Walia, *Border and Rule*, loc. 1428–1439; Harsha Walia, "There Is No 'Migrant Crisis,'" *Boston Review*, November 16, 2022, www.bostonreview.net/articles/there-is-no-migrant-crisis/.

23. Identifying with the nation is a choice, one as arbitrary as any other. As Malm and the Zetkin Collective noted, "If identification with the nation came naturally, by origin and birth, nationalists would never need to say anything at all (hence every exertion on their part is a performative contradiction)." Further, "people could just as well identify with their neighbourhood or gender or dietary habits or pets or class, but nationalists interpellate them as—above every other loyalty—subjects of the nation, and only insofar as they respond to the call do they become subjects of a nation that they know and love and will defend against adversaries with all the requisite harshness." Malm and Zetkin Collective, *White Skin, Black Fuel*, loc. 4128–4168; Gilmore, *Golden Gulag*, loc. 11; Walia, *Border and Rule*, loc. 319.

24. Malm and Zetkin Collective, *White Skin, Black Fuel*, loc. 4164–4168; Walia, *Border and Rule*, loc. 2147–2188, 2210, 2236; Rackete with Weiss, *Time to Act*, loc. 1492–1494; Grandin,

"American Extremism"; Al Jazeera and News Agencies, "Israel Completes 'Iron Wall' Underground Gaza Barrier," Al Jazeera, December 7, 2021, www.aljazeera.com/news/2021/12/7/israel-announces-completion-of-underground-gaza-border-barrier.

25. Jessica Bruder, "Meet the Immigrants Who Took On Amazon," *Wired*, November 12, 2019, www.wired.com/story/meet-the-immigrants-who-took-on-amazon/; Abdirahman Muse, Emma Green-man, and Erin Murphy, "Minnesota Enacts Landmark Protections for Amazon Warehouse Workers," *Nation*, May 17, 2023, www.thenation.com/article/politics/amazon-warehouse-workers-minnesota/.

26. Billy Perrigo, "Exclusive: 'I Feel Like I'm Drowning'; Survey Reveals the Toll of Working for Amazon," *Time*, January 19, 2023, https://time.com/6248340/amazon-injuries-survey-labor-osha/.

27. In the *Nation*, Abdirahman Muse, Emma Greenman, and Erin Murphy explain further:

> The bill requires employers to provide warehouse workers with written information about all quotas and performance standards they are subject to, in addition to how those quotas and standards are determined. Employers must provide this information in the worker's primary language—a crucial requirement for warehouses in our state, where more than 86,000 Somali-born immigrants and family members live.
>
> Importantly, the bill also stipulates that employers cannot fire or take disciplinary action against a worker who fails to meet a quota that wasn't disclosed, disarming one of the primary excuses Amazon may use to punish or fire workers who seek better conditions or organize. The bill also mandates that if Amazon or a particular worksite has a rate of injury 30 percent higher than that year's industry average, the Minnesota commissioner of labor and industry will open an investigation.
>
> Finally, the bill establishes a private right of action for workers—meaning current or former workers can bring a civil suit for damages and injunctive relief to obtain compliance with this law. And this bill doesn't just cover Amazon workplaces—it applies to all warehouses with more than 250 workers at a site or 1,000 across the state. ("Landmark Protections")

28. Jason Del Rey, "Leaked Amazon Memo Warns the Company Is Running Out of People to Hire," *Vox*, June 17, 2022, www.vox.com/recode/23170900/leaked-amazon-memo-warehouses-hiring-shortage.

29. Alfonso Galvan, "Amazon Shutters Shakopee Facility, Agrees to Transfer Hundreds of Workers," *Sahan Journal*, March 31, 2023, https://sahanjournal.com/business-work/amazon-closes-shakopee-sort-center-transfers-workers-minnesota/.

30. Maya Goodfellow, *Hostile Environment: How Immigrants Became Scapegoats* (London: Verso, 2019), 152; Walia, "There Is No Migrant Crisis"; Gordon, *Ghostly Matters*, loc. 5, 15–16.

31. Dalia Gebrial, "Racial Platform Capitalism: Empire, Migration and the Making of Uber in London," *EPA: Economy and Space* (2022): 1–25, doi: 10.1177/0308518X221115439, journals.sagepub.com/home/epn.

32. Gebrial, "Racial Platform Capitalism"; Katherine Long, "Amazon Unveiled a New Warehouse Robot That Can Identify and Pick 65% of the Items It Sells: 'This Will Take My Job,' One Warehouse Worker Said," *Business Insider*, November 11, 2022, www.businessinsider.nl/amazon-unveiled-a-new-warehouse-robot-that-can-identify-and-pick-65-of-the-items-it-sells-this-will-take-my-job-one-warehouse-worker-said/.

33. Saidiya Hartman wrote: "Vagrancy was a status, not a crime. It was not doing, withholding, nonparticipation, the refusal to be settled or bound by contract to employer (or husband). The statutes targeted those who maintained excessive notions of freedom and imagined that liberty included the right not to work." Vagrants, she wrote, were "migrants, wanderers, fugitives, displaced persons, and strangers." Hartman, *Wayward Lives*, loc. 2993–3007; Silvia Federici, "On Primitive Accumulation, Globalization, and Reproduction," in *Re-enchanting the World*, loc. 586; Adler-Bolton and Vierkant, *Health Communism*, loc. 850–888.

34. Pew Research Center, "The Military-Civilian Gap: Fewer Family Connections," Pew Research Center, November 23, 2011, www.pewresearch.org/social-trends/2011/11/23/the-military-civilian-gap-fewer-family-connections/.

35. Butler, *Frames of War*, loc. 57–59, 121–123, 166–167, 197, 209, 700–701, 789–791, 950–955; Ali Vitali, Kasie Hunt, and Frank Thorp V, "Trump Referred to Haiti and African Nations as 'Shithole' Countries," NBC News, January 11, 2018, www.nbcnews.com/politics/white-house/trump-referred-haiti-african-countries-shithole-nations-n836946; see also Jeremy Scahill, *Dirty Wars: The World Is a Battlefield* (New York: Bold Type Books, 2013).

36. Grandin, "American Extremism."

37. Walia, *Border and Rule*, loc. 675–686, 958–960, 979; Julian Borger, "Fleeing a Hell the US Helped Create: Why Central Americans Journey North," *Guardian*, December 19, 2018, www.theguardian.com/us-news/2018/dec/19/central-america-migrants-us-foreign-policy; Huma Gupta and China Sajadian with Ruth Wilson Gilmore, "Green, Red and International," Environment in Context Podcast, August 25, 2021, www.jadaliyya.com/Details/43252.

38. Borger, "Fleeing a Hell the US Helped Create"; Walia, *Border and Rule*, loc. 961–982.

39. Osterweil, *In Defense of Looting*, loc. 3577–3578; Denvir, *All-American Nativism*, loc. 1389–1392, 2545–2553; Borger, "Fleeing a Hell the US Helped Create"; Walia, *Border and Rule*, loc. 889; Ruth Wilson Gilmore wrote:

> According to a presentation given by a JfJ organizing committee in Los Angeles in March 1993, organizing has in some cases stretched back to immigrant janitors' towns of origin in Mexico and El Salvador.
>
> Insofar as it is common for people from a particular region to migrate to both the same area and labor-market niche as their friends and families who precede them, JfJ started to work backward along the migratory path in an attempt to incorporate the wider-than-daily labor market into the movement's sphere of influence. During this same presentation, when challenged by a Sandinista cadre who asked an apparently simple question ("What became of the people who used to be janitors?"), JfJ acknowledged that its organizing had not extended to the former workers. JfJ pledged to expand its Southern California scope of activity and reach out to former janitors in the community, who are, as noted above, mostly African Americans, in a project that many hoped would revive submerged knowledge from earlier labor and antiracist struggles. (*Golden Gulag*, loc. 274)

Anna Lekas Miller, *Love and Borders*, 111; Walia, *Border and Rule*, loc. Walia, *Border and Rule*, 883–888, 1789; Denvir, *All-American Nativism*, loc. Denvir, *All-American Nativism,* 3431; Borger, "Fleeing a Hell the US Helped Create."

40. Gilroy, *Postcolonial Melancholia*, loc. 22, 59; Day and McBean, *Abolition Revolution*, loc. 2318–2347; Malm and Zetkin Collective, *White Skin, Black Fuel*, loc. 805–940.

41. Malm and the Zetkin Collective further noted: "Just like Jews, Muslims had slid from a religious into a racial genus, presumed to have their most defining characteristics conferred to them from their source of origin. . . . The people in question had been racialised, although

not so much on the basis of somatic features, the absence of which might elicit nervousness about the hidden, invisible Muslim or Jew; in Nazi Germany, Jewish bodies had to be marked out with yellow stars of David. . . . Neither race nor capital exists in nature. They are not 'natural phenomena, like comets or quarks' but *social artefacts*, a distinction presupposed by every critical theory of race." Malm and Zetkin Collective, *White Skin, Black Fuel*, loc. 1568–1596, 1902, 4203–4205, 4663, 5058–5072; Paul Hanebrink, *A Specter Haunting Europe* (Cambridge, MA: Belknap Press, 2018), loc. 96–101, 4750–4767; Walia, *Border and Rule*, loc. 2443; Goodfellow, *Hostile Environment*, 53, 147, 185.

42. El Paso, Monica Muñoz Martinez noted, "was selected to pilot the inhumane family separation policy that eventually removed nearly 5,500 children from their guardians." Monica Muñoz Martinez, "El Paso in Mourning," in Barnes, Merritt, and Williams, *After Life*, loc. 492–517; Julio Cesar-Chavez, "Texas Shooting Suspect Told Police He Targeted 'Mexicans,'" Reuters, August 9, 2019, www.reuters.com/article/us-texas-shooting-idUSKCN1UZ28K; Meredith Deliso, "El Paso Walmart Gunman Patrick Crusius Given 90 Life Sentences in Federal Trial," ABC News, July 7, 2023, https://abcnews.go.com/US/el-paso-walmart-gunman-patrick-crusius-sentenced-90/story?id=100776455; Purnell, *Becoming Abolitionists*, loc. 3178–3272.

43. Gilroy, *Postcolonial Melancholia*, loc. 149–150; Jaden Edison and Patrick Sviek, "At Least 50 People Found Dead in Abandoned 18-Wheeler in San Antonio," *Texas Tribune*, June 27, 2022, www.texastribune.org/2022/06/27/bodies-18-wheeler-san-antonio-lackland/.

44. Butler, *Frames of War*, loc. 915–917; Gilroy, *Postcolonial Melancholia*, loc. 150.

45. I am using his first name only to protect his safety.

46. Just a quick web search for "gassing the Kurds" turns up thousands of results, including Juan Cole, "Did Saddam Gas the Kurds," History News Network, 2002, http://hnn.us/articles/1242.html; Kendal Nazan, "When Our 'Friend' Saddam Was Gassing the Kurds," Le Monde Diplomatique, March 1998, https://mondediplo.com/1998/03/04iraqkn; Parliamentary debate in Britain on January 20, 2003, https://publications.parliament.uk/pa/cm200203/cmhansrd/vo030120/debtext/30120-12.htm; "The Moral of Saddam Hussein," *Economist*, December 18, 2003, www.economist.com/leaders/2003/12/18/the-moral-of-saddam-hussein.

47. Sarhang Hamasaeed and Garrett Nada, "Iraq Timeline: Since the 2003 War," United States Institute of Peace, May 29, 2020, www.usip.org/iraq-timeline-2003-war.

48. Goodfellow, *Hostile Environment*, 2, 6; Lekas Miller, *Love and Borders*, 195; "The Hostile Environment Explained," Joint Council for the Welfare of Immigrants, www.jcwi.org.uk/the-hostile-environment-explained.

49. Goodfellow, *Hostile Environment*, 16–17, 20–25, 110; Gebrial, "Racial Platform Capitalism."

50. Day and McBean, *Abolition Revolution*, loc. 1986–1995; Olivia Petter, "Windrush Scandal: Everything You Need to Know About the Major Political Crisis," *Independent*, May 31, 2022, www.independent.co.uk/life-style/windrush-day-2022-scandal-history-b2090931.html; Lekas Miller, *Love and Borders*, 189–190; Amelia Gentleman, "'I Feel Such Indignation': Windrush Victims on the Compensation Process," *Guardian*, June 22, 2023, www.theguardian.com/uk-news/2023/jun/22/windrush-victims-on-compensation-process; El-Enany, "From Love to Justice"; Caolan Magee, "Record Number of Windrush Compensation Claims Rejected," iNews, January 21, 2024, https://inews.co.uk/news/huge-leap-number-windrush-scandal-zero-compensation-2860787; Goodfellow pointed to the story of Abdillaahi Muuse, who, when "detained for common assault, he gave his Dutch passport and driving licence as proof that as an EU citizen he couldn't be deported. But officials from what was then the UK Border Agency were to have bluntly told Muuse, a Dutch national of Somali reported origin: 'Look at you, you're African.' They held him for four months and told him they would send

him to Africa. He successfully challenged detention, but if immigration had nothing to do with race, why did Muuse, an EU citizen, end up in detention?" Goodfellow, *Hostile Environment*, 3, 188–189.

51. The environment is hostile across western Europe: Malm and the Zetkin Collective wrote that in Denmark, "the Danish state started confiscating jewellery and cash from refugees upon arrival (supposedly to make them pay for the services rendered). Then it designated twenty-five predominantly low-income Muslim neighbourhoods as 'ghettos,' whose inhabitants were subjected to a series of special laws, including harsher punishments for crimes and mandatory separation of children from their parents for a period every week (although the DF failed to convince the government to put all 'ghetto children' under curfew from 8 p.m. by fitting them with electronic bracelets). . . . The Danish state proceeded to isolate asylum-seekers convicted of crimes on a tiny island previously used for researching contagious animal diseases, ferry them to their new abodes in a ship called 'Virus' and proclaim that the time had come to give up on integrating refugees in Danish society: they should henceforth be kept apart from the autochthonous population until they could be sent packing." Malm and Zetkin Collective, *White Skin, Black Fuel*, loc. 2625–2643; American Immigration Council, "The Real Meaning of 'Self-Deportation,'" press release, January 26, 2012, www.americanimmigrationcouncil.org/news/real-meaning-%E2%80%9Cself-deportation%E2%80%9D; Goodfellow, *Hostile Environment*, 32–33.

52. Andrew McDonald, "Britain's Plan to Deport Migrants to Rwanda Will Cost £169,000 per Person," *Politico*, June 27, 2023, www.politico.eu/article/uk-plan-to-deport-migrants-to-rwanda-will-cost-169000-per-person-migration-asylum/; Kiran Stacey, "Home Office Hires Hangar for Staff to Practise Rwanda Deportations," *Guardian*, January 19, 2024, www.theguardian.com/politics/2024/jan/19/home-office-hires-hangar-for-staff-to-practise-rwanda-deportations; May Bulman and Bel Trew, "'Like I Was Going to Be Executed': On Board the Failed Rwanda Deportation Flight," *Independent*, www.independent.co.uk/news/uk/politics/rwanda-flight-refugees-deportation-migrant-b2102064.html; Maya Goodfellow, "Think Priti Patel Was Bad? Suella Braverman Wants to Make Claiming Asylum Near-Impossible," *Guardian*, October 5, 2022, www.theguardian.com/commentisfree/2022/oct/05/priti-patel-suella-braverman-claiming-asylum-home-secretary; Harsha Walia notes that the EU and the United States as well have extended bordering into Africa, training border patrol agents, forcing African countries to implement migration controls as well as agreements like the one with Rwanda. Walia, *Border and Rule*, loc. 1773–1776; Butler, *Frames of War*, loc. 955–966.

53. For more on Occupy Homes and Occupy, see Jaffe, *Necessary Trouble*.

54. Gilroy, *Postcolonial Melancholia*, loc. 123; Garza, *Grieving*, 144; Victoria Chang, *Dear Memory: Letters on Writing, Silence, and Grief* (Minneapolis, MN: Milkweed Editions, 2021), 22, 49, 80.

55. For more on IX's fight against Apartment Shop, see Roberto Edward de la Riva Rojas, "Tenants Took On the Biggest Landlord in Minneapolis—and Won," *Forge*, October 21, 2021, https://forgeorganizing.org/article/tenants-took-biggest-landlord-minneapolis-and-won; Matthew Desmond, "The Tenants Who Evicted Their Landlord," *New York Times Magazine*, October 13, 2020, www.nytimes.com/2020/10/13/magazine/rental-housing-crisis-minneapolis.html; Inquilinxs Unidxs Por Justicia, www.inquilinxsunidxs.org/en/about.

56. Butler, *Frames of War*, loc. 557–561, 652–655.

57. Day and McBean, *Abolition Revolution*, loc. 2090–2109; Rivkah Brown, "Couriers Stunt Dalston's Gentrification: The Police and Council Want Them Gone," Novara Media, May 17, 2022, https://novaramedia.com/2022/05/17/couriers-stunt-dalstons-gentrification-the-police-and-council-want-them-gone/.

58. Walia, "There Is No Migrant Crisis."

59. Denvir, *All-American Nativism*, loc. 379, 3642; Walia, *Border and Rule*, loc. 363–370, 2604; Laura Briggs, *How All Politics Became Reproductive Politics: From Welfare Reform to Foreclosure to Trump* (Berkeley: University of California Press, August 2018), 85, 86; Walia, "There Is No Migrant Crisis"; Gebrial, "Racial Platform Capitalism."

60. After Hurricane Katrina, Lydia Pelot-Hobbs wrote, immigrant workers came to the city to do disaster cleanup only to wind up harassed and arrested. Organizer Jacinta Gonzalez told her, "People would be picked up for looking for work and we would go find them in the jail." Pelot-Hobbs, *Prison Capital*, 301; Walia, *Border and Rule*, loc. 779, 1145, 1694–1701.

61. Denvir, *All-American Nativism*, loc. 309–332.

62. Lekas Miller, *Love and Borders*, 98; Briggs, *How All Politics Became Reproductive Politics*, 87–89; Denvir, *All-American Nativism*, loc. 332–364.

63. Sarah Jaffe and Michelle Chen, "Belabored: How Workers Escape, with Saket Soni," *Dissent*, June 2, 2023, www.dissentmagazine.org/blog/belabored-how-workers-escape-with-saket-soni/; Saket Soni, *The Great Escape: A True Story of Forced Labor and Immigrant Dreams in America* (New York: Algonquin Books, 2023), 58, 284, 308, 324; Denvir, *All-American Nativism*, loc. 347; Briggs, *How All Politics Became Reproductive Politics*, 91; Walia, *Border and Rule*, loc. 2495–2579, 2737–2769.

64. Emiliano Mellino, "'It's Almost the Same as Living on the Street': This Is How the People Picking Your Vegetables Have to Live," Bureau of Investigative Journalism, April 13, 2023, www.thebureauinvestigates.com/stories/2023-04-13/its-almost-the-same-as-living-on-the-street-this-is-how-people-picking-your-vegetables-have-to-live; Prem Thakker, "Florida Republicans Admit They Made a Big Mistake with Anti-immigrant Law," *New Republic*, June 5, 2023, https://newrepublic.com/post/173247/floida-republicans-admit-made-big-mistake-anti-immigrant-law.

65. Researcher Hilary Goodfriend wrote of the deportation-to-call-center pipeline:

> For bilingual workers, the industry offers relatively advantageous conditions, with starting salaries of around $600 per month versus the miserable $295 in the maquilas. Nevertheless, call centers follow the same maquila labor model: constant surveillance, limited bathroom access, demanding quotas, minimal break time, scarce promotion opportunities, and strict anti-union practices. . . . In addition to attracting university students and frustrated recent graduates, El Salvador's call centers have been a central economic and social hub for the country's ballooning deportee population since their inception. Indeed, call centers are some of the only workplaces that will open their doors to deportees, who are commonly associated with gang activity and face widespread discrimination. In the call centers, 1.5 generation deportees find an opportunity to commercialize their linguistic and cultural skills in a space uniquely tolerant of their highly stigmatized tattoos, shaved heads, baggy clothes and, in many cases, criminal records.

Hilary Goodfriend, "Deportation as Outsourcing in El Salvador's Call Center Industry," *Viewpoint Magazine*, February 1, 2018, https://viewpointmag.com/2018/02/01/deportation-outsourcing-el-salvadors-call-center-industry/.

66. I am using their first names only to protect their safety.

67. Garza, *Grieving*, 68–69; Arlie Russell Hochschild, "Global Care Chains and Emotional Surplus Value," in *Justice, Politics, and the Family*, ed. Daniel Engster, Tamara Metz (New York: Routledge, 2014); see also Barbara Ehrenreich and Arlie Russell Hochschild, eds., *Global Woman: Nannies, Maids and Sex Workers in the New Economy* (New York: Henry Holt), 2004; Briggs, *How All Politics Became Reproductive Politics*, 79–95.

68. Briggs, *How All Politics Became Reproductive Politics*, 79; Lynn May Rivas, "Invisible Labors: Caring for the Independent Person," in Ehrenreich and Hochschild, *Global Woman*, loc. 1416; Barbara Ehrenreich, "Maid to Order," in Ehrenreich and Hochschild, *Global Woman*, loc. 1576.

69. Ociel Alí López, "A New Colombia: The Rise of the Left," NACLA, June 30, 2022, https://nacla.org/new-colombia-left-elections; Joshua Collins and Daniela Diaz, "Petro's 'Total Peace' in Colombia: Essential, but Not Easy," NACLA, August 18, 2022, https://nacla.org/petro-new-peace-plan-colombia.

70. "The Evil Eye," *Jewitches* (blog), https://jewitches.com/blogs/blog/the-evil-eye.

71. Gilroy, *Postcolonial Melancholia*, loc. 67–70, 79.

72. Butler, *Frames of War*, loc. 752–756.

Break III

1. Butler, *Precarious Life*, loc. 476–477.

Chapter 3: Dig: Deindustrialization, work, and meaning

1. Joe Hill, "Don't Mourn, Organize!," *Jacobin*, November 19, 2015, https://jacobin.com/2015/11/joe-hill-songs-utah-iww-union-labor-haywood; Joe Hill, *The Letters of Joe Hill: Centenary Edition*, ed. Alexis Buss and Philip S. Foner (Chicago: Haymarket Books, 2015).

2. Mary Harris "Mother" Jones, *The Autobiography of Mother Jones*, complete and unabridged (first published by Charles Kerr in 1925, proofed and corrected by Hakan Erbil), https://archive.iww.org/history/library/MotherJones/autobiography/6/.

3. Sarah Jaffe, "Back at the Carrier Plant, Workers Are Still Fighting on Their Own," *Nation*, April 20, 2017, www.thenation.com/article/archive/back-at-the-carrier-plant-workers-are-still-fighting-on-their-own/.

4. Tony Cook, "Trump Campaigned on Saving Jobs at Indianapolis' Carrier Plant: This Is What It's like Now," *Indianapolis Star*, October 30, 2020, https://eu.indystar.com/story/news/politics/2020/10/30/trump-campaigned-saving-jobs-carrier-what-its-like-there-now/6010437002/.

5. Jaffe, "Back at the Carrier Plant."

6. Benjamin, "Theses on the Philosophy of History," loc. 202–203.

7. Gordon, *Ghostly Matters*, loc. 29.

8. Clover, *Riot. Strike. Riot*, loc. 139–140, 202–204; Gavin Mueller, *Breaking Things at Work: The Luddites Are Right About Why You Hate Your Job* (New York: Verso, 2021), loc. 190–192, Kindle.

9. Marx wrote, "By turning his money into commodities that serve as the material elements of a new product, and as factors in the labour-process, by incorporating living labour with their dead substance, the capitalist at the same time converts value, i.e. past, materialized, and dead labour into capital, into value big with value, a live monster that is fruitful and multiplies." Marx, *Capital*, loc. 1:3558–3561. Mario Tronti added:

> Capital sees the labour process solely as a process of valorization, it sees labour-power solely as capital; it alters the relation between living labour and dead labour, between the creative force of value and value; it can do so to the degree in which it is able to recuperate the whole process of social labour within the process of valorization of capital, in the degree that it can integrate labour-power within capital. . . . As a result, dead labour, like any natural force, provides a free service to capital: and when it is invested and put into motion by living labour, it accumulates and reproduces itself as capital.

Mario Tronti, "Factory and Society," trans. Guio Jacinto, June 13, 2013, https://operaismoinenglish.wordpress.com/2013/06/13/factory-and-society/; Aaron Benanav, *Automation and the Future of Work* (New York: Verso, 2020), loc. 27–34, 42–45, 201–202, Kindle; Mueller, *Breaking Things at Work*, loc. 450–463; Clover, *Riot. Strike. Riot*, loc. 202–204.

10. Anna Tsing noted that "plantations were organized to further alienation to better control," that later "factories built plantation-style alienation into their plans." Tsing, *The Mushroom at the End of the World*, 39–40; Aaron Benanav wrote, "Excitement about a coming age of automation can be traced back to at least the mid nineteenth century, with the publication of Charles Babbage's *On the Economy of Machinery and Manufactures* in 1832, John Adolphus Etzler's *The Paradise within the Reach of All Men, without Labour* in 1833, and Andrew Ure's *The Philosophy of Manufactures* in 1835." Benanav, *Automation*, loc. 202–207; Meredith Whittaker in turn noted, "Babbage's early nineteenth-century theories of worker control helped shape industrial factory management and predated methods later codified under the term 'scientific management' by Frederick Winslow Taylor. Babbage documented his ideas on labor discipline in his famous volume *On the Economy of Machinery and Manufactures*, published a year before Britain moved to abolish West Indian slavery. His work built on that of Adam Smith, extolling methods for labor division, surveillance, and rationalization that have roots on the plantation." Meredith Whittaker, "Origin Stories: Plantations, Computers, and Industrial Control," *Logic(s) Magazine*, May 17, 2023, https://logicmag.io/supa-dupa-skies/origin-stories-plantations-computers-and-industrial-control/; Mueller, *Breaking Things at Work*, loc. 363–370. See also Ed Baptist, *The Half Has Never Been Told: Slavery and the Making of American Capitalism* (New York: Basic Books, 2015); Helen Hester and Nick Srnicek, *After Work: A History of the Home and the Fight for Free Time* (London: Verso, 2023); Illouz, *Cold Intimacies*, loc. 259–353, Kindle; Craig Gent, *Cyberboss: The Rise of Algorithmic Management and the New Struggle for Control at Work* (London: Verso, 2024).

11. Workers have rebelled against work even before the dominance of the thing we call wage labor: as Beatrice Adler-Bolton and Artie Vierkant wrote, the first statute compelling labor was passed in England in 1349 in the wake of the Black Death. "The point was not just to regulate the non-working poor but to establish a categorical distinction between the 'idle' or 'vagrant' poor and unemployed workers, all of whom were seen as greedily withholding their labor power from the ruling class." Adler-Bolton and Vierkant, *Health Communism*, loc. 850–888; Clover, *Riot. Strike. Riot*, loc. 872–874; Mueller, *Breaking Things at Work*, loc. 132–147, 189–190, 211–218.

12. Murch, *Assata Taught Me*, loc. 230–248, 828; Gilmore, *Golden Gulag*, loc. 45–54.

13. W. E. B. Du Bois, in a much-cited passage, wrote, "It must be remembered that the white group of laborers, while they received a low wage, were compensated in part by a sort of public and psychological wage. They were given public deference and titles of courtesy because they were white." Du Bois, *Black Reconstruction in America*, loc. 16468–16469. Lip service as substitute for real wages is not limited to white workers; it was used also to motivate women workers in various caring and service professions. See Bethany Moreton, *To Serve God and Wal-Mart: The Making of Christian Free Enterprise* (Cambridge, MA: Harvard University Press, 2010); also my previous writing on the subject in *Work Won't Love You Back*; Clover, *Riot. Strike. Riot*, loc. 1971–1974.

14. Joshua Clover explained, "The strike is the form of collective action that 1) struggles to set the price of labor power (or the conditions of labor, which is much the same thing: the amount of misery that can be purchased by the pound); 2) features workers appearing in their role as workers; 3) unfolds in the context of capitalist production, featuring its interruption at the source via the downing of tools, cordoning of the factory floor, etc." Clover, *Riot. Strike. Riot*, loc. 287–291, 821–847, 1652–1654, 1759–1761, 1861–1877, 1899–1900; Sarah Jaffe and Josh Eidelson, "Belabored Podcast, Episode 1: 'We Will Shut Down Your City,'" *Dissent*, April 12, 2013.

15. Mike Davis noted, "Most importantly, however, the Reagan NLRB, with the support of the Burger Court, has created broad legal justification for the runaway shop and concessionary bargaining. The cornerstone of the new doctrine is the notorious Milwaukee Spring case of 1984 which, by reversing earlier NLRB judgments, found that employers need not bargain over plant closure and relocation to non-union sites if the closure does not 'turn' on labor costs. In cognate rulings, the Board has allowed employers to contract out work without bargaining with unions, and supported their right to reopen contracts to demand concessions." Mike Davis, *Prisoners of the American Dream: Politics and Economy in the History of the US Working Class* (New York: Verso, 2018), loc. 2443–2446, Kindle; Gilmore, *Golden Gulag*, loc. 45; Melinda Cooper, "Infinite Regress: Virginia School Neoliberalism and the Tax Revolt," *Capitalism: A Journal of History and Economics* 2, no. 1 (Winter 2021): 41–87, doi: https://doi.org/10.1353/cap.2021.0002; Denvir, *All-American Nativism*, loc. 862–866, 1005–1008, 1013; Gabriel Winant, *The Next Shift: The Fall of Industry and the Rise of Health Care in Rust Belt America* (Cambridge, MA: Harvard University Press, 2021), loc. 2924–2925, Kindle. Harsha Walia wrote:

> The cumulative impacts of NAFTA led to a crisis of displacement. Millions of Indigenous people, farmers, peasants, and ejidatarios from rural areas were dispossessed and then proletarianized into low-wage factory and farm work. Employment in the maquiladora industry exploded by 86 percent within the first five years of NAFTA and, exemplifying the growing feminization of precarious work worldwide, 85 percent of the workforce was women. 57 Maquila border towns were also key sites in the drug war, fueling a crisis of femicide in cities like Ciudad Juárez that continues today. By the year 2000, more than 1.6 million workers toiled in four thousand maquiladoras, 90 percent of which were US-owned, and set the de facto wage floor for manufacturing across the continent. (*Border and Rule*, loc. 352–355, 1066–1127)

16. Benanav, *Automation*, loc. 298–288, 302–388, 588–604, 705–731.

17. Jefferson Cowie, *Stayin' Alive: The 1970s and the Last Days of the Working Class* (New York: New Press, 2010), loc. 6077, Kindle.

18. David Shepardson, "Last Chevrolet Cruze in Ohio Built amid GM Restructuring," Reuters, March 6, 2019, www.reuters.com/article/us-gm-jobs/last-chevrolet-cruze-in-ohio-built-amid-gm-restructuring-idUSKCN1QN2LL.

19. Tom Perkins, "In America's 'Voltage Valley', Hopes of Car-Making Revival Turn Sour," *Guardian*, July 15, 2023, www.theguardian.com/us-news/2023/jul/15/ohio-voltage-valley-lordstown; Brian Merchant, "Life and Death in Apple's Forbidden City," *Guardian*, June 18, 2017, www.theguardian.com/technology/2017/jun/18/foxconn-life-death-forbidden-city-longhua-suicide-apple-iphone-brian-merchant-one-device-extract; Ross Perlin, "Chinese Workers Foxconned," *Dissent*, Spring 2013, www.dissentmagazine.org/article/chinese-workers-foxconned/; Jameson Dow, "GM's Ultium Battery Plant Votes Overwhelmingly to Unionize with UAW," Electrek, December 9, 2022, https://electrek.co/2022/12/09/gms-ultium-battery-plan-votes-overwhelmingly-to-unionize-with-uaw/.

20. Vince Guerrieri, "On the 40th Anniversary of Youngstown's 'Black Monday,' an Oral History," *Belt Magazine*, September 19, 2017, https://beltmag.com/40th-anniversary-youngstowns-black-monday-oral-history/; Winant, *The Next Shift*, loc. 3104–3106.

21. Sarah Jaffe, "Last Stand in Lordstown," *New Republic*, October 23, 2019, https://newrepublic.com/article/155466/lordstown-ohio-general-motors-strike-contract-vote.

22. Historian Jefferson Cowie, in his oft-cited and necessary book *Stayin' Alive*, wrote of Lordstown:

Commentators often referred to the unruliness on the assembly lines as the "Lordstown syndrome," after the infamous three-week-long strike in 1972 by a group of young, hip, and inter-racial autoworkers at a General Motors (GM) plant in Lordstown, Ohio, who battled the fastest—and most psychically deadening—assembly line in the world. "With all the shoulder-length hair, beards, Afros and mod clothing along the line," explained Newsweek of the notorious GM plant, "it looks for all the world like an industrial Woodstock"—suggesting the possibility of an upheaval in class relations for the seventies equal to those of race and culture of the 1960s. (loc. 212)

Johnny Reed Collective, "Workers Strike GM," *Industrial Worker* 69, no. 4 (April 1972).

23. Mike Davis noted that at various points, CIO union leaders, including Walter Reuther of the UAW, pitched closer collaboration between union leadership, management, and the state as a way to control dissidents and subversives among the workers. Mike Davis, *Prisoners of the American Dream*, loc. 1372–1382; Gilmore, "Abolition Geography and the Problem of Innocence," loc. 7222; Judith Stepan-Norris and Maurice Zeitlin, *Left Out: Reds and America's Industrial Unions* (Cambridge: Cambridge University Press, 2002), loc. 1287, 1290, 1327, 3017–3019, Kindle.

24. Alex N. Press, "Can the UAW Rise Again?," *Jacobin*, March 31, 2023, https://jacobin.com/2023/03/uaw-convention-bargaining-shawn-fain-reform; Lee Harris, "How Autoworkers' Democratic Tactics Reversed a Humiliating Loss," *American Prospect*, November 2, 2023, https://prospect.org/labor/11-02-2023-uaw-strike-stellantis-belvidere-reopening/; Lee Harris, "Union Leader: Stellantis Will Send Electric Vehicle Jobs to Mexico," *American Prospect*, December 14, 2022, https://prospect.org/labor/stellantis-will-send-electric-vehicle-jobs-to-mexico/.

25. Luis Feliz Leon, "The UAW Just Secured a Landmark Win in the Fight for a Pro-worker Green Transition," *Jacobin*, October 6, 2023, https://jacobin.com/2023/10/uaw-strike-gm-electric-vehicle-battery-plants-union; Mike Gauntner, Alex Kamczyc, and Erin Simonek, "Lordstown Ultium Workers Vote to Join GM Master Agreement," WFMJ, November 15, 2023, www.wfmj.com/story/49989467/lordstown-ultium-workers-vote-to-join-gm-master-agreement.

26. David Roediger, *The Sinking Middle Class: A Political History of Debt, Misery and the Drift to the Right* (Chicago: Haymarket Books, 2022), loc. 2253–2282, Kindle; Sarah Jaffe, "Whose Class Is It Anyway? The 'White Working Class' and the Myth of Trump," in *Labor in the Time of Trump*, ed. Jasmine Kerrissey, Eve Weinbaum, Clare Hammonds, Tom Juravich, and Dan Clawson (Ithaca, NY: Cornell University Press, 2019), 87–105; Cowie, *Stayin' Alive*, loc. 927–941; Craig Gent, "The Deindustrial Divide: Why Northern England Is a Political Problem," Novara Media, October 6, 2021, https://novaramedia.com/2021/10/06/the-deindustrial-divide-why-northern-england-is-a-political-problem/.

27. Roediger, *Sinking Middle Class*, loc. 421–422, 2369–2370; Gabriel Winant, "We Live in a Society," *n+1*, December 12, 2020, www.nplusonemag.com/online-only/online-only/we-live-in-a-society/.

28. Du Bois, *Black Reconstruction in America*, loc. 1360–1362, 1551–1584, 5740–5744; Gilmore, "Abolition Geography and the Problem of Innocence," loc. 6509–6510, 6610.

29. Ruth Wilson Gilmore explains: "Within any system of production, the idling, or surplusing, of productive capacities means that the society dependent on that production cannot reproduce itself as it had in the past. . . . Such inability is the hallmark of crisis, since reproduction, broadly conceived, is the human imperative." Gilmore, "Globalization and US Prison Growth: From Military Keynesianism to Post-Keynesian Militarism," loc. 2798–2878; Gilmore, "Abolition Geography and the Problem of Innocence," loc. 6509–6510, 6610; Gilmore, "Fatal Couplings of Power and Difference: Notes on Racism and Geography," loc. 1821; Gilmore, "You Have Dislodged a Boulder," loc. 4924–4936, 5175; all in Gilmore,

Abolition Geography; Du Bois, *Black Reconstruction in America*, loc. 1360–1362, 1551–1584, 5740–5744; Davis et al., *Abolition. Feminism. Now.*

30. In *Golden Gulag*, Gilmore wrote, "Finally, Black men are 30 percent more likely than their white counterparts to have lost permanent jobs between 1979 and 1989, with the long-term effect that only 51 percent of Black men have steady employment, compared with 73 percent twenty-five years ago—although 90 percent of all Black men work at least part of the time (Nasar 1994)" (75, 38). Gilmore, "Race and Globalization," loc. 1675; Gilmore, "Globalization and US Prison Growth," loc. 2873.

31. Jason Read, "The Principle of Our Negative Solidarity," *New Inquiry*, January 24, 2014, https://thenewinquiry.com/the-principle-of-our-negative-solidarity/; Asad Haider, "Class Cancelled," *Substack*, August 17, 2020, https://asadhaider.substack.com/p/class-cancelled; Gilmore, "Race, Capitalist Crisis, and Abolitionist Organizing: An Interview with Jenna Loyd," in *Abolition Geography*, loc. 6121–6150; Sarah Jaffe, "Forever Temp?," *In These Times*, January 6, 2014, https://inthesetimes.com/article/permatemps-in-manufacturing. See Jaffe, *Work Won't Love You Back*.

32. Or, in Peter Linebaugh's eloquent phrasing, "A word which at the end of the nineteenth century had attained all the nobility pertaining to the class that would bring to birth a new society from the ashes of the old, actually had its origins in the counter-revolution of a class that went to Roman history to find a term adequate to express its contempt (and fear) of those 'lawless' or 'loose and disorderly' persons whom it had just vanquished." Linebaugh, *The London Hanged*, loc. 486–488, 2273, 2346–2371, 2623–2675. Clover, *Riot. Strike. Riot*, loc. 1895–1900, 2026–2031; Winant, *The Next Shift*, loc. 2223–2224.

33. Gent, "Deindustrial Divide."

34. Walia, *Border and Rule*, loc. 1291–1293.

35. Oscar Holland, "10 Years After Rana Plaza, Is Bangladesh's Garment Industry Any Safer?," CNN, April 23, 2023, https://edition.cnn.com/style/article/rana-plaza-garment-worker-rights-accord/index.html.

36. Clean Clothes Campaign, "Ten Years After Groundbreaking Factory Safety Pact Signed, Major Fashion Brands Still Refuse to Join," https://cleanclothes.org/news/2023/ten-years-after-groundbreaking-factory-safety-pact-signed-major-fashion-brands-still-refuse-to-join; Elizabeth Paton, "Fears for Bangladesh Garment Workers as Safety Agreement Nears an End," *New York Times*, May 28, 2021, www.nytimes.com/2021/05/28/business/bangladesh-worker-safety-accord.html/; Walia, *Border and Rule*, loc. 1296.

37. Shuprova Tasneem, "There Is a Long Way to Go Yet," *Dhaka Tribune*, September 22, 2016, www.dhakatribune.com/feature/5750/there-is-a-long-way-to-go-yet; Walia, *Border and Rule*, loc. 1300–1303.

38. Frase, "The Garage Sale, and Other Utopias"; Tasneem, "There Is a Long Way to Go Yet."

39. Historian Erik Loomis explained, "That's especially true in the apparel industry, which developed what historians call 'merchant capitalism' during the nineteenth century. In this system, which has come back in the global supply chains of the twenty-first century economy, traders and financiers have more control over the labor market than manufacturers. Rather than own their factories, clothing companies contract with manufacturers to make clothing to order. A contractor's profit is generated from reduced labor costs." Loomis, *Out of Sight*, 62.

40. Paton, "Fears for Bangladesh Garment Workers."

41. Walia, *Border and Rule*, loc. 1355–1397; S. M. Najmus Sakib, "Climate Change Displaced Millions of Bangladeshis in 2022: WHO," aa.com, November 29, 2022, www.aa.com.tr/en/asia-pacific/climate-change-displaced-millions-of-bangladeshis-in-2022–who/2750491.

42. Gebrial, "Racial Platform Capitalism"; Walia, *Border and Rule*, loc. 1414–1426; Sarah Jaffe, "A Moment of Urgency: A Conversation with Bhairavi Desai," *Baffler*, February 16, 2017, https://thebaffler.com/latest/interviews-for-resistance-desai.

43. Dana Thomas, "Why Won't We Learn from the Survivors of the Rana Plaza Disaster?," *New York Times*, April 24, 2018, www.nytimes.com/2018/04/24/style/survivors-of-rana-plaza-disaster.html; Akhter, "From Triangle to Rana Plaza"; Walia, *Border and Rule*, loc. 1426.

44. Leila Taylor, *Darkly*, loc. 1512–1530, 1644–1646, 1662.

45. Or sometimes the people are generously acknowledged at the edges; Christina Sharpe wrote of Kara Walker's massive sugar sculpture in Brooklyn's former Domino factory as an attempt at acknowledging the Black women and men who made the sugar industry in conditions of slavery. She pointed out: "We are, though, living in the afterlives of that brutality that is not in the past: Robert Shelton, a former Domino Factory employee and a docent for Walker's exhibition, 'recalls the difficulty of the work, the ways it was hard on the body and soul.' He recalls, too, 'a co-worker who continued to come to the refinery in spite of being diagnosed with terminal liver cancer in the hopes of enabling his wife to receive the $20,000 death benefit available to families if workers died on the premises. He got his wish.'" Sharpe, *In the Wake*, loc. 1954; Gordon, *Ghostly Matters*, loc. 134; Cowie, *Stayin' Alive*, loc. 4581.

46. Gibbs, *Coal Country*, loc. 1203–1205, 3196–3198, 3404–3406; Winant, *The Next Shift*, loc. 437–438.

47. Miners fought for their lives and their communities, but their efforts were often ignored; instead, one reporter suggested "these people" might have "gotten to where they're so used to living in the shadow of disaster, floods, coal mine tragedies, that they kind of take it for granted." Trish Kahle, *Energy Citizenship: Coal and Democracy in the American Century* (New York: Columbia University Press, 2024 [forthcoming]), loc. 103–105, 146–148, 313–314, 548–548, 817–824, 3951–3987, 6132–6135, 6412–6414, 8672–8673; Gent, "Deindustrial Divide"; Elizabeth Catte, *What You Are Getting Wrong About Appalachia* (Cleveland: Belt, 2018), 59; "Longannet: Nicola Sturgeon Ignites 700kg of Explosives to Raze Scotland's Last Coal Power Station," ITV.com, December 9, 2021, www.itv.com/news/2021-12-09/sturgeon-ignites-700kg-of-explosives-to-raze-scotlands-last-coal-power-station; Kahle, *Energy Citizenship*.

48. Trish Kahle noted that "by the late 1960s, black lung was the most prevalent occupational disease in the United States." Kahle, *Energy Citizenship*, loc. 804–805, 4136–4137. As Erik Loomis wrote in *Out of Sight*, the passing of the Occupational Safety and Health Act in 1970 and creation of the Occupational Safety and Health Administration "was the greatest victory in the history of American workplace safety," and yet organized labor was lukewarm on its achievement, partly because capital mobility was by then very obviously a real threat. "The United Paperworkers' International Union refused to fight against asbestos in a Johns Manville paper mill it represented. Workers knew that asbestos was dangerous, but they feared the factory would move if they united with environmentalists to clean up the factory." Loomis, *Out of Sight*, 66–67.

49. Holdren, *Injury Impoverished*, loc. 11–21; Loomis, *Out of Sight*, 62; Meredith Tax, *The Rising of the Women: Feminist Solidarity and Class Conflict, 1880–1917* (New York: Verso, 2022), 206–207.

50. Holdren wrote, "To underscore this loss of rights, Bellamy refers to compensation laws as turning US working-class people into a proletariat, in the sense of people without rights. Bellamy's remarks recall Marx's description of the working class as free and rightless. Marx meant free in the sense of free to enter the market, an ironic point on Marx's part intended to point out that the working class is in fact compelled to be in the market. That freedom is in a sense the flip side of proletarian rightlessness: calling the market voluntary serves to minimize rights

claims by working-class people." Holdren, *Injury Impoverished*, loc. 1825, 1895, 2059–2064, 2266, 2359, 4317–4352; Linebaugh, *The London Hanged*, loc. 2842–2844.

51. Holdren pointed to a strike statement by miners organized with the Industrial Workers of the World against the physical examinations: "We do not propose to be stripped before going to work and then be stripped again when we get our paycheck. One of the strippings must be abolished now. We will tend to the other later." Holdren, *Injury Impoverished*, loc. 4507–4522, 4595, 5238–5269.

52. Daphne Carr, *Nine Inch Nails' Pretty Hate Machine (33 1/3)* (New York: Continuum, 2011), 69–75.

53. Carr, *Nine Inch Nails' Pretty Hate Machine*, 69–75.

54. The opioid crisis deserves its own book, and in fact it has many. My favorite is Sam Quinones's *Dreamland*, named for a community pool closed down in deindustrialized Portsmouth, Ohio, which became home to many pill mills. It was a kind of ground zero (though of course there were many) for prescription opioid addiction and the way it turned people toward illegal drugs and toward overdose and death. Sam Quinones, *Dreamland, The True Tale of America's Opiate Epidemic* (New York: Bloomsbury, 2015). In an interview with NPR, Quinones described the Mexican workers who did the distribution for the cartels:

> All these guys don't like selling heroin. But here's the thing: Back in the town where they're from they have been humiliated all their lives. Their jobs are dead-end jobs. They work as bakers, they work as farm boys, they work as butchers—they don't have anything pushing them ahead.
>
> As this business model began to take hold, the effects were immediately seen in the town. People began to do better. They began to build big houses, they began to have nice trucks, nice cars. And all around them young men saw this. They saw that this was a route to real economic progress.

"How Heroin Made Its Way from Rural Mexico to Small-Town America," *Morning Edition*, NPR, May 19, 2015, www.npr.org/2015/05/19/404184355/how-heroin-made-its-way-from-rural-mexico-to-small-town-america. James D. Walsh, "One Million Dead: *Dreamland* Author Sam Quinones on the Opioid Epidemic's Toll and Why It's Time to Attack Cartels," *New York Magazine*, January 16, 2022, https://nymag.com/intelligencer/2022/01/dreamlands-sam-quinones-on-opioids-drug-cartels-new-book.html; Roediger, *Sinking Middle Class*, loc. 1406–1408.

55. Steven Thrasher's excellent book *The Viral Underclass* delves into the overlap among HIV infection, opioid use, and austerity at length, but I was particularly struck by this passage about coal country:

> I thought addiction in Appalachia typically began when workers were prescribed opioid painkillers while injured on the job in the region's diminishing coal mines. But the number of actual mining jobs in West Virginia had peaked decades prior. Many of the newer jobs are in the health care industry. Those could make for well-paying careers if so much of the profits weren't being funneled toward upper management and corporate earnings.
>
> West Virginia laborers who did physical work did get pain prescriptions for work-related injuries. But by the twenty-first century, that work was more likely in informal construction jobs or as day laborers. But more than that, economic precarity coupled with depression and other mental distress created fertile ground for addiction to flourish. Many workers found the opioids didn't relieve only physical pain; the comforting euphoria also helped them cope with the emotional conditions that austerity had created: alienation and depression. (122–125)

See also Keri Leigh Merritt, "Suicide and Survival: Deaths of Despair in the 2020s," in Barnes, Merritt, and Williams, *After Life*, loc. 2942–2956.

56. Deaton, Scottish by birth, noted the role of the East India Company in the opium trade and noted too that "Scotland shows that you do not need an out-of-control health care sector to produce drug overdoses—that deindustrialization and community destruction are important here just as they are in the United States." Angus Deaton, "How Misreading Adam Smith Helped Spawn Deaths of Despair," *Boston Review*, August 2, 2023, www.bostonreview.net/articles/how-misreading-adam-smith-helped-spawn-deaths-of-despair/; Ehrenreich, *Natural Causes*; A. S. Venkataramani, E. F. Bair, R. L. O'Brien, and A. C. Tsai, "Association Between Automotive Assembly Plant Closures and Opioid Overdose Mortality in the United States: A Difference-in-Differences Analysis," *JAMA Internal Medicine* 180, no. 2 (2020): 254–262, doi:10.1001/jamainternmed.2019.5686; Katherine McLean, "'There's Nothing Here': Deindustrialization as Risk Environment for Overdose," *International Journal of Drug Policy* 29 (2016): 19–26, https://doi.org/10.1016/j.drugpo.2016.01.009; Gabor Scheiring, Aytalina Azarova, Darja Irdam, Katarzyna Doniec, Martin McKee, David Stuckler, and Lawrence King, "Deindustrialization and the Postsocialist Mortality Crisis," working paper, Political Economy Research Institute, University of Massachusetts Amherst, April 2021, https://peri.umass.edu/economists/lawrence123/item/1423–deindustrialization-and-the-postsocialist-mortality-crisis.

57. Mike Stobbe, "US Overdose Deaths Hit Record 93,000 in Pandemic Last Year," Associated Press, July 15, 2021, https://apnews.com/article/overdose-deaths-record-covid-pandemic-fd43b5d91a81179def5ac596253b0304.

58. Mark Brown, "'There Is Anger': Durham Miners' Gala Returns amid Cost of Living Crisis," *Guardian*, July 9, 2022, www.theguardian.com/uk-news/2022/jul/09/durham-miners-gala-returns-amid-cost-of-living-crisis.

59. On the colliery brass bands, immortalized in the 1996 film *Brassed Off*, many reports say that they were supported by mine companies to discourage the workers from political troublemaking yet they were funded by the miners themselves, and band members would be employed as miners but given work time to play music instead; like so much of the coalfields' history, these contradictions are themselves illuminating. See Christopher Werth, "Britain's Brass Bands: A Working-Class Tradition on the Wane," *All Things Considered*, NPR, March 6, 2013, www.npr.org/2013/03/06/173642709/britains-brass-bands-a-working-class-tradition-on-the-wane.

60. Marx, *Capital*, loc. 1:400.

61. Bright described the experience of attending one of the "funerals" for Margaret Thatcher:

> The Goldthorpe Thatcher funeral took a lot of us by surprise, as it seemed to come from nowhere. Even a week or so ago at the OTJC11 meeting, there were a few rumours that there might be a bonfire in one of the villages but nobody expected anything like this. What took place at Goldthorpe was extraordinary—a spectacular, improvised re-embodiment of the resistant, sometimes riotous, energy of the 84–85 strike. The pillocking slogans on home made banners—"The Lady's not Returning!," "Iron Lady, Rust in Peace" and so on—the rows of blackened, boarded-up terraced pit houses strung with bunting; a "miner" in black-face; a Thatcher effigy leaning against the wall of the Comrades Club prior to being loaded onto a horse-drawn hearse and carried in procession by a crowd of men, women, kids and old folks through the village to waste land where it was set alight to cheers and cries of "Scab! Scab! Scab!" Watching the TV coverage—which has gone viral—the shock of this carnival of cathartic release

is obvious: a TV presenter is heard saying to a retired miner she interviews: "It's as if you're in a time warp."

N. Geoffrey Bright (2016) "'The Lady Is Not Returning!' Educational Precarity and a Social Haunting in the UK Coalfields," *Ethnography and Education* 11, no. 2 (2016): 142–157, https://doi.org/10.1080/17457823.2015.1101381.

62. Seumas Milne, *The Enemy Within: The Secret War Against the Miners* (London: Verso, 2014), loc. 116, 477–481, Kindle.

63. Gavin Hawkton wrote in *Tribune* magazine:

> After just three weeks on strike, Yorkshire miner Stan Whitworth told ITN that food was already being rationed: "Everybody's had to cut back, there's no money coming into the house. We've got to live on, more or less, fresh air. It's hitting everyone very hard." But the resolve to continue the strike was clear: miners would "stick it out as long as needs be," he said, "even with no money."
>
> Feeding these communities therefore became an epic task, one taken up by women's support groups across the country. Run mostly by miners' wives, soup kitchens were opened and ration bags distributed which kept whole communities from starvation. In the process, they effectively created an alternative welfare state.

Gavin Hawkton, "Pits Against the State," *Tribune*, November 2, 2022, https://tribunemag.co.uk/2022/11/miners-strike-1984-food-hunger-solidarity-organising-welfare; Jason Dean, "Steel in the UK: A Timeline of Decline," *Guardian*, March 30, 2016, www.theguardian.com/business/2016/mar/30/steel-in-the-uk-a-timeline-of-decline; TUC Union History, "The 1984–85 Miners' Strike," UnionHistory.info, www.unionhistory.info/timeline/1960_2000_Narr_Display_2.php?Where=NarTitle+contains+%27The+1984-85+Miners+Strike%27+; University of Oxford, "The Miners' Strike of 1984–5: An Oral History," www.history.ox.ac.uk/miners-strike-1984-5-oral-history; Gibbs, *Coal Country*, loc. 1056–1061; Milne, *The Enemy Within*, loc. 613–651; Foot and Livingstone, *Charged*, loc. 740–743.

64. Thatcher used the term "the enemy within" in a speech, equating the miners to the Argentinians in the lopsided Falklands War the country had just fought, and the term still holds extraordinary resonance. Sinead Kirwan and Mike Simons, "Still the Enemy Within: The Strike That Split Britain," OpenDemocracy, March 4, 2016, www.opendemocracy.net/en/opendemocracyuk/still-enemy-within-strike-that-split-britain/; "Outrage and Fury as Thatcher Calls Strikers the Enemy Within," *Northern Echo*, April 9, 2013, www.thenorthernecho.co.uk/news/indepth/margaret_thatcher/herlifeandtimes/10342224.outrage-fury-thatcher-calls-strikers-enemy-within/; see Milne, *The Enemy Within*; David Conn, "The Scandal of Orgreave," *Guardian*, May 18, 2017, www.theguardian.com/politics/2017/may/18/scandal-of-orgreave-miners-strike-hillsborough-theresa-may; Foot and Livingstone, *Charged*, loc. 706.

65. Historian Tristram Hunt described the battle of Orgreave as "one of the great set-piece confrontations of the miners' struggle. Almost medieval in its choreography, it was at various stages a siege, a battle, a chase, a rout and, finally, a brutal example of legalised state violence." Tristram Hunt, "The Charge of the Heavy Brigade," *Guardian*, September 4, 2006, www.theguardian.com/theguardian/2006/sep/04/features5; Foot and Livingstone, *Charged*, loc. 808–887.

66. The BBC clips of the battle of Orgreave have long been a point of contention: everyone I spoke to referred to the footage as having been reversed deliberately, showing bricks thrown at police before the horse charge that actually happened after it. The BBC has not accepted this argument; one article noted:

A spokesman for the BBC said: "Thirty years on, it is difficult to reach definitive conclusions, but our investigations have uncovered no evidence of any deliberate attempt to mislead viewers in the coverage of the Battle of Orgreave."

He said the BBC had "failed to record some of the violence due to a camera error."

Minutes from an editorial meeting the day after the clashes record that concerns were raised about impartiality in some of the coverage, he said.

But they appeared to conclude that any problem amounted to a "marginal imbalance" and did not justify the NUM's claims of BBC bias.

"Orgreave Campaigners Call for BBC Strike Coverage Apology," BBC, June 18, 2014, www.bbc.co.uk/news/uk-england-south-yorkshire-27893072. According to David Conn at the *Guardian*, the Independent Police Complaints Commission found that the BBC had reversed its footage (David Conn, "We Were Fed Lies About the Violence at Orgreave: Now We Need the Truth," *Guardian*, July 22, 2015, www.theguardian.com/commentisfree/2015/jul/22/orgreave-truth-police-miners-strike). Foot and Livingstone, *Charged*, loc. 914–930.

67. Foot and Livingstone, *Charged*, loc. 681, 896–907.

68. Conn described the trial:

The South Yorkshire police force's version of events had already begun to unravel under questioning. But when the arresting officers were called as witnesses to present their evidence against the individual miners, the full scale of alleged police malpractice became clear.

Cross-examination of the officers by the miners' lawyers revealed that there had been an orchestrated operation by South Yorkshire police to dictate identical opening paragraphs for separate statements by dozens of different police officers. Furthermore, the evidence against the accused individuals was then shown to be unreliable, often contradicted by film or photographs of where they were—and there were to be worse embarrassments for some police witnesses.

David Conn, "The Scandal of Orgreave," *Guardian*, May 18, 2017, www.theguardian.com/politics/2017/may/18/scandal-of-orgreave-miners-strike-hillsborough-theresa-may; Foot and Livingstone, *Charged*, loc. 190–203, 936–946, 981–986, 1091.

69. Foot and Livingstone, *Charged*, 703, 989–1013; Milne, *The Enemy Within*, loc. 712–716.

70. Scottish government, "Miners' Strike Pardon," August 24, 2022, www.gov.scot/publications/miners-strike-pardon/; Foot and Livingstone, *Charged*, loc. 1014–1018, 1042.

71. Nicholas Watt, "Labour Calls on Government to Apologise over Miners' Strike," *Guardian*, January 29, 2014, www.theguardian.com/politics/2014/jan/29/labour-calls-apology-miners-strike; Conn, "Scandal of Orgreave"; Foot and Livingstone, *Charged*, loc. 722–743, 950, 1025–1029, 1046–1052, 1072–1076, 1617–1619; Milne, *The Enemy Within*, loc. 488–498.

72. Interview with Ronald Butt, *Sunday Times*, May 3, 1981, www.margaretthatcher.org/document/104475.

73. Ewan Gibbs, citing E. P. Thompson, explains the moral economy framework thus:

Thompson later summarized his conception of the moral economy at a theoretical level. It centred on claims of "non-monetary rights" to resources predicated on traditions of "community membership [which] supersedes price as a basis of entitlement." . . .

Perchard and Phillips defined the coalfield moral economy's contours as: Joint regulation, through agreement between managers and union representatives, of workplace affairs, including pit closures, job transfers, substantial alterations to production

> and the labour process; and guaranteed economic security, so that miners displaced by colliery closures could find equally well-remunerated alternative employment, at other pits or elsewhere in industry. . . . Like Thompson's moral economy of plebeian consumers, the coalfield moral economy was instigated by communitarian claims to economic resources: collieries and the employment they sustained. (*Coal Country*, loc. 280–281)

See also Gibbs, *Coal Country*, loc. 97–100, 134–136, 141–148, 161, 188–189, 268–284, 540–543, 729–730, 1051–1052, 1112–1113, 1159–1162; Bright, "The Lady Is Not Returning"; see Naomi Klein, *The Shock Doctrine: The Rise of Disaster Capitalism* (New York: Picador, 2008).

74. One of the demands the United Mine Workers would eventually win, Trish Kahle wrote, was for "mourning periods" that could halt production to honor those killed on the job—a way not only to publicly grieve but to incentivize managers to take care with the living, since death would cost them precious mining time. Kahle, *Energy Citizenship*, loc. 293–295, 572–574, 640–642, 733–754, 814–815, 874–877, 998–1000, 2232–2234; Holdren, *Injury Impoverished*, loc. 8–9; Catte, *What You Are Getting Wrong About Appalachia*, 44–47.

75. *Harlan County USA*, dir. Barbara Kopple, Cabin Creek Films, 1976, www.criterion.com/films/777-harlan-county-usa; Kahle, *Energy Citizenship*, loc. 831–834, 7533–7535. In addition to all of this I recommend the film *Matewan*, a fictionalized but stirring rendition of the mine wars starring luminaries like James Earl Jones. Make it a double bill with *Pride*. *Matewan*, dir. John Sayles, Cinecom Pictures, 1987; *Pride*, dir. Matthew Warchus, Pathé, 2014.

76. Gibbs, *Coal Country*, loc. 1970–1972, 2037–2038.

77. Denis Campbell, Matthew Weaver, and Anna Bawden, "NHS Leaders Voice Alarm as 10 More Ambulance Strikes Planned," *Guardian*, January 20, 2023, www.theguardian.com/society/2023/jan/20/nhs-leaders-unite-union-ambulance-strikes-planned; Andrew Gregory and Jamie Grierson, "Nurses Across UK to Strike for First Time on 15 and 20 December," *Guardian*, November 25, 2022, www.theguardian.com/society/2022/nov/25/nurses-across-uk-to-strike-for-first-time-on-15-and-20-december; Andrew Gregory, "Junior Doctors in England to Stage Four-Day Strike in August," *Guardian*, July 26, 2023, www.theguardian.com/society/2023/jul/26/junior-doctors-england-to-stage-four-day-strike-in-august-bma.

78. Trish Kahle captured this tension in the story of a striking miner during World War II who, while being interviewed about the strike, got the call telling him his son had been killed in the Pacific. "It was rare indeed to have a reporter close by to capture the raw reaction, as the fight in the mines collided with human cost of combat. Overcome with grief, Servaczgo cried out, 'I ain't a traitor, damn'em, I ain't a traitor. I'll stay out till hell freezes over. . . . Dickie was fighting for one thing. I'm fighting for another. And they ain't so far apart.'" Kahle, *Energy Citizenship*, loc. 2428–2432. Other references to soldiering: Gibbs, *Coal Country*, loc. 2538–2539, 2555–2557; Kahle, *Energy Citizenship*, loc. 2045–2047.

79. For more on LGSM and Mike Jackson, obviously the thing to do is watch *Pride*. See also Kate Kellaway, "When Miners and Gay Activists United: The Real Story of the Film *Pride*," *Observer*, August 31, 2014, www.theguardian.com/film/2014/aug/31/pride-film-gay-activists-miners-strike-interview.

80. Winant, *The Next Shift*, loc. 1420–1421.

81. Or, in Gabriel Winant's words, "The factories did not just make metal goods; they made people, institutions, a way of life, and a system of relationships—a social world." Winant, *The Next Shift*, loc. 128–129, 796–800, 3258–3259, 1427–1428, 1440–1441, 1597–1598; Jaffe, *Work Won't Love You Back*; Gibbs, *Coal Country*, loc. 226–228, 339–386, 2516–2516; Kahle, *Energy Citizenship*, loc. 3216–3218; For more on Ford's social engineering, see Greg Grandin, *Fordlandia: The Rise and Fall of Henry Ford's Forgotten Jungle City* (New York: Picador, 2010).

82. In the early days of the proletariat, Linebaugh reminded us, reproduction was difficult to impossible, babies a drain on the family even when parents were stable enough to keep them alive in the first place. "Demographically speaking, London in the early eighteenth century was a killer because deaths far exceeded births. Therefore, as a labour pool, from which sailors, like other workers, were recruited, it had to be maintained by migration into the city." The crisis was so severe that the state stepped in, though not to increase wages: it created orphanages and paid nurses through an Act for Keeping Children Alive. Linebaugh, *The London Hanged*, 2675, 2772–2803; Gibbs, *Coal Country*, loc. 438–439, 2098–2100, 2341–2343, 2346–2359, 2363–2372, 2409–2410; Winant, *The Next Shift*, loc. 190–191, 218–221, 229–230; Andrew J. Cherlin, *Labor's Love Lost: The Rise and Fall of the Working-Class Family in America* (New York: Russell Sage Foundation, 2014), 1–2, 4, 11, 88, 92; Angela Y. Davis, "Women and Capitalism," 165; Cowie, *Stayin' Alive*, loc. 4873; Friedrich Engels, *The Origin of the Family, Private Property, and the State*, trans. Ernest Untermann (Public Domain Books, 2011), loc. 44–45, 50, 64, Kindle; Cherlin, *Labor's Love Lost.*

83. Marcus, *Political Disappointment*, 80; Gibbs, *Coal Country*, loc. 2372–2383, 2489–2538; Kahle, *Energy Citizenship*, loc. 2044–2045.

84. As Gabriel Winant noted, steelworkers and miners and factory workers were deeply ambivalent about the work itself. It was, he wrote, "easy to miss how many workers hated the jobs they defended—a hate that bound workers together and made their defense formidable." Winant, *The Next Shift*, loc. 687–688, 985–992, 1000–1003, 1011–1015; Gibbs, *Coal Country*, loc. 2516–2525; E. P. Thompson, *The Making of the English Working Class* (New York: Open Road Media, 2016), loc. 88, Kindle.

85. Cowie, *Stayin' Alive*, loc. 302, 359, 1137, 3901, 4205, 4660, 4680, 4799, 4872.

86. Eva Illouz noted that this is a long process with roots in the rationalization of labor itself: "In parallel to the engineers' rhetoric or in its aftermath another discourse emerged, spearheaded by psychologists, which paid a great deal of attention to the individual, to the irrational dimension of work relationships, and to workers' emotions . . . productivity increased if work relationships contained care and attention to workers' feelings." Illouz, *Cold Intimacies*, loc. 257–353. In philosopher Donna Haraway's words, written in 1985 around the time of the miners' strike, "To be feminized means to be made extremely vulnerable; able to be disassembled, reassembled, exploited as a reserve labor force; seen less as workers than as servers; subjected to time arrangements on and off the paid job that make a mockery of a limited workday; leading an existence that always borders on being obscene, out of place, and reducible to sex." Donna Haraway, "Manifesto for Cyborgs," in *Simians, Cyborgs, and Women: The Reinvention of Nature* (New York: Routledge, 1991), 149–182. Thanks to Gabriel Winant for pointing me back to Haraway here, cited in *The Next Shift*, 4067–4071.

87. Cara Daggett called it "petro-masculinity," explaining, "In these spaces, fossil fuels can serve as potent conservative symbols that represent masculinity, autonomy, and self-sufficiency, even when they are not real economic interests for most of the public. In other words, fossil fuels matter to new authoritarian movements in the global North not only because of profits and consumer lifestyles, but also because privileged subjectivities are oil-soaked and coal-dusted. It is no coincidence that White, conservative American men—regardless of class—appear to be among the most vociferous climate deniers, as well as leading fossil fuel proponents in the West." This could, of course, also be named for coal. Cara Daggett, "Petro-Masculinity and the Politics of Climate Refusal," Autonomy, May 1, 2022, https://autonomy.work/portfolio/petro-masculinity-climate-refusal/; Gibbs, *Coal Country*, loc. 2990–2993; Martin Gelin, "The Misogyny of Climate Deniers," *New Republic*, August 28, 2019, https://newrepublic.com/article/154879

/misogyny-climate-deniers; Malm and Zetkin Collective, *White Skin, Black Fuel*, loc. 4273–4295, 4353, 4545–4568.

88. Malm and Zetkin Collective, *White Skin, Black Fuel*, loc. 5238–5243, 5364, 5442–5451, 5557, 5582, 5803–5943, 6035–6087, 6429; Gent, "Deindustrial Divide."

89. As Malm and the Zetkin Collective pointed out, the weakness of organized labor in recent years leads to workers being drawn into other collectivities. "One of the mechanisms has been noticed frequently, to the point of truism: when workers are no longer interpellated as comrades in a class with a mission, the far right fills the vacuum and interpellates them as members of a white nation." This of course works only for white workers, hence the perniciousness of "white working class" as an idea: it divides workers precisely where they should be strong. "Workers who have lost hope of ever wresting back some of the surplus-value from the class enemy switch to going after refugees. At last they can be beaten." Malm and Zetkin Collective, *White Skin, Black Fuel*, loc. 6975–7024.

90. Kevin Horne's experience is just one example of the possibilities of a changed understanding of gender and care. Nancy Fraser suggested a "universal caregiver" model in which men take on more care work, but, she wrote, "this, however, is tantamount to a wholesale restructuring of the institution of gender. The construction of breadwinning and caregiving as separate roles, coded masculine and feminine respectively, is a principal undergirding of the current gender order. To dismantle those roles and their cultural coding is in effect to overturn that order. It means subverting the existing gender division of labor and reducing the salience of gender as a structural principle of social organization. At the limit, it suggests deconstructing gender." Nancy Fraser, "After the Family Wage: Gender Equity and the Welfare State," *Political Theory* 22, no. 4 (1994): 591–618, www.jstor.org/stable/192041; Kenway, *Who Cares*, 89. For much more on the undervaluing of care work, see Jaffe, *Work Won't Love You Back*; Gibbs, *Coal Country*, loc. 2705–2707.

91. Winant, *The Next Shift*, loc. 25–27, 38–44, 65–66, 3003–3003.

92. Winant noted, "Like the expansion of the prison system in the final decades of the twentieth century, the rise of the health care industry offered an economic fix to the social crisis brought about by deindustrialization, channeling public expenditure and state power into the management of surplus population, generating employment, profits, and social stability." He added later, "In capitalist societies, where survival is linked to market employment, job loss wreaks havoc on working-class people's physical and mental health—an effect powerful enough that social scientists and epidemiologists have measured it in one form or another across widely disparate capitalist societies in different historical moments." Winant, *The Next Shift*, loc. 68–69, 85–87, 123–124, 239–265, 295–296, 302–306, 318–320, 344–346, 2514–2519, 3021–3023, 3347–3349, 3368–3369.

93. James McCarthy, "Now Down to Just 100 Active Members—the Decline of the Once-Mighty NUM," Wales Online, December 26, 2015, www.walesonline.co.uk/news/wales-news/now-down-just-100-active-10653263.

94. See Dana Frank, *Women Strikers Occupy Chain Store, Win Big: The 1937 Woolworth's Sit-Down* (Chicago: Haymarket Books, 2012); Marjorie Murphy, *Blackboard Unions: The AFT and the NEA, 1900–1980* (Ithaca, NY: Cornell University Press, 1992), 12–13; Cowie, *Stayin' Alive*, loc. 1238, 7049; Mike Davis, *Prisoners of the American Dream*, loc. 2547–2579.

95. As Aviah Sarah Day and Shanice Octavia McBean note, even when women of color were theoretically industrial workers within the bounds of the Global North they still were often discarded by the labor movement: the Grunwick Film Processing Laboratory strikers won solidarity from the community and other workers but were eventually sold out by their

own union and the Trades Union Congress, who cut a deal rather than back the striking Asian women. Day and McBean, *Abolition Revolution*, loc. 2819–2828; Mike Davis, *Prisoners of the American Dream*, loc. 3616–3632, 3705–3777, 4039; Roediger, *Sinking Middle Class*, loc. 502–503.

96. The full Marx quotation, from the *Grundrisse*:

> Capital itself is the moving contradiction, [in] that it presses to reduce labour time to a minimum, while it posits labour time, on the other side, as sole measure and source of wealth. Hence it diminishes labour time in the necessary form so as to increase it in the superfluous form; hence posits the superfluous in growing measure as a condition—question of life or death—for the necessary. On the one side, then, it calls to life all the powers of science and of nature, as of social combination and of social intercourse, in order to make the creation of wealth independent (relatively) of the labour time employed on it. On the other side, it wants to use labour time as the measuring rod for the giant social forces thereby created, and to confine them within the limits required to maintain the already created value as value. Forces of production and social relations—two different sides of the development of the social individual—appear to capital as mere means, and are merely means for it to produce on its limited foundation.

Karl Marx, *Grundrisse: Foundations of the Critique of Political Economy (Rough Draft)*, trans. Martin Nicolaus (Penguin Books in association with New Left Review, 1973), available online at www.marxists.org/archive/marx/works/1857/grundrisse/ch14.htm.

Joshua Clover, glossing all this for today's era, wrote, "The rise in the ratio of dead to living labor undermines the capacity for value production, living labor in the production process being the sole source of surplus value." Clover, *Riot. Strike. Riot*, loc. 326–328, 373–401, 412–415, 455–456, 647–648, 657–659, 1668–1675, 1692–1710, 1731–1737, 1806–1838.

If you're really interested in all of this stuff, it's worth reading some of the books cited here in full: Gilmore, "Globalization and US Prison Growth," loc. 2807; Mueller, *Breaking Things at Work*, loc. 314–327; Benanav, *Automation*, loc. 831–922; Phil Jones, *Work Without the Worker: Labour in the Time of Platform Capitalism* (London: Verso, 2021), loc. 285–287, Kindle; Clover, *Riot. Strike. Riot*, loc. 1921–1922; Eidelson and Jaffe, "We Will Shut Down Your City"; Roediger, *Sinking Middle Class*, loc. 975–985.

97. Berardi, *After the Future*, loc. 55, 89, 103; Jones, *Work Without the Worker*, loc. 34–47, 63–81, 146–148, 304–306, 309–311, 565–584, 687–688, 875–875; Penny, "Abolition Geography"; Tsing, *Mushroom at the End of the World*, 132–133, 278; see also Gent, *Cyberboss*.

98. Penny, "Abolition Geography"; Mitchell, *Imperial Nostalgia*, 158, 173–175.

99. Mitchell, *Imperial Nostalgia*, 20.

100. The word "strike," Joshua Clover noted, comes to us from the sea, in English from sailors "striking" sails to prevent ships from moving. The French, *grève*, from the place that cargo was unloaded. Clover, *Riot. Strike. Riot*, loc. 821–830. It was London river workers in 1768, aligned with the rest of the ragged proletariat, who connected "striking" sails to refusing to work, hoisting a red flag and giving the international working class both a symbol and a tactic for future struggles. Linebaugh, *The London Hanged*, loc. 5457–5626, 5721–5757; Butler, "Between Grief and Grievance," 14–15.

101. The system's critics have always seen through it: George Orwell wrote in 1937, "But the beauty or ugliness of industrialism hardly matters. Its real evil lies far deeper and is quite uneradicable. It is important to remember this, because there is always a temptation to think that industrialism is harmless so long as it is clean and orderly." Orwell, *Road to Wigan Pier*, loc. 2106–2109;

Dan Hancox, "'Who Remembers Proper Binmen?' The Nostalgia Memes That Help Explain Britain Today," *Guardian*, November 15, 2022, www.theguardian.com/news/2022/nov/15/who-remembers-proper-binmen-facebook-nostalgia-memes-help-explain-britain-today.

102. John Maynard Keynes, "Economic Possibilities for Our Grandchildren (1930)," in *Essays in Persuasion* (New York: Harcourt Brace, 1932), 358–373, www.aspeninstitute.org/wp-content/uploads/files/content/upload/Intro_and_Section_I.pdf; Du Bois, *Darkwater*, 56–59, 69, quoted in Benanav, *Automation*, loc. 70–73, 1013–1019; Alex Q. Arbuckle, "Cigar Factory Lectors," *Mashable*, https://mashable.com/feature/cigar-factory-lectors. For a great collection of one dissident autoworker's publication, read Gregg Shotwell, *Autoworkers Under the Gun: A Shop-Floor View of the End of the American Dream* (Chicago: Haymarket Books, 2012); John Merrick, "Good Bourgeois Subjects," *Soft Punk*, October 27, 2021, www.softpunkmag.com/criticism/good-bourgeois-subjects.

103. Ruth Milkman's book changed how I thought about industrial work, and her insights are worth reproducing at a bit of length here: she wrote that to take the perspective of autoworkers seriously "is to abandon any effort to restore the world of mass production industry as it existed in the past—which is probably impossible in any case. If we look forward rather than backward, the real challenge is how to enhance the resources with which workers might confront the newly transformed world of work now taking shape." Elsewhere, she continued, "With appropriate policies in place—either public policies or, as in this instance, private ones achieved through collective bargaining—the inevitable shrinkage of the nation's industrial base might be achieved with far less pain to its potential victims than has typically been the case." Ruth Milkman, *Farewell to the Factory* (Berkeley: University of California Press, 1997), 12–13, 19, 96–98; Roediger, *Sinking Middle Class*, loc. 777–778.

104. In *Capital*, Marx noted: "We there saw how machinery, by annexing the labour of women and children, augments the number of human beings who form the material for capitalistic exploitation, how it confiscates the whole of the workman's disposable time, by immoderate extension of the hours of labour, and how finally its progress, which allows of enormous increase of production in shorter and shorter periods, serves as a means of systematically getting more work done in a shorter time, or of exploiting labour-power more intensely" (loc. 1:218). Dan Georgakas and Marvin Surkin, *Detroit: I Do Mind Dying: A Study in Urban Revolution* (Chicago: Haymarket Books, 2012), 37, 85–88; Clover, *Riot. Strike. Riot*, loc. 1475–1509, 2026–2031, 2100–2101; Cowie, *Stayin' Alive*, loc. 1180; Mueller, *Breaking Things at Work*, loc. 764–840.

105. Gabriel Winant noted that Sadlowski, while losing, won "the majority of votes in basic steel—the great integrated mill complexes in places like Pittsburgh, Youngstown, and Chicago. His own ambivalence about the industry's future seemed, at least, to match that of the largest bloc of workers." Winant, *The Next Shift*, loc. 3066–3101; Cowie, *Stayin' Alive*, loc. 455, 518, 739, 4926–4934, 7550; Kahle, *Energy Citizenship*, loc. 4373–4375, 4510–4708, 5398–5399, 6607–6609; Les Leopold, *The Man Who Hated Work and Loved Labor: The Life and Times of Tony Mazzocchi* (White River Junction, VT: Chelsea Green Publishing, 2011), loc. 167, 172–192, 202, 229, 249, 281–282, 302, 312–324, 410–417, Kindle; Loomis, *Out of Sight*, 57. Since I am recommending films here, let me say that I have never seen *Silkwood*, starring Meryl Streep as OCAW member and whistleblower Karen Silkwood, who died under mysterious circumstances while in the midst of a campaign with Mazzocchi to expose dangerous plutonium levels at her workplace. Her family won a $10.5 million judgment against the company for negligence after her death. The story is also told in Leopold's book, but perhaps we can convince someone to put *Silkwood* out on a streaming service . . .

106. Baker, "The Right to Grieve"; Nunes, *Neither Vertical nor Horizontal*, loc. 1693–1715; Dario Azzellini, "The 'Tute Bianche' = White Overalls: Interview with Chiara Cassurino and Federico Martelloni," Azzellini, July 22, 2001, www.azzellini.net/zapatisten/die-tute-bianche-weisse-overalls; Berardi, *After the Future*, loc. 111–112.

107. Chris Isidore, "Shawn Fain, CNN Business' Labor Leader of the Year, Plans to Keep Automakers Sweating," CNN Business, December 27, 2023, www.cnn.com/2023/12/27/success/shawn-fain-labor-leader-of-year/index.html; John Merrick, "The Language of Your Fathers," *Soft Punk*, June 12, 2021, www.softpunkmag.com/essay/the-language-of-your-fathers.

108. As Linebaugh wrote, "That the world can be hostile and capricious the proletarian knows, but he or she also knows that this need not always be so, because it is the work of his hands and the labour of her body that have created it in the first place." Linebaugh, *The London Hanged*, loc. 2852–2865; Clover, *Riot. Strike. Riot*, loc. 2026–2031; Friedrich Engels and Karl Marx, *The Communist Manifesto* (Public Domain Books, 2019), 38; Simon Childs and Polly Smythe, "Hundreds of Amazon Workers Stage Wildcat Strike over 'Kick in the Teeth' Pay Offer," Novara Media, August 4, 2022, https://novaramedia.com/2022/08/04/hundreds-of-amazon-workers-stage-wildcat-strike-over-kick-in-the-teeth-pay-offer/; Gilmore, *Golden Gulag*, loc. 192–193; Ruth Wilson Gilmore and Craig Gilmore, "Restating the Obvious," in Gilmore, *Abolition Geography*, loc. 3806–3810; Gilmore, "What Is to Be Done?" in *Abolition Geography*, loc. 545.

Chapter 4: Breathe: Pandemic, communities, and care

1. Francesca Nava, "Coronavirus Anno Zero, quel 23 febbraio all'ospedale di Alzano Lombardo: Così Bergamo è diventata il lazzaretto d'Italia," *Post Internazionale*, March 17, 2020, www.tpi.it/cronaca/coronavirus-caos-ospedale-alzano-lombardo-cosi-bergamo-epicentro-pandemia-20200317567879/.

2. Mirco Nacoti, Andrea Ciocca, Angelo Giupponi, Pietro Brambillasca, Federico Lussana, Michele Pisano, Giuseppe Goisis, Daniele Bonacina, Francesco Fazzi, Richard Naspro, et al., "At the Epicenter of the COVID-19 Pandemic and Humanitarian Crises in Italy: Changing Perspectives on Preparation and Mitigation," *NEJM Catalyst*, March 21, 2020, https://catalyst.nejm.org/doi/full/10.1056/CAT.20.0080.

3. Noi Denunceremo, Facebook, www.facebook.com/groups/noidenunceremo/.

4. "Anti-Vax Protesters in Rome Target PM's Office and Trade Union Headquarters," *Local*, October 9, 2021, www.thelocal.it/20211009/anti-vax-protesters-in-rome-target-pms-office-and-trade-union-headquarters/; Hannah Brenton, "Italian Police Arrest Two Anti-vaxxers for Fire Bombing of Vaccination Hub," *Politico*, May 1, 2021, www.politico.eu/article/italy-police-arrest-coronavirus-vaccination-hub-bomb-brescia/; Ryan Broderick, "Italy's Anti-vaccination Movement Is Militant and Dangerous," *Foreign Policy*, November 13, 2021, https://foreignpolicy.com/2021/11/13/italy-anti-vaccination-movement-militant-dangerous/; Malm and Zetkin Collective, *White Skin, Black Fuel*, loc. 7914–7922.

5. As of spring 2023, the region of Lombardy had 45,781 COVID-19 deaths, more than twice as many as the next largest region, nearby Emilia-Romagna. Juliette Gagliardi, "Coronavirus (COVID-19) Deaths in Italy as of April 13, 2023, by Region," Statista, April 17, 2023, www.statista.com/statistics/1099389/coronavirus-deaths-by-region-in-italy/.

6. Francesca Nava, "COVID, la perizia di Crisanti: La zona rossa in Val Seriana avrebbe potuto salvare 4mila vite," *Post Internazionale*, June 10, 2022, www.tpi.it/cronaca/covid-crisanti-zona-rossa-val-seriana-20220610906989/; Corrado Zunino, "Miozzo: 'Macché piano segreto. Abbiamo taciuto i numeri per non seminare il panico,'" *La Reppublica*, September 5, 2020, www

.repubblica.it/cronaca/2020/09/05/news/miozzo_macche_piano_segreto_abbiamo_taciuto_i_numeri_per_non_seminare_il_panico_-301039673/.

7. Francesca Nava, "Esclusivo TPI—coronavirus, lavoratori finiti in terapia intensiva e giovani ricattati: Così la Dalmine in Lombardia ha tenuto aperte anche le attività produttive non essenziali. Gli operai: 'Abbiamo paura di contagiare le nostre famiglie,'" *Post Internazionale*, April 17, 2020, www.tpi.it/cronaca/coronavirus-lombardia-azienda-dalmine-aperta-rischi-fase-2-20200417587096/.

8. Scholar David Broder wrote of the Fratelli D'Italia:

> Brothers of Italy is rooted in the Movimento Sociale Italiano (MSI), a neo-fascist party created in 1946 which ran in elections but retained a deep hostility toward the republic created at the end of the anti-fascist resistance. During Berlusconi's governments, MSI leaders formally accepted liberal-democratic values, dropped their old name and condemned Mussolini's antisemitism. Yet many still cherished the legacy of postwar neo-fascism, and Brothers of Italy was created in 2012 as an explicit reassertion of the MSI tradition. This is a party that seeks to rewrite history textbooks to highlight the crimes of anti-fascist partisans. But it also draws on other, more international far-right memes like the "great replacement" of Europeans by immigrants—a conspiracy theory that has inspired multiple terrorist attacks.

David Broder, "Italy's Drift to the Far Right Began Long Before the Rise of Giorgia Meloni," *Guardian*, September 26, 2022, www.theguardian.com/commentisfree/2022/sep/26/italy-far-right-before-giorgia-meloni-berlusconi-brothers-of-italy.

9. Sarah Jaffe, "Who Cares," *Baffler*, May 2021, https://thebaffler.com/salvos/who-cares-jaffe; Garza, *Grieving*, 8.

10. Marya and Patel, *Inflamed*, loc. 283–284; Vikas Shah, "A Conversation with Noreena Hertz on Loneliness and How to Restore Human Connection in a World That's Pulling Apart," ThoughtEconomics, March 26, 2021, https://thoughteconomics.com/noreena-hertz/; Malkia Devich-Cyril, "Loss Runs Like a River Through My Life," *Nation*, June 16, 2021, www.thenation.com/article/society/covid-california-facebook-quarantine/.

11. Alan Yu, "6.8 Million Expected to Lose Medicaid When Paperwork Hurdles Return," Shots at NPR, January 24, 2023, www.npr.org/sections/health-shots/2023/01/24/1150798086/6-8-million-expected-to-lose-medicaid-when-paperwork-hurdles-return.

12. Adam Gaffney, "COVID-19 Coverage for the Uninsured Is Ending," *Nation*, March 29, 2022, www.thenation.com/article/society/covid-uninsured/.

13. Andrea Capocci, "Italians Are Angry About Wages and Healthcare, and Meloni Knows It," *il manifesto*, global ed., October 5, 2023, https://global.ilmanifesto.it/italians-are-angry-about-wages-and-healthcare-and-meloni-knows-it/; Francesca Piscioneri and Crispian Balmer, "Italy Looks to Foreigners for Quick Fix to Sickly Health Service," Reuters, October 4, 2023, www.reuters.com/world/europe/italy-looks-foreigners-quick-fix-sickly-health-service-2023-10-04/; Adler-Bolton and Vierkant, *Health Communism*, loc. 64–70; 140–145, 229–237, 364–365, 370–371, 470–471, 496–510; see also Ehrenreich, *Natural Causes*; and Nadasen, *Care*.

14. Thrasher, *Viral Underclass*, 7–9.

15. Lekas Miller, *Love and Borders*, 15; Kenway, *Who Cares*, 9–10.

16. Kenway, *Who Cares*, 143.

17. Portions of this section were previously published in Sarah Jaffe, "The Great Ungrieving," *New York Review of Books*, April 22, 2022, https://www.nybooks.com/online/2022/04/22/the-great-ungrieving/.

18. Rupa Marya and Raj Patel wrote, "As COVID spread around the world, it was people's stories that helped scientists understand how the virus was attacking different parts of the body impacting various systems—the dry cough, the lack of smell, the brain fog, the recurrent flushes of inflammation. Before there were tests and vaccines and treatments, there were stories." Marya and Patel, *Inflamed*, loc. 177.

19. COVID death totals taken from the World Health Organization, "WHO Coronavirus (COVID-19) Dashboard," accessed February 2, 2024, https://covid19.who.int/; Mary L. Dudziak, "An Uncountable Casualty: Ruminations on the Social Life of Numbers," in Barnes, Merritt, and Williams, *After Life*, loc. 2310–2349.

20. Heather Hollingsworth, Grant Schulte, "Health Workers Once Saluted as Heroes Now Get Threats," Associated Press, September 29, 2021, www.pbs.org/newshour/nation/health-workers-once-saluted-as-heroes-now-get-threats.

21. Thrasher, *Viral Underclass*, 47, 70; Polly Smythe, "How COVID Turned Cashiers into Carers," *Tribune*, December 9, 2020, https://tribunemag.co.uk/2020/12/how-covid-turned-cashiers-into-carers.

22. Thrasher, *Viral Underclass*, 70; Marya and Patel, *Inflamed*, loc. 10–13, 26, 230.

23. Marya and Patel, *Inflamed*, loc. 230; Tera W. Hunter, "COVID-19: A New 'Negro Servants' Disease,'" in Barnes, Merritt, and Williams, *After Life*, loc. 1428–1558; Thrasher, *Viral Underclass*, 41.

24. "Health Disparities: Provisional Death Counts for Coronavirus Disease 2019 (COVID-19)," CDC, April 19, 2023, www.cdc.gov/nchs/nvss/vsrr/covid19/health_disparities.htm; Stuart Hall, Chas Critcher, Tony Jefferson, John Clarke, and Brian Roberts, *Policing the Crisis: Mugging, the State, and Law and Order*, 2nd ed. (London: Palgrave Macmillan 2017), 394.

25. Kim Moody, "How 'Just-in-Time' Capitalism Spread COVID-19," *Spectre*, April 8, 2020, https://spectrejournal.com/how-just-in-time-capitalism-spread-covid-19/; Karen Weise, "Somali Workers in Minnesota Force Amazon to Negotiate," *New York Times*, November 20, 2018, www.nytimes.com/2018/11/20/technology/amazon-somali-workers-minnesota.html; Marya and Patel, *Inflamed*, loc. 80–82; Thrasher, *Viral Underclass*, 29–30, 71; Amitav Ghosh, *The Nutmeg's Curse: Parables for a Planet in Crisis* (Chicago: University of Chicago Press, 2021).

26. Marya and Patel, *Inflamed*, loc. 10, 44, 50, 153, 230, 231; Devich-Cyril, "Loss Runs Like a River."

27. Allison L. Skinner-Dorkenoo, Apoorva Sarmal, Kasheena G. Rogbeer, Chloe J. André, Bhumi Patel, Leah Cha, "Highlighting COVID-19 Racial Disparities Can Reduce Support for Safety Precautions Among White U.S. Residents," *Social Science & Medicine* 301 (2022): 114951, https://doi.org/10.1016/j.socscimed.2022.114951.

28. Kelly Hayes and Mariame Kaba wrote:

> In spring 2020, Health Affairs published a study that found that "jail-community cycling was a significant predictor of cases of [COVID-19], accounting for 55 percent of the variance in case rates across ZIP codes in Chicago and 37 percent of the variance in all of Illinois." The study also found that jail-community cycling "far exceeds race, poverty, public transit use, and population density as a predictor of variance." The authors of the study suggested that the cycling of people through Cook County Jail was associated with 15.7 percent of all documented COVID-19 cases in Illinois and 15.9 percent of all documented cases in Chicago as of April 19, 2020. As of this writing, one in seven people in the 60623 zip code, which encompasses

> most of Little Village, has had a confirmed case of COVID-19, making it the hardest-hit zip code in Chicago. (Hayes and Kaba, *Let This Radicalize You*, 166–167)

Steven Thrasher found the pattern held across the country: "One day in August 2020, I logged on to the *New York Times*'s coronavirus tracker, which, among other factors, displayed how many COVID-19 cases could be traced to institutions. Besides a pork-processing plant in South Dakota and a chicken plant in Iowa, fifteen of the seventeen institutions on that date with a thousand or more coronavirus cases traced to them were jails or prisons." Thrasher, *Viral Underclass*, 168.

29. As Amitav Ghosh wrote, "The usual conclusion is that disasters and outbreaks of new diseases will not only take a terrible toll of lives in poor countries, but will also lead to riots and uprisings that could culminate in the collapse of state structures." Yet the reality was that it was not African countries but America and Western Europe where "posse-like mobs, armed with automatic weapons and bedecked with fascist paraphernalia, besieged state capitols; where large numbers of people refused to comply with lockdowns; where doctors and experts were belittled and derided; where violence against people of color continued apace." Ghosh, *Nutmeg's Curse*, loc. 2409–2424; Thrasher, *Viral Underclass*, 10–12, 72, 187; Malm and Zetkin Collective, *White Skin, Black Fuel*, loc. 7914–7922.

30. Governor Doug Ducey pushed forward with reopening against the recommendations of experts in public health from his state. The *Washington Post* reported in early May 2020:

> On Monday night, the eve of President Trump's visit to the state, Ducey's health department shut down the work of academic experts predicting the peak of the state's coronavirus outbreak was still about two weeks away.
>
> "We've been asked by Department leadership to 'pause' all current work on projections and modeling," Steven Bailey, the bureau chief for public health statistics at the Arizona Department of Health Services, wrote to the modeling team, composed of professionals from Arizona State University and the University of Arizona, according to email correspondence reviewed by The Washington Post.

Isaac Stanley-Becker and Rachel Weiner, "Arizona Halts Partnership with Experts Predicting Coronavirus Cases Would Continue to Mount," *Washington Post*, May 6, 2020, www.washingtonpost.com/politics/arizona-halts-partnership-with-experts-predicting-corona-virus-cases-would-continue-to-mount/2020/05/06/d7a97c46-8fc2-11ea-a9c0-73b93422d691_story.html.

31. Governor Douglas A. Ducey, State of Arizona Executive Order 2020–43, "Pausing of Arizona's Reopening," June 29, 2020, https://azgovernor.gov/sites/default/files/eo_2020-43.pdf.

32. Steven Thrasher noted:

> Though it got only passing mention in the news at the time, George Floyd died with SARS-CoV-2 antibodies in his system. This meant he had recently contracted the virus that was a leading cause of death in the United States that summer, especially among Black men. . . . The budget priorities of Minneapolis increased the odds that its police would have a deadly encounter with someone like Floyd and increased the odds that Floyd would encounter the novel coronavirus. It was no coincidence that in the summer of Floyd's murder, the United States represented less than 5 percent of the world's population, but was home to about 25 percent of global COVID-19 deaths and 25 percent of the world's incarcerated people. (*Viral Underclass*, 21–23)

33. "We're Not All in This Together: Reckless Protest Flaunts Brookfield's White Privilege During Pandemic," *Milwaukee Independent*, April 19, 2020, www.milwaukeeindependent.com/special/covid-19/not-together-reckless-protest-flaunts-brookfields-white-privilege-pandemic/.

34. Pierre Bourdieu, "The Essence of Neoliberalism," *Le Monde diplomatique*, December 1998, https://mondediplo.com/1998/12/08bourdieu; Cooper, *Family Values*.

35. David Wojnarowicz, *Close to the Knives: A Memoir of Disintegration* (New York: Open Road Media, June 2014), loc. 121–122, Kindle. Mourning, Sara Marcus noted, was fraught for AIDS activists: they often, she wrote, preferred "the active energies of rage." Yet Wojnarowicz and others, including Douglas Crimp, pointed to a political mourning, yet another form of praying for the dead and fighting like hell for the living, in a moment when "gay lives were considered neither worth saving nor worth grieving." Marcus, *Political Disappointment*, 158–159; see also Douglas Crimp, *Melancholia and Moralism: Essays on AIDS and Queer Politics* (Cambridge, MA: MIT Press, 2002).

36. Act Up NY, "The Ashes Action," https://actupny.org/diva/synAshes.html; s. e. smith, "Tired of Dying: Ashes Action, COVID-19, and Protesting Under a Pandemic," *Catapult*, June 15, 2020, https://catapult.co/stories/tired-of-dying-ashes-action-covid-19-and-protesting-under-a-pandemic-column-s-e-smith; Jason Silverstein, "Why the Ashes of People with AIDS on the White House Lawn Matter," *Vice*, August 20, 2016, www.vice.com/en/article/vdqv34/why-the-ashes-of-aids-victims-on-the-white-house-lawn-matter.

37. Sarah Jaffe, "Mourning and Organizing," *Progressive*, May 28, 2020, https://progressive.org/latest/mourning-organizing-jaffe-200528/.

38. Hayes wrote in a memorial zine for the event:

> There is a reason our collective grief has been suppressed with lies and political circus acts during this pandemic. It's because there is power in solidarity and collective memorialization, and the powerful are afraid of that empathy and solidarity. This pandemic, like the horrors of the prison system, has demonstrated how harmful it is to human beings to be deprived of connection. We were already being starved of it by the cult of individualism.
>
> The answer is more empathy and connection. The answer is to become an immovable force when we are together and a constellation of power and empathy when we are apart. (Hayes and Kaba, *Let This Radicalize You*, 148–152)

39. Simon G. Talbot and Wendy Dean, "Physicians Aren't 'Burning Out': They're Suffering from Moral Injury," Stat News, July 26, 2018; A. Rimmer, "COVID-19: Eight in 10 Doctors Have Experienced Moral Distress During Pandemic, BMA Survey Finds," *BMJ* 373, no. 1543 (2021), doi:10.1136/bmj.n1543.

40. Thomas Colson, "Boris Johnson Opposed a Lockdown Last Year Because People Dying Were Mostly over 80 Anyway, Leaked Messages Say," *Business Insider*, July 20, 2021, www.businessinsider.com/boris-johnson-opposed-2nd-lockdown-as-those-dying-were-over-80-texts-2021-7; Joshua Nevett, "Boris Johnson Thought Old People Should Accept COVID Fate, Inquiry Told," BBC, November 1, 2023, www.bbc.com/news/uk-politics-67278517; Bess Levin, "Texas Lt. Governor: Old People Should Volunteer to Die to Save the Economy," *Vanity Fair*, March 24, 2020, www.vanityfair.com/news/2020/03/dan-patrick-coronavirus-grandparents.

41. Rhae Lynn Barnes and Keri Leigh Merritt, "The Present Crisis," in Barnes, Merritt, and Williams, *After Life*, loc. 364–368; Marya and Patel, *Inflamed*, loc. 171.

42. See also Kenway, *Who Cares*.

43. Tamara Keith, "Biden's Message Shifts from Mourning the Dead to the Tactical Fight Against COVID," *Morning Edition*, NPR, December 22, 2021, www.npr.org/2021/12/22/1066642230/bidens-message-shifts-from-mourning-the-dead-to-the-tactical-fight-against-covid.

44. Keith, "Biden's Message Shifts"; Maya Binyam, "You Pose a Problem: A Conversation with Sara Ahmed," *Paris Review*, January 1, 2022, www.theparisreview.org/blog/2022/01/14/you-pose-a-problem-a-conversation-with-sara-ahmed/. See also Sara Ahmed, *Complaint!* (Durham, NC: Duke University Press, September 2021).

45. Sarah Jaffe and C. M. Lewis, "Nurses Are Striking Across the Country over Patient Safety," *Nation*, May 6, 2021, www.thenation.com/article/activism/nursing-strike-massachusetts-covid/; Ed Yong, "America Is Zooming Through the Pandemic Panic-Neglect Cycle," *Atlantic*, March 17, 2022, www.theatlantic.com/healthcarchive/2022/03congress-covid-spending-bill/627090/.

46. Thrasher, *Viral Underclass*, 6, 198; Beatrice Adler-Bolton, "Deaths Pulled from the Future," *Blind Archive*, Substack, January 3, 2022, https://blindarchive.substack.com/p/deaths-pulled-from-the-future; Adler-Bolton and Vierkant, *Health Communism*, loc. 229–230, 203–205, 232–242, 248–251.

47. Adler-Bolton, "Deaths Pulled from the Future"; Shannon Brownlee and Jeanne Lenzer, "How Mistreating Nursing Home Staff Helped Spread COVID-19," *Washington Monthly*, April 16, 2021, https://washingtonmonthly.com/2021/04/16/how-mistreating-nursing-home-staff-helped-spread-covid-19/; Adler-Bolton and Vierkant, *Health Communism*, loc. 374–421, 1311–1327; Thrasher, *Viral Underclass*, 198–204; Priya Chidambaram, "Over 200,000 Residents and Staff in Long-Term Care Facilities Have Died from COVID-19," Kaiser Family Foundation PolicyWatch, February 3, 2022, www.kff.org/policy-watch/over-200000-residents-and-staff-in-long-term-care-facilities-have-died-from-covid-19/; "Timeline: New York Gov. Andrew Cuomo Resigns in Wake of Sexual Harassment, Nursing Home Scandals," CBS News, January 7, 2022, www.cbsnews.com/newyork/news/cuomo-nursing-home-and-sexual-harassment-allegations-timeline/; Luis Ferré-Sadurní, "Health Agency Under Cuomo 'Misled the Public' on Nursing Home Deaths," *New York Times*, March 15, 2022, www.nytimes.com/2022/03/15/nyregion/nursing-home-deaths-cuomo-covid.html. It's worth noting of course that Andrew Cuomo also lost his job over quite a few accusations of sexual harassment. Joanna Walters, "Andrew Cuomo Resigns in Wake of Damning Report on Sexual Harassment," *Guardian*, August 10, 2021, www.theguardian.com/us-news/2021/aug/10/andrew-cuomo-resigns-sexual-harassment-intimidation.

48. Jessie Hellmann, "Biden's Long-Term Care Agenda Faces Headwinds," *Roll Call*, July 11, 2023, https://rollcall.com/2023/07/11/bidens-long-term-care-agenda-faces-headwinds/; Brandon Lee, "Health Care Briefing: Home Health Groups Look to Revive Agenda," Bloomberg Government, March 31, 2022, https://about.bgov.com/news/health-care-briefing-home-health-groups-look-to-revive-agenda/; Jonathan Cohn, "The Legislation Joe Manchin Is Holding Up Would Help His State—a Lot," *HuffPost*, September 26, 2021, www.huffingtonpost.co.uk/entry/manchin-biden-west-virginia-child-care-hcbs-poverty_n_614e2e70e4b03dd7280afa11.

49. Jonathan Pie and Adam Westbrook, "The First Thing You Need to Know About Boris Johnson Is He's a Liar," *New York Times*, February 4, 2022, www.nytimes.com/2022/02/04/opinion/boris-johnson-party-scandal.html; Balani, "Without Mourning"; Kevin Rawlinson, "Johnson and Sunak Must Go, Say 'Disgusted' Families of COVID Victims," *Guardian*, April 12, 2022, www.theguardian.com/politics/2022/apr/12/johnson-and-sunak-must-go-disgusted-covid-victims-families.

50. Rawlinson, "Johnson and Sunak Must Go."

51. Quotation is from Angela Giuffrida, "Former Italian PM Giuseppe Conte Faces Investigation over COVID Response," *Guardian*, March 2, 2023, www.theguardian.com/world/2023/mar/02/italy-former-pm-giuseppe-conte-investigation-covid-response. See also sources Nava shared at the time: Agence France Presse, "Former Italy PM Under Investi-

gation over COVID Response," Barron's, March 1, 2023, www.barrons.com/news/former-italy-pm-under-investigation-over-covid-response-aa92d38e; and "Coronavirus Investigation Completed in Italy," *WestObserver*, March 2, 2023, https://westobserver.com/news/europe/coronavirus-investigation-completed-in-italy-breaking-news/.

52. Douglas Starr, "How Italy's 'Father of the Swabs' Fought the Coronavirus," *Science*, August 27, 2020, www.science.org/content/article/how-italy-s-father-swabs-fought-coronavirus; Gregorio Sorgi, "Former Italian PM Faces Probe over Lombardy COVID Outbreak," *Politico*, March 2, 2023, www.politico.eu/article/giuseppe-conte-lombardy-former-italy-pm-faces-probe-over-covid-outbreak/; E. Lavezzo, E. Franchin, C. Ciavarella, et al., "Suppression of a SARS-CoV-2 Outbreak in the Italian Municipality of Vo," *Nature* 584 (2020): 425–429, https://doi.org/10.1038/s41586-020-2488-1.

53. Giselda Vagnoni, "Families of Italian COVID-19 Victims Seek $122 Million from Government," Reuters, December 23, 2020, www.reuters.com/article/us-health-coronavirus-italy-lawsuit-idUSKBN28X1PQ.

54. Engels, *Condition of the Working Class in England.*

55. Adler-Bolton and Vierkant, *Health Communism*, loc. 254–263, 2080–2088; see also Jasbir Puar, *The Right to Maim: Debility, Capacity, Disability* (Durham, NC: Duke University Press, 2017).

56. "Press Briefing by Press Secretary Jen Psaki, December 6, 2021," White House, www.whitehouse.gov/briefing-room/press-briefings/2021/12/06/press-briefing-by-press-secretary-jen-psaki-december-6-2021/.

57. Devich-Cyril, "Loss Runs Like a River."

58. George Walker, "Nurses Tell of Disappointment with Latest NHS Pay Offer," Novara Media, April 6, 2023, https://novaramedia.com/2023/04/06/nurses-tell-of-disappointment-with-latest-nhs-pay-offer/; Barnes and Merritt, "The Present Crisis," in Barnes, Merritt, and Williams, *After Life*, loc. 291–293; Bradley Jolly, "Junior Doctors and Young Medics Confirm Exactly How Much They Earn as New Strikes Launched," *Mirror*, August 11, 2023, www.mirror.co.uk/news/politics/junior-doctors-young-medics-confirm-30678038; Priya Bharadia, "'Daunted': New Junior Doctors in England Voice Worries as Strike Begins," *Guardian*, August 11, 2023.

59. Cherie Renfro, "Production Didn't Stop When Line Worker Died and More: Frito-Lay Employee Gives Glimpse Behind the Scenes," *Capital-Journal*, July 2, 2021, https://eu.cjonline.com/story/opinion/2021/07/02/frito-lay-employee-topeka-shares-complaints-working-conditions/7838411002/.

60. Sarah Jaffe, "Sephora Makes Plans to Reopen," *Dissent*, May 8, 2020, www.dissentmagazine.org/blog/belabored-stories-sephora-makes-plans-to-reopen/; Michelle Chen, "I'm Not Going to Risk My Life for Lipstick," *Dissent*, August 5, 2020, www.dissentmagazine.org/blog/im-not-going-to-risk-my-life-for-lipstick/.

61. Marked By COVID, "Policy Platform" (May 2022), https://docs.google.com/document/d/1gjM-AB-1tS0cfoWrBu2g1OnrDIgkZShbyXRtOgWh1X8/edit; Adler-Bolton and Vierkant, *Health Communism*, loc. 98–99, 104–107, 796–797, 806–807, 822–824, 842–843.

Break V

1. Muna Mire, "How I Used Makeup to Heal from Loss," *Vice*, August 22, 2019, www.vice.com/en/article/gyzgwx/extreme-makeup-lets-me-quietly-express-grief.

Chapter 5: Weather: Climate catastrophe, the web of life, and salvage

1. Philip Hoare, "Orcas Are Ramming Yachts off the Spanish Coast—Is the Whale World Rising Up?," *Guardian*, May 25, 2023, www.theguardian.com/commentisfree/2023/may/25

/orcas-ramming-yachts-spanish-whale-behaviour-trauma-humans; Jessica Hamilton, "Killer Whale Named White Gladis Who 'Started the Trend' of Animals Ramming Boats off the Coast of Spain and Portugal 'Was Pregnant When She Began the Orca Uprising,'" *Daily Mail*, August 28, 2023, www.dailymail.co.uk/news/article-12246987/Killer-whale-named-White-Gladis-started-trend-animals-ramming-boats-pregnant.html; Sascha Pare, "Orcas Have Sunk 3 Boats in Europe and Appear to Be Teaching Others to Do the Same: But Why?," LiveScience, May 18, 2023, www.livescience.com/animals/orcas/orcas-have-sunk-3-boats-in-europe-and-appear-to-be-teaching-others-to-do-the-same-but-why; Emma Beddington, "The Orca Uprising: Whales Are Ramming Boats—but Are They Inspired by Revenge, Grief or Memory?," *Guardian*, July 11, 2023, www.theguardian.com/environment/2023/jul/11/the-orca-uprising-whales-are-ramming-boats-but-are-they-inspired-by-revenge-grief-or-memory.

2. Ghosh, *Nutmeg's Curse*, loc. 3534; Ed Yong, "What a Grieving Orca Tells Us," *Atlantic*, August 14, 2018, www.theatlantic.com/science/archive/2018/08/orca-family-grief/567470/. Orcas are not the only creatures that mourn: Donna Haraway noted that corvids—crows, magpies, and such—also grieve their dead. Haraway, *Staying with the Trouble*, loc. 1046–1049.

3. Alexis Pauline Gumbs, "Heat Is Not a Metaphor," *Harper's Bazaar*, August 16, 2023, www.harpersbazaar.com/culture/features/a44819303/climate-crisis-maui/.

4. Matthew J. Haugen, "Alyssa Battistoni on Care Work, Organizing, and the 'Free Gift of Nature,'" *Terrain*, August 17, 2022, www.terrain.news/p/alyssa-battistoni-on-care-work-organizing; Federici, "Re-enchanting the World," in *Re-enchanting the World*, loc. 3873; Damian Carrington, "Earth's Sixth Mass Extinction Event Under Way, Scientists Warn," *Guardian*, July 10, 2017, www.theguardian.com/environment/2017/jul/10/earths-sixth-mass-extinction-event-already-underway-scientists-warn; Haraway, *Staying with the Trouble*, loc. 1046–1049; Kate Soper, *Post-growth Living: For an Alternative Hedonism* (London: Verso, 2020), loc. 1756–1758, Kindle.

5. John Barry explained what happened during the Great Flood thus:

> In 1927, New Orleans was the most vital economic city in the South by far, and it was run entirely by bankers who didn't not even bother to consult elected officials; they simply decided they were going to dynamite the levee to reassure their correspondent banks in New York, London and Boston that they would never allow the Mississippi River to threaten the city. It was a strictly political power play. They promised reparations to the people they flooded out, and they stiffed them. They reneged on all their promises, written promises; they controlled the state Supreme Court, so the lawsuits against them went nowhere.

John M. Barry on Weekend Edition, "The Mississippi Flood of 1927," NPR.org, September 3, 2005, https://www.npr.org/2005/09/03/4831423/the-mississippi-flood-of-1927; see also John M. Barry, *Rising Tide: The Great Mississippi Flood of 1927 and How It Changed America* (New York: Simon & Schuster, 1998); Thrasher, *Viral Underclass*, 6.

6. Sharpe, *In the Wake*, loc. 781; Soni, *The Great Escape*, 1–2; Gilmore, "Race, Prisons, and War: Scenes from the History of US Violence," in *Abolition Geography*, loc. 2373–2385, 2515–2523; Osterweil, *In Defense of Looting*, loc. 3380–3381, 3614–3645; Pelot-Hobbs, *Prison Capital*, 268–269; Ko Bragg, "The Lie of the Storm," *Columbia Journalism Review*, November 10, 2021, https://www.cjr.org/special_report/new-orleans-hurrcane-katrina-ida-looting.php.

7. Helen A. Regis, "Second Lines, Minstrelsy, and the Contested Landscapes of New Orleans Afro-Creole Festivals," *Cultural Anthropology* 14, no. 4 (November 1999): 478, 484, 489.

8. Regis further wrote:

> I would argue that, in New Orleans, it is those very cultural processes that have been labeled as detracting from the proper "work ethic" in the population which work

> to create positive experiences of community in the inner city. For example, the practice of leaving work to attend a jazz funeral on a weekday is hardly a prized cultural practice in the production of a positive business climate (Thompson 1967). But this is a narrow and wrongheaded view. Participation in funerals, in New Orleans as in many other cultures, is a profound way of strengthening and repairing the social fabric, which is severely weakened by poverty, joblessness, violence, class- and race-based segregation, and racism. ("Second Lines," 478, 480–481)

See also Marya and Patel, *Inflamed*, loc. 261–265.

9. William Archambeault, "Vinyl Is Final for Sinking City Records & Special Man Industries," *Anti-Gravity Magazine*, June 2019, https://antigravitymagazine.com/feature/vinyl-is-final-for-sinking-city-records-special-man-industries/; Sinking City Records, https://sinkingcityrecords.bandcamp.com/.

10. Audrey Mcavoy and Claire Rush, "Lahaina Residents Worry a Rebuilt Maui Town Could Slip into the Hands of Affluent Outsiders," CTV News, August 13, 2023, www.ctvnews.ca/climate-and-environment/lahaina-residents-worry-a-rebuilt-maui-town-could-slip-into-the-hands-of-affluent-outsiders-1.6517220; "Mayor Bloomberg Rings Opening Bell at NYSE," CBS News, October 31, 2012, www.cbsnews.com/newyork/news/mayor-bloomberg-rings-opening-bell-at-nyse/; Sarah Jaffe, "Power to the People," *Jacobin*, November 3, 2012, https://jacobin.com/2012/11/power-to-the-people.

11. Sharpe, *In the Wake*, loc. 2493.

12. Soni, *Great Escape*, 1–2.

13. Soni, *Great Escape*, 2–3, 6.

14. Soni, *Great Escape*, 1–3, 6, 326; "This New Orleans Statue Honors the Latino Workers Who Helped Rebuild the City After Hurricane Katrina," *Remezcla*, November 12, 2018, https://remezcla.com/culture/hurricane-katrina-new-orleans-statue/; Salvage editorial collective, "Perspectives 1: Amid This Stony Rubbish," *Salvage* 1, July 2015, https://salvage.zone/issue-one/.

15. Nik Theodore, "Recovering from Climate Disasters: Immigrant Day Laborers as 'Second Responders,'" Center for Urban Economic Development, University of Illinois Chicago, and National Day Laborer Organizing Network (NDLON), April 2022, https://ndlon.org/wp-content/uploads/2022/04/Recovering-from-Climate-Disasters-Report-2.26.22.pdf.

16. Theodore, "Recovering from Climate Disasters"; Erik Villalobos, "New Report Finds 'State of Emergency' for immigrant workers in Florida," National Day Laborer Organizing Network (NDLON), June 29, 2023, https://ndlon.org/new-report-finds-state-of-emergency-for-immigrant-workers-in-florida/.

17. Theodore, "Recovering from Climate Disasters"; Villalobos, "New Report"; PBS News Hour, "Timeline: Guatemala's Brutal Civil War," March 7, 2011, https://www.pbs.org/newshour/health/latin_america-jan-june11-timeline_03-07.

18. Marx, in *Capital*, explained it thus: "He opposes himself to Nature as one of her own forces, setting in motion arms and legs, head and hands, the natural forces of his body, in order to appropriate Nature's productions in a form adapted to his own wants. By thus acting on the external world and changing it, he at the same time changes his own nature." Marx, *Capital*, loc. 1:97; Táíwò, *Elite Capture*, loc. 1243–1244.

19. Donna Haraway noted that Andreas Malm coined the term, which was then taken up by Moore and others. Haraway, *Staying with the Trouble*, loc. 1229–1260, 3865; Daniel Hartley, "Against the Anthropocene," *Salvage* 1 (July 2015): 107–117, https://salvage.zone/wp-content/uploads/2019/08/Salvage-1.pdf; Tsing, *Mushroom at the End of the World*, loc. 122; Patel and Moore, *A History of the World*, 2–3; see also Jason W. Moore, ed., *Anthropocene or Capitalocene? Nature, History, and the Crisis of Capitalism* (Oakland, CA: PM Press, 2016);

Jason W. Moore, *Capitalism in the Web of Life: Ecology and the Accumulation of Capital* (London: Verso, 2015).

20. Or, in Anna Tsing's words, "Nature was a backdrop and resource for the moral intentionality of Man, which could tame and master Nature. It was left to fabulists, including non-Western and non-civilizational storytellers, to remind us of the lively activities of all beings, human and not human." Tsing, *Mushroom at the End of the World*, loc. 123–125; Patel and Moore, *A History of the World*, 3, 21, 50; Hartley, "Against the Anthropocene"; China Miéville, "The Limits of Utopia,*" *Salvage* 1 (July 2015): 177–189.

21. Patel and Moore, *A History of the World*, 22, 24–25; Moore, "Introduction: Anthropocene or Capitalocene? Nature, History, and the Crisis of Capitalism," in Moore, *Anthropocene or Capitalocene?*

22. Kahle, *Energy Citizenship*, loc. 236–272.

23. Naomi Klein wrote: "So another way of thinking about this history is that, starting two centuries ago, coal helped Western nations to deliberately appropriate other people's lives and lands; and as the emissions from that coal (and later oil and gas) continually built up in the atmosphere, it gave those same nations the means to inadvertently appropriate their descendants' sky as well, gobbling up most of our shared atmosphere's capacity to safely absorb carbon." Naomi Klein, *This Changes Everything: Capitalism vs. the Climate* (New York: Simon & Schuster, 2015), 416; Patel and Moore, *A History of the World*, 35; Ghosh, *Nutmeg's Curse*, loc. 1787–1818; Kahle, *Energy Citizenship*, loc. 316–317, 548–623, 841–842, 1085–1086, 1245–1246, 1733–1805, 2987–2989, 3452–3454, 4011–4012, 4602–4605, 4925–4926.

24. Kahle, *Energy Citizenship*, loc. 7281–7285, 7876–7880, 8002–8004; David Biello, "Where Did the Carter White House's Solar Panels Go?," *Scientific American*, August 6, 2010, www.scientificamerican.com/article/carter-white-house-solar-panel-array/; Loomis, *Out of Sight*, 133–138, 140–142.

25. Thea Riofrancos, Alissa Kendall, Kristi K. Dayemo, Matthew Haugen, Kira McDonald, Batul Hassan, Margaret Slattery, *Achieving Zero Emissions with More Mobility and Less Mining*, Climate & Community Project, January 2023, https://www.climateandcommunity.org/more-mobility-less-mining; Alyssa Battistoni, "The Lithium Problem: An Interview with Thea Riofrancos," *Dissent*, Spring 2023, https://www.dissentmagazine.org/article/the-lithium-problem/; see Thea Riofrancos's book, forthcoming, www.theariofrancos.com/extraction; Haugen, "Alyssa Battistoni on Care Work"; Kahle, *Energy Citizenship*, loc. 8694–8697.

26. Martin Gelin, "The Misogyny of Climate Deniers," *New Republic*, August 28, 2019, https://newrepublic.com/article/154879/misogyny-climate-deniers; Cara Daggett, "Petro-masculinity and the Politics of Climate Refusal," Autonomy, May 1, 2022, https://autonomy.work/portfolio/petro-masculinity-climate-refusal/; Malm and Zetkin Collective, *White Skin, Black Fuel*, loc. 1008, 1469–1470, 4233–4248, 7533–7725.

27. Klein wrote, "Because of those decades of hardcore emitting exactly when we were supposed to be cutting back, the things we must do to avoid catastrophic warming are no longer just in conflict with the particular strain of deregulated capitalism that triumphed in the 1980s. They are now in conflict with the fundamental imperative at the heart of our economic model: grow or die." Klein, *This Changes Everything*, 21; for more on destruction and freedom see Greg Grandin, *The End of the Myth: From the Frontier to the Border Wall in the Mind of America* (New York: Metropolitan Books: 2019); Nunes, *Neither Vertical nor Horizontal*, loc. 2549–2551.

28. Berardi, *After the Future*, loc. 134; Loomis, *Out of Sight*, 146–153.

29. Loomis, *Out of Sight*, 148; Ghosh, *Nutmeg's Curse*, loc. 2686–2754; Goodfellow, *Hostile Environment*, 32–33, 41; Miéville, "Limits of Utopia*"; Gilroy, *Postcolonial Melancholia*," 72–75.

30. Marya and Patel, *Inflamed*, loc. 4–5, 9; Sarah Jaffe, "Post-Occupied," *Truthout*, May 19, 2014, https://truthout.org/articles/post-occupied/.

31. Patel and Moore, *A History of the World*, 27; Hartley, "Against the Anthropocene," 107–117; Miéville, "Limits of Utopia.*"

32. Ricia Anne Chansky and Marci Denesiuk, eds., *Mi María: Surviving the Storm: Voices from Puerto Rico* (Chicago: Haymarket Books, 2021), 2–3.

33. Elizabeth Chuck, "Where Is Disgraced Former FEMA Chief Michael Brown Now?," NBC News, August 27, 2015, www.nbcnews.com/storyline/hurricane-katrina-anniversary/heck-job-brownie-where-disgraced-fema-head-now-n400436.

34. Klein, who after all wrote the book on disaster capitalism, wrote of Puerto Rico:

> You just have to move your company's address to Puerto Rico and enjoy a stunningly low 4 percent corporate tax rate—a fraction of what corporations pay even after Donald Trump's recent tax cut. Any dividends paid by a Puerto Rico–based company to Puerto Rican residents are also tax-free, thanks to a law passed in 2012 called Act 20. . . .
>
> Thanks to a clause in the federal tax code, U.S. citizens who move to Puerto Rico can avoid paying federal income tax on any income earned in Puerto Rico. And thanks to another local law, Act 22, they can also cash in on a slew of tax breaks and total tax waivers that includes paying zero capital gains tax and zero tax on interest and dividends sourced to Puerto Rico. And much more-all part of a desperate bid to attract capital to an island that is functionally bankrupt.

Naomi Klein, *Battle for Paradise* (Chicago: Haymarket Books, 2018), 12, 17–18, 25–27, 58.

35. Klein, *Battle for Paradise*, 29; David Cordero Mercado and Laura M. Quintero, "Las muertes por el paso del huracán Fiona son más de las que se han contado hasta la fecha," *El Nuevo Dia*, October 31, 2022, www.elnuevodia.com/noticias/locales/notas/las-muertes-por-el-paso-del-huracan-fiona-son-mas-de-las-que-se-han-contado-hasta-la-fecha/; David Cordero Mercado and Laura M. Quintero, "Traspiés en el operativo de contar las muertes a causa del huracán Fiona," *El Nuevo Dia*, November 2, 2022, www.elnuevodia.com/noticias/locales/notas/traspies-en-el-operativo-de-contar-las-muertes-a-causa-del-huracan-fiona/; Mel Leonor, "Study: 4,645 People Died After Hurricane Maria, Far More Than Official Estimate," *Politico*, May 29, 2019, www.politico.com/story/2018/05/29/puerto-rico-hurricane-maria-death-toll-610265.

36. For much more on the special economic zone and its place in modern capitalism, see Quinn Slobodian, *Crack-Up Capitalism: Market Radicals and the Dream of a World Without Democracy* (New York: Macmillan, 2023); Klein, *Battle for Paradise*, 6, 28; Chansky and Denesiuk, *Mi María*, 273–281; Marya and Patel, *Inflamed*, loc. 64–66.

37. Charo Henríquez, "Puerto Rico Protesters Got Creative: Dancing, Singing, Diving . . . ," *New York Times*, July 24, 2019, www.nytimes.com/2019/07/24/us/puerto-rico-governor-ricky-renuncia.html.

38. Ghosh, *Nutmeg's Curse*, loc. 2251–2275, 2492; Tracy Jan, Arelis R. Hernández, Josh Dawsey, and Damian Paletta, "After Butting Heads with Trump Administration, Top HUD Official Departs Agency," *Washington Post*, January 16, 2019, www.washingtonpost.com/business/economy/top-hud-officials-departure-follows-disagreements-over-housing-policy-and-puerto-rico-disaster-funds/2019/01/16/e6ba5be4-1839-11e9-9ebf-c5fed1b7a081_story.html; Nicole Acevedo, "New Probe Confirms Trump Officials Blocked Puerto Rico from Receiving Hurricane Aid," NBC News, April 22, 2021, www.nbcnews.com/news/latino/new-probe-confirms-trump-officials-blocked-puerto-rico-receiving-hurri-rcna749; Chansky and Denesiuk, *Mi María*, 7; Frances Robles and Deborah Acosta, "Puerto Rico Cancels Whitefish

Energy Contract to Rebuild Power Lines," *New York Times*, October 29, 2017, www.nytimes.com/2017/10/29/us/whitefish-cancel-puerto-rico.html.

39. Chansky and Denesiuk, *Mi María*, 7, 68.

40. Ricia Anne Chansky wrote, "Resilient is a word that has often been used to describe the people of Puerto Rico in the aftermaths of Hurricane María. This label is problematic, though, as it sidesteps the reality that this resiliency is born of repeated abandonment by the federal government during the almost 125 years that Puerto Rico has been a part of the United States. What is named 'resilience' is in actuality what occurs when a people are taught not to expect equitable treatment from their own government, developing a necessary understanding that they must be largely self-reliant in order to survive." Chansky and Denesiuk, *Mi María*, 10, 310; Klein, *Battle for Paradise*, 2–3, 10, 33–38, 40, 50; Sarah Jaffe, "Teachers in Puerto Rico Demand an End to School Closures and Privatization," *Truthout*, April 11, 2018, https://truthout.org/audio/teachers-in-puerto-rico-demand-an-end-to-school-closures-and-privatization/; Hayes and Kaba, *Let This Radicalize You*, 57–58.

41. Jason Schachter and Antonio Bruce, "Revising Methods to Better Reflect the Impact of Disaster," United States Census Bureau, August 19, 2020, www.census.gov/library/stories/2020/08/estimating-puerto-rico-population-after-hurricane-maria.html; "Puerto Rico: The Exodus After Hurricane Maria," CBS News, September 21, 2018, www.cbsnews.com/news/puerto-rico-exodus-after-hurricane-maria-cbsn-originals/.

42. Maroon is a reference to the communities created by people who fled slavery, created their own culture, and carved out spaces of resistance in a broader slave society. Loiza was home to one such community, and the people who live there today might be descended from those who built a space of freedom there. Olasee Davis, "Open Forum: Puerto Rico Shares Some of St. Croix's Rich Maroon History," *St. Thomas Source*, August 11, 2022, https://stthomassource.com/content/2022/08/11/open-forum-puerto-rico-shares-some-of-st-croixs-rich-maroon-history/.

43. Marya and Patel, *Inflamed*, loc. 14, 64; Patel and Moore, *A History of the World*, 28; Klein, *This Changes Everything*, 416; Marya and Patel, *Inflamed*, 14; see also, Marx, *Capital*, vol. 1; and Raj Patel, *The Value of Nothing: How to Reshape Market Society and Redefine Democracy* (New York: Picador, 2010).

44. Walia, *Border and Rule*, loc. 618; Marya and Patel, *Inflamed*, loc. 196; Patel and Moore, *A History of the World*, 91; Ghosh, *Nutmeg's Curse*, loc. 460.

45. Patel and Moore, *A History of the World*, 51, 94–95, 99; Ghosh, *Nutmeg's Curse*, loc. 451–465, 643.

46. It's worth including the longer quotation here from Hall:

> I am the sugar at the bottom of the English cup of tea. I am the sweet tooth, the sugar plantations that rotted generations of English children's teeth. There are thousands of others beside me that are, you know, the cup of tea itself. Because they don't grow it in Lancashire, you know. Not a single tea plantation exists within the United Kingdom. This is the symbolization of English identity—mean, what does anybody in the world know about an English person except that they can't get through the day without a cup of tea? Where does it come from? Ceylon—Sri Lanka, India. That is the outside history that is inside the history of the English. There is no English history without that other history. The notion that identity has to do with people that look the same, feel the same, call themselves the same, is nonsense. As a process, as a narrative, as a discourse, it is always told from the position of the Other.

Stuart Hall, "Old and New Identities, Old and New Ethnicities," in *Essential Essays*, ed. David Morley, vol. 2: *Identity and Diaspora* (Durham, NC: Duke University Press, 2018), https://doi.org/10.1215/9781478002710-005; Ghosh, *Nutmeg's Curse*, loc. 164; Loomis, *Out of Sight*, 110, 131; Federici, *Caliban and the Witch*, 111.

47. Federici, *Caliban and the Witch*, 104, 220, 225, 237; Federici, "Re-enchanting the World," loc. 3887–3900; Klein, *This Changes Everything*, 159; Ghosh, *Nutmeg's Curse*, 643–684.

48. Rackete with Weiss, *Time to Act*, loc. 1682; Silvia Federici, "Feminism and the Politics of the Commons in an Era of Primitive Accumulation," in *Re-enchanting the World*, loc. 2282; Federici, *Caliban and the Witch*, 11–12, 63, 66, 69, 87–88, 97, 165; Ghosh, *Nutmeg's Curse*, loc. 2038–2054, 4408–4459; See also Friedrich Engels, *The Origin of the Family, Private Property, and the State*, trans. Ernest Untermann (Public Domain Books, 2011), Kindle.

49. Federici, *Caliban and the Witch*, 141–144, 170, 186, 203; Carol Rosenberg, "What the C.I.A.'s Torture Program Looked like to the Tortured," *New York Times*, December 4, 2019, www.nytimes.com/2019/12/04/us/politics/cia-torture-drawings.html; Ghosh, *Nutmeg's Curse*, loc. 4476.

50. Federici, *Caliban and the Witch*, 165–166, 174.

51. Descartes quoted in Patel and Moore, *A History of the World*, 51–54; Federici, *Caliban and the Witch*, 149; Carolyn Merchant, "'The Violence of Impediments' Francis Bacon and the Origins of Experimentation," *Isis* 99 (2008): 731–760, https://nature.berkeley.edu/departments/espm/env-hist/articles/90.pdf; Malm and Zetkin Collective, *White Skin, Black Fuel*, loc. 3015.

52. Frederick Engels, "Dialectics," in *Socialism: Utopian and Scientific*, vol. 3 of *Selected Works*, by Karl Marx and Frederick Engels (Progress, 1970), 95–151, www.marxists.org/archive/marx/works/1880/soc-utop/index.htm.

53. In similar terms to Federici's "re-enchanting," Kate Soper calls for "an alternative hedonist turn to the spirit [that] would seek to redress this imbalance and to restore sources of direct spiritual well-being that have been sacrificed to the commodifying logic of consumer culture," and a "more spiritual consumption, when conceived along these lines, would introduce new thinking about what constitutes a distinctively human flourishing." Soper, *Post-growth Living*, loc. 1929–1967; Ghosh, *Nutmeg's Curse*, loc. 3217, 3235, 3244, 3261, 3291; Federici, "Re-enchanting the World," loc. 3835–3852, 3870.

54. Fanon, *Wretched of the Earth*, loc. 182; Malm and Zetkin Collective, *White Skin Black Fuel*, loc. 2510–2520.

55. Reuters, "Pakistan Authorities Breach Lake to Save Other Areas from Floods," *Guardian*, September 4, 2022, www.theguardian.com/world/2022/sep/04/pakistan-more-floods-lake-manchar-swells-monsoon-rains.

56. Patel and Moore, *A History of the World*, 59; Federici, "The Debt Crisis, Africa, and the New Enclosures," in Federici, *Re-enchanting the World*, loc. 911–959, 2410–2417; Walia, *Border and Rule*, loc. 1456–1504; Kristen Lyons and Peter Westoby, "Carbon Colonialism and the New Land Grab: Plantation Forestry in Uganda and Its Livelihood Impacts," *Journal of Rural Studies* 36 (2014): 13–21, https://doi.org/10.1016/j.jrurstud.2014.06.002. Harvey explained that Marx's idea of "primitive accumulation," so called because it was assumed to be setting the ground for capitalism to grow, was insufficient to understand the way that capitalism continues to enclose land, resources, and even intellectual property through "predation, fraud, and violence." He described it as "accumulation by dispossession." The forms of violence discussed in the beginning of this section—colonial occupation, the enclosures, the witch hunts, the suppression of alternate ways of living and relating to the natural world outside of the property relation—have not stopped, as Silvia Federici also documented in the texts cited above, and indeed now, Harvey wrote, "Wholly new mechanisms of accumulation by dispossession have also opened up."

> The emphasis on intellectual property rights in the WTO negotiations (the so-called TRIPS agreement) points to ways in which the patenting and licensing of genetic materials, seed plasmas, and all manner of other products, can now be used against whole populations whose environmental management practices have played a crucial role in the development of those materials. Biopiracy is rampant and the pillaging of the world's stockpile of genetic resources is well under way, to the benefit of a few large multinational companies. The escalating depletion of the global environmental commons (land, air, water) and proliferating habitat degradations that preclude anything but capital-intensive modes of agricultural production have likewise resulted from the wholesale commodification of nature in all its forms. The commodification of cultural forms, histories and intellectual creativity entails wholesale dispossessions—the music industry is notorious for the appropriation and exploitation of grassroots culture and creativity. The corporatization and privatization of hitherto public assets (like universities) to say nothing of the wave of privatization of water and other public utilities that has swept the world, constitute a new wave of "enclosing the commons." As in the past, the power of the state is frequently used to force such processes through even against the popular will.

David Harvey, "The 'New' Imperialism: Accumulation by Dispossession," *Socialist Register* 40 (2004), https://socialistregister.com/index.php/srv/article/view/5811.

57. Amitav Ghosh wrote:

> It is instructive, in this regard, to compare the world's military expenditures with its spending on climate change mitigation. At the UN climate summit in Copenhagen in 2009, it was agreed that wealthy countries would channel $100 billion a year to poorer nations, to help them cope with the impacts of climate change. But the Green Climate Fund set up by the UN succeeded in raising only $10.43 billion and is now running out of money: it never came close to being funded at the level envisaged at the summit. In that same period the world's annual military expenditure has risen from slightly above $1.5 trillion to almost $2 trillion. The total costs of the US's post-9/11 wars have been estimated as over $6 trillion. Yet the subject is so little studied that, according to three leading scholars in the field, "research on the environmental impacts of militarism [is] non-existent in the social sciences." (*Nutmeg's Curse*, loc. 2161–2169, 2844)

See also Walia, *Border and Rule*, loc. 1512–1538.

58. Marya and Patel, *Inflamed*, loc. 217.

59. Nick Estes, *Our History Is the Future: Standing Rock Versus the Dakota Access Pipeline, and the Long Tradition of Indigenous Resistance* (New York: Verso Books, 2019), 96, 99–104, 298, 953; Riverkeeper, "Newburgh Drinking Water Crisis," www.riverkeeper.org/campaigns/safeguard/newburgh-2/; Sarah Jaffe, "Standing Firm at Standing Rock: Why the Struggle Is Bigger Than One Pipeline," *Moyers & Company*, September 28, 2016, https://billmoyers.com/story/standing-firm-standing-rock-pipeline-protesters-will-not-moved/.

60. Estes, *Our History Is the Future*, loc. 109–113, 981–987; Marya and Patel, *Inflamed*, loc. 345; Federici, introduction to *Re-enchanting the World*, loc. 299.

61. Estes, *Our History Is the Future*, loc. 113–115, 140, 158–160, 307–313, 443–481, 812–832, 877, 943–981, 3881–3889; Marya and Patel, *Inflamed*, loc. 63; "Cowboy and Indian Alliance Stands Against Pipeline," CBS News, April 23, 2014, www.cbsnews.com/pictures/cowboy-and-indian-alliance-stands-against-pipeline/; Mary Kathryn Nagle, "A Year for Epic Victories amid Historic Loss," in Barnes, Merritt, and Williams, *After Life*, loc. 648–649, 702–705, 719–725; Alleen Brown, Will Parrish, and Alice Speri, "Leaked Documents Reveal Counterterrorism Tactics Used at Standing Rock to 'Defeat Pipeline Insurgencies,'" *Inter-*

cept, May 27, 2017, https://theintercept.com/2017/05/27/leaked-documents-reveal-security-firms-counterterrorism-tactics-at-standing-rock-to-defeat-pipeline-insurgencies/; Ruth Wilson Gilmore, "Race, Prisons, and War: Scenes from the History of US Violence," in *Abolition Geography,* loc. 2434–2438; Walia, *Border and Rule,* loc. 622.

62. Estes, *Our History Is the Future,* loc. 477; Ghosh, *Nutmeg's Curse,* loc. 4176–4200.

63. Some scientists have argued that the Great Dying, which killed perhaps 90 percent of the Native people in the Americas, contributed to the period of climate change known as the Little Ice Age. According to *Live Science,* "Essentially, once these tens of millions of people died in North, Central and South America, they could no longer farm. The forest then crept in, taking over farmland and doing what plants and trees do best: breathe in carbon dioxide (CO_2). This process decreased the amount of CO_2 in the atmosphere, leading to widespread cooling, the researchers said." Other researchers disputed the claim. Laura Geggel, "European Slaughter of Indigenous Americans May Have Cooled the Planet," *Live Science,* February 8, 2019, www.livescience.com/64723-great-dying-little-ice-age.html; Ghosh, *Nutmeg's Curse,* loc. 742–792, 875, 882, 896, 902–921, 946, 954–1018, 1077–1107, 1239, 2857; Estes, *Our History Is the Future,* loc. 224, 1387–1407; Gilmore, "Race, Prisons, and War," in Gilmore, *Abolition Geography,* loc. 2442–2444; Hayes and Kaba, *Let This Radicalize You,* 153.

64. Estes, *Our History Is the Future,* loc. 219–222, 281–285, 321–396, 1949–2087; Gordon, *Ghostly Matters,* loc. 171–173.

65. Marya and Patel, *Inflamed,* loc. 216–217; Estes, *Our History Is the Future,* loc. 794–796, 195, 530–531, 1280–1298; Julia Stern, "Pipeline of Violence: The Oil Industry and Missing and Murdered Indigenous Women," *Immigration and Human Rights Law Review,* May 28, 2021, https://lawblogs.uc.edu/ihrlr/2021/05/28/pipeline-of-violence-the-oil-industry-and-missing-and-murdered-indigenous-women/.

66. Estes, *Our History Is the Future,* loc. 938, 1036–1038, 1836, 3861.

67. Estes, *Our History Is the Future,* loc. 3923–3925; Nagle, "A Year for Epic Victories," loc. 686–688; Robinson Meyer, "Oil Is Flowing Through the Dakota Access Pipeline," *Atlantic,* June 9, 2017, www.theatlantic.com/science/archive/2017/06/oil-is-flowing-through-the-dakota-access-pipeline/529707/.

68. Estes, *Our History Is the Future,* loc. 1836; Ruth Wilson Gilmore, "Forgotten Places and the Seeds of Grassroots Planning," in Gilmore, *Abolition Geography,* loc. 5532.

69. Estes, *Our History Is the Future,* loc. 232.

70. Gilmore noted that the prison-siting process followed almost exactly the recommendations of the Cerrell Report, locating humans deemed surplus and waste similarly: "It might be coincidence that California's prison-building frenzy began the year Cerrell released its report and that the state's new prison towns match the criteria in that report—rural, poor, Catholic, agricultural, modestly educated." Gilmore, "The Other California (w/ Craig Gilmore)," in Gilmore, *Abolition Geography,* loc. 3332–3335; Miéville, "Limits of Utopia*"; Shahir Masri, "The Environmental Side of Racism," *Hill,* June 10, 2020, https://thehill.com/opinion/energy-environment/501991-the-environmental-side-of-racism/; Loomis, *Out of Sight,* 92–92; Office of Environmental Justice, Department of Justice, www.justice.gov/oej.

71. Masri, "Environmental Side,"; Office of Environmental Justice, Justice.gov, https://www.justice.gov/oej; Gilroy, *Postcolonial Melancholia,* loc. 10–11; Loomis, *Out of Sight,* 85–85.

72. Tom Miles, "In 'Climate Apartheid', Rich Will Save Themselves While Poor Suffer: U.N. Report," Reuters, June 25, 2019, www.reuters.com/article/us-climate-change-un-idUSKCN1TQ1KY; "German Leaders Agree on €30 Billion for Flood-Hit Regions," *DW,* August 10, 2021, www.dw.com/en/german-floods-leaders-agree-on-30-billion-reconstruction-fund/a-5882

2602; IMF Press Center, "IMF Executive Board Approves US$3 Billion Stand-By Arrangement for Pakistan," July 12, 2023, www.imf.org/en/News/Articles/2023/07/12/pr23261-pakistan-imf-exec-board-approves-us3bil-sba.

73. "Summary for Policymakers Headline Statements," *IPCC Sixth Assessment Report*, February 28, 2022, www.ipcc.ch/report/ar6/wg2/resources/spm-headline-statements/; Chaudhary, "The Long Now."

74. Loomis, *Out of Sight*, 85.

75. Mike Davis, "The Case for Letting Malibu Burn," *Ecology of Fear: Los Angeles and the Imagination of Disaster* (New York: Metropolitan Books, 1998), https://longreads.com/2018/12/04/the-case-for-letting-malibu-burn/.

76. Marya and Patel, *Inflamed*, loc. 237; Julia Shipley, Brian Edwards, David Nickerson, Robert Benincasa, Stella M. Chávez, and Cheryl W. Thompson, "Heat Is Killing Workers in the U.S.—and There Are No Federal Rules to Protect Them," NPR, August 17, 2021, www.npr.org/2021/08/17/1026154042/hundreds-of-workers-have-died-from-heat-in-the-last-decade-and-its-getting-worse.

77. As Andreas Malm and the Zetkin Collective, citing research that found that "individuals who questioned the full humanity of people of colour were also unbothered by the state of the environment," note, "Now if the early impacts of climate change are primarily an affliction for black and non-white people, one could imagine some people beholden to this long tradition thinking, 'Oh, that's just another piece of bad news for the wretched of the earth. Why bother?'" Malm and Zetkin Collective, *White Skin, Black Fuel*, loc. 4857–4898.

Ghosh, *Nutmeg's Curse*, loc. 2958–2986; Adler-Bolton, "Deaths Pulled from the Future."

78. Michael Whitney, "BP Failing to Report Workers Sick from Pollutants," Shadowproof, June 18, 2010, https://shadowproof.com/2010/06/18/bp-failing-to-report-workers-sick-from-pollutants/.

79. Gilmore, "Forgotten Places and the Seeds of Grassroots Planning," in Gilmore, *Abolition Geography*, loc. 5507–5553; Frank Perez, "What's in a Name? Bulbancha and Mobilian Jargon," *French Quarter Journal*, March 2023, https://www.frenchquarterjournal.com/archives/whats-in-a-name-bulbancha-and-mobilian-jargon.

80. If you're interested in this history, I highly recommend beginning with the Bucket Brigade's reports. The Shell refinery report closes with a photo of the refinery manager's home, noting that it is twenty-five miles from the facility, in an area free of chemical and oil plants. Anne Rolfes, "Shell Games: Divide and Conquer the Diamond Community," Louisiana Bucket Brigade, 2000, https://labucketbrigade.org/wp-content/uploads/2020/08/Shell-Games-2000.pdf; Emily Sanders, "How Shell Is Selling the Petrochemical Buildout as 'Sustainable,'" *DeSmog* (blog), April 5, 2023, www.desmog.com/2023/04/05/shell-norco-louisiana-petrochemical-sustainable/.

81. Pelot-Hobbs, *Prison Capital*, 22.

82. Gilmore, "Forgotten Places," in Gilmore, *Abolition Geography*, loc. 5433–5450; Pelot-Hobbs, *Prison Capital*, 22, 57–58, 107, 276.

83. Arlie Russell Hochschild, *Strangers in Their Own Land: Anger and Mourning on the American Right* (New York: New Press, 2016), 61–68, 74–77, 200.

84. Stephen Jay Gould, *The Panda's Thumb: More Reflections in Natural History* (New York: W. W. Norton, 1992), 151; for more on New Orleans music history, I recommend Ned Sublette, *The World That Made New Orleans: From Spanish Silver to Congo Square* (Chicago: Chicago Review Press, 2008).

85. John Burnett and Marisa Peñaloza, "Descendants of Slaves Say This Proposed Grain Complex Will Destroy the Community," NPR, July 7, 2021, www.npr.org/2021/07/07/1012609448/descendants-of-slaves-say-this-proposed-grain-factory-will-destroy-the-community; Janet McConnaughey, "Fight over $400M Grain Terminal Turns to 'Corrupt Zoning,'" AP, November 10, 2021, https://apnews.com/article/business-louisiana-new-orleans-slavery-formosa-plastics-corp-4d0bbf3931e2d75cc62a813d234a99e4.

86. See Tiya Miles, *Tales from the Haunted South: Dark Tourism and Memories of Slavery from the Civil War Era* (Chapel Hill: University of North Carolina Press, 2018).

87. On the pandemic effects, CNN reported:

> The numbers are "tremendous" for a parish this size, said Dr. Christy Montegut, the parish coroner. "This virus is just overwhelming people," he added. Montegut has worked at the coroner's office for 32 years and has run a primary care practice in town for nearly 40 years. "It's just been a real surge, like an onslaught."
>
> Montegut said the vast majority of people who died from coronavirus also had underlying health issues like hypertension, diabetes, kidney disease, and obesity. So far, he said in an interview last week, he had only seen a couple of coronavirus victims who also had cancer.
>
> Still, activists who've been long frustrated by the air pollution here argue the correlation to a high coronavirus death rate couldn't be clearer. They point to a recent nationwide study by Harvard that found a small increase in long-term exposure leads to a large increase in the coronavirus death rate.
>
> "We are suffering at this great percentage because . . . (of) the battle we have been in for years in our systems," said Robert Taylor, Jr., who leads the group called Concerned Citizens of St. John, which has been targeting a chemical plant in LaPlace, formerly owned by DuPont for decades and now owned by Denka.

Ashley Killough and Ed Lavandera, "This Small Louisiana Parish Has the Highest Death Rate per Capita for Coronavirus in the Country," CNN, April 16, 2020, https://edition.cnn.com/2020/04/15/us/louisiana-st-john-the-baptist-coronavirus/index.html; Marya and Patel, *Inflamed*, loc. 170.

88. Sabrina Wilson, "Ida Recovery Drags On for Some St. John Parish Residents," Fox 8 News, August 30, 2023, www.fox8live.com/2023/08/30/ida-recovery-drags-some-st-john-parish-residents/.

89. Chaudhary, "The Long Now." See also Ajay Singh Chaudhary, *The Exhausted of the Earth: Politics in a Burning World* (London: Repeater Books, 2024).

90. Violina R. Angelova, Dimitar F. Grekov, Veselin K. Kisyov, and Krasimir I. Ivanov, "Potential of Lavender (Lavandula vera L.) for Phytoremediation of Soils Contaminated with Heavy Metals," 2015, https://doi.org/10.5281/zenodo.1105651.

91. Eleanor Penny, Tina Ngata, and Raj Patel, "Against Nature," Verso Podcast, April 20, 2023, https://www.versobooks.com/en-gb/blogs/news/against-nature-raj-patel-tina-ngata-1.

92. Julie Weitz, "Doikayt Dispatch," Ayin Press, December 27, 2022, https://ayinpress.org/doikayt-dispatch/; Estes, *Our History Is the Future*, loc. 3980; Kim Tallbear, "The US-Dakota War and Failed Settler Kinship." *Unsettle*, April 23, 2021, https://kimtallbear.substack.com/p/the-us-dakota-war-and-failed-settler; Ghosh, *Nutmeg's Curse*, loc. 4144–4164.

93. Richard Seymour, "Welcome to the Inferno," *New Statesman*, July 2022, www.newstatesman.com/ideas/2022/07/climate-change-welcome-to-the-inferno.

94. Georgina Kenyon, "Have You Ever Felt 'Solastalgia'?" BBC, November 2, 2015, https://www.bbc.com/future/article/20151030-have-you-ever-felt-solastalgia.

95. Ghosh, *Nutmeg's Curse*, loc. 2556–2568; Chaudhary, "The Long Now"; Ed Struzik, "Fire-Induced Storms: A New Danger from the Rise in Wildfires," *Yale Environment 360*, January 24, 2019, https://e360.yale.edu/features/fire-induced-storms-a-new-danger-from-the-rise-in-wildfires; Nouran Salahieh, Gene Norman, Christina Maxouris, and Dakin Andone, "'We're Not Built for This': Tropical Storm Hilary Batters California with Heavy Rain and Catastrophic Floods," CNN, August 21, 2023.

96. As Andreas Malm and the Zetkin Collective note, "each moment of sustained business-as-usual is the outcome of conflict." Malm and Zetkin Collective, *White Skin, Black Fuel*, loc. 170; Lisa Friedman, "Biden Administration Approves Huge Alaska Oil Project," *New York Times*, March 12, 2023, www.nytimes.com/2023/03/12/climate/biden-willow-arctic-drilling-restrictions.html; Jennifer Scott, "Rishi Sunak Stands By Oil Drilling Expansion as Critics Warn of Climate Consequences," SkyNews, August 1, 2023, https://news.sky.com/story/rishi-sunak-heads-to-scotland-for-net-zero-energy-policy-push-12930459; Holly Evans, "Starmer 'Ditches Commitment to Ulez-Style Clean Air Zones Across Country,'" *Independent*, August 12, 2023, www.independent.co.uk/news/uk/politics/keir-starmer-labour-sadiq-khan-ulez-b2392162.html; Kristin Askelson, "Louisiana's Largest Fire, at 33,000 Acres, Will Likely Burn Until 'We Get Some Good, Long Rain,'" *Acadiana Advocate*, August 27, 2023, www.theadvocate.com/acadiana/news/tiger-island-fire-fueled-by-drought-windy-conditions/article_d85711bc-44ff-11ee-926d-bb5ea48acba5.html; "Louisiana Refinery Fire Mostly Contained but Residents Worry About Air Quality," Associated Press, August 26, 2023, https://apnews.com/article/louisiana-refinery-fire-marathon-garyville-b9bc66c602768ddf0e6d439d532b7f01; Haraway, *Staying with the Trouble*, loc. 2203.

97. Joshua Clover, "The Roundabout Riots," *Verso* (blog), December 9, 2018, www.versobooks.com/en-gb/blogs/news/4161-the-roundabout-riots; Simon Pirani, "End of the World, End of the Month—One Fight!," *Resurgence*, September/October 2022, www.resurgence.org/magazine/article5996-end-of-the-world-end-of-the-month-one-fight.html.

98. Pirani, "End of the World"; Keir Milburn, "Don't Pay Took Down Kwasi Kwarteng," Novara Media, October 18, 2022, https://novaramedia.com/2022/10/18/dont-pay-took-down-kwasi-kwarteng/; Isabeau van Halm, "Big Oil Profits Soared to Nearly $200bn in 2022," Energy Monitor, February 8, 2023, www.energymonitor.ai/finance/big-oil-profits-soared-to-nearly-200bn-in-2022/.

99. Rithika Ramamurthy, "Personal Hell," *Drift*, May 6, 2021, www.thedriftmag.com/climate-anxiety/; Bridget Read, "Weathering the Weather: Mental-Health Professionals Are Trying to Figure Out How to Talk About the Climate," *Cut*, October 28, 2021, www.thecut.com/2021/10/climate-change-mental-health-therapy.html; Pelot-Hobbs, *Prison Capital*, 270–271.

100. Alyssa Battistoni, "A Green New Deal for Care: Revaluing the Work of Social and Ecological Reproduction," in *The Green New Deal and the Future of Work*, ed. Craig Calhoun and Benjamin Y. Fong (New York: Columbia University Press, 2022), 105–117; Rackete with Weiss, *Time to Act*, loc. 819–845; Read, "Weathering the Weather."

101. Aaron Bady, "The Trap of Climate Optimism," *Nation*, December 23, 2021, www.thenation.com/article/culture/dan-sherrell-warmth-qa/; Nunes, *Neither Vertical nor Horizontal*, loc. 591–593.

102. Estes, *Our History Is the Future*, loc. 1737; Food and Agriculture Organization of the United Nations, "Voices from Arctic Nomads: An Ancestral System Facing Global Warming," in *Indigenous Peoples' Food Systems: Insights on Sustainability and Resilience in the Front Line of Climate Change* (Rome: FAO and Alliance of Bioversity International and CIAT, 2021), chapter 2, https://doi.org/10.4060/cb5131en, Federici, *Re-enchanting the World*,

loc. 2628–2781; Dan Collyns, "Ecuadorians Vote to Halt Oil Drilling in Biodiverse Amazonian National Park," *Guardian*, August 21, 2023, https://www.theguardian.com/world/2023/aug/21/ecuador-votes-to-halt-oil-drilling-in-amazonian-biodiversity-hotspot; Meztli Yoalli Rodríguez Aguilera, "Everyday Resistances to Environmental Racism, Mestizo Geographies and Toxicity in Oaxaca," The Funambulist, May/June 2021, https://thefunambulist.net/magazine/decolonial-ecologies/everyday-resistances-to-environmental-racism-mestizo-geographies-and-toxicity-in-oaxaca; Ayana Young and Meztli Yoalli Rodríguez Aguilera, "Transcript: YOALLI RODRIGUEZ on Grief as an Ontological Form of Time /306," For The Wild Podcast, September 28, 2022, https://forthewild.world/podcast-transcripts/yoalli-rodriguez-on-grief-as-an-ontological-form-of-time-306.

103. Rodríguez Aguilera, "Everyday Resistances"; Young and Rodríguez Aguilera, "Transcript."

104. Rodríguez Aguilera, "Everyday Resistances"; Young and Rodríguez Aguilera, "Transcript"; Szerszynski, "Drift as a Planetary Phenomenon."

105. Patel and Moore, *A History of the World*, 102; Klein, *This Changes Everything*, 169–170, 177, 285; Ghosh, *Nutmeg's Curse*, loc. 1471, 1513–1537; Gordon, *Ghostly Matters*, loc. 48; Leila Taylor, *Darkly*, loc. 1645–1648; Marya and Patel, *Inflamed*, loc. 217; Haraway, *Staying with the Trouble*, loc. 1946.

106. Ghosh, *Nutmeg's Curse*, loc. 2518–2522, 3899–3903; Ehrenreich, *Natural Causes*, 208; Barbara Ehrenreich, *Living with a Wild God: A Nonbeliever's Search for the Truth About Everything* (New York: Twelve, 2015).

107. Ghosh, *Nutmeg's Curse*, loc. 1457; Miéville, "Limits of Utopia.*"

108. Bady, "The Trap of Climate Optimism"; Nunes, *Neither Vertical nor Horizontal*, loc. 591–593.

109. Soper, *Post-Growth Living*, loc. 52–64, 694–697, 2066–2069; Benjamin, "Paralipomena to 'On the Concept of History'"; Bue Rübner Hansen, "The Kaleidoscope of Catastrophe," *Viewpoint Magazine*, April 14, 2021, https://viewpointmag.com/2021/04/14/the-kaleidoscope-of-catastrophe-on-the-clarities-and-blind-spots-of-andreas-malm/.

Break VI

1. Butler, *Undoing Gender*, loc. 337–338.
2. Gordon, *Ghostly Matters*, 45.

Conclusion: Walking with Ghosts

1. Zapata's legacy was brought into the consciousness of the world and a new generation of post–Cold War radicals with the rise of the Ejército Zapatista de Liberación Nacional (Zapatista Army of National Liberation, EZLN), who began their struggle in Chiapas as the North American Free Trade Agreement (NAFTA) was launched. See Hilary Klein, "A Spark of Hope: The Ongoing Lessons of the Zapatista Revolution 25 Years On," NACLA, January 18, 2019, https://nacla.org/news/2022/12/21/spark-hope-ongoing-lessons-zapatista-revolution-25-years; Eduardo Barraza, "'Zapata vive, la lucha sigue': Cien años de la muerte de Emiliano Zapata," *Barriozona*, April 13, 2019, https://barriozona.com/cien-anos-despues-emiliano-zapata-vive-la-lucha-sigue/.

2. Amna A. Akbar, "The Fight Against Cop City," *Dissent*, Spring 2023, www.dissentmagazine.org/article/the-fight-against-cop-city/; Natasha Lennard, "Police Shot Atlanta Cop City Protester 57 Times, Autopsy Finds," *Intercept*, April 20, 2023, https://theintercept.com/2023/04/20/atlanta-cop-city-protester-autopsy/; Timothy Pratt, "'Sadness in the Whole Forest':

Family of Cop City Activist Killed by Police Seeks Answers," *Guardian*, February 12, 2023, www.theguardian.com/environment/2023/feb/12/cop-city-manuel-paez-teran-family-mourns; Micah Herskind, "A Solidarity That Is Only Growing," Welcome to Hell World, March 16, 2023, www.welcometohellworld.com/the-movement-to-stop-cop-city-isnt-going-anywhere/.

3. Mark Fisher, *k-punk: The Collected and Unpublished Writings of Mark Fisher (2004–2016)*, ed. Darren Ambrose (London: Repeater Books, 2018), loc. 12594–12698, Kindle; Mark Fisher, *Ghosts of My Life: Writings on Depression, Hauntology and Lost Futures* (London: Zero Books, 2014), 26; Fisher, *Postcapitalist Desire*, loc. 42, 47–48, 53, 173–174; Haraway, *Staying with the Trouble*, loc. 2782–2785.

4. In Anna Tsing's evocative words, "Freedom/haunting: two sides of the same experience. Conjuring a future full of pasts, a ghost-ridden freedom is both a way to move on and a way to remember." Tsing, *Mushroom at the End of the World*, 73, 76, 79. Derrida, *Specters of Marx*, loc. 178–187, 11, 16–17, 48, 142–143.

5. Gordon, *Ghostly Matters*, loc. 12, 18, 22–23; Huw Lemmy and Ben Miller, "Jack Saul Live! At Foyles in London with Shon Faye," *Bad Gays* (podcast), December 25, 2022, https://badgayspod.com/episode-archive/jack-saul-live-at-foyles-in-london-with-shon-faye.

6. Gordon, *Ghostly Matters*, loc. 22–23, 27, 57–58, 62, 98, 180, 183, 191, 201–202, 204; Butler, *Undoing Gender*, loc. 337–338; Michael Löwy, "The Libertarian Marxism of Andre Breton," in *Morning Star: Surrealism, Marxism, Anarchism, Situationism, Utopia*, republished at SurrIV, March 9, 2012, https://surriv.wordpress.com/2012/03/09/the-libertarian-marxism-of-andre-breton/.

7. Karl Marx, "Theses on Feuerbach," in *Ludwig Feuerbach and the End of Classical German Philosophy in 1888*, vol. 1 of Marx and Engels, *Selected Works*, 13–15, www.marxists.org/archive/marx/works/1845/theses/theses.htm; Gordon, *Ghostly Matters*, loc. 205–208; Benjamin, "Theses on the Philosophy of History," loc. 199–200; Gayatri Chakravorty Spivak, "Ghostwriting," *Diacritics* 25, no. 2 (1995): 64.

8. Adam Kaszynski, a union leader with IUE-CWA Local 201 in Lynn, Massachusetts, told me in 2020 of the workers' decision to picket the plant where they made military aircraft, demanding to put the machines to work making ventilators rather than warplanes. The union, he said, has been "fighting to keep union jobs and manufacturing jobs in the United States for as long as we've been here. Right now, there's an opportunity for these lifesaving ventilators and where there's skilled manufacturing workers and idle capacity. It feels like a perfect fit." Sarah Jaffe, "Belabored Stories: On the Picket Line for Ventilators," *Dissent*, April 9, 2020, www.dissentmagazine.org/blog/belabored-stories-on-the-picket-line-for-ventilators/; see also Mohamed Mire's story in Chapter 2; Federici, "Marxism, Feminism, and the Commons," loc. 3256–3266; Federici, "From Crisis to Commons," loc. 3637; Federici, "Re-enchanting the World," loc. 3965–3975; Marya and Patel, *Inflamed*, loc. 13.

9. Benjamin, "Paralipomena to 'On the Concept of History,'" 4:402; Federici, "Marxism, Feminism, and the Commons," loc. 3133. Capitalism is a process rather than a static affair, the process of accumulation. Marx, in *The German Ideology*, explained communism thus: "Communism is for us not a *state of affairs* which is to be established, an *ideal* to which reality [will] have to adjust itself. We call communism the *real* movement which abolishes the present state of things. The conditions of this movement result from the premises now in existence." Karl Marx, with Friedrich Engels, *The German Ideology: Critique of Modern German Philosophy According to Its Representatives Feuerbach, B. Bauer and Stirner, and of German Socialism According to Its Various Prophets* (first published 1932), www.marxists.org/archive/marx/works/1845/german-ideology/ch01a.htm; Fisher, *Postcapitalist Desire*, 178; Chaudhary, "The Long Now"; Táíwò, *Elite Capture*, loc. 705–770. Kelley, *Freedom Dreams*, loc. 223–224; William Davies,

"The New Neoliberalism," *NLR* 101 (September/October 2016); Ruth Wilson Gilmore, "Decorative Beasts: Dogging the Academy in the Late 20th Century," in Gilmore, *Abolition Geography*, loc. 948; Winant, "We Live in a Society"; Kotsko, *Neoliberalism's Demons*, loc. 2354; Butler, *Undoing Gender*, loc. 504–509.

10. Butler, *Undoing Gender*, loc. 355–465, 514; Garza, *Grieving*, 7–8, 47.

11. Hayes and Kaba, *Let This Radicalize You*, 199–200, 210; Fisher, *Capitalist Realism*, 16–17.

12. See Jenny Odell, *Saving Time: Discovering a Life Beyond the Clock* (New York: Random House, 2023); Ehrenreich, *Natural Causes*, 194–195, 189; Sarah Jaffe, "Worker Centers: Where Causes Cohere, and Forge Power," *American Prospect*, April 21, 2021, https://prospect.org/labor/the-alt-labor-chronicles-america-s-worker-centers/worker-centers-where-causes-cohere-and-forge-power/.

13. Frederick Douglass, "The Dred Scott Decision" (speech delivered before American Anti-Slavery Society, New York, May 14, 1857), University of Rochester Frederick Douglass Project, https://rbscp.lib.rochester.edu/4399; Marcus, *Political Disappointment*, loc. 22–37.

14. Antonio Gramsci, *Selections from the Prison Notebooks*, ed. Quintin Hoare and Geoffrey Nowell Smith (New York: International, 1971), loc. 7398–7402; Nancy Fraser, *The Old Is Dying and the New Cannot Be Born: From Progressive Neoliberalism to Trump and Beyond* (New York: Verso, 2019), loc. 54–58, 242–244.

15. The mistranslation or loose translation is often attributed to Slavoj Žižek, "A Permanent Economic Emergency," *New Left Review*, no. 64 (2010), https://newleftreview.org/issues/ii64/articles/slavoj-zizek-a-permanent-economic-emergency.

16. Gramsci, *Prison Notebooks*, loc. 199–200.

17. Ruth Wilson Gilmore, "Terror Austerity Race Gender Excess Theater," in Gilmore, *Abolition Geography*, loc. 2179; Alex Doherty, "Politics Theory Other: Fascist Echoes w/ Adam Tooze," *Politics Theory Other* (podcast), March 17, 2023, https://soundcloud.com/poltheoryother/fascist-echoes-w-adam-tooze; see also Adam Tooze, *The Wages of Destruction: The Making and Breaking of the Nazi Economy* (New York: Penguin, 2007); Gilroy, *Postcolonial Melancholia*, loc. 64. Jacqueline Rose suggested, "At this level fascism could be described as the historical annexing, or collective seizure, of unconscious drives (this does not, of course, exhaust the historical reality of fascism). In fascism, the realm of politics reveals itself as massively invested with the most private and intimate images of our fantasy life." Jacqueline Rose, *The Haunting of Sylvia Plath* (Cambridge, MA: Harvard University Press, 1992), 7, 235–236; Mbembé and Meintjes, "Necropolitics"; Butler, *Precarious Life*, loc. 60–64, 90; Walter Benjamin, "The Work of Art in the Age of Mechanical Reproduction," in *Illuminations*, 193, loc. 2310–2313; George Orwell, *The Road to Wigan Pier* (New York: HarperCollins, 1972), loc. 3041–3049, Kindle.

18. Malm and Zetkin Collective, *White Skin, Black Fuel*, loc. 3475–3495; Orwell, *Road to Wigan Pier*, loc. 4080–4086; Mitchell, *Imperial Nostalgia*, 7, 16, 23, 114, 119, 128, 185.

19. Michael Azar describes a scene from Italian fascism:

> Rome, 28th October, 1932. Benito Mussolini inaugurates the exhibition *Mostra della Rivoluzione Fascista* as a part of the ten-year jubilee of the Fascist Party march on Rome. The absolute core of the exhibition, its most sacred room, is the so-called *Sacrario dei Martiri* (Sanctuary of the Martyrs). On a blood-red podium in the vaulted centre of the room stands a lone crucifix with the inscription *Per la Patria Immortale* (For the Immortal Fatherland), and along the walls the word *Presente* (Presence) is repeated thousands of times, like a mantra. The martyr is the one who cannot die, who always rises again. In the six-month period of the exhibition, four million people pass

through this exhibition space, with its presentation of an intensified fascist revolutionary image of national history.

Michael Azar, "Presente! Western Martyrdom and the Politics of Memory and Death," trans. Henning Koch, *Eurozine*, July 7, 2011, www.eurozine.com/presente/ (first published in Swedish in *Glänta* 3/4 [2010]). Later in the same piece, Azar noted, "It is not unusual for a deep ambivalence to emerge as a result of this synthesis between the discourses of nationalist martyrdom ('pro patria mori') and the internationalism of revolutionary martyrdom." Mitchell, *Imperial Nostalgia*, 114; Jordy Rosenberg, "The Daddy Dialectic," *Los Angeles Review of Books*, March 11, 2018, https://lareviewofbooks.org/article/the-daddy-dialectic/; Malm and Zetkin Collective, *White Skin, Black Fuel*, loc. 3521–3583, 3636.

20. Classical fascism, Malm and the Zetkin Collective pointed out, "was a reaction against limits." Thinking of this, its affinity with fossil fuels makes sense. And thus its reemergence at a moment when we confront planetary limits makes sense as well. "In the light of the genealogies we have sketched, there is nothing surprising about the grandchildren of classical fascism returning to protect the automobile and the aeroplane and the burning of coal against meddlesome hands." Malm and Zetkin Collective, *White Skin, Black Fuel*, loc. 6900–6921.

See Juliet Hooker, "White Grievance and the Problem of Political Loss," in Enwezor, Beckwith, and Gioni, *Grief and Grievance*, 23; and Juliet Hooker, *Black Grief / White Grievance: The Politics of Loss* (Princeton, NJ: Princeton University Press, 2023); Mitchell, *Imperial Nostalgia*, 184; Gilroy, *Postcolonial Melancholia*, loc. 146.

21. As Harsha Walia noted, the far right is networked around the world:

> Brexit cheerleader Nigel Farage appeared at a Trump rally in 2016, former executive chairperson of Breitbart News Steve Bannon became the cochair of the Republican Hindu Coalition in 2019, President Jair Bolsonaro in Brazil was the guest of honor at India's Republic Day celebration hosted by Prime Minister Narendra Modi in 2020, and the Christchurch shooter as well as Norwegian killer Anders Breivik both glorified the Bosnian Serb army's ethnic cleansing of Bosnian Muslims and the creation of the ethnostate Republika Srpska. (*Border and Rule*, loc. 3107)

Stephen Berry, "Confederates Take the Capitol," in Barnes, Merritt, and Williams, *After Life*, loc. 1298–1301; Sarah Jaffe, "In GOP Country, a Small Labor Organization Offers a Model for Fighting Trumpism," *Nation*, November 4, 2016, www.thenation.com/article/archive/in-gop-country-a-small-labor-organization-offers-a-model-for-fighting-trumpism/; Fisher, *Postcaptalist Desire*, 156; Fisher, *Ghosts of My Life*, 25; Wendy Brown, "Wounded Attachments," *Political Theory* 21, no. 3 (August 1993): 390–410, www.jstor.org/stable/191795.

22. Miéville, "Limits of Utopia*"; Berardi, *After the Future*, loc. 52; Samuel Fishwick, "The Truth Behind Silicon Valley's Obsession with Immortality," *Evening Standard*, January 21, 2022, www.standard.co.uk/insider/jeff-besoz-altos-labs-silicon-valley-peter-thiel-b977992.html; Ehrenreich, *Natural Causes*, 77–79, 94–97; Émile P. Torres, "Longtermism Poses a Real Threat to Humanity," *New Statesman*, August 3, 2023, www.newstatesman.com/ideas/2023/08/longtermism-threat-humanity; Fisher, *Postcapitalist Desire*, 77; Marya and Patel, *Inflamed*, loc. 175.

23. Jade Bremner, "William Shatner Fans Hit Out at Jeff Bezos for Interrupting His Emotional Space Speech to Spray Champagne," *Independent*, October 14, 2021, www.independent.co.uk/news/world/americas/william-shatner-fans-bezos-blue-origin-b1938422.html.

24. Samantha Lock, "'It Felt like a Funeral': William Shatner Reflects on Voyage to Space," *Guardian*, October 11, 2022, www.theguardian.com/culture/2022/oct/11/it-felt-like-a-funeral-william-shatner-reflects-on-voyage-to-space; Miéville, *A Spectre, Haunting*, loc. 2427–2428, 2442.

25. Defend Atlanta Forest [@defendatlantaforest], Fight Like Hell photo, Instagram, August 10, 2023, www.instagram.com/p/CvvkO3Cu549/?hl=en; Jack Crosbie, "The Battle for 'Cop City,'" *Rolling Stone*, September 3, 2022, www.rollingstone.com/culture/culture-features /defend-atlanta-forest-copy-city-climate-change-defund-the-police-1397188/; Nadasen, *Care*, loc. 176–180, 124–125, 176–180, 2935–3149; Riley Clare Valentine, "Radicalizing Care: Street Medics and Solidarity," *Activist History Review*, June 1, 2020, https://activisthistory.com/2020/06/01 /radicalizing-care-street-medics-and-solidarity/; Olivia B. Waxman, "With Free Medical Clinics and Patient Advocacy, the Black Panthers Created a Legacy in Community Health That Still Exists amid COVID-19," *Time*, February 25, 2021; see also Donna Murch, *Living for the City: Migration, Education, and the Rise of the Black Panther Party in Oakland, California* (Durham: University of North Carolina Press, 2010); and Bryan Shih and Yohuru Williams, *The Black Panthers: Portraits from an Unfinished Revolution* (New York: Bold Type Books, 2016).

26. Nadasen, *Care*, loc. 3077–3125.

27. Melissa Gira Grant and Sarah Jaffe, "For Love or Money," Guillotine, 2016; Federici, "Feminism and the Politics of the Commons," loc. 2249; Federici, "Re-enchanting the World," loc. 3980–3989.

28. Kenway, *Who Cares*, loc. 202–204, 268–271, 1017–1395, 1616–1774; Nadasen, *Care*, loc. 2987–2988.

29. Sophie Lewis, "With-Women: Grieving in Capitalist Time," *e-flux*, September 2020, www.e-flux.com/journal/111/343916/with-women-grieving-in-capitalist-time/; Sophie Lewis, "Mothering Against the World: Momrades Against Motherhood," September 18, 2020, https:// salvage.zone/mothering-against-the-world-momrades-against-motherhood/; Donna Haraway, *Staying with the Trouble: Making Kin in the Chthulucene* (Durham, NC: Duke University Press, 2016). Jodi Dean, *Comrade: An Essay on Political Belonging* (New York: Verso Books, 2019).

30. Butler, *Frames of War*, loc. 1020–1035; Shih and Williams, *Black Panthers*; M. T. Bassett, "Beyond Berets: The Black Panthers as Health Activists," *American Journal of Public Health* 106, no. 10 (October 2016): 1741–1743, doi: 10.2105/AJPH.2016.303412, PMID: 27626339, PMCID: PMC5024403; Gilroy, *Postcolonial Melancholia*, loc. 4, 54, 56, 71; Gilmore, "Forgotten Places and the Seeds of Grassroots Planning," in Gilmore, *Abolition Geography*, loc. 5460; Gilmore, "Abolition Geography and the Problem of Innocence," loc. 6407.

31. Gilmore, "Abolition Geography and the Problem of Innocence," loc. 6527–6559; Pelot-Hobbs, *Prison Capital*, 276.

32. Gilmore, "Abolition Geography and the Problem of Innocence," loc. 6527–6559; Pelot-Hobbs, *Prison Capital*, 276–277; Sophie Lewis, "Grief Circling," *Dissent*, Summer 2020, www.dissentmagazine.org/article/grief-circling/; Butler, "Between Grief and Grievance," 15; Balani, "Without Mourning"; Ehrenreich, *Natural Causes*, 97; Baker, "The Right to Grieve."

33. Garza, *Grieving*, 123–124; Hayes and Kaba, *Let This Radicalize You*, 79.

34. Daniel Denvir, "Making Sense of Antonio Gramsci: An Interview with Michael Denning," *Jacobin*, June 11, 2023, https://jacobin.com/2023/06/michael-denning-antonio-gramsci-strategy -intellectuals-coalitions-theory; Nunes, *Neither Vertical nor Horizontal*, loc. 268–274, 702–704.

35. Haraway, *Staying with the Trouble*, loc. 372.

36. Malkia Devich-Cyril, "Grief Belongs in Social Movements: Can We Embrace It?," *In These Times*, July 28, 2021, https://inthesetimes.com/article/freedom-grief-healing-death -liberation-movements.

37. Gargi Bhattacharyya, in her beautiful book *We, the Heartbroken*, wrote something very similar: "Heartbrokenness might be seen as the complex grief of a broken world, necessarily resistant to therapeutic interventions because there is no reasonable response to what we know

of the world other than heartbreak." Bhattacharyya, *We, the Heartbroken*, loc. 945; Butler, *Precarious Life*, loc. 832–837, 1669.

38. I take the idea of fugitivity from Fred Moten, who explained it as "a desire for and a spirit of escape and transgression of the proper and the proposed. It's a desire for the outside, for a playing or being outside, an outlaw edge proper to the now always already improper voice or instrument." Quoted in Hugo Canham, "Thanatopolitics and Fugitive Mourning in Pandemic Death," *Social and Health Sciences* 19 (2021): 1–17, doi: 10.25159/2957–3645/10329; Marya and Patel, *Inflamed*, loc. 297, 326, 333; see Fred Moten, *Stolen Life* (Durham, NC: Duke University Press, 2018); Davis et al., *Abolition. Feminism. Now.*, 14, 31–32.

39. Crawley, *The Lonely Letters*, loc. 516, 522, 537, 1422–1427, 1448–1450, 2098, 2514, 3005; Miéville, *A Spectre, Haunting*, loc. 2277–2285; Haraway, *Staying with the Trouble*, loc. 371–375, 392, 2212–2219.

40. Eva Kittay, *Love's Labor: Essays on Women, Equality and Disability* (London: Routledge, 1999), 68, 70, 107; Federici, "Feminism and the Politics of the Commons," loc. 2269–2279.

41. Marya and Patel, *Inflamed*, loc. 349–350; Miéville, *A Spectre, Haunting*, loc. 2286–2287, 2324–2398.

42. Benjamin, "Paralipomena to 'On the Concept of History,'" 4:402; Benjamin, *One Way Street*, loc. 93–96.

43. The full Marx quotation that I gloss here is from *Capital*, vol. 3, and is one of my favorites despite its dated language, and so I am including it here:

> In fact, the realm of freedom actually begins only where labour which is determined by necessity and mundane considerations ceases; thus in the very nature of things it lies beyond the sphere of actual material production. Just as the savage must wrestle with Nature to satisfy his wants, to maintain and reproduce life, so must civilised man, and he must do so in all social formations and under all possible modes of production. With his development this realm of physical necessity expands as a result of his wants; but, at the same time, the forces of production which satisfy these wants also increase. Freedom in this field can only consist in socialised man, the associated producers, rationally regulating their interchange with Nature, bringing it under their common control, instead of being ruled by it as by the blind forces of Nature; and achieving this with the least expenditure of energy and under conditions most favourable to, and worthy of, their human nature. But it nonetheless still remains a realm of necessity. Beyond it begins that development of human energy which is an end in itself, the true realm of freedom, which, however, can blossom forth only with this realm of necessity as its basis. The shortening of the working-day is its basic prerequisite.

Karl Marx, *Capital*, vol. 3, ed. Friedrick Engels (1894; New York: International, 1959), Marxists.org, 1999, www.marxists.org/archive/marx/works/1894-c3/ch48.htm; Angela Y. Davis, "Women and Capitalism," 179; Butler, *Precarious Life*, loc. 789.

44. Kenway, *Who Cares*, loc. 2072–2080, 3257–3301; Bhattacharyya, *We, the Heartbroken*, loc. 650, 835.

45. Devich-Cyril, "Grief Belongs in Social Movements."

46. Tender-Heart Press, "Enormity," www.countrycounterculture.com/product-page/enormity-oranges; Ehrenreich, *Natural Causes*, 192–193, 203.

47. Mitchell, *Imperial Nostalgia*, 187–188; Ehrenreich, *Natural Causes*, 208.

48. Butler, *Precarious Life*, loc. 800–814; Gilmore and Gilmore, "Beyond Bratton," loc. 4107; Marcus, *Political Disappointment*, loc. 264–268, 282, 331–335, 390–394.

49. Pacinthe Mattar, "Beautiful like the Moon," *The New Quarterly*, retrieved February 27, 2024, https://tnq.ca/story/beautiful-like-the-moon/; Hala Alyan, "'I Am Not There and I Am Not Here': A Palestinian American Poet on Bearing Witness to Atrocity," *Guardian*, January 28, 2024, https://www.theguardian.com/world/2024/jan/28/gaza-palestine-grief-essay-poetry.

50. Marcus, *Political Disappointment*, loc. 2802–2949, 3395–3399.

51. Marcus, *Political Disappointment*, loc. 3406–3407.

52. Kotsko, *Neoliberalism's Demons*, loc. 2622–2628; Nancy Fraser, *The Old Is Dying*, loc. 252–254, 313–314, 318–322; Nunes, *Neither Vertical nor Horizontal*, loc. 3538–3540.

53. As Walter Benjamin reminded us, the experience of his generation was "that capitalism will not die a natural death," and it is no more willing to do so now. Walter Benjamin, *The Arcades Project*, Howard Eiland and Kevin McLaughlin, trans. (Cambridge: Belknap Press, 2002), 667. Miéville, *A Spectre, Haunting*, loc. 1260–1271; Clover, *Riot. Strike. Riot*, loc. 1865–1867.

54. Day and McBean, *Abolition Revolution*, loc. 463–476.

55. Nunes, *Neither Vertical nor Horizontal*, loc. 2720–2871, 3044–3170, 3269–3270, 3471–3508.

56. Nunes, *Neither Vertical nor Horizontal*, loc. 2720–3270.

57. Nunes, *Neither Vertical nor Horizontal*, loc. 3507–3532; Alex N. Press, "The UAW Strike Matters for the Entire US Working Class," *Jacobin*, September 14, 2023, https://jacobin.com/2023/09/the-uaw-strike-matters-for-the-entire-us-working-class.

58. Nunes, *Neither Vertical nor Horizontal*, loc. 2217–2227; Campbell Kwan, "Gurner Says Unemployment Needs to Rise," September 12, 2023, www.afr.com/politics/federal/albanese-dodges-on-qatar-defends-qantas-stance-20230912–p5e3vb?post=p557gn; Roediger, *Sinking Middle Class*, loc. 187–189.

59. Kelley, *Freedom Dreams*, loc. 70–72, 177–188, 1710–1713, 1932–1939, 2810–2816; Hartman, *Wayward Lives*, loc. 61–62, 482, 2799–2803; Garza, *Grieving*, 153, 169, 174; Miéville, *A Spectre, Haunting*, loc. 575–582, 1919–1932, 2458–2465; Clover, *Riot. Strike. Riot*, loc. 1327–1328, 2432–2436.

60. Jamie Allinson, China Miéville, Richard Seymour, and Rosie Warren, *The Tragedy of the Worker: Towards the Proletarocene* (London: Verso/Salvage, 2021); Miéville, *A Spectre, Haunting*, loc. 2169–2174; Táíwò, *Elite Capture*, loc. 190–192.

61. Benjamin, "Theses on the Philosophy of History," loc. 207–209; Chaudhary, "The Long Now"; Adam Turl, "A Thousand Lost Worlds: Notes on Gothic Marxism," *Red Wedge Magazine*, June 4, 2015, www.redwedgemagazine.com/evicted-art-blog/a-thousand-lost-worlds-notes-on-gothic-marxism.

62. Butler, *Undoing Gender*, loc. 347–351, 580–586.

63. Crawley, *The Lonely Letters*, loc. 485, 513, 3038–3031.

Index

Credit: Salem Rizk

Sarah Jaffe is an independent journalist covering the politics of power, from the workplace to the streets. She is the author of *Work Won't Love You Back: How Devotion to Our Jobs Keeps Us Exploited, Exhausted, and Alone* and *Necessary Trouble: Americans in Revolt*. Her work has appeared in the *New York Times*, *Nation*, *Guardian*, *Washington Post*, *New Republic*, *American Prospect*, and many other publications. She is the cohost, with Michelle Chen, of the *Belabored* podcast, as well as a columnist at the *Progressive*. You can find her on various social media sites as sarahljaffe and online at sarahljaffe.com.